MYTHS OF THE MODOCS

MYTHS OF THE MODOCS

BY

JEREMIAH CURTIN

Author of "The Mongols, A History," "The Mongols in Russia," "Myths and Folk-Lore of Ireland," "Creation Myths of Primitive America," etc.

TRANSLATOR OF THE WORKS OF HENRY SIENKIEWICZ

BOSTON
LITTLE, BROWN, AND COMPANY
1912

Published, November, 1912

THE COLONIAL PRESS
C. H. SIMONDS & CO., BOSTON, U. S. A.

INTRODUCTION

THE majority of Americans know who the Modocs are and where they live, for on a time their bravery and so-called treachery gave them widespread notoriety; but for those who do not know, the following sketch may be helpful.

The Old Modoc Country was the valley of Lost River in Oregon, and the country adjacent to the shores of Little Klamath Lake, and Tula Lake which in main lies within the boundary of California.

The country around Tula Lake is of volcanic formation and at the southern end of the lake are the lava beds about which so much was written during the Modoc War of 1872–1873. Along the rivers and lakes the scenery is pleasing and in places, grand. Lake Klamath, nearly surrounded by mountains, is as beautiful as are the famed lakes of Italy and Switzerland. Mount Pitt, which, from a distance, seems to rise from the very shore of the lake, is snow-crowned except for a few weeks in midsummer. Mount Shasta is seen from its summit to the snow line.

The Modoc people believe that Kumush created the world — the world in Modoc myth means the country inhabited by the Modocs and the tribes they come in contact with. — He made the mountains, lakes and rivers and gave them names. We are not told about the creation of the "first people," those wonderful beings who inhabited the world before man was created and were "so numerous that if a count could be made of all the stars in the sky, all the feathers on birds, all the hairs and fur on animals, and all the hairs on our heads, they would not be as numerous." No man knows how long those "first people" lived, but after countless ages a time came when they were transformed into beasts, reptiles, birds, fishes, insects, plants, stones, snow, earthquake, sun, moon and stars, in fact into every living thing, object, phenomenon and power outside of man. This transformation took place about the time that Kumush created the Modoc and other Indian tribes and gave them names, told them where their homes would be — designated the Klamath country for the Modocs — and established the present order of things.

For the Modocs the valley of Lost River and the lands around Klamath and Tula Lake are sacred. We, who endeavor to trace our origin back to a monkey or, still farther, to a bit of protoplasm, or who believe in and search far and wide for the Garden of Eden, cannot revere a country which is ours simply by chance of birth as the Indian reveres the country where his tribe originated. We cannot estimate the love an Indian has for his country. His holy places are not in far-off Palestine; they are before his eyes in his own birthplace, where every river, hill and mountain has a story connected with it, an account of its origin. No people could be more religious than were the Indians before the advent of the white man; they had no observance, rite, or custom which they did not believe to be God-given.

Into this country that Kumush gave to the Modocs came white settlers. To protect the lives and property of the intruders it was necessary for the United States government to establish a fort and garrison it. Thenceforth the Indians could not subsist by fishing and hunting. At last, to obtain food, supplies and annuity, they were forced to sign the Treaty of 1864. That treaty outlines the limits of a reservation where the Modocs can live, take fish and gather edible seeds, roots and berries. As a payment for lands they gave up they received eight thousand dollars per annum, for a period of five years, five thousand per annum for the next five years, and three thousand per annum for the five years next succeeding. The treaty provided thirty-five hundred dollars for removing the Indians to the reservation, giving them rations for the first year, and furnishing them with clothing, tools and teams. It reserved the right to the government to provide each Indian family with land in severalty to the extent of from forty to a hundred and twenty acres.

The Modocs pledged themselves to commit no depredation upon the persons or property of the settlers.

The amounts stipulated were insignificant for a body of Indians considered as numbering two thousand, and they were to be paid only after the Senate and the President had ratified the treaty, which did not take place till five years after the Indians signed it. The Modocs were not forced to leave their land, now ceded to the United States, till 1869. At the end of that year, two hundred and fifty-eight dissatisfied and unhappy Indians were on the reservation. In April, 1870, rations gave out, and a considerable number of the reservation Indians went back to Lost River Valley; others went to Yaneks on Sprague River. They were permitted to stay in their old homes till the autumn of 1872, then steps were taken to drive them to the reservation. They resisted, and the President ordered the commander at Fort Klamath to have them removed from Lost River Valley: "peaceably if you can, forcibly if you must."

November 29, 1872, troops surrounded the Modoc camp on Lost River. When the men escaped to the hills, soldiers and settlers fired upon the unprotected women and children of a camp farther north. The Indians retaliated by killing fourteen settlers, then they retreated to the lava beds south of Tula Lake and selected as headquarters a cave called Ben Wright. There they remained undisturbed till January 17. Then, in spite of a fog so dense that the lake and lava beds were shrouded as with a pall, Colonel Wheaton ordered an attack. Four hundred men moved against seventy, but fog forced them to withdraw.

After this defeat, General Gillen was placed in command, and his troops were reenforced by four companies from San Francisco. The new commander decided to negotiate for peace. A few of the Indians were willing to listen to overtures; others, having no confidence in the promises of the United States government, were opposed to wasting time in parley, but at last April 11, 1873, was appointed for a peace meeting. But before the day came, Kintpuash's ponies were captured by the troops, in spite of General Canby's promise of a total suspension of hostilities.

That act so roused and enraged the chief that he determined to kill the peace commissioners, whom he now thought to be planning treachery in place of peace. General Canby and Doctor Thomas were murdered; the others fled. Wright's Cave was bombarded on April 16, 17 and 18. On April 19 the Modocs left the cave. At Sand Hill, April 26, an encounter took place which was more disastrous for the troops than for the Indians, but at a battle fought May 10 the Indians were forced to retreat.

May 25 a number of the warriors, dissatisfied with their leader and considering their cause hopeless, surrendered to General Davis, who was then in command of the government troops. June 1 Kintpuash, and the men who had remained faithful to him, betrayed by an Indian, gave themselves up to a scouting party of cavalry.

The men who killed General Canby were condemned and hung; those accessory to the deed were incarcerated at Fort Alcataz; the other warriors, with their wives and children, numbering about one hundred and forty-five, were removed to the Quapaw Agency in the Indian Territory (now Oklahoma) and are still there.

Exile for the Modocs was a crushing sorrow. When I saw them, in 1884, they were still mourning over their changed condition, and for the Klamath country, — the country Kumush created and gave to them.

A large number of the myths in this volume were related to Mr. Curtin, in 1884, by one of the exiles, Ko-a-lak′-ak-a, a woman who was then old and feeble, but who as late as Aug. 1, 1912, was still living, the oldest woman of the Klamath-Modoc tribe of Indians. At the time she told the myths she was remarkable for her intelligence and her wonderful memory. In childhood her grandfather had instructed her in the religion of her people, in other words, taught her all the myths of the Modocs, and to old age her tenacious memory retained many of them. For years Ko-a-lak′-ak-a was the most unhappy of all the exiles.

Later in 1884, Mr. Curtin visited the Modocs who were left in the Klamath country. There is much that could be written regarding the treatment those poor, unhappy creatures were receiving from the professedly Christian men and women who were in power on the reservation. Such abuses existed, that Mr. Curtin mentioned them to the proper officials in Washington, and changes were made.

Sconchen, the oldest Indian there, related to Mr. Curtin a number of the myths which are in this volume, and also told him a good deal about the customs of the Modocs. Though old and infirm, his mind was still clear and active. For years, in the prime of his life, he was chief of his people, and in his old age they revered him.

M. A. Curtin.

Pasadena, California,
March, 1912.

CONTENTS

CONTENTS

MYTHS OF THE MODOCS

LÁTKAKÁWAS

CHARACTERS

Dásläts	California lion	Lok	Bear
Djakkonus	A duck	Mówatwas	South wind place people
Dohos	A duck		
Dútûte	A duck	Mukus	Owl
Isis		Nada	A bird
Kai	Jack rabbit	Skakas	Free toad
Kládo	Duck	Tcfkas	Wren
Kols	Badger	Tókwa	Mole
Kumush		Wálwilegas	Butterfly
Látkakáwas			

LÁTKAKÁWAS and her five brothers lived on the south side of Klamath Lake. The brothers went every day to fish from an island in the middle of the lake. Látkakáwas stayed at home; she gathered wiwhi seeds and burned the down from them to prepare them as food for her brothers and for herself.

When Látkakáwas was at work, she looked like a common old woman, but when she shook herself and went out of the house, she was young, blue and beautiful.

The "Old Man" (Kumush) lived on the eastern side of Klamath Lake. On the western side of the lake lived many people. Those people often saw Látkakáwas standing on the top of her house, looking blue and nice, but as soon as they went toward her she changed to an old hunchback woman.

The young men of the western village counseled together;

then each day they sent one of their number to try to steal up to Látkakáwas and catch her before she could make herself old and ugly. They wanted to talk to her; they wanted to ask her to take one of them for a husband. — Every young man in the western village tried, but Látkakáwas was never young when they came toward her.

One man started before daybreak; he wanted to get near the house and hide till Látkakáwas came out. That day she stayed inside, an old hunchback woman stringing beads. She knew when people were looking at her or thinking of her; she even knew where they were.

Each morning Látkakáwas' brothers went to the island to catch salmon, and dry them, but as soon as it was dark they came home. One night Látkakáwas said to her eldest brother: "Men come here to watch me, and try to catch me; when they find me hunchback and ugly to look at, they make fun of me. I don't like that. It makes me feel badly."

"How soon will you have seeds enough gathered?" asked her brother.

"To-morrow," said Látkakáwas.

"When the seeds are ready, you will go with us to the island where nobody can bother you," said her brother.

On the west side of the lake there was a young man as blue and beautiful as Látkakáwas herself. His father kept him in an underground place; no one ever saw him except when he went out to bathe or swim. When all the other young men had tried to get near Látkakáwas, and had failed, the people said to this young man's father: "Why don't you send your son? Maybe he could catch that beautiful blue woman."

When the old man told his son about Látkakáwas, the young man said: "There is no use of my going there. If all the others have failed I should fail, too."

"You are as blue and nice to look at as Látkakáwas is," said his father; "maybe she will like you and take you for a husband."

The old man took his son out of the underground place, washed him and got him ready, made him clothes from a wonderful cap, a cap that could never be destroyed. When the young man put on those clothes, he was beautiful beyond anything in the world; he was blue and gold and green, like the clouds in the sky. He could run in the air and under the ground. He had great power.

When he was ready to start, his father said to him: " When the sun comes to the edge of the sky, Látkakáwas shakes herself and goes to the top of the house to watch it. If you travel under the ground you will get near her before she sees you."

When Látkakáwas shook herself and stood on top of the house to watch the sun, the young man was near by, under the ground, with one eye looking out. She knew that he was there, but she didn't change to an old woman. She said to herself: " This man pleases me; he is not like the others. He is the first man who hasn't laughed and made fun of me."

The young man watched Látkakáwas for a time and then went home.

When Látkakáwas' brothers came, she said: " A young man, all blue and gold and green, nice to look at, has been here to watch me, but he didn't make fun of me as the others did."

The eldest brother said: " We will move to the island tomorrow. Just at sundown we caught two big salmon; we will go early and dress them, then we'll come for you. While we are gone, you must pack up the beads and skins."

In the morning, before it was light, the brothers started for the island. Just as the sun looked up over the edge of the sky, the young man from the west came again. As Látkakáwas shook herself and came out at the smoke hole on top of the house, a light shone in her face. It was so strong that it dazzled her and she turned back. The young man was brighter than before, for he was out of the ground.

When Látkakáwas went into the house, he peeped through a crack and watched her. She knew he was there, but she didn't turn old; she sat down and assorted her beads according to color. Then she picked up her mats and got ready to go to the island.

Early in the forenoon the five brothers came and began to pull down the house.

The people on the west side of the lake saw them at work and asked one another: " Where are those brothers going? Why are they pulling down their house? "

At midday, when the brothers were ready to start, they spread mats from the house to the canoe, for Látkakáwas to walk on. When she got into the canoe at the edge of the lake, she forgot all about the young man, forgot that she had fallen in love with him that morning.

The brothers pushed the canoe to get it into the water, but they couldn't move it; the young man was holding it. He was right there by them, but they didn't see him. They worked for a long time. Finally he let go of the canoe, and it started, but he pulled it back. He let them push it out a second time, and a second time he pulled it back. They started many times but each time, before they could get out into the lake, they were back at the shore. They strove in that way till the middle of the afternoon, then the young man freed the canoe and the brothers rowed toward the island.

As the canoe went on, the young man swam behind it in the form of a salmon. He was in love with Látkakáwas, and he wanted to look at her. She sat in the middle of the canoe with one of her brothers; two brothers sat at the end of the canoe and two in front.

As they rowed along, one of the brothers saw a beautiful salmon, all blue and gold and green. He speared it and pulled it into the canoe, and that moment the salmon turned to a young man; but right away he died.

Látkakáwas cried and blamed her brothers. She knew the young man, and she felt badly. The brothers felt badly, too. They went back to the shore and the next day they put their beads and mats in one big pile and burned them, together with the young man's body. When the pile was burned, there was a bright disk in the ashes. The disk was as bright as the sun in the heavens. This was the crown of the young man's head.

Látkakáwas saw it, and said: " Look, what is that bright thing in the ashes? "

The brother who had speared the salmon took up the disk, gave it to Látkakáwas, and said: " Take it to Kumush. He is in his sweat-house at Nihlaksi. Kumush can bring a man to life if he has only one hair from his head."

Látkakáwas put the disk in her bosom, then she gave each of her brothers a bundle of bone head-scratchers, and said: "If Kumush doesn't bring my husband to life, you will never see me again."

Látkakáwas traveled all day; when night came she camped at Koáskise, not far from Kumush's sweat-house.

The next morning, just as the sun came up, Látkakáwas gave birth to a child, a wonderfully beautiful boy. She strapped the baby on a board, put the board on her back and went to Kumush's sweat-house.

When Kumush asked why she came, she took the disk out of her bosom, and said: "I want you to bring this to life."

When Kumush saw the disk, he thought he had never seen anything that was half as bright and beautiful. Látkakáwas wanted to gather wood to build a fire in the sweat-house, but Kumush said: "You stay here; I will get the wood."

Right away he had a big fire; then he heated stones, and when they were ready to put in the basket of water, he said to Látkakáwas: "Take your baby and lie down in the corner; wrap yourself up and keep still."

When she was wrapped up tight, Kumush put the hot stones into the basket, and when the water boiled, he put in the disk. After a little while the disk came to life, and became the young man again.

When Kumush saw how beautiful the man was, he wanted him to die, and never come to life again. He thought he would get the disk and the young man's beauty. As Kumush wanted, so it was. The young man died.

When Látkakáwas unwrapped herself and saw that her husband was dead, she cried, she felt so lonesome. She cried all the time Kumush was gathering wood to burn the body.

When the body was half consumed, Látkakáwas asked Kumush to put more wood on the fire. While he was picking up the wood, she strapped the baby on to the board, put the board on her back and sprang into the fire. Kumush saw her just in time to snatch the baby from her back. Látka-káwas and the young man's body were burned to ashes.

The baby cried and cried. Kumush called it by every name he could think of. He called it Wanaga, Lákana, Gailalam-tcaknoles. When he called it Isilámlĕs, it didn't cry quite as hard; when he said Isis Uknóles, it cried only a little; when he said Isis, the child stopped crying. The name pleased it.

Kumush put the child on the ground and looked in the ashes for the disk. He found it and was glad, but he didn't know where to put it. He put it on his knee, under his arm, on his breast, on his forehead, and on his shoulders, but it wouldn't stay anywhere. At last he put it on the small of his back. The minute he put it there it grew to his body, and right away he was beautiful and young and bright, the brightest person in the world. The disk had become a part of him, and he was the father of Isis, for the disk was the father of Isis.

Then Kumush left Nihlaksi and traveled toward the north. On the road he kept thinking where he was to hide the baby. At last he hid it in his knee, where it appeared as a boil. That night he stayed with two old women who lived in a house at the edge of a village. All night he groaned and complained of the boil on his knee. In the morning he asked one of the old women to press the boil.

As soon as she began to press it, she saw bright hair. "What is this?" asked she.

"I told you that wasn't a boil," said the other old woman.

They both pressed, and soon the baby came out. The women washed the child, wrapped it up in a skin blanket and fed it.

Right away people found out that old man Kumush had a baby and everybody wanted to know where he got it.

Kumush said: "The earth is kind to me. The earth gave this baby to me."

Kumush took Isis and went to live on the southeast side of

Tula Lake,[1] and there he fished and worked and reared Isis.

When Isis was old enough to marry, the Mówatwas, a people from the south, brought him a woman named Tókwa (mole). A great many people came with her, for she was a powerful woman, the best worker in the world.

When the Mówatwas came, Kumush and Isis were at home. Isis was asleep; he had been fishing, and children were carrying fish from the canoe to the house. As the Mówatwas came in sight, Gäk saw them and said to the children: "I wonder where all those people came from? They will never come here again!"

That minute the Mówatwas and Tókwa turned to stone. Kumush and Isis turned to stone, too, but their spirits came out and were men again. Their bodies and the body of Tókwa are at Tula Lake now, near the bodies of the Mówatwas people, who came with Tókwa.

Kumush took Isis to Lĕklis,[2] where he had a house. Then he said to him:

"You must be wise, you must be great and powerful and strong. You must go to the top of Lâniswi and swim in the pond of blue water that is there. When you get to the pond, you must pile up stones and then stand and talk to the mountain. Tell it what you think. The mountain will hear you. Everything in the world will hear you and understand you. After you have talked to the mountain, you must dive in the pond. Dive five times to the bottom, and each time drink of the lowest water. When you come out of the pond, build a fire, warm yourself and then sleep. If you dream, don't tell the dream to any one. When you wake up, start for home. On the road don't talk to any one, or drink any water. If you do as I tell you, you will be as great as I am and do the things that I do. You will live always. You will be the brightest

[1] Different events in the lives of Isis and Kumush are represented by rocks on that side of Tula Lake. Half-way up a high mountain is the house in which Kumush and Isis lived (a large rock); near Deus (Stork's bill), is Isis (a rock of peculiar shape), and at the northwest corner of Tula Lake is Kumush himself.

[2] The rocky summit of a mountain near Lake Tula.

object in the world. If you endure these things, you will be able to bear every suffering."

Isis put on a dress made of the red bark of the teskot tree, and went to the swimming place on the mountain. At night he piled up stones till he was sleepy; then he stood by the pond and talked to the mountain. After that he dived five times in the swimming pond. The fourth time he felt something big and heavy, but he thought: "My father does not want me to have riches in this world; he wants me to have mind." The fifth time he felt five kinds of gambling sticks and a large white feather.

He came out of the pond, built a fire and warmed himself; then he lay down and went to sleep. He dreamed that he saw the gambling sticks and the feather that he had felt in the water. When he woke up, he started down the mountain. As soon as he got home, he began to tell his dream, but Kumush said: "Don't tell your dream now. If you were to gamble with some one, then you might tell it."

After this Kumush sent Isis to Slákkosi, a swimming place in a deep basin on the top of a mountain. Kumush said: "When you get there, make a rope of willow bark, tie one end around a tree and the other around your body, and let yourself down into the whirlpool."

When Isis got to the top of the mountain, he went five times around the basin, then he made the rope and let himself down into the water. He went five times around inside the basin. Five times he saw a bright house that was nice to look at, and he saw lights burning in the water. After swimming, he drew himself up and started down the mountain.

When Isis got home, Kumush sent him to Gewásni, a pond deep down among the rocks on the summit of Giwásyaina.[1]

Kumush said: "Lok and Dásläts used to swim in Gewásni. When you get to the top of the mountain, you must hold your right hand up and talk to the mountain; ask it for mind and power. The mountain will hear you and great thoughts will go in through the top of your head. When you have talked to

[1] A mountain in Oregon.

Giwásyaina, you can talk all day to other mountains and not get tired or hoarse."

When Isis got to the swimming place, he let himself down with a bark rope, sat on a rock at the edge of the water and washed himself. Then he drew himself up to the top and lay down. He couldn't go to sleep. He went to the place where he stood when he talked to the mountain, lay down there and tried to sleep, but couldn't; so he started for home.

When Kumush saw Isis coming, he washed himself, and used nice smelling roots; then he took food and went to meet him and fix a resting place for him.

After Isis had eaten and rested, Kumush said: "I want you to go to Adáwa. You must go to all the gauwams (swimming places); you will find something in each one. Adáwa is Lok's pond. He stays in the water there. You must swim on the western side."

When Isis got to the pond, he thought there was a great rock out in the water. He swam out and stood on it. It was Lok and right away he began to shake and move. Isis jumped into the water; into the middle of a terrible whirlpool; the whirlpool was Lok's medicine. It made Isis' head feel queer and dizzy. He swam to the western side of the pond, dived five times, got out of the water and went home.

Kumush said: "Now you must go to old man Mukus. Before Gäk turned him into a rock Mukus was the greatest gambler in the world. Around him are many rocks, the men he was gambling with when Gäk's word was spoken.

When Isis started, Kumush put the back of his hand across his forehead, looked toward the place and talked to Mukus, asking him to be good to Isis and give him whatever he had to give.

When Isis got to the rock, he stood and waited. After a while old Mukus asked: "What did you come for?"

Isis made no answer.

Then the old man moved a little, and said: "I heard Kumush talking. I have nothing but gambling to give, — my work. I will give you that."

When Isis got home, he lay down. Kumush washed himself,

then gave his son food and drink. The next morning he sent him to get Tcok, the great gambling medicine.

Kumush said: "Tcok is round and bright, like the sun. If a lazy man tries to catch it, it will show itself in two or three places at the same time, and he can't overtake it; but if a strong man, who has been to the swimming ponds, follows it, it will let itself be caught."

Isis went for Tcok, caught it and brought it home. He held it so tightly in his hand that it burned him, and blistered his hand.

Kumush said: "You must kill Tcok; if you don't it will get away from you. You want it, for if a man has it when he is gambling, it gives him strength."

When Isis had killed Tcok, Kumush said: "Now you must go to Káimpeos. On the way you will come to a small pond. Don't stop there, for it is a bad place. In Káimpeos there are five Kais; they belong to the pond."

When Isis got to Káimpeos, he saw the sun, the moon, the stars and big fires down under the water. He dived five times; each time he felt a Kai right near him. Under the arm of the fifth Kai there were gambling sticks. When Isis came out of the water, he lay down on a rock and tried to go to sleep, but he couldn't, so he got up and went home.

While Isis was gone, Kumush made a sweat-house, and when Isis returned, he said: "Take off your bark clothes and sweat, then paint your face and body red and put on buckskin clothes and nice beads. You have been to all the swimming places, and you might be a big chief, but I don't want that. Other people will come and it will be bad here. We will go away where you can keep all the strength the mountains and swimming places have given you, where you won't get bad and dirty from the earth and people."

They went to the top of a high mountain and built a house among the rocks. The house was red and nice to look at. Kumush thought that people around Tula Lake would see his house, but couldn't climb up to it. Kumush had the north side, Isis the south side of the house; the door opened toward the east.

Kumush didn't know that Skakas and Nada lived on that mountain, but they did, and both of them fell in love with Isis. They came to the house and neither one of them would go away.

"What do you want?" asked Kumush.

"I want Isis for a husband," said Skakas. Nada gave the same answer.

"Well," said Kumush, "I will find out what you can do. Which of you can bring water first from that lake down there?"

Both started. Skakas found water on the way, turned around and was back first. When Nada came, she said to Skakas: "I didn't see you at the lake."

"I got there first; I took some water and came back. We were not there at the same time."

"I am a fast traveler," said Nada. "It is strange that you got back first."

Isis drank the water Nada brought, but wouldn't touch the water Skakas gave him.

Nada said: "We will go again. This time we will take hold of hands." They started in the morning, got the water and Nada flew back. Skakas didn't get back till midday.

Isis drank the water Nada brought, and said it was good, but he wouldn't drink the water Skakas brought. Kumush tore Skakas in pieces and threw the pieces over the cliff into the lake. The pieces are in the lake now; they became rocks.

Isis and Kumush didn't want to live where people could come, so they left their home and traveled toward the north-east. Not far from the house they put down their baskets, fish-spears, canoes and everything they had used in fishing. Those things turned to stone and are there on the cliff to-day. Kumush and Isis traveled for a long time before they came to the river that is now called Lost River. Kumush made a basket and caught a salmon in it. Then he said: "I want salmon always to be in this river, and many of them, so people will have plenty to eat." At Nusâltgăga he made a basket and caught small fish, and said the same thing, so that there should always be plenty of small fish in the river. He multiplied the histis, a kind of fish which Klamath Indians like.

When Isis and Kumush got to the third camping place, Kumush called it Bláielka and the mountain he called Ktáilawetĕs. He said to Isis: " You must swim in the swimming pond on this mountain, and pile up stones, and talk to the mountain."

Isis went to the pond and while he was in the water he saw nice gambling sticks and felt them touch his body. When he was through swimming and was coming out, Gäk flew by. He saw Isis standing in the water, and he thought: " I wonder where that bright thing in the water came from. It won't come here again! " That minute Isis was turned to stone, but his spirit escaped, and went to his father's camping place.

Isis and Kumush stayed a long time at Bláielka, then Kumush said: " I must travel around and work; you can stay here." Kumush left Isis on Dúilast, a mountain on the eastern side of Tula Lake and he started off for the west.

While Kumush was gone, many women came to live with Isis. Among his wives were Tókwa, Wéakûs, Djakkonus, Tcíktcikûs, Kládo, Tseks, Dohos, Dúdûte, Tcíkas, Kols, Nada and Wálwilegas. The first wife to have a child was Tcíkas, who had a little boy. Tcíkas was uneasy about Kumush; she was afraid something had happened to him.

Isis said: " Nothing can hurt Kumush. He will be here soon. He can go around the world in two days."

The next morning Kumush came, bringing in his hands little bundles of seeds of every kind. He threw those seeds in different directions, and talked to the mountains, the hills, the rivers and springs, to all places, telling them to take the seeds, to care for them and keep them forever. And he told them not to harm his grandson.

Isis' wives were so nice to look at that Kumush fell in love with them and began to think how to get rid of Isis.

One day when he was hunting, Isis used his last arrow. Kumush said: " I will make some arrows, but you must get eagle feathers to put on them. When I was coming home I saw an eagle's nest on the top of a tree. There were eggs in it; the eggs are hatched by this time. You can get some of the young eagles." And he told him where the tree was.

When Isis came to the tree, he took off his buckskin clothes and climbed up to the nest. He found the eagles and threw them to the ground. As he threw the last one, he looked down, and he nearly lost his mind, for at Kumush's word the tree had grown so tall that it almost touched the sky. Isis' clothes were under the tree. He saw Kumush come and put them on, then pick up the eagles, and start for home.

Before leaving the house, Kumush had said to Isis' wives: "I am going for wood." When he came back, the women thought he was Isis. When he asked: "Where is Kumush?" they said: "He went for wood and hasn't come back."

Kumush hurried the sun down and right away it was dark. All the women except Wálwilegas, Kols, Tcíkas and Tőkwa thought he was Isis.

The next morning Tcíkas asked Wálwilegas what she thought.

"He isn't Isis," said Wálwilegas.

"That is what I think," said Tcíkas.

Kols cried and tears ran down her cheeks. "Tears," said she, "are a sign that Isis is in trouble."

"What are you talking about?" asked Kumush. "Hurry up and get me something to eat. I don't want people to come here to gamble; we will go where they are."

After Kumush had eaten enough, he and all the women, except Wálwilegas, Kols and Tcíkas, started for Pitcowa, the place where Isis always went to gamble. (A broad flat northeast of Tula Lake.)

As Kumush traveled, he set fire to the grass; the smoke went crooked. People saw it, and said: "That is not Isis. Isis' smoke always goes straight up to the sky."

Kumush knew their thoughts. He tried to make the smoke go straight; part went straight and part went crooked.

Then they said: "Maybe that is Isis."

When he got near, the people asked: "Where is Kumush?"

"He stayed at home; he didn't want to come."

Some thought: "This man doesn't look just like Isis," but they began to gamble with him.

When all the women had gone except Wálwilegas and Tcíkas and Kols, Kols began to track her husband. Wálwilegas followed her. Tcíkas put her baby on her back and started for Pitcowa. She felt lonesome. She traveled slowly, digging roots as she went along.

Kols tracked Isis to the tree. Then she said: "He is up in this tree, but he must be dead."

"He is alive," said Wálwilegas. "I hear him breathe. He loved his other wives and didn't care for us. They have gone off with another man; now he will find out who loves him."

Kols tried to dig the tree up, but couldn't; then Wálwilegas began to make a basket. When the basket was ready, Kols strapped it on her back and flew up part way to try it. She came back, got something for Isis to eat and bear's fat to rub him with, then she started again. She flew in circles around the tree, camped one night and reached Isis the next night. He was almost dead. She gave him seeds and rubbed him with bear's fat. The next morning she put him in the basket and started down; she got home at midday.

Kols and Wálwilegas fed Isis well. Every night they rubbed him with bear's fat and soon he was well again. Then they fixed a sweat-house and he sweated till his skin was nice and soft. It became rough while he was on the tree. After he had sweated, they put nice clothes on him.

Isis asked: "How did Tókwa and Nada and the others act while I was lost?"

"They didn't care much," said Kols; "they were not sorry."

When the people at Pitcowa had gambled long enough, they began to play ball. Some thought that the man they were playing with was Isis; others thought he was Kumush.

Kumush had the disk on his back. It looked like a great scar. One day, while the people were disputing, some saying that he was Isis, others that he was Kumush, a man hired a doctor to make the south wind blow. When Kumush ran north after the ball and stooped down to pick it up, the wind raised his blanket and everybody saw the scar. Then they knew Kumush. They shouted, whooped and laughed. They stopped the game and gathered around him.

After Isis had sweated, he said: " We will go and see what Kumush is doing." He went ahead of Kols and Wálwilegas, and as he traveled he set fire to the grass. The smoke went straight up to the sky. People saw the smoke, and said: " That is Isis! Isis is coming now! " Kumush saw the smoke and was scared; he trembled and almost lost his mind.

Tcíkas had been camping and digging roots. She was mourning for Isis. The child saw Isis coming and called out " Tsutowas " (father).

" Don't call your father," said Tcíkas, " your father is dead."

The boy called again, and again. Tcíkas shook him and scolded him.

" Why do you do that? " asked Isis.

Tcíkas turned and saw Isis. She was glad, for she thought he was lost or dead. " Where were you? " asked she. " How did you get back? "

" Wálwilegas and Kols, the wives I didn't care for, saved me." Then he told her how Wálwilegas found him in the eagle's nest, and how she and Kols carried him home and cured him.

When Isis got to the gambling place, Kumush wanted to talk to him, wanted to be friendly. But Isis was angry; he wouldn't let Kumush come near him. He had Kols and Wálwilegas gather wood and build a big fire; then he called to his wives who were with Kumush and told them to come to him. They wouldn't come, for they were afraid. Then he willed that they should come, and they had to; his word drew them, and they couldn't help going.

He burned their feet and made them red; then he said: " You will no longer be people; you will be birds and will scatter over the world. People will kill you, for you will be good to eat." They turned into ducks and water birds and flew away. Then Isis threw Kumush into the fire and covered him with burning wood. He burned him to ashes, but in the ashes was the disk.

The next morning the morning star, Kumush's medicine, called out to the disk: "Why do you sleep so long? Get up, old man!" That minute Kumush was alive — he will last as long as the disk and the morning star.

Isis knew now that Kumush would never die, that nothing could kill him. Isis wandered off among the mountains, and as he traveled he sang a beautiful song, that no one else could sing. People could imitate it, but they couldn't repeat it or understand it.

Kumush followed Isis everywhere for years. At last he overtook him. He wanted to be kind, and live as before, but Isis said: "After what you did to me you may go wherever you want to in the world, and I will go where I want to. You are not my father. I feel that. I hope that of the people, who are to come into the world hereafter, no father will ever treat his son as you have treated me."

Kumush went to Tula Lake to live. Then Isis turned one of his three faithful wives to a butterfly, another to a badger and the third to a wren, and then he went to live alone on Tcutgósi, a high mountain.

THE FIVE BROTHERS OF LÁTKAKÁWAS

CHARACTERS

Blaiwas	Eagle	Lĭsgaga	
Dûnwa	Stone Mortar	Lóluk	Fire
Gäk	Crow	Naulintc	
Gáukos	Moon	Wekwek	Magpie
Kaiutois	Wolf	Wûlkûtska	Marten

WHEN Látkakáwas went to Kumush's sweat-house with the disk, her five brothers started for the east, traveling a little toward the north. After a long time they came to a village where there were many people. All those people had their heads shaven and covered with cedar pitch, for they were mourning.

In the house at the edge of the village lived three orphans, the Naulintc children, two girls and a boy. They were so poor that they had nothing to eat.

Látkakáwas' brothers went in and sat down by the fire. They put their elbows on their knees and their heads on their hands. They felt lonesome, for they were mourning for their brother-in-law.

The little boy, Gáukos, began to cry, for he was scared. His elder sister scolded him, and said: "Be quiet; these men didn't come here to hurt you. If you don't stop crying, I will throw you out!"

Gáukos kept on crying, and at sunset his sister threw him out. She threw him his blanket and laughed at him, and said: "You can go to the gauwams [1] on the mountains, talk to the earth, and swim. Maybe you will be a great doctor, and know how to do things."

Lĭsgaga, the younger sister, went to Gáukos. She was cry-

[1] Gauwams, a pond or small lake.

ing, also. "Let us go to the village and stay with our friends," said the little girl.

"I don't want to go there," said Gáukos. "You must get a string and help me tie my blanket around my waist. I am going to the gauwams on the mountains, but I will come back."

"You are a little fellow," said his sister; "you are not old enough to go so far alone."

"I can take care of myself," said Gáukos. "I will make myself strong. I will talk to the earth and mountains and get them to give me power."

Lĭsgaga tied his blanket together and Gáukos walked off quickly. With every step he took, he grew. He had a song that he sang as he traveled; the song said: "I've been thrown out, I've been given to the earth!"

The trail Gáukos followed went into a ravine; when he came up on the other side of the ravine he was as large as a full-grown man.

Lĭsgaga was watching, and when she saw that her brother had grown large and strong, she went back to the house. The elder sister laughed, and said: "Our little brother has gone to get wise and great, but the crows will eat him." Lĭsgaga didn't say a word.

After a while Látkakáwas' five brothers went to Blaiwas' house. The eldest brother married Blaiwas' daughter; the second brother married Kaiutois' daughter; the third Wûlkûtska's daughter: the fourth Wekwek's; the fifth married the daughter of Kutyelolinas.

For five days Lĭsgaga sat on the top of the house, making a tula grass mat, and waiting for her brother. Often her sister threatened to push her off, made fun of her, and asked: "Who are you looking for? Your brother," said she, "has gone for wisdom and power, but some wild beast will eat him; you will never see him again."

The sixth morning, when Lĭsgaga went to the top of the house, she heard her brother's song. It sounded far away, near the mountains.

As Gáukos came along the trail, he saw nice things, — blankets worked with porcupine quills, buckskin dresses, beads, and bows and arrows. He took a wonderful buckskin dress, for his little sister. There were no seams in the dress and it was covered with beads; there was not another such a dress in the world. Gáukos thought he would be kind to his elder sister, so he took a buckskin dress for her, but it wasn't as nice as Lĭsgaga's.

When his little sister saw him coming, she went down the ladder into the house. Everybody in the village saw Gáukos coming and wondered who the stranger was. He was like the moon; his body was changed and he was bright and beautiful. When the elder sister saw him, she laughed and said to Lĭsgaga: "Maybe that young man is your brother. Maybe Gáukos looks like that now."

Lĭsgaga didn't say a word. She spread down the tula grass mat she had made and it became bright and beautiful. The elder sister took it up, and spread it on her own place for the stranger to sit on; she thought he might be coming to marry her.

Lĭsgaga said: "I made that mat for my brother to sit on. You have always said that he soiled your mats." She took the mat and put it down on her own side of the house.

The elder sister brought water from the spring, and then began to pound seeds to give to the stranger. Lĭsgaga took seeds from her own basket and put them in a basket for her brother.

When Gáukos got home, he left his presents on the top of the house and went in and sat down by Lĭsgaga. She was still small, but Gáukos was a full-grown man. She gave him the tula grass mat to sit on, and gave him seeds to eat.

The elder sister knew him now and was ashamed. After Gáukos had eaten the seeds, he asked Lĭsgaga to comb his hair.

When night came and Gáukos was going to lie down near Lĭsgaga, the elder sister said: "Why do you lie near that child? She will give you lice. I am glad to see you; I will lie on your mat," and she went to his side of the house.

"Don't come so near," said Gáukos. "It is too hot," and

he pushed her away. She came again, and again he pushed her away. In the night when he woke up, she was lying by his side; and he rolled over toward his little sister. The next morning he said to Lĭsgaga: " Wash your face and comb your hair. I have brought you a new dress."

He went to the creek and bathed, then he gave Lĭsgaga both dresses, and said: " Give this one to our sister." He gave Lĭsgaga a belt to wear when she danced her maturity dance, and porcupine quills for her hair.

When the little girl put on her new dress, she looked very nice. She gave the other dress to her sister, and said: " This is how our brother pays you for throwing him out."

" Why did you bring such a nice dress to this dirty child? " asked the sister. Gáukos didn't answer.

While Lĭsgaga was gone for wood, the elder sister put pounded ges [1] in a basket and placed the basket in front of Gáukos. He asked: " Why do you do this? I heard, when I was a child, that young women, when in their father's house, gave ges to their husbands. It should not be given to a brother." He pushed the basket away. His sister didn't say anything, but she was angry. When Gáukos went out, she said to Lĭsgaga: " He likes you, but he doesn't care for me."

" You threw him out," said Lĭsgaga. " I have always been kind to him; but he likes you, for he brought you a nice dress."

That night when Gáukos lay down on his mat, he told Lĭsgaga to lie near him, then he whispered to her, and told her his elder sister's thoughts; he knew them all. Lĭsgaga listened, but she didn't say anything.

In the night the elder sister tied three strands of her hair to Gáukos' hair. When he woke up and wanted to turn over he couldn't, for his hair was tied. In the morning he said to Lĭsgaga: " To-night I am going away; I can't stay here."

" If you go toward the east," said Lĭsgaga, " you will be safe, and will find people to help you."

When the elder sister came with water, and saw Gáukos talking to the little girl, she asked: " What are you saying

[1] The seed of a certain kind of weed.

to that child?" He did not reply. That night she again tied three strands of her hair to her brother's hair.

When he woke up he said to himself: "Let her sleep till I reach the first house." To Lĭsgaga he said: "I am going east and I must travel fast, for our sister will turn to a man-eater and follow me."

Gáukos crossed a wide flat at a step, sprang from one mountain to another, and early in the morning came to the first house. There were many mountains between it and his sisters' house. In that house lived two sisters, old women who were wise and had power; they could even make themselves young if they wanted to.

Gáukos said to the old women: "I am in trouble; you must save me."

"We don't know how to save you," said the sisters. He begged hard, and at last they turned him into a baby, put him on a board and swaddled him.

When the girl woke up and found her brother gone, she turned to a man-eater and followed him. She tracked him across flats and over mountains. In the evening she came to the house where the old women lived, and asked: "Where is the young man who came here?"

"We haven't seen a young man," said the sisters. "Nobody comes here."

"His tracks stop at your house," said the sister. She looked in, saw the baby, and said: "Oh, you have a baby!" She went in, picked up the child, and said: "He looks like the man I am following."

"That baby was born this morning," said one of the sisters.

The woman put the baby back where it had been, then she lay down and went to sleep. She couldn't help it, for the sisters made her sleep. One of them covered her, and said: "Let her sleep till her brother is near the place where he wants to go."

As soon as the woman was asleep, the sisters unswaddled the baby. That minute he was a man and started off, saying: "If I live, I will not forget you."

About daylight the sister woke up, and asked: "Where is your baby?"

"He has gone."

"I thought so. I should have eaten him last night. When I come back I will pay you for this!" She started off quickly; she could step and jump as far as Gáukos could.

"Oh," said the sisters, laughing, "you will not come back if you go where your brother is," and they threw ashes after her, that fire might burn her up.

When Gáukos came to the house where old Lóluk and his wife, Dûnwa, lived, he asked Dûnwa to save him. Dûnwa didn't speak. When Lóluk said "Um, um!" (he wanted his wife to save the young man) Dûnwa stood up and told Gáukos to go down in the hole where she had been sitting.

Gáukos thought: "Maybe she will sit on me and kill me."

Dûnwa said: "You mustn't think that; I won't hurt you."

He went into the hole, and Dûnwa sat down again.

Old Lóluk's daughters were out hunting. When they went off to track deer they left their clothes at home and wore only a breech-clout. The minute Gáukos hid in the hole, each sister's bowstring broke. The girls were frightened, for they knew that something had happened, and right away they started for the house. When they were putting on their clothes, the elder sister said: "I feel as if somebody were looking at me."

"I feel so, too," said the younger sister.

They went into the house. Just then Gáukos' sister came in like a whirlwind.

"Tell me where my brother is!" screamed she.

Nobody answered. The sisters didn't know what she meant.

"Where is he?" cried she. "I have tracked him to your house. Tell me where he is!"

The elder sister put back her hair, and said: "We have been hunting; we don't know anything about your brother. Ask our father or our mother."

Gáukos' sister didn't ask but she began to poke the fire

around. That made the girls angry, for she was scratching their father's face.

"Why do you scratch my father?" screamed the elder sister.

"This is not a living person; it is nothing but fire. I want to warm myself."

"That isn't a common fire," said the girl. "That's our father! Let him alone!" She pushed her away.

Gáukos' sister jumped on the girl, opened her mouth and was going to chew her up and swallow her but the younger sister pulled her back by the hair. Old Lóluk said "Um! um!" Dûnwa raised herself up, rolled over on the girl and broke her legs. The old man opened his mouth wide, like two walls, the sisters caught hold of the girl and threw her into his mouth. Lóluk swallowed her.

The elder sister said: "You will not do such things again. You will no longer be a person; you will be a bird, and lay eggs in the holes of cedar trees. People will kill you, for you will be good to eat."

Old Lóluk called Gáukos out of his hiding-place and fixed him a place between his two daughters. Dûnwa brought him seeds to eat; he was her son-in-law now.

The next morning Gáukos asked for a bow and arrows. The elder sister brought him hers.

He tried the string of the bow, and said: "This is not strong enough."

The younger sister brought her bow; he tried the string and said: "This will do." Then he started.

Dûnwa said to her elder daughter: "You must go, too. This place is new for him; he may have bad luck."

The young woman took her bow and arrows and followed Gáukos. When he looked back and saw her coming, he stopped and asked: "Why have you come?"

"I came to show you where the deer are."

Right away they saw under a tree two deer hiding from flies. Gáukos crept up and shot both of them with one arrow. Then he told the woman to stay by the two while he looked for others. Soon he shot two more, and again two, and farther on he killed five; he put the nine deer in his belt and went back to his wife.

"Put the deer down," said she, "I want to tell you about my father and mother. My sister and I kill ten deer each day. Each night our mother eats all the bones of those ten deer and in the morning not a bone is left; our father eats the meat and the livers. As soon as we get home, we cut the deer open, take out the livers and put five of them in our father's mouth. We give him meat three times each day. You mustn't think about my father or my mother, for they know your thoughts."

Gáukos said: "I will kill the deer for you; I am a good hunter." He put the eleven deer in his belt, and they went home.

Dûnwa asked: "How many deer did my son-in-law kill?"

"Eleven," said her daughter. The old woman was glad.

Gáukos cut open the deer and gave five of the livers to Lóluk; then he gave the back and leg bones and all the other bones to his mother-in-law; she pounded them fine and ate them.

The sisters cooked meat, for themselves and Gáukos, on their father's face, without scratching or hurting him.

When they were through eating, the elder sister asked: "Where shall we hang meat to dry?"

Gáukos went off a little way, pulled up a big tree, brought it to the house and stuck it down in the ground. On the branches of the tree they hung the meat of the eleventh deer.

That night Gáukos said: "I will stay ten days and hunt, then I must go and see my little sister."

He killed eleven deer each day for ten days. As soon as they had ten big trees full of meat, he started for home. He spent the first night with the two old women. When they asked about his sister, he said: "Lóluk ate her up." That night he heard singing and the rattle of a belt; Lĭsgaga was dancing her maturity dance. It was the fifth night. When young men came to ask the old women where the singing was, Gáukos told them.

Early the next morning Gáukos got home. Lĭsgaga was glad to see him; she had on her buckskin dress and her face was painted red. He said: " I have two wives now. I am going to make this house big enough for us all. I am afraid to live in the house with old Lóluk and my mother-in-law, for they know my thoughts. If I should think something bad about them, they might kill me." He thought hard, and right away the house was big and full of nice things.

The next morning he started back. He spent the first night with the two old women and was at Lóluk's house in the evening. That night he told Dûnwa's daughters that he wanted to live in his old home. When he talked, neither Lóluk nor his wife knew what he said, they knew only when he thought. The elder sister told her mother in thought what Gáukos said.

" Is he going to leave you here? " asked Dûnwa.

" No, he wants us to go with him."

" Our married daughters don't belong to us," said the old woman. " We keep them while they are single, but married they belong to another house."

The next morning the young man killed ten deer. For ten days he killed ten deer each day, and on the eleventh day he killed many more.

Old Lóluk and his wife never went out; they stayed always in one place. The girls went every day to dig roots. They put them in baskets of different sizes and arranged the baskets in a row, a large basket at one end, and a small one at the other end. The old woman put a cap on the head of the largest basket.

When Gáukos and the two sisters were ready to start, Dûnwa asked if they would come back. When her son-in-law said that one of her daughters would come and bring her deer meat, she was satisfied.

The three started and all the baskets followed; the basket with the cap went ahead.

Gáukos and the two sisters spent the first night with the old women. Gáukos gave the woman who had turned him into a baby and saved him from his sister, the second basket. It was full of roots that were sweet and tasted good.

The next morning the three went on, and the baskets followed. When Gáukos got home, Lĭsgaga stored away the roots and put up the baskets.

Gáukos hunted deer for ten days and killed twenty each day. In the largest basket, the one with the cap, he put all the bones; in the other baskets he put livers and meat. Then he said to the elder sister: "You must take these baskets to your father and mother."

The younger sister said: "She can stay here, I will go with the baskets."

"We had better do as we are told," said the elder.

"Make the journey in one day and don't camp anywhere," said Gáukos.

The elder sister started, and the baskets followed, walking one behind the other. The younger sister cried, for she was lonesome.

Gáukos said: "When we left your father and mother, I promised that one of you should go back with meat; that is why I sent your sister. If you want to go, get ready."

She started and overtook her sister. The elder sister went ahead of the baskets, the younger walked behind them. When the sisters were near Lóluk's house, old man Gäk saw them and was scared. He said: "B*e*-*e*-au! Where did all those baskets come from? And why are they walking? They will never do that again. Hereafter people will carry on their backs whatever they put into baskets. Baskets will not walk like that." Right away the baskets turned to stone.

Then Gäk said to the sisters: "You will no longer be living women; you will be rocks, and stay right here on the trail." When he came to Lóluk's house, he said: "Old woman Dûnwa, you will no longer be great. In later times people will pound roots on you." To old man Lóluk he said: "Hereafter you will be kin to no man; you will burn all alike." As Gäk spoke, Lóluk became common fire.

When Gáukos' wives were turned to stone his bowstring broke, and right away he knew what had happened.

ISIS AND YAULILIK'S DAUGHTERS

CHARACTERS

Isis . . . .
Kumush . . . .
Yaulilik . . . . Snowbird

Isis built a house on Teutgosi and lived there many years. Each day that he hunted for deer he killed three or four. He hung the deer on his belt as though they were rabbits and carried them home; then he cut up the meat and dried it.

Isis had so much deer meat that if all the people in the world had eaten of it there would have been plenty left.

While hunting Isis always sang, and his song was heard everywhere in the world. It was so beautiful that any one listening to it might have dropped asleep.

On one side of Isis' mountain lived old Yaulilik with her two daughters and her son. Yaulilik was so poor that she had to beg meat for herself and children. One day she said to her daughters:

" You ought to be sorry that your mother has to work so hard. For many years I've begged meat for you to eat. I am old now. You should find a good hunter to kill deer for us. I can't work for you much longer. You are old enough to have a husband."

" Where can we find a good hunter? " asked the elder sister.

" There is one on this mountain; I often hear his song. If you didn't always stay in the house, you would hear it. It is the song of a great hunter."

" Where is his house? " asked the elder sister.

" In the north. You will camp one night before you get there."

The sisters didn't want to go, for they didn't know about Isis; they were afraid and wanted to stay with their mother.

Old Yaulilik said: " Isis is the son of Kumush. He is the greatest hunter, the greatest ball player and the greatest runner in the world. He can run down deer and catch them." When the sisters heard this they were willing to go.

Yaulilik filled two baskets with roots and seeds, gave one to each of her daughters, and said: " Old man Kumush lives with Isis, and sometimes he pretends that he is Isis. He puts on Isis' clothes and tries to sing his song. You mustn't let him fool you. When Isis is at home there is always fresh deer meat hanging on the trees near the house."

The sisters traveled till the sun went down; then they camped. They started early the next morning and soon came to a large village. Blaiwas was chief of that village.

All the Blaiwas people came out of their houses to watch the sisters and see where they were going. When they got to Isis' house, they put their baskets down outside the door and listened; somebody inside was playing on a flute.

The elder sister said: " Isis is at home."

" That's not Isis," said the younger sister.

" How do you know? "

" Mother said that if Isis was at home there would be fresh deer meat hanging on the trees near the house. All the meat on these trees is dry."

" Don't you hear the nice music? "

" Yes, but mother said that Isis' song was so beautiful that one might fall asleep when they heard it."

The sisters disputed for a long time, then the elder one went in and sat down by the man who was playing on the flute; the younger followed her, but she was crying, for she knew that the man was not Isis.

Isis was away hunting for deer and just at the moment the girls put down their baskets outside his door his bowstring broke, then he knew that young women had come to him. He started for home, singing as he traveled. When he was on the top of a mountain where the sky came to the ground, all the people in the world heard his song, and said: "Isis is coming."

The old man kept playing on the flute. After a while he said to the girls: "I wonder why Kumush doesn't come?"

The elder sister nudged the younger, and said: "This man is Isis; Kumush has gone for wood."

"No," said the younger, "Isis is coming. I hear his song."

Soon Isis came in with his belt full of deer. He stood still and didn't know where to go, for the younger sister sat in his place. At last he went to the old man's side of the house, put down the deer, cut up one and cooked the ribs, then he asked Kumush if he had given the girls anything to eat.

"No," said Kumush. "I was playing on the flute."

Isis gave the girls meat. The elder ate, but the younger couldn't, for she was crying.

When it was growing dark, Isis said to Kumush: "Take off my clothes; you will break the beads if you sleep on them."

The girls went outside; then Isis gave Kumush a large mat and said: "Go outside with your young women."

The old man took his blanket and the mat and went outside.

The elder sister was angry; she knew now that she had been fooled. When Kumush lay down, she and her sister held him to the ground and began to scratch him with their bone head-scratchers. He screamed and called to Isis that the girls were killing him, but Isis didn't care. The girls scratched harder and harder; they wanted to scratch all the flesh off his bones. At daybreak, when they started for home, there was nothing left of old Kumush but bones and the disk.

Isis stayed in the house all night. He heard Kumush scream and knew that the girls were abusing him, but he was angry at the old man and wouldn't help him. In the morning when he went out to see what had happened, he found only a pile of bones and a disk. The girls were gone.

Isis felt badly; he was lonesome for his father. He strung his bow and shot an arrow through the air. The arrow struck the side of a mountain, split the mountain apart, and through the opening came a river so deep and wide that the girls couldn't cross it. They sat down on the bank, for they didn't know what to do. Soon Isis came and sat down near them. He called the elder sister to him, caught hold of her hair and cut her head off. Then he killed the younger sister and threw both bodies into the river.

Isis felt badly. He went to Mlaiksi (Mt. Shasta), lay on the top of the mountain and cried. He didn't want to go home.

One day, when old Yaulilik was fishing in the river that Isis had made, the head of one of her daughters floated into the net. When she sent Cogátkis, her little boy, to see if there were fish in the net he ran back crying: "There is something in the net that looks like my sister's head."

Yaulilik ran to the river, took the head out of the net and saw that it was the head of her elder daughter. She put the head in a basket and carried it home, then she sent Cogátkis to look for the body. Soon he called out: "Come quick, my sister's body is in the net!"

They carried the body to the house, then old Yaulilik sent the boy to watch for the head of his younger sister, and after a time her head and body floated into the net. Then the mother made a sweat-house, and built a big fire in it. She put the two heads and two bodies into a basket, and put the basket and Cogátkis into the sweat-house. She wrapped up Cogátkis, so that he couldn't move, and said: "No matter what your sisters say or do, you mustn't answer them or speak to them." She shut the sweat-house up tight, and started for Blaiwas' village to ask Blaiwas if he knew who had killed her daughters.

As Yaulilik traveled, she sang her snow song, and a great snow-storm came. When she stopped singing the snow stopped falling. When she got to Blaiwas' village she went into the first house.

The people living there asked: "Why did you come here? What do you want?"

Yaulilik said: "I came to find out who killed my daughters."

The people didn't know, but they gave her as much deer

meat as they could lift. Yaulilik made it small by her power, put it in her bosom and went on. She began to sing; snow fell again. She stopped at each house in the village, and asked: " Do you know who killed my daughters? "

At each house she got the same answer, and a gift of deer meat.

At the end of the village three houses stood near together. Blaiwas lived in the first house, Gäk in the second, and Ndúkis in the third. When Yaulilik asked Blaiwas who had killed her daughters, he said: " I don't know, you had better ask old man Gäk; he lives in the next house; maybe he will know."

Gäk didn't know, but told her to ask the old man who lived in the next house.

When Yaulilik went into the third house old Ndúkis looked up, and asked: " What have you come here for? " When she told him he asked: " What man did you send your daughters to? "

Yaulilik didn't answer.

" Well," said Ndúkis, " the man you sent them to killed them. Just after daylight I heard one woman scream and then another. The second screamed louder and longer than the first. The sound came from the northwest."

Yaulilik said: " I know now who killed my daughters." She thanked old Ndúkis and started for home. As soon as she started the snow disappeared, the ground was dry and the air warm and pleasant.

When half-way home Yaulilik took the deer meat out of her bosom, made it large and carried it on her back. When she was near the sweat-house she heard talking and laughing.

Yaulilik hadn't been gone long when the girls began to be noisy and to try to make their brother talk to them. The elder sister's voice called from the basket:

" Little brother, don't you want to see me? I have come back."

The younger one said: " Get up, little brother, and talk with us."

Cogátkis didn't look toward the basket or speak.

When Yaulilik was almost home, the girls got out of the basket and began to unwrap their brother, but he jumped up and ran away. He was afraid if he spoke his sisters would die again. When Yaulilik opened the sweat-house door, the three ran out; they were glad to see her. The girls were well, but their bodies were tender, and Yaulilik wouldn't let them go far from the house. One day, when the younger sister was digging roots, she looked toward Mlaiksi, and right away she wanted to go there. When she carried her roots home, she said to her mother: " To-morrow I am going to Mlaiksi to gather seeds."

Yaulilik said: " You can't go there; you are not strong enough."

The elder sister said: " Your feet are too tender to climb that mountain."

The girl waited two days, then she said: " To-morrow I am going to Mlaiksi to gather seeds." In the morning she asked her mother to feed her.

The elder sister said: " If you go, I shall go."

Then Cogátkis began to cry; he wanted to go with his sisters. When his mother gave each of the girls water for the road he screamed.

Yaulilik said to her daughters: " Your brother feels lonesome; let him go with you."

The elder sister said: " If the lolus seeds are not ripe, we shall come home. He is little; he can't travel fast."

The younger sister was sorry for her brother, so she tied his hair in a knot on the top of his head and told her mother to take him to Duilas (Little Shasta). From Duilas, through the power of his hair, he could see them when they were on the mountain.

The sisters started toward Mlaiksi, and Yaulilik took Cogátkis to Duilas. Cogátkis could watch his sisters, and he could talk with his mother, though the house was a long way off.

The sisters gathered seeds all day. When it was nearly dark, the elder sister asked: " Shall we stay here to-night? "

"We have only a few seeds," said the younger sister. "We can stay all night and fill our baskets in the morning."

When Cogátkis saw them picking up wood, he went home. Early the next morning he went again to Duilas. The girls were busy gathering seeds, so Cogátkis called to his mother: "They are at work again!"

At midday the younger sister said: "I want water; where can we get some?"

"I don't know. There is no water near here."

They were at the foot of Mlaiksi. The younger sister looked at the mountain, and said: "High up there is a green place; maybe there is water there. I will go and see."

She climbed the mountain till she came to soft ground, then went higher and came to a place where the ground was moist. She dug down and found mud, but no water; she went higher, and this time, when she came to moist earth and dug down, she found a little water. She called her sister, and both drank of the water and then filled their water baskets.

They gathered seeds a while. The younger sister kept going up the mountain. The elder sister said: "Don't go so high; you won't find any seeds up there. It is getting late. Let us go back to where we camped last night."

The younger sister heard a strange noise and wanted to find out what made it. She thought: "I will go back now, but to-morrow I will go to that green place that I can see way up there. Maybe I will find out what that noise is."

When they got to the foot of the mountain and began to pick up wood Cogátkis went home, and said to his mother: "My sisters have camped where they camped last night."

That night the younger sister couldn't sleep; she was thinking of the strange noise she had heard: she felt drawn toward the sound. The next morning they gathered seeds till their baskets were full, then the younger sister said: "I want water. I am going to the place where we got some yesterday."

They left their baskets and climbed up to where they had dug the hole; there was no water in it. They went higher, came to moist ground, dug down and got a little water. The younger sister again heard the strange sound. She went higher and listened; then she heard, far away, a weak voice saying: " Kĕlmas popanwe. Kĕlmas popanwe! " (You are drinking nothing but tears. You are drinking nothing but tears.)

The girl followed the sound, and saw a bright red hair on the ground. When she picked it up she knew it was a hair from the head of the man who had killed her and her sister. The place where she found the hair was level and smooth, without a blade of grass or a weed on it. In the middle of that space was a skeleton. All the bones were dead but the eyes were living. It was Isis' skeleton. Thousands of deer had been there and danced around the man who had killed so many of their people. With their hoofs they had stamped down the grass and beaten the ground level.

When the elder sister saw the skeleton she was frightened and wanted to run away, but the younger sister spread out her wolf skin blanket and put the skeleton on it.

" What are you going to do with that? " asked her sister. " It smells badly. It makes me sick." She wanted to snatch the skeleton and break it up.

" Go away! " said the younger girl. " I will bring this to life." She wrapped the bones up carefully and started down the mountain, her sister following.

When they got to their camp the elder said: " Let me have those bones; they are the bones of the man who killed us. I'll pound them up and burn them."

The younger sister didn't listen to what the elder said. She got deer fat, rubbed the skeleton with it, and pushed some of the fat between the teeth. She worked over the skeleton all night. In the morning there was a little flesh on the bones; at midday the skeleton was a man again.

The younger sister fed him, and the elder gathered seeds for him, for she liked him now.

Cogátkis called to his mother: " I see two persons sitting in the shade while my elder sister gathers seeds." The next morning he called to his mother: " The stranger is alone; both my sisters are gathering seeds."

Isis drank water, then lay down and slept. While he was sleeping porcupines danced around him, and sang. The sisters came at midday, and when the porcupines saw them coming they ran away.

The next morning the younger sister said to Isis: " This is the last day we can gather seeds near by. We must go farther up the mountain."

When Isis was left alone, he fell asleep. The porcupines came and danced around him and sang, and each one's song was: " Who can cut off my feet and hands and eat them? "

Isis woke up, struck the chief of the porcupines with his cane, killed him, cut off his feet and hands, pulled the quills out of his back and tied them up in ten bunches. He wanted to give the quills to his wives and his mother-in-law. Isis was well now, and could hunt for deer.

Soon the elder sister had a child. Isis stayed in the camp till the child was five days old; then he went out to hunt. He killed a deer, but he let it stay where it fell, for it wasn't right to bring it home or say anything about it. The next day he killed two deer at a shot, left them and went home.

When the first child was seven days old, the younger sister had a little boy. When the last child was eight days old, Isis said to his wives: " Your mother and brother are lonesome, we must go and see them."

The next day they started. The sisters complained of the weight of the seeds, and Isis said: " I will make them light." As soon as he said that, their baskets were as light as feathers.

When Cogátkis saw his sisters and the stranger coming, he called to his mother: " My sisters are coming, and there is a beautiful blue man with them! "

Old Yaulilik spread out nice mats and her daughters' bead dresses and ornaments. When near the house, Isis stopped and the sisters went on. Cogátkis ran to meet them; he was glad, but he was afraid of Isis. The sisters said: " Go and lead your brother-in-law into the house."

When they were in the house, Cogátkis told Isis how deer ran around him while he was out on the mountain watching his sisters.

Isis said: " I want to go and hunt for deer, but I haven't arrows enough."

" I will give you all the arrows you want," said old Yaulilik, and she gave him a quiverful that had been her husband's. Isis killed two deer.

" How can we carry them home? " asked Cogátkis.

Isis picked up the deer and put them in his belt. On the way home he killed a third deer, and he put that in his belt also. When Cogátkis told his younger sister how many deer Isis had killed, she said: " Maybe he will go away. Maybe he doesn't want to stay here."

Isis pulled up six big trees, brought them to the house, and set them up to dry meat on. The next morning he killed a deer and said to Cogátkis: " Stay here and see that nobody steals the deer while I am gone." When he came back, he had ten deer in his belt. He put the first deer with them and went home. Old Yaulilik cut up the meat and hung it on the trees to dry, and Isis stretched the skins.

The next day when he was going home, with his belt full of deer, he wanted water and went to Tsiwisa to get it. After he had drunk, he remembered that the spring was near the place where Kumush had made the tree, with the eagle's nest on it, grow up to the sky. He didn't like the place, for it made him feel lonesome. That night he said to the sisters: " I am going away. You have plenty of meat; you can stay here with your mother and brother."

The elder sister didn't want to stay, and Isis said: " I am going a long way. The children are heavy; you couldn't carry them."

" We can carry them easily," said the elder sister. " I don't want to stay here."

" Then you can go," said Isis, for he wasn't willing to show that he wanted them to stay.

Her sister said: " He is going to a strange country; something may happen to me. I don't want to go."

" You must go with us, so get ready," said the elder sister.

The younger sister said to her mother: " I didn't ask to go with them; she makes me go."

" You can stay with me," said her mother.

"No, maybe they will be gone a long time. I will go with them, and it won't be my fault if something happens."

The three traveled one day, then camped at Blaiaga, the mountain where Isis and Kumush had lived. Isis said to his wives: "The spring here is bad. When you go for water you must take the children with you."

Each day for three days Isis killed deer. The fourth day, while he was hunting, the younger sister put her child on her back and went for wood. The elder sister wanted water and she ran to the spring to get it. She forgot that Isis had told her not to leave her child alone. The boy was beginning to walk. He tried to follow his mother, but he fell and hit his head on a stone. He gave one loud scream and died. The younger sister heard the scream and ran to the child. The mother heard it, too, and came back quickly. Her sister said: "I told you we had better stay with our mother; that we didn't know this country. See what trouble has come to us." They set bushes on fire to let Isis know what had happened.

The moment the child fell, Isis struck his foot against a stone and stumbled. Right away he knew that something had happened to one of his boys. When he saw the smoke, he left the deer he had killed and went home.

When the younger sister told him that his child was dead, he said: "I didn't think that my wives would cause me greater grief than my father did, but you have. I thought my children would live, that they would go to the swimming places and talk to the earth and mountains, that they would be wise and able to do things. If my first child is dead, I don't want to live in this world. Bring me the other boy."

When the younger wife brought her child, Isis took it in his arms, put the top of its head to his mouth and drew a long breath. He took the breath out of the child and it was dead. He put the second child by the first, and said:

"These children are half mine, and half yours. The breath is mine, the body is yours. I have taken the breath into myself. You can have the bodies. This is the last time I will have a wife. If I live forever I shall never have a woman again. This place where my children died will be called

Yaulilikumwas. People who come in after times will find you under the bushes. They will make sport of you and call you Yaulilikumwas. You will die from the cold and snow which you yourselves make. Your brother will run around the world and be Kĕngkong'kongis (a medicine) and doctors will dream of him."

Right away Isis' wives and their mother turned to snowbirds and Cogátkis became Kĕngkong'kongis. Sometimes ordinary people see him in their dreams. Doctors always see him in the country where his mother and sisters lived. Isis went north, went far away.

KUMUSH AND HIS DAUGHTER

CHARACTERS

Kumush . . . . The Creator, according to Indian myths
Skoks . . . . Spirit

KUMUSH (our Father) left Tula Lake and wandered over the earth. He went to the edge of the world and was gone a great many years; then he came back to Nihlaksi, where his sweat-house had been; where Látkakáwas brought the disk; where the body of the beautiful blue man was burned, and where Isis was saved.

Kumush brought his daughter with him from the edge of the world. Where he got her, no one knows. When he came back, Isis and all the people he had made were dead; he and his daughter were alone. The first thing he did was to give the young girl ten dresses, which he made by his word. The finest dress of all was the burial dress; it was made of buckskin, and so covered with bright shells that not a point of the buckskin could be seen.

The first of the ten dresses was for a young girl; the second was the maturity dress, to be worn while dancing the maturity dance; the third was the dress to be put on after coming from the sweat-house, the day the maturity dance ended; the fourth was to be worn on the fifth day after the dance; the fifth dress was the common, everyday dress; the sixth was to wear when getting wood; the seventh when digging roots; the eighth was to be used when on a journey; the ninth was to wear at a ball game; the tenth was the burial dress.

When they came to Nihlaksi Kumush's daughter was within a few days of maturity. In the old time, when he was making rules for his people, Kumush had said that at maturity a girl should dance five days and five nights, and while she was dancing an old woman, a good singer, should sing for her. When the five days and nights were over she should bathe in the sweat-house, and then carry wood for five days. If the girl grew sleepy while she was dancing, stopped for a moment, nodded and dreamed, or if she fell asleep while in the sweat-house and dreamed of some one's death, she would die herself.

Kumush was the only one to help his daughter; he sang while she danced. When the dance was over and the girl was in the sweat-house, she fell asleep and dreamed of some one's death. She came out of the sweat-house with her face and hands and body painted with wáginte.[1] As she stood by the fire to dry the paint, she said to her father: "While I was in the sweat-house I fell asleep and I dreamed that as soon as I came out some one would die."

"That means your own death," said Kumush. "You dreamed of yourself."

Kumush was frightened; he felt lonesome. When his daughter asked for her burial dress he gave her the dress to be worn after coming from the sweat-house, but she wouldn't take it. Then he gave her the dress to be worn five days later, and she refused it. One after another he offered her eight dresses — he could not give her the one she had worn when she was a little girl, for it was too small. He held the tenth dress tight under his arm; he did not want to give it to her, for as soon as she put it on the spirit would leave her body.

"Why don't you give me my dress?" asked she. "You made it before you made the other dresses, and told me what it was for; why don't you give it to me now? You made everything in the world as you wanted it to be."

He gave her the dress, but he clung to it and cried. When she began to put it on he tried to pull it away. She said: "Father, you must not cry. What has happened to me is your will; you made it to be this way. My spirit will leave the body and go west."

At last Kumush let go of the dress, though he knew her spirit would depart as soon as she had it on. He was crying

[1] A red root.

as he said: "I will go with you; I will leave my body here, and go."

"No," said the daughter, "my spirit will go west without touching the ground as it goes. How could you go with me?"

"I know what to do," said Kumush. "I know all things above, below, and in the world of ghosts; whatever is, I know."

She put on the dress, Kumush took her hand, and they started, leaving their bodies behind. Kumush was not dead but his spirit left the body.

As soon as the daughter died, she knew all about the spirit world. When they started she said to her father: "Keep your eyes closed; if you open them you will not be able to follow me, you will have to go back and leave me alone."

The road they were traveling led west to where the sun sets. Along that road were three nice things to eat: goose eggs, wild cherries and crawfish. If a spirit ate of the wild cherries it would be sent back to this world, a spirit without a body, to wander about homeless, eating wild cherries and other kinds of wild fruit. If it ate of the goose eggs, it would wander around the world, digging goose eggs out of the ground, like roots. It would have to carry the eggs in a basket without a bottom, and would always be trying to mend the basket with plaited grass. If it ate of the crawfish it would have to dig crawfish in the same way.

A Skoks offered Kumush's daughter these three harmful things, but she did not look at them; she went straight on toward the west, very fast.

After a time Kumush asked: "How far have we gone now?"

"We are almost there," said the girl. "Far away I see beautiful roses. Spirits that have been good in life take one of those roses with the leaves, those that have been bad do not see the roses."

Again Kumush asked: "How far are we now?"

"We are passing the place of roses."

Kumush thought: "She should take one of those roses."

The girl always knew her father's thoughts. As soon as that thought came into his mind, she put back her hand and, without turning, pulled a rose and two leaves. Kumush did not take one. He could not even see them, for he was not dead.

After a time they came to a road so steep that they could slide down it. At the beginning of the descent there was a willow rope. The girl pulled the rope and that minute music and voices were heard. Kumush and his daughter slipped down and came out on a beautiful plain with high walls all around it. It was a great house, and the plain was its floor. That house is the whole underground world, but only spirits know the way to it.

Kumush's daughter was greeted by spirits that were glad to see her, but to Kumush they said "Sonk!" (raw, not ripe), and they felt sorry for him that he was not dead.

Kumush and his daughter went around together, and Kumush asked: "How far is it to any side?"

"It is very far, twice as far as I can see. There is one road down, — the road we came, — and another up. No one can come in by the way leading up, and no one can go up by the way leading down."

The place was beautiful and full of spirits; there were so many that if every star of the sky, and all the hairs on the head of every man and all the hairs on all the animals were counted they would not equal in number the spirits in that great house.

When Kumush and his daughter first got there they couldn't see the spirits though they could hear voices, but after sunset, when darkness was in the world above, it was light in that house below.

"Keep your eyes closed," said Kumush's daughter. "If you open them, you will have to leave me and go back."

At sunset Kumush made himself small, smaller than any thing living in the world. His daughter put him in a crack, high up in a corner of the broad house, and made a mist before his eyes.

When it was dark, Wus-Kumush, the keeper of the house, said: "I want a fire!" Right away a big, round, bright fire sprang up in the center, and there was light everywhere in the house. Then spirits came from all sides, and there were so many that no one could have counted them. They made a great circle around Kumush's daughter, who stood by the fire, and then they danced a dance not of this world, and sang a song not of this world. Kumush watched them from the corner of the house. They danced each night, for five nights. All the spirits sang, but only those in the circle danced. As daylight came they disappeared. They went away to their own places, lay down and became dry, disjointed bones.

Wus-Kumush gave Kumush's daughter goose eggs and crawfish. She ate them and became bones. All newcomers became bones, but those who had been tried for five years, and hadn't eaten anything the Skoks gave them, lived in shining settlements outside, in circles around the big house. Kumush's daughter became bones, but her spirit went to her father in the corner.

On the sixth night she moved him to the eastern side of the house. That night he grew tired of staying with the spirits; he wanted to leave the underground world, but he wanted to take some of the spirits with him to people the upper world. "Afterward," said he, "I am going to the place where the sun rises. I shall travel on the sun's road till I come to where he stops at midday. There I will build a house."

"Some of the spirits are angry with you," said Wus-Kumush. "Because you are not dead they want to kill you; you must be careful."

"They may try as hard as they like," said Kumush; "they can't kill me. They haven't the power. They are my children; they are all from me. If they should kill me it would only be for a little while. I should come to life again."

The spirits, though they were bones then, heard this, and said: "We will crush the old man's heart out, with our elbows."

Kumush left Wus-Kumush and went back to the eastern side of the house. In his corner was a pile of bones. Every bone in the pile rose up and tried to kill him, but they couldn't hit him, for he dodged them. Each day his daughter moved him, but the bones knew where he was, because they could see him. Every night the spirits in the form of living people danced and sang; at daylight they lay down and became disconnected bones.

"I am going away from this place," said Kumush, "I am tired of being here." At daybreak he took his daughter's bones, and went around selecting bones according to their quality, thinking which would do for one tribe and which for another. He filled a basket with them, taking only shin-bones and wrist-bones. He put the basket on his back and started to go up the eastern road, the road out. The path was steep and slippery, and his load was heavy. He slipped and stumbled but kept climbing. When he was half-way up, the bones began to elbow him in the back and neck, struggling to kill him. When near the top the strap slipped from his forehead and the basket fell. The bones became spirits, and, whooping and shouting, fell down into the big house and became bones again.

"I'll not give up," said Kumush; "I'll try again." He went back, filled the basket with bones and started a second time. When he was half-way up he said: "You'll see that I will get to the upper world with you bones!" That minute he slipped, his cane broke and he fell. Again the bones became spirits and went whooping and shouting back to the big house.

Kumush went down a second time, and filled the basket. He was angry, and he chucked the bones in hard. "You want to stay here," said he, "but when you know my place up there, where the sun is, you'll want to stay there always and never come back to this place. I feel lonesome when I see no people up there; that is why I want to take you there. If I can't get you up now, you will never come where I am."

When he put the basket on his back the third time, he had no cane, so he thought: "I wish I had a good, strong cane." Right away he had it. Then he said: "I wish I could get up with this basketful of bones."

When half-way up the bones again tried to kill him. He struggled and tugged hard. At last he got near the edge of the slope, and with one big lift he threw the basket up on to level ground. "Maklaksûm káko!" (Indian bones) said he.

He opened the basket and threw the bones in different directions. As he threw them, he named the tribe and kind of Indians they would be. When he named the Shastas he said: " You will be good fighters." To the Pitt River and the Warm Spring Indians he said: " You will be brave warriors, too." But to the Klamath Indians he said: " You will be like women, easy to frighten." The bones for the Modoc Indians he threw last, and he said to them: " You will eat what I eat, you will keep my place when I am gone, you will be bravest of all. Though you may be few, even if many and many people come against you, you will kill them." And he said to each handful of bones as he threw it: " You must find power to save yourselves, find men to go and ask the mountains for help. Those who go to the mountains must ask to be made wise, or brave, or a doctor. They must swim in the gauwams and dream. When you are sure that a doctor has tried to kill some one, or that he won't put his medicine in the path of a spirit and turn it back, you will kill him. If an innocent doctor is killed, you must kill the man who killed him, or he must pay for the dead man."

Then Kumush named the different kinds of food those people should eat, — catfish, salmon, deer and rabbit. He named more than two hundred different things, and as he named them they appeared in the rivers and the forests and the flats. He thought, and they were there. He said: " Women shall dig roots, get wood and water, and cook. Men shall hunt and fish and fight. It shall be this way in later times. This is all I will tell you."

When he had finished everything Kumush took his daughter, and went to the edge of the world, to the place where the sun rises. He traveled on the sun's road till he came to the middle of the sky; there he stopped and built his house, and there he lives now.

WANAGA BECOMES WUS - KUMUSH

Two brothers, Kumush and Wanaga, lived east of Tula Lake. Wanaga was uneasy; he didn't want to be always with Kumush, so one day he started off toward the northwest to hunt for woodchucks. When he had killed five, he took out the intestines, cleaned them, filled them with fat and cooked them in front of the fire. The bodies he cooked on hot stones. He was eating the intestines when his brother came up to the fire. Kumush's face was wet, he had run so fast.

Wanaga was mad, but he said: "Now you are here, come and eat some of these intestines."

Kumush didn't want a part of the intestines; he wanted them all, and wanted the woodchucks, too, so he asked: "Which way did you come?"

Wanaga told him, but told him wrong.

Kumush said: "I saw a long track the way I came. I thought it was yours."

"Why don't you eat?" asked Wanaga.

"I can't, my heart beats so. I am scared; I feel as if some one were near here, watching us. I will go down the hill and look around in the bushes."

Kumush went into thick bushes where Wanaga couldn't see him; he pulled every hair out of his head, eyebrows, eyelashes, ears, beard, armpits, pulled out every hair on his body, and said to them: "You must be people; you must scream and shout and run after me, as if you were going to catch me and kill me."

Right away the hairs became men, and pursued Kumush. As he ran, Kumush screamed: "Wanaga, save yourself! Wanaga, save yourself!"

Wanaga started up, then he remembered his bow and arrows. He got them, then he ran off as fast as he could; he forgot all about the five woodchucks.

As soon as Wanaga was out of sight, the hairs were back in Kumush's head and body, and he sat down to eat the woodchucks. As he ate he kept saying: "My brother, you shouldn't eat such nice things alone; I like woodchucks."

Wanaga felt lonesome, for he thought that Kumush had been killed. As he traveled along, he caught a woodchuck. Then he saw another one, and he followed it and killed it with a club; he killed a third one among the rocks. He built a fire and cooked the woodchucks. Just as he was beginning to eat the intestines, he heard Kumush call out: "Oh, I am glad you are alive. I was afraid those men had killed you."

When Kumush came up to the fire he said: "I hid under the bushes where they couldn't find me; that is how I got away! I saw tracks out here; are they yours?"

"I didn't come that way," said Wanaga.

"I feel queer," said Kumush; "I will go back and see if there is any one around. I am scared."

When he got where Wanaga couldn't see him, he pulled all his hair out again, and said: "Be men! As soon as you are near the woods, make a ring around me and act as if you were going to kill me."

When they surrounded him, Kumush screamed: "Save yourself, Wanaga! Run for your life! These men will kill you."

Wanaga took his bow, quiver and club and ran off as fast as he could; he forgot about his woodchucks again, and Kumush ate them, saying: "My brother, you shouldn't eat such good things alone."

The next day Wanaga kept thinking about Kumush. At last he said to himself: "If Kumush wasn't killed yesterday he is fooling me."

Wanaga killed five woodchucks and this time he cooked them without taking out the intestines. Just as he was ready to begin eating, he saw Kumush coming. When Kumush came up to the fire he pretended to cry, he was so glad that Wanaga was alive. Wanaga offered him part of a woodchuck, but he wouldn't take it. He said that he couldn't eat;

he had seen tracks, and the grass was trampled down as if people were around; he would go and see.

Wanaga thought: "You'll not fool me this time!" When Kumush screamed to him to run as fast as he could, he ran, but he took the woodchucks with him.

Wanaga traveled for two days without camping. Kumush was hungry, but he followed his brother. The third day Wanaga caught a woodchuck. He was cooking it when Kumush came up.

"I have been mourning for you," said Kumush. "I thought you were killed. Over there by the bushes I saw tracks; I will go and look at them." He tried the old trick, but Wanaga wasn't fooled; he took the woodchuck with him.

It was cold, but Kumush followed Wanaga. He followed him all winter. In the spring, when Kumush was only one day behind, Wanaga came upon porcupine tracks. He made a fire near an old tree where he thought the porcupines would come when it began to grow dark. He hadn't been there long before he saw a porcupine and killed it; then he saw another and killed it. The next day, when he was cooking the porcupines, Kumush came up. "How did you kill those porcupines?" asked he.

Wanaga was mad, but he said: "Sit down and eat, then I will tell you how I catch porcupines." When they were through eating, Wanaga said: "If I want to kill porcupines, I find a tree where I think they live; I set fire to the tree, then I wrap my blanket tight around me and lie down under it; when the tree gets to burning well, the porcupines fall out of it."

Wanaga traveled on, and Kumush stopped to kill porcupines. He set a tree on fire, wrapped his blanket tight around him and lay down. The tree burned quickly, and soon limbs began to fall. A heavy bough fell on Kumush, and he thought: "That is a big porcupine!" Another fell. Kumush lay still; he thought: "Oh, I shall have lots of big, fat porcupines!" At last the tree fell and killed him. His body was burned up, nothing was left of it but the skull and the disk. They lay in the ashes for a long time; at last the morning star saw them and called out: " What is the matter, old man? Why do you sleep so long? Get up! "

Kumush sprang up, and right away began to track Wanaga. It was warm weather, and Wanaga was hunting woodchucks among the rocks. He had killed five when Kumush came. Wanaga divided the meat with his brother, and the two spent the night together.

" How do you kill woodchucks? " asked Kumush.

" When I see one among the rocks, I jump down and catch it. It is easy for me; I am used to it."

They started on together, Wanaga ahead. Kumush saw a woodchuck; he jumped and caught it, then he cooked and ate it, for Wanaga had told him he must eat the first one he caught before he tried to catch another. When his stomach was full, he saw a woodchuck down in a hole between high rocks; he jumped, struck on the rocks, burst open and died.

His body lay there a long time; then crows came and ate it up, till only the disk was left. They tried to eat that, but couldn't. At last the morning star saw the disk and cried out: " What are you doing down there, old man? Get up. Wanaga has gone far; you must hurry! "

Kumush sprang up. " Oh, I was sleeping! " said he.

Wanaga turned back. He wished for a wide river to flow between him and his brother, and right away it was there. Kumush traveled up and down the river. After a long time he found a ford and crossed. Wanaga was on Pitcowa flat, where a great deal of ges was growing. He got two sticks, umda, sharp at both ends, took them out on the flat, showed them the ges, and said: " Work hard. Dig lots of ges! "

They dug fast and made a great many piles of ges. At sundown, Wanaga went to the flat; he washed a few roots and ate them; they were nice and white, and the skin came off of itself. He carried the sticks back to his camp. The next day, when Kumush came, Wanaga gave him plenty of roots to eat.

" How did you get all of these roots? " asked Kumush.

" I made two sticks, one straight, the other bent. Then I took them to the flat and told them to dig."

Kumush cut five sticks and sharpened them at both ends.

Wanaga said: " You must take them to the flat and leave them; you mustn't go near them till sundown."

Kumush took his sticks to the flat, put a basket by each stick, and said: " You must work hard; you must dig plenty of roots." He went back, but he couldn't wait, and in a few minutes he ran over to see if the umda were digging fast. That made them mad and they stopped digging. He went back again, for he thought that when he was out of sight they would go to work, but they didn't.

The next morning Wanaga made small, and put into two baskets, the piles of ges his sticks had dug. (When he wanted to, he poured out the ges, thought hard, and it was big again.)

Kumush was so mad that he broke up his sticks and threw them away.

Wanaga took his sticks to the flat, stuck them in the ground, and said: " Grow here and be of use to people in later times."

The sticks grew, and are the kind that are used in digging roots now. When he had planted the sticks, Wanaga said: " Hereafter I will be Wus-Kumush." Then he left Kumush, stole away in the night. Kumush stayed two or three days. When he had eaten all the ges Wanaga left, he went off toward the east. Thenceforth he traveled about in the world, alone.

STEALING FIRE

CHARACTERS

Blaiwas	Eagle	Nébăks	Sickness
Dásläts	California Lion	Sältgăls	The Red of Morning
Gowwá	Swallow	Súbbas	Sun
Kāhkaas	Stork	Tcanpsaudewas	The People to Come
Kânoa	A Small Bird	Tcwais	Turkey Buzzard
Káwhas	Blackbird	Tsīhläs	Red Squirrel
Kéis	Rattlesnake	Tusasás	Skunk
Kékina	Lizard	Tskel	Mink
Kówe	Frog	Wámanik	Bull Snake
Kûlta	Otter	Wûlkûtska	Black Marten
Lok	Bear	Wus	Black Fox
Moi	Squirrel		
Múkus	Owl		

THE ten Nébăks brothers, who lived in the east at the edge of the world, and the ten Súbbas brothers, who lived in the west, where the sky touches the earth, were the owners of fire.

Other people had no fire, they ate their meat raw; but they knew about fire, and were thinking how to get it; they knew that those men owned it.

At last Wus called a council of all the people in the world. When they had assembled, he said: " I feel sorry for the people who are to come." (He had heard that people would come soon, and that he and his people would no longer be persons. He called the people who were to come Tcanpsaudewas.) " It will be hard for them in the world if they have no way of keeping warm. I know where fire is, and if you will help me I will get it."

All promised to help, then Wus said: " You must stand in a line, one person a long running distance from another, and the line must reach from here to within one running distance of the place where the Nébăks have their house. I will go to the house and steal fire, but you must bring it home."

Wus sent the best runner to the farthest station, the second fastest runner to the second station and so on, till near home he placed men who could run only a little, men who soon tired out. The Kéis family he sent underground. People who traveled in the air formed a line above the earth.

"We will tell you how the Nébăks brothers live," said the people of the air, "for we see them often. Every morning they build fires on the mountains to drive deer to their snares. When you see a big smoke, you will know that you are near their house. Two Moi brothers are the servants of the Nébăks. The Mois never hunt; they stay in the house and watch that no one steals fire."

Wus traveled toward the east for a good many days. At last he reached the Nébăks' house without being seen by the brothers, or by their servants. When he went through the smoke hole into the house, the Moi brothers were terribly scared; one ran out to call the Nébăks, but Wus drove him back.

"Why are you frightened?" asked he. "I have come to talk to you. Sit down. Why don't you have your faces painted? you would look nice. I know how to paint; I will paint them for you."

He took dead coals, drew long lines across their faces and said: "Go to the spring and look at yourselves." (From that time those people have stripes on their faces.)

As soon as they were out of the house, Wus took the largest piece of fire, put it behind his ear and ran off as fast as he could. When he picked up the coal, the fires on the mountains died down.

"Somebody is in our house," said the Nébăks brothers. "Somebody has stolen fire!" And they hurried home.

When Wus had fire behind his ear, he ran a long distance, ran till he met Tskel. Tskel took fire and ran till he came to Kaiutois; the next man to carry fire was Dásläts. Dásläts carried it till he came to Wámanik, who was stationed under the ground.

The Nébăks brothers were fast runners and they nearly caught Wámanik. He was so scared that he was just going to drop fire and run off when he met Tsĭhläs and gave it to him. The next to carry fire was Lok. Lok was a slow runner and the Nébăks nearly came up to him before he met Moi, a fast runner. When Moi was getting tired, and was running slower, he came to Kékina. Kékina sprang away and was soon far ahead. When he reached Wûlkûtska the Nébăks brothers were a long way off, but Wûlkûtska was not a good runner, and the Nébăks gained on him fast. They got so near that he hid in the bushes and gave out a frightened call. Kûlta was waiting right there; he snatched fire and ran as fast as he could till he was tired and was thinking: "Where is the man who is going to take fire? I can't hold out much longer."

Then he met Tusasás. Blaiwas took fire from Tusasás; he went up in the air and carried fire a long distance, until Gowwá took it. When darkness came, Múkus was there to carry fire, and he and his people carried it till daylight. Then Sältgăls took it, and afterward Káwhas. Káwhas was about to drop it, when he saw Tcwais and called: "Take it quick! I am tired! I can't hold it; I shall let it drop."

Tcwais looked back as he started. The Nébăks were so near that his head turned yellow from fright, but he reached the next man — and so they carried fire day after day, till the ocean was not far off. Only a few runners were left, and some of them couldn't run ten steps.

At last wood dove took fire, but the Nébăks brothers were so near that he hid in the bushes. He thought: "Now they will kill me, and then people will never have fire." It made him feel lonesome; and he cried, not loud, but down in his throat.

The Nébăks heard his cry, and said: "We can never overtake these people; that cry is far off. We can't get fire back, but the people who have stolen it will have us with them always. We will stay in their country; we won't go back to our old place; we will scatter and live everywhere in the world."

Till that time the Nébăks brothers had lived by themselves, and had never troubled people. After fire was stolen, they were everywhere in the world. People had fire, but they had sickness too.

Wus-Kumush saw this race, but he didn't help, for at the council, when he told the people what would happen, they wouldn't listen to his words. They liked the words of Wus better.

Now Wus called a second council of all the people in the world, and when they came he said: "What else shall we do for the people who are coming? I think we should steal fire from the brothers who live in the west, at the edge of the world. I can go there and get it."

"Kāhkaas, Súbbas' servant, will see you," said the people; "you will never get there."

"Oh, I can get there," said Wus. "I will kill the ten brothers and come back. It will not be hard."

"What will you do when you get to the house? No person has ever been there."

"Don't kill all the brothers," said Wus-Kumush. "If you do it will be dark here. There will never be any light again. It will always be night."

"You will freeze to death," said some of the people. "There is deep snow along that trail."

"I will build ten houses, where I can rest and get warm."

"Before you get to Súbbas' house there is a long, broad flat," said Blaiwas. "The brothers dig roots there. I often see them when I am up in the air. Near the house there is a high mountain. You must go to the top of it and watch the brothers from there. When they start for home, there is always a terrible snowstorm. The eldest brother goes first, and one follows another. In the morning, when they start to hunt for roots, the youngest goes first."

When Wus came to the mountain he talked to it and asked it for help; then he watched for the brothers. Soon he saw the youngest brother come out of the house and start toward the flat. One brother followed another till all ten had gone to dig roots; then Wus went toward the house. The house was made of dirt and covered with turf. Kāhkaas didn't see Wus coming; when he sprang in at the smoke hole Kāhkaas screamed out. Wus jumped on him, choked him and scolded him; then he threw him into a corner, and said: "When I come to see you, what makes you scream? I want to talk nice to you; I want you to go home with me. This is a bad place. I will give you shells and nice beads."

"I will go out and make just a little noise," said Kāhkaas, "and then the brothers won't come home; that is the way I do."

Wus let him go out, but he followed him so he wouldn't scream loud.

The brothers heard Kāhkaas and one said: "What's the matter? I heard something." When they heard him the second time they said: "Oh, that is Kāhkaas at play."

"How do these men live?" asked Wus.

"Every morning they go early to dig roots; they dig all day, then one brother comes home. When he gets to the house, he puts down his basket of roots, comes to the smoke hole and looks all around to see if any one is here; then he comes in. Each brother comes in the same way; each one brings a basketful of roots, and each looks around the house before he comes in. The five oldest brothers come first, then the five youngest follow. As each one starts for home, there is a terrible snowstorm. I build a big fire from that pile of sticks outside the house. The snow and cold almost put the fire out, but I keep putting on sticks."

"Where can I hide, so that they won't see me when they look around?" asked Wus.

"They don't look toward the east," said Kāhkaas; "you must hide in the east part of the house, in the hole where we keep roots."

"Hide me there," said Wus. "I am going to take you home with me. You must tie up a bundle of roots for us to eat on the road. You will have to eat a good deal or you will give out. It is a long road."

The eldest brother was coming, so Kāhkaas built a great fire. When the man got to the house he put down his basket of roots and looked in at the smoke hole; he looked all around, then asked: "Why did you scream?"

"It was getting late; I wanted you to come home," said Kāhkaas.

Just then Wus sprang at Súbbas and cut off his head. He and Kāhkaas pulled the body in and hid it; then they put the head in the hole where the roots were.

Again it began to snow; the second brother was coming. Soon he looked in at the smoke hole, and asked: "Why did you scream?"

"I missed the step and fell into the house," said Káhkaas.

"We have always told you to be careful," said Súbbas.

That moment Wus sprang up. Súbbas screamed, but Wus cut his head off and dragged the head and the body to the hole where the roots were.

When the third brother came he asked: "What noise was that? I thought I heard my brother scream."

"I was screaming," said Kāhkaas. "I wanted to hurry you home."

Wus killed the third brother, as he had the other two.

Again it began snowing; the fourth brother was coming. Wus told Kāhkaas that he must work around as he always did. "You must not talk," said Kāhkaas; "he will hear you. He is stronger than the other brothers."

Súbbas looked in at the smoke hole, and asked: "Why don't you brush up the snow? What makes it so yellow?"

"I've been walking in the ashes," said Kāhkaas.

Súbbas was just going to draw his head up out of the smoke hole and come down into the house, when Wus sprang at him and cut his head off. That time a good deal of blood was left. Kāhkaas couldn't clean it up; it made the snow yellow.

Wus was afraid the fifth brother would see the blood. "I will go outside and kill him," said he.

"You mustn't do that," said Kāhkaas. "If you do the other brothers will see you."

Súbbas was at the house now; he left his basket outside and looked in. "Why does it look so around here?" asked he. "It looks queer."

"Oh, I've worked around a good deal," said Kāhkaas, "that is why it looks queer."

Súbbas stretched half his length in to see that no one was there and Wus sprang at him and cut his head off.

"Now the other five brothers will come," said Kāhkaas. "They come quicker, for it is getting late." The fifth brother had screamed louder when Wus killed him. His brothers had heard his scream and they were running.

Wus jumped out of the house and started for home. Kāhkaas picked up the bundle, put it on his back and followed. Both ran as fast as they could; sometimes Kāhkaas got ahead of Wus, then Wus was ahead. The wind blew terribly. Wus' ears were filled with snow, and he was almost frozen. They were giving out when they reached the last house that Wus had built; the fire was still burning. They had just got warm when they heard the brothers coming, and started off again. They ran till Kāhkaas said: "I'm so tired I can't run any farther!"

"Hurry," said Wus. "They won't overtake us. We are near the next house." They reached the ninth house, and the fire was burning.

"Look and see if they are coming," said Wus.

"Not yet."

After a while Kāhkaas looked again. "They are coming!" called he. And off the two ran as fast as they could. When they got near the eighth house, the brothers were close behind.

"I am afraid!" said Kāhkaas.

"I am not," said Wus, but he kept on running, though snow was in his ears and in his hair; he was almost frozen. They stopped at the seventh house, but Kāhkaas looked back and said: "They are coming; they are not far away!"

The brothers were tired. They began to think that they couldn't overtake Wus and Kāhkaas. They still carried their baskets. Wus didn't stop at the sixth or fifth house.

"Don't open your mouth so wide," said Kāhkaas; "if you do, it will fill with snow."

"No matter," said Wus, "that will help me to run."

When the brothers reached the fifth house and found it empty, the elder said: "Let us be only five. We can never catch up with the man who killed our brothers, and stole our servant. Let us go back, but we will always watch this country. We won't let any one come here again. I thought we were the strongest people in the world. I wonder who this man is."

They didn't know the people of this world; they had always lived by themselves. The only man they knew about was Kāhkaas.

When the people saw Wus coming, they went to one place to wait for him. They talked about him, and said: "Wus is a smart man; we couldn't have done what he has done." When Wus came up to them, they saw that he had Kāhkaas with him. Kāhkaas still had his bundle of roots, for he hadn't had time to eat many. Everybody was glad now, for there was summer and winter. Up to that time people had had only clouds and storms.

After a while Wus said: "We must do another thing for the Tcanpsaudewas. We have done a good deal, — they will have two kinds of fire, — but there is too much cold. We must hold a council and decide how much cold they can have, — how long winter will be."

Wus sent for all the people in the world. Every one came; every one thought: "What will Wus say?" But nobody talked; they all sat still waiting. At last Wus said: "There should be ten months of cold." Then everybody began to talk. Nobody wanted ten months. Some said: "If there are ten months of cold, people will starve to death; they can't lay up roots and seeds enough. Let us have five months." Others said: "Two months are enough." Wus kept saying: "There should be ten." When they couldn't agree, some one said: "Let the oldest man here decide." There was one very old man there, — the oldest of all, but he only listened, he didn't say a word. Again Wus said: "There should be ten months."

The council lasted all night; then people asked: "Where is Kânoa? Why doesn't he talk?" It was getting daylight, and Wus still insisted on ten months. "The months can be short," said he, "not many days long." Now the people said to Kânoa: " Speak, old man; maybe you have something in your mind to say." He started to go, and just then he called out: " Danwacuk " (three months).

Wus was mad, but the other people were glad, and said: " The old man is right. There will be three months of winter."

" I am afraid people will not be thankful for what we have done," said Hedgehog, " and will eat us." Porcupine was afraid, too, but others said: " We have got fire for them; we have killed five of the Súbbas brothers; we have made winter short; they will be thankful."

The council broke up, and soon after all those people turned to common animals, for real people were coming.

The five Súbbas brothers lived in their house in the west, but they watched the world. And since then things have been as they are now.

HOW SICKNESS CAME INTO THE WORLD

CHARACTERS

Gletcówas		Snoútiss	Blowsnake
Kéis	Rattlesnake	Wéwenkee	Whipsnake
Nébăks	Sickness		

Kéis and his brother, Snoútiss, lived on the southwest side of Little Shasta. The three Gletcówas brothers lived on the northwest side.

The Gletcówas brothers were great hunters; they made snares of grass ropes knotted and tied together, and fastened them between trees. Each morning they drove deer into the snares. As the brothers traveled, they called out their own name, "Gletcówas," and they called it as they went home at night. When they had snared as many deer as they wanted, they packed them up and carried them to the house; they never skinned or cut up a deer in the woods. The Gletcówas brothers were so small that they looked like children, but they were young men.

Kéis, the elder of the two brothers who lived on the southwest side of the mountain, always sat at home making bows and arrows. Snoútiss, his little brother, dug roots, and while he was digging he listened to the Gletcówas brothers. He heard their song, and knew that they were great hunters. One day he said to Kéis: "The Gletcówas brothers have plenty of meat."

"Let us go to their snares and get some," said Kéis.

"They never cut up their deer in the woods," said the younger brother; "if they did, they couldn't catch any more; they carry them home whole. You might go to their house and ask for meat, but don't go near their snares; if you do you will get into trouble."

Kéis went, but he didn't do as his brother told him. He went straight to the snares the Gletcówas brothers had set. In one of the snares was a large fat deer. Kéis tried to untie the knot in the rope around its neck; he couldn't do it; so he pulled at it till he broke out all but two of his teeth.

"We will go to the snares, and see if we have caught anything," said the eldest of the Gletcówas brothers.

"I will stay and dry meat," said the youngest. There was a great deal of meat hanging on trees near the house.

When the two brothers came to where their snares were, they saw a man. "Who are you?" asked one of them.

Kéis didn't answer, but as soon as they untied the deer he sprang upon it and cried: "This is mine!"

"No, it is ours!" said the eldest brother, "but if you will come with us, we will give you some of the meat. We can't cut the deer up here; it would spoil our snares."

Kéis didn't listen to them; he went off. His mouth was bleeding, and he was mad. When he got home, he sat down and began to make poison — fever and black vomit and terrible things.

"What is the matter?" asked Snoútiss. "What makes your mouth bleed? Why are you working so hard over that bad stuff? It is wrong to make that. It may get out of our house and spread everywhere; then the people to come will have these terrible things and die."

"Those brothers in the northwest took my deer from me, — a large, fat one," said Kéis, and he kept on making the medicine.

"You must have gone to their snares," said the boy. "They couldn't cut the deer up there in the woods."

Kéis didn't answer, and Snoútiss thought: "I will go and find out what has made Kéis so mad." When he got to the house of the three brothers, they said: "Come in, little boy. What is the trouble with your brother?"

"All his teeth are out, but two, and with those he is making bad medicine. He is mad; he says that you took a deer away from him."

"We took our own deer. We told him to come and get

some of the meat, but he wouldn't; he went away without saying a word."

The brothers gave Snoútiss meat; he took it and started for home. When he got to the house he looked in at the smoke hole and he was frightened. His brother was hard at work; the whole house was dripping with sores; there were aches and pains of all kinds, and terrible sickness.

"I can't come in," cried the little boy. "You have made those things and now they will be here always, and will make trouble. You got mad for nothing. I can't stay with you; I will go to my uncle."

When Snoútiss came in sight of Wéwenkee's house, a little boy saw him, and called to his father: "A boy is coming!"

"That is Snoútiss," said Wéwenkee. "He has never been here before; he wouldn't come now if he wasn't in trouble."

When Snoútiss got to the house, he stood outside, crying.

"Tell him to come in," said Wéwenkee to his son. Snoútiss went in. "What is the matter? Why do you cry?" asked his uncle.

"My brother is mad. He has made all kinds of terrible sores and sickness. I feel badly, for those things can never be got rid of; they will live always to trouble the people who are to come. It looks badly and smells badly in our house. My brother got mad for nothing."

"Those Gletcówas brothers are mean men," said Wéwenkee, "but if Kéis wanted meat he should have gone to their house. I am stronger than your brother; I have a wildcat skin blanket, all painted. I will go home with you. How far away is your house?"

"On the other side of a flat there are big rocks, our home is under those rocks. I don't want to go there. I can't go in the house, it smells so badly."

"I will go alone," said his uncle.

When Wéwenkee got to the house, he crawled in through a crack in the wall. His nephew didn't see him, didn't know that he was there. There was such a terrible smell in the house that Wéwenkee couldn't stay; so he got out quickly. The only way he could look in was by painting red stripes across his forehead and around his wrists. When he got home, he said to Snoútiss: "You told me the truth. Hereafter there will be all kinds of sickness. Sickness will spread everywhere. Does Kéis think he is more powerful than I am? I can do all that he can do. I know that what he has made will live always. Will you go home now?" asked Wéwenkee.

"I don't want to go," said Snoútiss.

Wéwenkee started off again. After he had gone, his wife said to Snoútiss: "You should have gone with your uncle. Do you think that he has only one blanket? His blankets are doubled around his body, one over another, and one is worse than another. They are blankets of sickness and sores. Wéwenkee is chief of those things; he can make more bad medicine than your brother can. When he is mad, he can raise a terrible whirlwind. That is the kind of man he is. You should have gone with him."

Snoútiss went out then and followed his uncle, but Wéwenkee didn't see him. As the old man traveled, sores came out all over him. He cried, and his tears were drops of matter. When he went into his nephew's house, he said: "You have done wrong; now all this bad stuff will soak into the earth and make great trouble."

Wéwenkee made a big ball of soft bark, rolled it around and gathered on it all the sores and sickness that were on the top and sides of the house, and on the ground. "Don't you wink again and let that stuff fall," said he to his nephew.

He rolled the bark ball over Kéis' body, cleaned him of sores, and then he squeezed the ball over his own head and said: "This is mine. How did you dare to let this out? Sickness belongs to Nébăks. It is only loaned to us; we had no right to let it out till he told us to. Now it has gone from us; I have saved some, but a great deal has scattered and gone through the world. You have frightened your brother so he won't come back to you" — Wéwenkee didn't know that Snoútiss was on top of the house listening to what he said.

"Will you change skins with me?" asked Wéwenkee.

"No," said Kéis, "I want my own skin."

"It is too bad I can't get up all this sickness," said Wéwenkee, — he was still rolling the bark ball, — "it has soaked into the ground, and in hot weather and in winter it will come out."

Kéis didn't say much, for he didn't want Wéwenkee to see that his teeth were gone.

"The Gletcówas brothers are bad men, but you should have asked them for meat, not tried to steal it," said Wéwenkee.

"They wanted to kill me."

"How many teeth have you?" asked Wéwenkee.

"Two."

"Let me have them for a little while."

"No, I want them myself; people will always hate me, these teeth will defend me. If I want to kill any one I can do it with my teeth. I can throw medicine at them and kill them. I shall keep poison medicine in the ends of my teeth; I will be as bad as others are."

"I will always be good, unless somebody makes me mad," said Wéwenkee. "In later times people will like my skin and want to take it. Maybe they will throw dirt at me so they can hide my face and eyes from them, but they can do me no harm. I will not be a servant to any one; but those who go to the swimming ponds on the mountains, and those who are willing to travel at night, I will like. I will give them my skin, and the earth will give me another.[1] I shall never appear to any one, who is not a doctor."

"I will do just as I have done," said Kéis. "If I get mad, I will kill people by throwing out sickness."

"If you do, you will be hated, and you will always be in trouble," said Wéwenkee. And he begged hard for Kéis to put away sickness. "You are my nephew," said he; "you should do as I say. I am a chief, too. I am sorry for the people who are to come, and you ought to think of them. Let us put sickness back in our bodies, and never use it unless this earth tells us to. It won't be long that we shall be persons; soon we shall live under rocks and in holes in the ground. When the people to come take our places, they will hate you. I am sorry for your little brother. I would go away now, but

[1] Doctors often rub a whipsnake in dust and pull off his skin, then he gets a new skin, so what Wéwenkee said was true.

I don't want to be changed till some one comes to tell me what I shall be."

So Wéwenkee talked to his nephew, and at last Kéis took off all his sicknesses and tied them up in a bundle. He put the bundle in his quiver, and said: "I will only take these out when people abuse me." Then he told his brother to come in.

"My little nephew," said Wéwenkee, "those Gletcówas can turn to anything; sometimes they are fish and sometimes they are bugs or ticks. You might catch one of them and think that you were holding him in your hand, but he would be gone. You can remember better than Kéis; that is why I tell you about those brothers. Sometimes they are large animals, sometimes they are a straw on a trail, or a stump of burnt wood, or lice. Often, in the night, they are wind; or they are mole hills for men to fall over. I can't tell you all that they turn to. I know they are going to kill your brother, for he has tried to kill them." Then he said to Kéis: "Stand up." When his nephew stood up, Wéwenkee turned him around, looked at him on every side, and said: "I don't like any part of your skin, and your mind is mean. What part of my skin do you like?"

Kéis said: "I like the spots on your breast and the gloss on your body."

"Lie down," said Wéwenkee, "and cover yourself up and sleep all day; then maybe your mind will be better and you won't get mad so easily." He told him over and over not to open the bundle of sickness, then he told Snoútiss to watch Kéis, and if he started to untie the bundle to come and tell him. He said: "Nobody will be able to kill sickness; your brother has spoiled the world. In later times we may have no mind, but we may want to go near houses. People will hate Kéis, but they will say: 'His uncle was chief before we came,' and they will know that I won't hurt them."

Kéis slept till night, then he woke up and sent his brother for water. "I wonder why he sent me for water when there was water in the house," thought Snoútiss, and he hurried back and looked in at the smoke hole. Kéis was sitting by the fire, untying his bundle. When he heard Snoútiss on the top of the house, he tied up the bundle and pulled his blanket around him.

"What were you doing?" asked Snoútiss.

"I was covering myself up."

"I know what you were doing," said the boy; "you were letting out sickness. Our uncle told you never to untie that bundle."

Snoútiss ran off to his uncle's house and told him what Kéis had done. Wéwenkee was so mad at his nephew that he stretched himself out full length; then he made a circle around the world and pressed everything together, but Kéis went in among rocks and Wéwenkee couldn't press hard enough to break them.

"What are you doing?" asked Wéwenkee.

"What I want to," said Kéis.

"If you want to be great of your own strength, I will leave you," said Wéwenkee, and he started for home.

Now Kéis began to sing like a doctor; the three Gletcówas brothers heard his song, and wondered who was around among the rocks singing.

"I will find out," said the eldest brother, and he went toward the rocks.

The second brother followed him. When near they smelt smoke, — Kéis was smoking Indian tobacco, — and they knew who was singing. "I wonder what that man is doing," said one of the brothers; "we must think how to kill him."

Now Wéwenkee sent Snoútiss to see what Kéis was doing; he came back, and said: "My brother is among the rocks, singing."

Wéwenkee rubbed himself around in the dirt, and said: "This is what I knew would happen when he went by his own strength. All that I have talked to your brother I will take off and give to the dirt. I will rub off all that I promised to help him, and give it back to the ground. We will no longer be living persons. You will remember me in later times, for I have been a great chief. You will be near me always, for you will be my brother. Hereafter you will be only a little snake and blow with your mouth." Right away Snoútiss became a common little snake. Then Wéwenkee turned himself into a whipsnake.

The youngest of the Gletcówas brothers listened to Kéis' song and watched for him to come out from among the rocks. As he ran back and forth he called: "Gletcówas! Gletcówas!"

"What is the matter?" asked his brothers.

"I have no father or mother; that is why I cry all the time."

The brothers said to one another: "Kéis is the man who killed our father and mother; we must kill him."

As Gletcówas went toward the rocks, he hit against a mole hill and fell; then he talked to the earth, and said: "You shouldn't treat me in this way. I have no father or mother; you should carry me safely."

As Gletcówas fell, Kéis came out from among the rocks. He had grown so tall that he almost touched the sky. His song was loud and nice.

The brothers hid behind rocks and tied cross sticks to their arrows. "Go up to the sky," called they to their youngest brother, for Kéis was just going to throw his medicine at him.

The brothers shot their arrows and hit Kéis. He fell, but he kept singing. The eldest brother pulled up a tree stump and pounded him on the head till he died. They cut Kéis into small pieces, threw the pieces over the rocks, and said: "You will no longer be great; even old women will kill you." The pieces became rattlesnakes.

Then the three brothers went north. Kéis had made them lose their minds. They crossed the Shasta River and became birds.

HOW OLD AGE CAME INTO THE WORLD

CHARACTERS

Komúchass	Old Age
Nébăks	Sickness

FIVE brothers and their sister lived alone on a mountain; the brothers had killed a great many people in the country around.

The sister gathered the wood and cooked the meat. When it was time for her maturity dance, she asked: "How can I dance when there is nobody to sing for me?"

"Walk around all the time," said her eldest brother; "pile stones, and don't sleep for five nights."

The girl kept awake four nights, then she was so tired that she fell asleep. She dreamed that her brothers were covered with sores and were starving. When she woke up, she cried and said: "I wish I had died long ago, then I shouldn't have brought trouble on my brothers. I have done this by not dancing and by going to sleep."

When she got home, she found that Sickness had been in the house. Sickness came every day for five days. Then each one of the five brothers had great sores on his body. There was nobody to hunt for deer, or rabbits, and soon the brothers were starving. The sister brought wood and kept the fire, but she couldn't find anything to eat. Everybody was glad that the brothers were sick and hoped they would die.

One of the brothers saw two swans on a pond near the house, and when the sister came with a load of wood on her back, he said: "I wish we could kill one of those swans."

"Maybe I can kill one," said the sister. She got her brothers' bows and tried the strings to see which string was the strongest. She put down one bow after another, saying:

"That isn't strong." The strings had been strong enough for her brothers, but for her they were weak. She took the bow that belonged to her youngest brother, pulled the string, and said: "This will do."

When she started for the pond, one of the brothers watched her, he said: "Now she is near the pond; now she is sitting down on the bank!" She drew the bow, and when he thought she had missed the swan, he nearly fell, he was so sorry. He didn't look out again. The arrow went through both swans.

The sister brought the swans home and left them outside; she took the bow and arrow in and put them away. Her brothers felt badly; they were disappointed. When she asked: "Shall I cook them in the house?" they were glad. They tried to get up, but they couldn't stand on their feet, they were so weak.

The girl cooked the swans and gave her brothers some of the meat. She said: "Eat a little at a time, so it will last longer." She saved the fat and rubbed her brothers with it, to heal their sores.

"Now I am stronger," said the eldest brother. "Give me my bow; I feel as if I could shoot something." Each brother said the same.

When the people at the foot of the mountain heard that the five brothers were sick, they were glad and sent a young man to find if it were true. He came back, and said: "They are sick and are going to die."

When the sister had gone for wood, the eldest brother said: "I know that somebody is coming; I want to be strong." They all had the same feeling, and each one tried his bow-string. When the sister came back, the eldest brother said: "You must roll us up in our blankets, and tie them around us as though we were dead. Put our bows and arrows and beads near us."

When she had done that, she went off to the mountains, for she felt badly and didn't want to stay with her brothers; she didn't want to live any longer.

The brothers waited for her, and when it was dark and she

didn't come, one said: "Our sister is always talking about dying; maybe she is dead."

Now the people at the foot of the mountain sent a little boy to see if the five brothers were alive. He crossed the pond in a canoe; he rowed the canoe by saying: "Peldack! Peldack!" (Go fast). When the boy saw the men tied up in their blankets, he went back, and said: "They are dead. In their house there are bows and arrows and nice beads. You must go and get them."

The chief said: "Get ready; we will go and scalp those men, and take their things."

When the brothers saw the men coming, they said: "We will lie here as if we were dead, and when they pack up our things and start away, we will spring up and fight them with knives."

The men came into the house. They unrolled the brothers and kicked them around; they took their blankets, bows, arrows and beads, took everything they could find, and started off.

Then the five brothers jumped up and ran at them with knives. They killed every man, threw the bodies into the pond, and started off to hunt for their sister. They hunted a long time. At last they found her body and burned it; then the eldest brother said: "Let us leave this country and kill every man we can find."

They started and traveled toward the west. They killed every man or woman they met. When people saw them coming they ran and hid, they were so afraid of them. The brothers traveled a long time, and killed a great many people. At last they came to a big lake. They made a canoe and started to cross it, but before they got to land, the canoe sank. It went under the water and under a mountain and out into another lake. There they met Storm.

He was a man then and could kill anybody he could catch and draw into the water. He tried to kill the five brothers, but the youngest brother fought with him, cut him to pieces with his knife, and said: "You will be a person no longer; you will only be something to scare people," and he drove him away. All the people under the water hid, for they were afraid of the brothers.

When the brothers couldn't find any one to kill, they turned toward the east and traveled till they came to a country where they found a very old man and a very old woman. They said: "We have come to fight you."

"I don't want to fight," said the old man. "We have always lived here, this is our place; nobody ever came here before to trouble us. We don't bother any one. Go away and leave us."

"You must fight," said the brothers. "If you don't, we will kill you; we kill every one we meet."

"You can't kill us or harm us, no matter what you do," said the old man. "We are Komúchass (Old Age). We shall live always."

The five brothers were mad; they didn't listen to the old man, but shot at him with arrows, and pounded him with clubs; then they built a fire and tried to burn him. When they couldn't kill him in any way, they got scared and ran off.

The old man called to them to stop, but they didn't listen; then he said: "We shall follow you; you cannot get away; wherever you go we shall go. You will never get home."

The old man and old woman followed the brothers for a long time, and at last they caught up with the eldest brother. Right away he was old and weak. He stumbled along for a little way, then fell to the ground and died.

They overtook the second brother; he also grew old and weak, fell to the ground and died. The third brother reached the lake; he was running on the ice when Komúchass overtook him; he grew weak and fell; the ice broke and he was drowned. The fourth brother died in the same manner. The youngest brother thought he was going to get away from the old man; he was only a few steps from home when Komúchass overtook him. Right off he was an old man; he stumbled along a step or two, then fell to the ground and died.

This is how old age came into our world. If the five brothers had let the old man and his wife alone, they would have stayed in their own country, and there would have been no such thing as old age.

Komúchass turned the bodies of the five brothers into five rocks, and those rocks are still to be seen in the Klamath country.

LEMÉIS AND NUL-WE

CHARACTERS

Kókolaileyas	The Necklace (Kŏko means bone)
Leméis or Limālimáas	Thunder
Nul-we	

OLD Limālimáas was a man-eater. He lived among big rocks at one end of a long, swampy flat. At the other end of the swamp lived an old woman and her little grandson. Limālimáas had killed all the old woman's kin, except the boy. He had strung their elbow and ankle bones on a grass rope and he wore them for a necklace. People called him Kókolaileyas, (Bone Necklace).

The grandmother was too old to dig roots, so the little boy dug them for her. One day Limālimáas saw the boy digging; he crept up and lay down near him, and when the boy's basket was full of nice, white roots, he ate them all at a mouthful. After that, he came every day. No matter where the boy went to dig, Limālimáas followed him. If the boy ate a root while he was digging, Limālimáas struck him on the forehead with his hammer. He listened and knew when he took a root. The little boy felt badly; he wanted to carry roots to his grandmother, for he knew she was hungry. He cried all the time he was digging, cried "Nul-we! Nul-we!" (that was his name). He always went home at sundown.

One day he cried on the way home. His grandmother heard him, and said: "My grandson, you mustn't cry so loud. A bad man lives among the big rocks. He will hear you and come where you are digging. Maybe he will kill you; he has killed your father and your mother and all your kin."

The next morning, when Nul-we went to dig roots, Limālimáas came, and said: "Little Nul-we, I am waiting for you; I am hungry. I want you to grow fast and get big, then I will kill you and eat you. I will put your bones in my necklace, between the bones of your father and the bones of your mother, and they will make my necklace nice and long."

That evening, when Nul-we went home without any roots, his grandmother said: "When you were a little fellow, you brought your basket full of roots. Now it is always empty. I am hungry. I have only dry, old roots to eat."

"I eat all the roots I dig," said Nul-we; then he cried, he was so sorry for his grandmother. He didn't want to tell her about Limālimâas.

The next morning, as soon as Nul-we began digging, Limālimâas came, rattling his bone necklace as he traveled. He lay down right by Nul-we, and said: "Little boy, I am tired; peel me some nice, white roots." When he had eaten the roots, he took hold of his necklace, rattled it, and said, as he divided the bones: "These are your father's bones; these are your mother's bones; these are your sister's bones; these are your brother's bones; these are your grandfather's bones. Now dig away, little boy; when you are big enough, your bones will be in my necklace."

That day Nul-we dug four basketfuls, and Limālimâas ate them all. Then he said: "Little boy, you should kill me, for I have eaten your father and your mother and all your kin." Then Nul-we thought: "Maybe I could kill this bad old man; I will get a bow and arrow and try."

The next day, when Limālimâas had eaten all the roots, he said: "Little boy, you should kill me; I have killed all your kin. You must shoot me in the body; that is where I keep my heart."

That night the grandmother asked: "Why don't you bring me roots? I am hungry; you shouldn't eat them all."

"I dig roots early in the morning," said Nul-we, "then I eat them and lie down and sleep all day."

"That isn't true," said his grandmother, "you don't deceive me; somebody takes your roots away from you."

"I want you to make me a bow and arrow," said Nul-we, "and put poison in the end of the arrow. I miss all the birds I shoot at with sticks."

In the morning Limālimáas said to him: "I think you are about big enough to eat."

That night Nul-we said to his grandmother: "I dig a great many roots, but a bad man comes and eats them all. He wears a necklace made of bones. He says they are the bones of my father and of my mother and of all my kin, and that my bones will make the necklace nice and long."

The grandmother was frightened, for she knew it was old Limālimáas, the man who lived among the rocks. She gave Nul-we his father's strong bow and put fresh points on the arrows; then she made the bow and arrows look like a little boy's first bow and arrows, and said: "That man's heart isn't in his body; it's in the end of his first finger; you must shoot him there."

When Limālimáas came, the boy fed him lots of roots. He dug fast and gave the old man all he could eat. Then Limālimáas lay down to sleep. Usually he lay with his head on his hands, but that time he lay with his face up and his hands spread out. Nul-we got his arrow ready, and made up his mind which way to run; then, when he saw something moving in Limālimáas' finger, he shot. The heart came out on the end of the arrow.

Limālimáas sprang up and ran after the boy. Ever so many times he almost caught him, but each time Nul-we dodged and got away. At last they came to a dried up river-bed where there were big rocks and deep holes. Limālimáas was getting weak; he stumbled and fell into a hole. Nul-we ran across the river-bed; then he turned and called to Limālimáas: "You shall not live in this world and kill people. Hereafter you will make a great noise, but you will not have the power to harm anybody. When another strikes, you will shout for him; that is all you will be able to do."

Nul-we took the heart off the end of his arrow, blew it up into the sky, and said: "You can go up there and live; you can't live down here any longer."

Now Nul-we could dig roots and carry them to his grandmother; he was glad, and he didn't cry any more.

The old man-eater became Thunder.

WIND AND THUNDER

CHARACTERS

Galaíwa	Mouse	Tániäs Sléwis .	North Wind
Káwhas	Blackbird	Tcûskai	Weasel
Leméis	Thunder	Tskel	Mink
Mówas Sléwis .	South Wind		

TCÛSKAI and Tskel lived together on North Wind Mountain (east of Klamath marsh). Tskel thought it was time to have a wife. He knew there were women off in the north, so he said to Tcûskai: " Go to Sycan and get two women." When Tcûskai got to the place, the women were digging roots. He snatched their caps and ran home with them. All the women followed him. In that old time this was one way of getting a wife. A man stole something a woman was wearing; then she knew he wanted her, and she followed him home.

When Tcûskai brought so many caps, Tskel was angry. He said: " Why do you always make trouble? I sent you for two women, and you have brought a great many. What will you do now? "

Tcûskai kept two of the caps and threw the other ones away. When the women came, they picked up their caps and went home; only two women stayed. After a while each woman had a little boy. They rubbed the children with ashes, and they grew fast.

As soon as the boys could run around and play, they began to quarrel. Tcûskai made them arrows to shoot birds and squirrels with; after that, when they got angry, they shot at each other. Then Tcûskai made them arrows with poisoned points, and one day when they were fighting, they killed each other.

Tcûskai stayed in the house, but he knew what had happened; he always knew everything. Tskel was away hunting for deer. As soon as he came home, he looked around for his boys; when he found that the two boys were dead, he called Tcûskai and they burned the bodies. Then Tskel said to his brother: "I want you to travel in the mountains and swim in the ponds. After that you can go south and cut off Mówas Sléwis' head."

Tcûskai wanted to go north.

Tskel said: "If Tániäs Sléwis should put out his head, you would die. He would cover everything with ice, and you would freeze to death."

"I can go north as well as you can," said Tcûskai. "I don't want to go south; you can go there."

"Go north if you want to," said Tskel. "It won't be my fault if you are killed."

They went to all the high mountains and swam in the swimming pools, then Tcûskai went to Tániäs Sléwis' home, and his brother went south to Mówas Sléwis' home.

When Tcûskai got near Tániäs Sléwis' house, he rolled himself up tight in his blanket, but as soon as Tániäs Sléwis stuck his head out to see who was around, Tcûskai died. Wind and cold cut through his body and killed him. When Tániäs Sléwis drew his head in, Tcûskai came to life.

Tskel was at Mówas Sléwis' place, but he saw Tcûskai and knew what was happening. Mówas Sléwis put his head out, Tskel cut it off, skinned it, and made himself a cap of the skin. Tskel had his emi [1] in his hand. Nothing in the world could break that knife, but whatever it was thrown at broke — Tskel made it that way by thinking hard. As soon as he had cut off Mówas Sléwis' head, he went north to help his brother. When he got to Tániäs Sléwis' house, he put Tcûskai under his blanket, and watched for Sléwis to put his head out. Tskel could endure the cold, for he had on the cap made of the skin of Mówas Sléwis' head.

As soon as Tániäs Sléwis put his head out, Tskel cut it off. Now both Mówas Sléwis and Tániäs Sléwis were killed, and that is why it is not as cold in winter, or as hot in summer as it used to be. Their bodies are dead, but their spirits are

[1] Obsidian knife.

alive. The wind that blows from the south is Mówas Sléwis' spirit, and the wind that comes from the north is Tániäs Sléwis' spirit.

Tskel skinned Tániäs Sléwis' head, and now he had two caps. When they got home Tcûskai wanted the cap made of Tániäs Sléwis' head, for whenever he put it on he could freeze people to death, but Tskel wouldn't give it to him. He was afraid that Tcûskai wasn't strong enough to wear it; that it would freeze him to death.

Tskel said: " The five Leméis brothers are bad men; they kill people and eat them. Their house is in a deep place, and there are great rocks around it. The tallest tree in the world wouldn't reach to the bottom of the house. Our sister, who married Kaiutois lives there with her husband and his five brothers; we will go and visit her."

Gäk and Káwhas went with Tcûskai and Tskel. When they came to the house the men were off hunting; only old Leméis and his wife and daughter and Kaiutois' wife were at home. Tskel had on the cap made of Tániäs Sléwis' head. The minute he went into the house ice was everywhere. Old Leméis and his wife were terribly scared; they thought somebody had come who was stronger than they were. They wanted to get away as soon as they could, but the ladder was covered with ice, and they kept slipping back into the house. At last they got out.

Kaiutois' wife and children were warm. Tskel made it so, for she was his sister.

Old Leméis' daughter was meaner than her brothers. The belt around her waist was made of men's bones; she killed men by making them put on that belt. As soon as the belt was around a man's waist, the bones pressed together until they cut him in two. She handed the belt to Tskel and told him to put it on.

He said: " I will put on your belt, if you will put on my cap first." She put the cap on. It pressed her head and almost froze her to death, but she snatched it off and ran out of the house. She was scared.

Outside old Leméis and his wife were crying with cold. The

eldest of the five brothers came with two men in his belt. His father said: "There is somebody in our house who is stronger than we are."

"There is nobody in the world stronger than I am," said the young man. "I will kill the man who is in there." He put one foot on the ladder, but sprang back and began to scream.

The second brother came with dead men in his belt. He said he was the strongest person in the world, but the minute he put one foot on the ladder, he sprang back, crying with cold.

The third brother put his foot on the second rung of the ladder, then he turned back. He roared terribly; he tried to frighten Tskel, but Tskel wasn't afraid.

The fourth brother came with four dead men in his belt; one was kin to Tskel. He went down four rungs of the ladder, then sprang back; the dead man who was kin to Tskel slipped out of his belt and fell inside. Tskel made that so by thinking. Then he brought the dead man to life.

When the youngest and strongest one of the brothers came, he got down the ladder into the house, but he was out as soon as he was in. Just at sundown Kaiutois came with a deer on his back. Tskel took his cap off and Tcûskai put on his cap made of South Wind's head. Right away all the ice was gone.

Now the Leméis brothers came inside. They built a big fire and heated rocks, put the rocks in a basket of water, and boiled pieces of the men they had brought home. Kaiutois roasted deer meat and gave it to his brothers-in-law. Gäk and Káwhas ate the meat old Leméis gave them. That is why crows and blackbirds eat any dead thing they can find.

After eating, everybody lay down. The five Leméis brothers lay in a row; they were watching, for they wanted to kill Tskel.

Káwhas had bright eyes; when he was asleep the Leméis brothers thought he was awake. Tskel made the five brothers go to sleep. They had long hair and Tskel tied one brother's hair to another's, till he had the five tied together. He did this so that when they woke up each one would think that his brother was pulling his hair, and all of them would get to fighting. Tcûskai, Tskel, Gäk, Káwhas, Kaiutois and his wife went outside. Tskel hired Galaíwa to fill all the holes in the house with pitch and pile pitch wood up around it; when that was done he set fire to the place.

When the house began to burn, the five brothers sprang up; that made their hair pull and they began to fight one another with their long flint knives. Soon they were all dead. Their bodies were burned up, but their hearts flew out of the fire. Tcûskai and Tskel were watching, and as soon as a heart came out they pushed it back into the fire. They did this till each heart burst and the spirit came out and went away. Four of the hearts were destroyed, but the heart of the youngest and strongest brother got away from Tskel. It went up to the sky and became Leméis. Leméis is up there yet; we hear him when he travels around.

Klamath Indians think that Thunder is a little fellow with very long hair.

GÁUKOS AND KÛLTA

CHARACTERS

Gáukos	Moon	Lok	Bear
Kówe	Frog	Weketas	A Small Green Frog
Kûlta	Otter		

GÁUKOS and Kûlta had a house among the rocks on the east side of Klamath Lake. On the west side of the lake lived the ten Kówe sisters, beautiful little women. Their clothes were covered with beads and porcupine quills. They were powerful women, too; they could do anything they wanted. A Weketas woman lived with the ten sisters. She was big and ugly, and the only thing she could do was to bring people to life.

Gáukos grew lonesome. He was tired of living in the world. Kûlta said: "I will go and tell the ten sisters that you want a wife. With a woman to cook for us, it won't be lonesome."

Kûlta went to the ten sisters, and said: "A young man on the east side of the lake wants one of you for a wife, but he don't know which one."

Each one of the ten sisters got ready to go; they cooked nice roots and pounded sweet seeds. They put on new moccasins and dresses, pulled their canoe into the water, and started. Weketas had nothing to cook and nothing new to wear. She had on a ragged old cap, and was half naked, but she went to row the canoe. The sisters kept pushing her, and saying: "Row faster, ugly thing! Row faster!"

Gáukos sat on the rocks where he could watch the sisters. When they reached land, they left the canoe, one by one. To the first one Gáukos said: "Not you; another." To the second sister he said the same, and so on to the last.

Kûlta told them to go back to the canoe; then he said to Gáukos: "Tell me which one you want."

"The one at the end of the canoe."

"What do you want of that ugly thing?" asked Kûlta. "You should take one of those nice girls."

"I will take the one I know will be best for me, the one that will live in my heart and always save me."

"Don't take that ugly Weketas woman," said Kûlta.

"I don't want to live around here," said Gáukos. "Every night, I see some of the big-mouthed people. They are watching me; they like to eat such men as I am."

"How can that ugly Weketas woman save you?" asked Kûlta.

"If there should be only a little bit of me left in Lok's mouth, she would bring me to life," said Gáukos.

Kûlta was willing now, but the ten sisters wouldn't let the Weketas woman pass them. She crept along on the edge of the canoe, and each sister pinched her as she passed; they made her arms and legs bleed.

Gáukos wiped the blood off, rubbed her with deer tallow, and gave her a nice blanket. Then he put her in his bosom and started off toward the east. As he left, he said to Kûlta: "You will see me every month; I shall live always and will always travel on the sky."

To this day Gáukos travels and he always will travel. People can see Weketas, for Gáukos still carries her in his bosom. Sometimes they can see Weketas' children lying near her. When Súbbas comes, and Gáukos is still in the west, he gets eaten up by the big-mouthed people, but Weketas always brings him to life and will do so just as long as he carries her in his bosom.

TCOITCAK AND HIS PACK

CHARACTERS

Tcoitcak	A Bird (English name unknown)
Tcûskai	Weasel
Tskel	Mink

ONCE Tcoitcak was going along near the house where two brothers, Tcûskai and Tskel, lived. He was carrying a big pack on his back. Tcûskai liked to stay outside the house looking around. Tskel scolded him for not staying at home, so when he went away he always left his tail hanging down inside the smoke hole and left his voice with his tail. He said: "If Tskel calls me, you must answer: 'I am here'!"

When Tcûskai saw the man coming with a big pack, he went to meet him. "What are you packing?" asked he.

Tcoitcak didn't answer.

"Let me see what you have in your pack," said Tcûskai.

The man kept walking along, but didn't speak. Tcûskai followed him and teased him to tell what he was carrying. "Sit down and rest," said Tcûskai. "That pack is too heavy to keep on your back all the time."

At last Tcoitcak got angry; he pulled the pack off his back and put it on the ground. In that big bundle Tcoitcak had lots and lots of little bundles. Tcûskai untied the big bundle, snatched one of the little bundles and opened it. Out came Darkness, and that minute it spread all over the world. It was black everywhere. Tcûskai couldn't see, but he snatched a second bundle and pulled it open. A crowd of stars came out.

In the big pack there were bundles of all kinds. Twilight was in one bundle, Daybreak in another. Each big star that has a name was tied up in a separate bundle, — Morning Star in one, Evening Star in another. Whatever time there is of day or night was in Tcoitcak's pack. Clouds, Rain, Snow, everything was there.

Tcûskai was lost in the darkness. He ran around everywhere, but couldn't find his way home.

Tskel knew what Tcûskai had done, and that he couldn't find his way home. He let him run around for a long time, then he pointed his flint knife toward the east, and cut a hole in the darkness to let light in.

It is because Tcûskai was running around so long in the dark that nights are so long and dark in winter time.

WITSDUK

CHARACTERS

Tcutûk . . . . Rock Squirrel
Witsduk . . . . Snow that the Wind Blows and Drifts
Wus . . . . Fox

WHEN Witsduk was a person, her home was in the Modoc country; she and her family were that snow which the wind carries in every direction. Wherever they went, they made people shiver, blinded them, and took their breath away. Everybody was tired of the Witsduks and wanted to get rid of them.

At last Tcutûk, an old medicine woman, said: "I can destroy Witsduk and her family, but I am afraid of Wus. He is a bad man; he likes to tease people, and he is always around. I can put Witsduk and her family in my bag and hide them under rocks where they can't get out, but if I meet Wus he will take the bag away from me, and untie it. Then the Witsduks will kill us."

The people were glad when Tcutûk said she could destroy the Witsduks; they promised to watch for Wus and kill him if he tried to get the bag away from her.

Tcutûk went to the mountain where the Witsduks lived. She opened her bag and waited for a long time. The Witsduks were going back and forth in every direction; Tcutûks was so cold that she was almost frozen. At last they came near her hiding-place, but they didn't see her. When they were right there, Tcutûk said magic words and the Witsduks began to go into the bag. They couldn't help going; Tcutûk pushed them down, crowded them, packed them solid. When they were all in and her bag was full, she tied it with a buckskin string, took it on her back, and went toward the rocks; she traveled fast.

When Tcutûk got to the foot of the mountain, she said to the people waiting for her: "I have every Witsduk in the world in this bag on my back; now you must come with me to the rocks where I am going to hide them. I am afraid of Wus; I am afraid that I will meet him. If he should open my bag and let the Witsduks out, I should feel badly, for then no one would be safe. The Witsduks are mad; they would come out and kill everybody. Then they would live forever; they would scatter and be everywhere."

The people said: "If we meet Wus, we will kill him," but they were afraid. They went a little way, then turned back. Tcutûk traveled on alone till she came to a log; when she was climbing over the log, she saw Wus; he was hunting for mice. Tcutûk stood still, for she didn't know what to do. As soon as Wus saw her, he came up, and right away he began to tease her to tell him what was in her bag, to open it and let him see.

At last Tcutûk said: "I am carrying off people you have met, and they have made you shiver. I am going to destroy them."

"Let me have them," said Wus, "I will eat them. I can eat anything in the world, all the people that crawl, or fly. I can eat Wind and Air. You haven't anything in that bag that I can't eat. I can eat Clouds and Rain, — everything."

"Are you sure that you can eat all kinds of people?" asked Tcutûk.

"There isn't anything in the world that I can't eat."

"I am carrying the Witsduks; you don't want to eat them, do you?"

"Yes. Open the bag and let them out; I will eat them right away."

Wus talked and teased. Tcutûk tried to make him let her pass. He got mad and caught hold of her head-strap and pulled on it till it cut her forehead. When she couldn't keep the bag any longer, she said: "Take the bag and untie it! But don't untie it till I am across the flat over there."

She dropped the bag from her back and ran as fast as she

could, but before she was half-way across the flat Wus loosened the string. Right away the Witsduks began to come out. Wus caught them, one by one, and ate them. Before Tcutûk reached the end of the plain, he loosened the string a little more; then the Witsduks came out fast. Wus caught them all; he ran around, snapped his mouth in every direction, ate as fast as he could, — ate till he was so full he couldn't eat any more. The string came off from the bag, and the rest of the Witsduks rushed out in a crowd. They were mad; they went everywhere, covered the whole world. Wus ran away, but they overtook him and killed him. The Witsduks he had eaten came out through his mouth and ears and nose and eyes.

All the people Tcutûk had tried to save, by catching the Witsduks in her bag, were killed. Tcutûk turned to a squirrel and hid among the rocks.

The Witsduks scattered everywhere, and they will live forever. Wus did this. If Tcutûk had hidden them under the rocks, there would have been no more Witsduks in the world. At the place where Wus was killed nobody can live to this day; every one dies from cold or starvation, for old woman Witsduk lives there yet.

DJÁKALIPS

CHARACTER

Djákalips . . . . Red Clouds

DJÁKALIPS lived on the west side of Klamath Lake. He had eyes as red as blood and he always looked down; he wouldn't look up at any time. When he ate, he closed his eyes, and when fishing he shaded them with his arm.

Two sisters went to live with Djákalips and be his wives. He said to them: " When you clean fish, you must not break the gall; if you do trouble will come."

One day one of the sisters said to the other: " Did you ever see Djákalips' face? "

" No, I don't lie as near him as you do; you must know how he looks."

" I don't, for I never see his eyes; he always covers them with his arm, or turns his face away from me."

" I want to see his eyes," said the younger sister; " I don't want a man who won't look at me."

" Maybe if we saw his eyes we would die," said the elder sister.

" Why do we stay here? " asked the younger sister. " Every woman has to look at her husband and every man at his wife. I feel as if something would happen to us, but I am going to see Djákalips' eyes."

They tried in every way to make Djákalips look up. Sometimes they told him that people were coming; sometimes they called out: " There is a deer! " But no matter what they said, he didn't look up.

One morning Djákalips went fishing. At midday he had a basketful of nice fish. The elder wife cooked some of the fish in the coals and gave them to her husband to eat; she spoke to him, but he didn't answer. He kept his arm over his eyes. The two sisters sat down in front of their straw house to dress fish and watch Djákalips. They were mad at him. They didn't like him any longer. The younger sister thought: "I will make him look up!" She broke the gall of a fish and screamed: "Oh! I've broken a gall!"

Djákalips looked up. His eyes were balls of fire, and his face was as red as blood.

The sisters were terribly frightened; they wanted to get away. The elder sister said: "We have no wood, you must come and help me get some." They ran off to the river and began to twist reeds to make a rope long enough to reach from the ground to the sky. They worked fast. When the rope was finished, they made it into a ball and threw the ball up till it caught in the sky; then they climbed on the rope that hung from the ball. As they climbed, they said: "We will leave the rope, and if Djákalips follows us, we will come down again." They left a little animal sitting on the ground near the end of the rope, and told him not to tell where they had gone.

Djákalips wondered why his wives didn't come. At last he tracked them to the place where they had made the ball; he saw the little animal, and asked: "Where are my wives?" It wouldn't tell. Djákalips pulled its hair, took out a handful; still it wouldn't tell. He looked everywhere for tracks; then he came back to the same place and asked again: "Where are my wives?" He got no answer. He pulled out another handful of the little animal's hair, then he went to hunt for tracks again. The tracks always led him back to the animal. When he had pulled all of the animal's hair out, it said: "They have gone to the sky."

"How did they go?" asked Djákalips.

"On a rope made of reeds. Here is the end of it. Look up and you will see where they are."

Djákalips climbed the rope. The sisters went far west, but he tracked them. They ran north and south, then they ran back to the rope and came down. As they touched the ground, the elder sister called to Djákalips: "You will never come back to this earth; you will always stay there in the sky. You will stay where the sun goes down, and in later times, when you look up and people see your red eyes, they will say: 'Djákalips is going to make water freeze.'"

Djákalips followed his wives north and south, but couldn't find them; then he went back to where the sun sets and stayed there. He turned into the red clouds which we see in the fall of the year. When Djákalips is seen in the west, water freezes.

MOASÄM BEPS, THE DAUGHTER OF SOUTH WIND

CHARACTERS

Moasäm Beps	South Wind's Daughter
Tsákiak	A Bird (English name unknown)

At Euks a great many people were starving to death; they were so weak they couldn't stand. It was winter; snow was falling all the time. The people were out of doors. They didn't live in houses. Tsákiak was the only person who had a house. He took people in, warmed them, and gave them a little to eat; he hadn't much.

One day, when it was cold and there was deep snow everywhere, Tsákiak went on top of his house and stood looking around. He felt badly, felt sorry for the people, they were so cold and hungry. Just then he saw Moasäm Beps coming from the south; she was bringing minnows, holding them out in her hand as she came along; when she passed Tsákiak's house, she gave him the minnows. He cooked them over his fire and gave them to the hungry people. He felt glad in his heart.

The next day, Moasäm Beps came again and brought many minnows; she had both hands full. When she passed Tsákiak, she gave them to him. He was hungry himself, but he gave all of the minnows to the starving people.

The next day Moasäm Beps' hands were empty, but she asked Tsákiak where the nut pine trees were. He said: "They are on both sides of the fire in my house."

Moasäm Beps went in and sat on a pine tree. As soon as she was there, the snow melted and went away. She said to Tsákiak: "Spread five blankets under each tree; then go out and don't look in."

Soon on each one of the ten blankets there was a big pile

of pine nuts. Then Moasäm Beps called the people in; those who were too weak to eat she fed.

Right away all the people were strong; they were happy, too. They gave Moasäm Beps wildcat skins and beads of every kind, and then they went their own way, for it was warm and they had plenty to eat. Tsákiak and Moäsam Beps went to Moasänik, her father's home, for Moasäm Beps was Tsákiak's wife now.

The day they got to Moasänik, Moasäm Beps gave her husband a pair of moccasins, and said: " You must wear these moccasins all the time you are here; if you take them off, you will die."

The next day she told him to go and hunt for deer. He went to the top of a high mountain, where there was snow. Tsákiak tracked a herd of deer and killed five.

Tsákiak went hunting every day for five days, — he started before it was light in the morning and came home in the evening. Each time he went Moasäm Beps told him not to take off his moccasins. The sixth morning, when he was ready to start, Moasäm Beps said: " Even if your feet are wet and cold, you mustn't take off your moccasins; if you do you won't come home; you will die on the mountain."

Tsákiak tracked deer for a long time. The ground was wet and muddy. At last he went to the other side of the mountain, where the ground was dry; it looked nice. Tsákiak said: " This is a good place to walk, the ground is dry. I will take off these wet moccasins and walk around a little."

He took off one moccasin. Snow began to fall and the wind to blow hard and cold. Tsákiak took off the other moccasin. " I don't care for you any longer," said he. " You are cold and wet." He picked up both moccasins and threw them as far as he could. Right away the wind blew furiously. It turned awfully cold, so cold that Tsákiak couldn't walk; his legs were stiff. Snow came down fast, like big basketfuls tipped over. Tsákiak couldn't get air, couldn't breathe; he died.

WEST WIND'S WIVES

CHARACTERS

Mówas Sléwis	South Wind
Tániäs Sléwis	North Wind
Tkálmas Sléwis	West Wind

TKÁLMAS SLÉWIS and his younger brother lived together. Tkálmas had two wives, Mówas Sléwis and Tániäs Sléwis; Mówas had a little baby.

Mówas was mild and kind and pleasant. The weather was nice when she was at home, but Tániäs was always cross and stormy.

Mówas went to visit her father at Moasänik, and only Tániäs was left at Tkálmas' house. Right away it grew cold in the house and there was snow and ice everywhere. Tkálmas' brother sat all the time looking toward the south, and kept saying: " I wish my sister-in-law would come. We shall die if she doesn't come soon; we shall freeze to death."

At last he saw Mówas coming. When she was still a long way off the snow on the top of the house began to melt, and water dripped down through the smoke hole, but as fast as it fell it dried up.

Tkálmas' brother said: " Oh my best sister-in-law, even if water freezes as hard as a rock, you can melt it. No matter how much ice there is, your soft breath thaws it. You are the kindest and the most useful woman in this world."

Tkálmas heard what his brother said, but he didn't care; he was glad that Mówas had come. The house was dry now and the sun was shining. Mówas gave them nice things to eat, things she had brought from Moasänik.

Tániäs was angry at her brother-in-law, and jealous of Mówas, so as soon as Mówas came home Tániäs took all of Tkálmas' beautiful beads, white, and yellow, and every color, took the nice things she had brought when she came to marry him, and went back to her home in the north. But once each year she goes to her husband, and stays with him till Mówas comes home from Moasänik; then she gets angry and jealous and goes back to her home in the north.

THE STAR BROTHERS

CHARACTERS

Gäk	Crow	Tekewas	
Gapni	Louse	Tohós	A Duck
Kaltsik	Spider	Tûtats	
Kûlta	Otter	Wámanik	Bull Snake
Skóla	Meadow Lark	Yaukûl	"One of the Stone People"

Yahyáhaäs or Yá-hi-yas or Yáhyahiyáas, always represented as a one-legged man

On the south side of Lake Klamath lived five brothers. The eldest was married to Skóla. Four of the brothers were without wives. Tekewas, their sister, was married to Kûlta, and lived not far away. The brothers were bad men. The name of the youngest brother was Tûtats. When he was a child his sister was fond of him; then her mother made her forget him, but after a long time she remembered him again, and thought: "I wonder where Tûtats is. I used to nurse him; he was nice when he was a baby. I will go and find him."

Tekewas got to her brothers' house at midday. When she had been there a while they asked: "Why don't you go home?"

"I am not going," said the sister. "I have come to stay all night."

They tried to drive her away, but she wouldn't go. The next day, when Tekewas' brothers told her to go home, she went to her mother, who was outside pounding seeds, and asked: "What have you done with Tûtats? Is he dead?"

"What do you care if he is?" said her mother. "You had better go home. The next time you come I will tell you about Tûtats."

Tekewas went home then, for she was glad. As soon as she was out of sight the old woman took Tûtats from under the ground, where she kept him in a big bark basket, and his brothers carried him to the river and let him swim.

The eldest brother said to his mother: " I am the only person who knows what my sister thinks. She thinks bad; she will come again. You must make Tûtats dry and put him back."

While swimming, Tûtats lost a hair out of his head. It was a beautiful, bright hair. The mother didn't notice it; she wiped him quickly, rubbed him with deer fat, put him in the basket, and carried him back under the ground.

The next morning, when Skóla was starting off to dig roots, she saw something red on the ridge of the mountains. Her husband said: " That is Tekewas lying there; she means to kill us." The brothers were so frightened that they wouldn't go out of the house, but sat inside; they wouldn't even look out. But Skóla watched.

When Tekewas came to the house, the eldest brother asked: " Why do you come so often? You were here yesterday."

Tekewas stayed all day; while she was swimming in the river she found the long bright hair. She took it to her mother and asked: " Who is so beautiful as to have this kind of hair? "

" No matter," said her mother. " Why do you come to trouble your brothers? You are Kûlta's wife; you should stay with him."

The next day Tekewas brought five pairs of nice moccasins, and told her mother to give them to her brothers, and tell one of them he must go home with her and get some of Kûlta's beads. The eldest brother said: " I will go."

" I don't want you to go," said Tekewas.

" Your second brother is ready to go," said her mother.

" I don't want him; he has enough of my beads." One after another, the brothers got ready, but Tekewas refused each one. " No," said she, " you have had enough of Kûlta's beads. I want Tûtats to go with me."

" Who is he? " asked her mother.

" You know that you can't fool me. I have a young brother;

I want him to go with me. It is getting late; where is he?" Every time Tekewas turned her body she talked to the sun, told it to go quick, so it would be dark soon.

Her brothers didn't want her to stay all night, so they took the basket from under the ground, and got Tûtats ready to go. They let down his hair and combed it. It was blue and beautiful, and reached to his feet. He cried all the time they were combing it, for he didn't want to go with his sister. When she started, he walked behind her, crying.

Tekewas talked to the sun, told it to go down, scolded it to make it hurry. The sun was scared and it went as though it were sliding down a slippery place. When they came to a clump of cedar trees, it was already dark. Tekewas stopped and said: "We will camp here."

"It is too near," said Tûtats; he was crying.

"It is too dark to follow the trail," said Tekewas. She built a fire and gave Tûtats roots from her basket. After eating, he lay down on one side of the fire and she on the other; then she thought: "Let him go to sleep quick." When he was asleep, she went over to lie by him.

He woke and got up; he was still crying. "Let her sleep till I get half-way to the sky," said he to himself. He found a log, put it by his sister's side, and told it to keep her asleep. Then he hurried home.

"What is the trouble?" asked his brothers. "Why did you come back?"

"I don't like my sister. I left her asleep. When she wakes up she will come to kill us. We must get away from here."

The brothers hired old man Kaltsik to help them. Kaltsik made a basket and put the five brothers into it; then he made a web, took the basket up into the air, let it down into the web, and started.

"Don't look down till I tie you to the sky," said the old man. "If you do, you will fall out and get killed."

When Tekewas woke up, she ran back to the house and asked: "Where are my brothers?"

"I don't know," said the old woman.

"Yes, you do. Here is a trail going up to the sky!"

Tekewas was so mad that she ran around the house so fast and so many times that she set it on fire.

Old man Kaltsik was half-way to the sky when he saw the blaze, and said: " Your house is burning! " The eldest brother forgot and looked down, over the edge of the basket. That minute the web broke, and the five brothers fell out, one after another.

The mother and daughter were fighting; each had a wooden paddle. When Tekewas saw her brothers falling, she said to her mother: " You mustn't say: ' Fall this side '; you must say: ' fall in the middle.' "

" Fall this side! Fall this side! " cried the mother.

Tekewas knocked the paddle out of her hand into the fire. Four of the brothers fell into the fire. When sparks flew out, Tekewas pushed them back with her paddle. As often as her mother got her paddle out of the fire, Tekewas knocked it in again. The youngest brother fell last.

" This side! This side! " cried his mother.

Tekewas jumped on her and fought with her. Tûtats swayed back and forth, back and forth, and fell outside the fire, but his sister pushed him into it, and he was burned up.

His mother ran to the south side of the fire, his sister to the north side. The old woman knocked Tûtats' heart out of the fire, for she was on the right side. She said to the heart: " We shall see who will live, you or your sister. You will be a great mountain with a white top, and will live always. In later times people will come to you to get wisdom, to be great talkers, and brave warriors, and you will talk to them and help them."

The heart flew north and became Mount Shasta; then the mother stirred the fire till four hearts flew out and off toward the north. Each heart became a mountain. The heart of the eldest brother went as far as the ocean. But the youngest brother is the largest of the five, and he is the only one who always has snow on his head.

Tekewas, when she thought she had killed her brothers, went home to Kûlta; then the old woman remembered Skóla, and hunted for her. At last she found her; she was dead, but by her side were two babies. The grandmother pressed them together with her hands, and they became one. She was glad and called the child Wéahjukéwas. She made a hole in the ground and hid him.

That night the old woman took the baby out and rubbed him with ashes. In the morning he noticed things. Each night she rubbed him with ashes; each morning he was larger and stronger. She talked to the earth, to the mountains, and to the springs, and asked them to make her grandson strong and make him grow fast.

One morning the grandmother saw Tekewas lying on the ridge of a hill; she was red and beautiful. The old woman was frightened; she thought Tekewas had seen the little boy.

Tekewas came to the grass house and asked for seeds and roots. The grandmother had forgotten the boy's deerskin blanket; she had left it in the house when she put him under the ground as she always did in the daytime. Tekewas saw the blanket, and said: "You have a baby! Whose is it?"

The old woman said: "My daughter, you shouldn't talk so to me. I am old; I had children, but now I am alone; you have killed all my sons. Go away! You know where the seeds and roots are; take them and go off."

Tekewas got the seeds and started, but she came back and said: "I know whose baby it is. It is Skóla's, and you must give it to me."

"Skóla is dead," said the old woman; "she had no children." She drove Tekewas away and followed her to see that she didn't stop on the mountain to watch the house. She was sorry that Tekewas had seen the blanket. When she came back, she rubbed the boy and talked to the earth, to the mountains, to the trees, to everything for a long time; then she put him away under the ground.

Each night and morning the old woman rubbed the little boy with deer's fat, and soon he was large enough to run around and play. Then she said to him: "My grandson, you mustn't show yourself; you must always play in the tall grass; never go away from it!"

Tekewas came every day; sometimes she wanted to stay, but her mother drove her off. When the boy was large enough to trap birds, his grandmother said: "Stay near the house; don't go far, for if you do, you will get killed." One evening she asked: "What have you been doing all day?"

"Playing with birds," said the boy. "They can talk to me now."

"The best way to play is with a bow and arrows. You can shoot an arrow toward the sky, then watch and see where it falls."

One day the boy noticed that his shadow was two, and he was one. The next morning, when he went out to play, he shot an arrow up to the sky; then he held his head down and listened. The arrow came back, hit him on the top of the head and split off one half of him; there was another boy just like him. He wished the second boy to be small, to be a baby. He called the baby by his own name. He went to a clump of brush, scratched a place in the middle of it, put his blanket down there, put the baby on it, and said: "Don't cry; if you do, our aunt will come and eat us up."

For a long time he sat and talked with his little brother, then he went home. It was night and his grandmother was frightened; she thought that Tekewas had killed the boy.

"Why did you stay so long?" asked she.

"I lost my blanket. I put it down in the brush and then couldn't find it."

The next morning his grandmother gave him a wildcat skin blanket, and he went out to play; but he didn't play, he sat by his little brother and cried, he was so sorry for him. When it was dark, he covered the child with brush and went home. "What is the matter?" asked his grandmother. "Why have you been crying?"

"I shot at a bird and then couldn't find my arrow."

"I can make you as many arrows as you want; don't cry," said his grandmother.

The next morning, when he was starting out, the boy said: "I must take a few seeds with me; I get hungry."

She gave him seeds, tied them up in a squirrel skin and said: " Be careful this time, don't lose your blanket or arrows."

When he came home in the evening, he said: " Grandmother, you must pound seeds for me to carry to-morrow. I don't like whole seeds, and I can't eat the roots in my arms, I bite myself."

The next day he took pounded seeds to his little brother, fed him, petted him, and talked to him till night, then he wrapped his wildcat skin blanket twice around the child, took his old blanket, and went home.

" Where is your new blanket? " asked his grandmother.

" I found my old one. I like it better. I left the new one in the brush."

When four days old, the little boy could walk. The fifth day the elder boy cried all the time; he was wondering who had killed his father and mother. His grandmother had never told him; she only frightened him to make him careful. His little brother could play with him now.

That night his grandmother asked: " What ails you? Why do you cry? "

" Because I have nobody to play with."

" You are a lonely child, but you mustn't think of that," said his grandmother, and she began to cry.

" To-morrow will you fill my sack full of pounded seeds? " asked the boy.

" You can't eat all I give you; you must waste it," said his grandmother, " but you shall have all you want."

The little boy could eat a great deal; he ate the pounded seed his brother brought and that afternoon he cried for more. The elder boy made five straw rings to shoot at and roll around to amuse the little fellow. The next day, when the child began to cry for more seeds his brother went home, and said: " Grandmother, you must give me more pounded seeds. I shot my arrow up, and when it was coming down to hit me on the head, I ran away and it hit my sack and spilt all the seeds."

" You must be more careful," said his grandmother.

" You told me you would give me all I wanted to eat."

"Yes, but you must not waste things."

She filled a willow pan, and told him to go away before any one saw him.

When night came, the boy gave his brother his bow and arrows, covered him with grass, and went home, crying.

"What is the matter?" asked his grandmother.

"I have lost my bow and arrow. I dropped them to follow a bird and kill it with a stone; when I came back I couldn't find them."

"Don't cry," said his grandmother. "I will make you another bow and more arrows. You shall have everything you want."

"I threw away my moccasins to-day; I want a new pair," said the boy.

The next morning he had a nice pair of new moccasins. The two boys played all day, rolling straw rings and shooting at them with arrows.

That night the old woman looked at her grandson and said: "You have only one head; where is the other?"

"I didn't have two heads," said the boy, and he began to cry.

"You had two heads."

"I had only one."

"You have always had two; now you have one. Where is the other?" At last he told her about his brother. "After it is dark," said she, "go and bring your brother to the house."

He brought the little boy on his back. The old woman cried when she saw him; she rubbed him with ashes, and talked to the earth and mountains, asking them not to hurt him. In the morning she put both of the children in the hole where the first child had been and threw a straw mat over the hole.

That day Tekewas came for roots. She saw the mat and asked: "Why did you throw away that nice mat?"

"Go off!" cried her mother. "Don't torment me. You have killed your brothers. My spirit is old; you can kill me if you want to, but don't torment me. Go away and let me alone!" She drove her off.

The next morning Tekewas went early to look for tracks.

She found the place where the boys had rolled straw rings and saw that some of the tracks were very small. She followed the larger tracks till she came to her mother's house. "You didn't tell me the truth!" cried she. "There are children here! Every afternoon I hear little boys laughing."

The old woman scolded her, drove her off, watched her till she was out of sight; then she took the boys out of the hole and told them to go and play, but not to run around; if they did a bad woman would catch them.

That day the boys followed a white-necked duck. They tried to shoot it but couldn't. At night the elder boy said: "Grandmother, you must give me an arrow with a strong head; then I can kill ducks."

She gave him one and all the next day he followed the duck; at last he hit it. The bird screamed like a man and hid in the bushes. Ever since that time ducks like that one scream in the same way. When the boy found the bird, it said: "Don't kill me. I always bring good news. Take this arrow out and I will talk to you."

The boy pulled out the arrow, then the bird said: "Little boys, don't think that you have a father and a mother. Your aunt killed them. She loved her youngest brother, but he didn't love her, so she killed him and all of her brothers. Now she is trying to kill you. I hear her sing in her heart: 'I will kill my nephews, I will kill my nephews!' When you are large enough to shoot ducks from a canoe, you can kill her if you try. She swims in the lake in the form of a duck; when she is in the form of a woman she has long red hair. She will call you as though she loved you, but you must remember my words. Don't tell your grandmother that you know about your aunt; she wouldn't let you kill her. She could have saved your father if she had killed her daughter."

"Grandmother," asked the boy that night, "is there any place around here where there are green-headed ducks?"

"Yes, but you can't kill them; you are too small."

The boy went to the lake, sat in the reeds, and watched till he saw two green-headed ducks and killed them. The next day he killed five green-headed ducks. The old woman was frightened. She didn't dare to let a feather drop or fly away for fear Tekewas would see it. She burned each feather and roasted the ducks in hot ashes.

"When I kill a duck, I shiver, and am cold," said the boy.

"Why is that?" asked the grandmother.

"Because I want a canoe."

"To-morrow, when you go to the lake, you will find a canoe."

He was glad. "I will take my brother," said he.

"No," said the grandmother, "he is too small; he might fall into the water and you couldn't get him out."

The boy started off alone, then he thought: "My arrows are not strong enough to kill big birds." He ran back and his grandmother gave him five strong arrows and a straw mat to wrap them in. That day he killed many ducks, and his grandmother was glad.

The next morning he said: "When I am in the reeds at the edge of the water, I always feel that somebody is looking at me to scare me."

"Don't be afraid," said his grandmother; "maybe the earth is trying to get hold of you." She thought of Tekewas, but she didn't want to tell the boys about her.

"No," said he. "I feel that somebody is looking at me. I want my brother to go with me."

"He can go, but be careful; don't let him fall into the water."

All day the little boy slept in the canoe; when the sun went down, his brother cooked him a duck to eat, and then the two went home.

That lake was their aunt's swimming-place. One day when the boy had killed a good many ducks, and had gone to the shore to cook one for his brother, he saw something swimming in the water; only a head could be seen, — a great, ugly head, with long red hair floating around it. As soon as the boys saw the head, they made themselves small. The little boy screamed. The woman called to them and tried to go to them, but she could only come up out of the water as far as her waist. "I shall see you another day," screamed she. "I will wait till you are larger."

When the boys got home, the grandmother asked: "Why did you scream so loud?"

"My brother swallowed a duck bone," said the elder boy. "You must cook seeds for him to eat."

Every day the brothers went for ducks. Many times the aunt floated up to their canoe, put her breast against the side of it, and almost tipped it over. Each time the little boy screamed. The elder boy drove her away. He was angry, but he was waiting for his brother to get older and stronger. Sometimes the woman didn't come; she was with Kûlta, who lived in the lake near the place where the boys hunted for ducks.

The grandmother gave the older boy a knife to sharpen his arrows. "I want a stronger one," said he. She gave him another, a very strong, sharp knife. That day Tekewas put her breast to the canoe and almost tipped it over. The little boy screamed, he was so scared.

When they went home, the grandmother asked: "Why did your brother scream so loud?"

"He cut his finger."

"That is because I gave you a sharp knife. You shouldn't let him have it."

The next day they killed a good many ducks. When the aunt came toward them the boy said to his little brother: "Don't scream." But when the head looked up over the edge of the canoe the child couldn't help screaming.

"Why does he always scream?" asked the grandmother. "You must be careful when you are down by the water."

"Why do you say that?"

"Because the earth sometimes has a pain, and wants people."

"Don't be afraid, grandmother, we belong to the earth; it won't hurt us."

One day when the grandmother asked why the little boy screamed, his brother said: "He got choked with a bone. I got it out, but he was almost dead, and I cried."

"You must leave him at home."

"No, the water looks ugly. I'm afraid when I'm alone."

The next time Tekewas came to the canoe and tried to tip it over, the boy cut her head off with his sharp knife. He threw the head down in the end of the canoe, then dragged the body into a deep hole among the rocks in the water. The water around that place is Tekewas' blood, and to this day it is as black as ink. As they pushed the body down into the hole, the elder boy said to it: "You will never be great again. You will be small and weak, and people will say you are too nasty to eat." The spirit came out of the body and flew around the lake, an ugly bird.

The brothers shot ducks and piled them up on the head in the end of the canoe. When they got home, the elder boy said: "Grandmother, give us plenty of seeds and roots to eat." While they were eating, the old woman began to bring in the ducks. Each time she went for a load, the elder brother talked to the fire, to the water, to the wood, to the bows and arrows, talked to the pounder, to the basket, and to the digging sticks, talked to everything in the house and everything outside, told them not to tell where he and his brother went, — but he forgot to tell awl. When he thought he had told everything, he took his brother and went down in the ground near the fire. He put a coal over the hole and started toward the east.

Each time the old woman brought in a basketful of ducks, she asked: "Are you here, boys?" and the spirit in the wood and the fire answered: "We are here."

She found blood in the canoe, and wondered where it came from. When she got hold of the head, she screamed and ran to the house. She pulled her clothes off and was going to kill her grandsons. "Where are you?" cried she.

"We are in the corner."

She went there, but didn't find them. Then she called again: "Where are you?"

"We are on the top of the house."

She looked for them there, then called: "Where are you?"

"We are in the grass of the house." The house was made of twigs and grass.

Then they said they were among the wood. She pulled the logs apart and threw them out, but she didn't find the boys. "We are in the canoe." She went there, and when she failed to find them, she screamed: "Where are you?"

"We are where your roots are."

She scattered the roots.

"We are sitting in the fire."

She threw out the wood and coals. She hunted all night but couldn't find them.

At last awl said: "What are you going to do, old woman? The boys are not to blame. Your daughter was a bad woman; she killed her brothers, and then she wanted to kill her nephews. Your grandsons are a long way off; you can't catch them. Look at that little coal. Under it is the hole where they went down in the ground."

The old woman saw the coal, picked it up, found the hole, and started to follow her grandsons.

The boys traveled toward where the sun comes up. They wanted to be servants of Sun, to be of use to him. The first house they came to was on the south side of Tula Lake; Tohós, Wâmanik's wife, lived there; she was their aunt.

Tohós had a great red lump on her forehead. The little boy laughed at her, and said: "That looks like a boil. It don't look well. I don't like to see it. People who come hereafter may look as you do." He took his fire-drill and pressed the swelling downwards. From that time fowls and beasts do not carry their young in their foreheads.

"Oh, my nephew," said his aunt, "what have you done? Your uncle is a bad man; he will be mad and maybe he will kill you."

Wâmanik was off hunting; when his bowstring broke he knew what had happened at home. He let himself out full length, then made a circle around the world and began to press in trees, rocks, mountains, everything. When he began to press his own house, the elder nephew went on the top of it, lay down, drew his bowstring, snapped it, and sent an arrow into Wâmanik's head and killed him. Then he cut his body into small pieces. Each piece turned to a rock, and the rocks made a great mountain. The spirit of Wámanik came out and was a snake. The nephew said: " You will be of no use; only dirty people will eat you."

When the boys started toward the east, Tohós' spirit followed them a while, then said: " My nephews, tell me where you are going and when you are coming back."

" We are not coming back," said the boys. " It is a lonesome world. We have no father or mother; our aunt has killed them. We don't want to live here any longer. We shall never come back; we are going to where the sun comes up." And they went on.

" I am dry," said the little boy; " I want to drink."

" I don't know this country," answered the elder boy. " I don't know where the springs are." As they traveled they came to a place where water flowed out of two holes in a rock. They drank there and the elder brother named the place Gádûm (Stone Springs). While they were drinking a little snake ran into the spring. The younger boy laughed and said to the snake: " In later time, if strangers come here to drink, you and your people will show yourselves and scare them."

They started on, but hadn't gone far when the little boy wanted water to drink. The elder boy shot his arrow off toward the east, but he saw no water. He shot a second arrow and a third; then he shot through a mountain and into a lake, and water came through the mountain and made a spring that he called Ktsiskăsalkis. (People have to crawl in under the rocks to drink from it.)

They crossed a high mountain and came to a lake. " I am hungry," said the little boy.

" Sit down, and I will go into the water and get tuls [1] for you," said his brother.

While they were eating the grass, they saw a catfish. When the elder brother shot at it, a great many fish came up out of the water. He caught some and cooked them. The place where the boys sat while eating is called Eŭdélis, and to this day a great many catfish are caught in the river near there.

As the boys traveled on, they came to a muddy stream. The

[1] A grass that grows in the water.

elder brother scratched the mud away, multiplied the fish that were there, and said: "You will be of use for my people." There were a good many eels in the water and along the bank, and the little boy was afraid of them. He took his fire-drill, picked them up, one by one, threw them off into the lake, and said: "You are not living people. I don't want you to be around here. In later times people will roast and eat you, and say you are good."

Near their camping-place that night there were a great many round, smooth stones. The younger brother didn't know that those stones were people, so he played with them, broke some of them, and struck one against another. When it grew dark, the stones began to fight; they flew at one another, pounded one another, and made a terrible clatter. The boy was frightened; he struck at them with his fire-drill, and said: "Hereafter you will be stones, not people! You will stay in the water, but in the evening and early in the morning you will make just such a noise as you have made to-night." To this day the noise made by those stones can be heard evening and morning. The place is called Dănwagáiyas.

As the brothers traveled east, they came to a place where there were large rocks. "I'm hungry," said the little boy. His brother scolded him for being always hungry, but said: "We will sit down by the rocks; perhaps we'll see a squirrel."

After a while a squirrel, on its way to the flat, passed them; they killed and roasted it, ate half of it, and took half with them. They came to a place on the top of smooth, level rocks, where at night there was a lake, and in the daytime only a little muddy water. There they caught one large fish. The little boy wanted to catch more, but his brother said: "No, this world was made before we came. Those fish were made for some purpose; we must leave them here."

They went on till they came to a hill. There were no trees on the hill, but it was covered with grass, and from the top of the hill they could see a long distance.

"Let us stay here," said the little boy. "Let us have this hill for our home."

"No," said his brother, "this is a lonely world; I don't

want to stay. We will go where we can be of use; we will go to where the sun comes up."

Then they talked about which one they would rather serve, Sun or Moon. The elder brother said: "I would rather serve Sun." The younger said: "I would like to serve Moon, for then people can't see me."

"People will always look at us," said his brother. "They will watch for us, and be glad when they see us."

Soon the boys came to a wide plain at the foot of a mountain. They dug roots, cleaned, and ate them, then climbed the mountain. "This mountain," said the elder boy, "is brother to Salwâhe. Hereafter people will come to this place for rock to make knives of."

"Let us stay here," said the little boy.

"No," said his brother. "I know what it is best to do; I am older than you are. This world isn't for us to live in always."

That night they camped at a place which the elder brother named Wélosina. The next morning they climbed a hill, and looking down into the valley on the other side, saw a great dirt house.

"When shall we get to that house?" asked the little boy.

"It isn't safe to go there in the daytime," said his brother. "Old Yaukùl, the man who lives there, kills people by twisting their wrists; he has a knife stuck in the ground near the fire, and after he kills a man he cuts him up and burns the pieces. No one ever comes away from his house. We will go there in the night."

"Don't go to that bad place," said the little boy.

"If I go, maybe I can kill that man; I don't think he has the power to live always."

The elder brother gathered the strongest wood he could find and made bones of it. He put the bones into his brother's wrists and into his own, and outside of those he put bones made of brittle wood. When night came, they went to the valley and climbed to the top of the house. Then they turned themselves into dead coals and dropped through the smoke hole.

Yaukûl had two servants, Gäk and Gapni. The old man and Gäk were asleep, but Gapni was awake and he called out: "Something fell in! Something fell in!" They didn't hear him; they were sound asleep: he had to call to them a good many times. Even if dust fell, Gapni heard it and called out: "Something fell in." At last they woke up. "What can you see with your little eyes?" asked Gäk.

"I can see everything in the world, and I can count everything." Gäk hated Gapni.

Yaukûl got a torch and looked around the fire. Gäk wouldn't look, for he didn't believe that anything fell in. Gapni kept repeating: "Dwûhélibina!" (Something fell in).

"I can look through the world," said Gäk; "I know that nothing fell in."

"I know for myself that something came in," said Yaukûl. He lighted the fire and hunted. At last the old man was tired; he put his hands on his knife, leaned on it, and rested. Then the elder brother changed into a man and stood in front of him.

"Oh, I am glad you have come!" said Yaukûl. (He thought he would have something to eat.) "Gäk," said he, "I knew that Gapni didn't lie; he never lies, he always tells the truth. He can see farther and hear better than you can; he shall be chief."

Gäk was ashamed and mad.

The younger brother then stood up. "I am glad that you have come," said Yaukûl. "Gapni was right; he said there were two. What do you want?"

"We came to visit you."

"Then I will play with you."

"I am too small to play with such a big man as you are," said the little boy. Yaukûl took hold of his wrists. When the brittle bones cracked, he was glad. "I can kill him easy," thought he.

"You can't play with him first," said the elder brother, "you must play with me; I am older than he is."

When Yaukûl took hold of the elder boy's wrists, the bones cracked, and he was glad.

"Now it is my turn," said the boy. He caught hold of Yaukûl's wrists, broke them, and killed him. Then he tore out the old man's arms, and said: "You will no longer be a person and have arms; you will be a bird with legs, and you will stand by the water to watch which way the wind blows, so as to find dead fish to eat. You, Gäk, will no longer be a man; you will fly in the air and go around among the rocks to watch for what hunters throw away, and what you find you will eat." Then he said to Gapni: "You will no longer be the wisest man in the world; you will live in people's heads. Some will crack you, like this" — he took him in his fingers and cracked him — "others will put you in the fire, and others will catch you in their heads and will bite you to pay you for biting them. You will waken people at night, and they will catch and kill you." He burned up the dirt house, and said: "Hereafter, Yaukûl, you will have no home, you will live everywhere in the world."

Tohós, their aunt, had told them that after passing Yaukûl's house, they would be out of their own country and must go along at the foot of mountains, for on the mountains a one-legged man was always walking around. But they were traveling east and couldn't go around the mountains. On the first one they came to, they met the one-legged man, Yahyáhaäs. He had a great, bushy head, his face and body were painted red, his blanket was made of untanned elk-skin, and rattled as he walked. On his back he carried a straw quiver. He had only one leg, but he traveled very fast. He came up to the boys, and sitting down said: "I didn't think that I should meet anybody."

"I didn't expect to see you," said the elder boy, "but a little while ago I felt that somebody was looking at me."

"Why don't you light your pipe?" asked Yahyáhaäs. (This was always his question.)

"I have no pipe," said the younger boy.

"Everybody who travels should have a pipe," said the man. He lighted his own and handed it to the elder brother. The first whiff the boy drew the pipe broke.

"Why did you bite my pipe and break it?" asked Yahyáhaäs.

"I didn't break it; I drew a whiff, and the pipe fell apart."

"You are the first man to break my pipe. Let me take your pipe." When he had it, he said: "I will keep this to pay for mine."

"No," said the boy, "that pipe rests me when I am tired; you can't have it."

"I shall keep it to pay for mine," said Yahyáhaäs. He drew a whiff, handed the pipe back, and said: "Put in more tobacco." When he had the pipe again, he struck it against a rock, but it didn't break; then he took a rock and pounded it.

"Don't break my pipe," said the boy. "I didn't mean to break yours."

Yahyáhaäs threw the pipe against a great rock, and the pipe rolled to its owner. He picked it up, put it in his pouch, and put the pouch into his quiver.

The one-legged man built a fire. "Now we will wrestle," said he.

"Why did you build the fire?" asked the boy.

"The one that gets beaten will be thrown into the fire and burned up."

While Yahyáhaäs was fastening his leg to a rock, the elder boy said to his little brother: "Take our quivers and bows and stand on the north side of the fire with your back toward us. When we begin to wrestle, run as fast as you can and don't look back, no matter who calls to you. Run till you are on the other side of that high mountain over there and then wait for me. I shall kill this man and burn up his body, but his spirit will follow us as far as we go."

The two began to wrestle. A good many times Yahyáhaäs swung the boy around and almost killed him, but the boy clung to him, and at last bent him back with a twist and broke his leg off. He threw the leg and the body into the fire, poked the fire up around them, and ran off as fast as he could toward the mountain, where he had told his brother to wait for him.

"Come back and wrestle with me," called Yahyáhaäs'

spirit. "You haven't thrown me. Come back!" Then he called to the younger brother: "Come back, little boy; I have thrown your big brother into the fire." The boy didn't turn. His brother soon overtook him, and they went on together.

"Yahyáhaäs' spirit will follow as far as we go," said the elder brother.

They traveled a good many days; one day Yahyáhaäs' spirit went ahead, then turned and came toward them. The spirit looked exactly as Yahyáhaäs had looked. Yahyáhaäs had a deer on his back. The boys couldn't turn, for they were always going east.

The spirit stopped on the trail, took the deer off his back and built a fire. When the boys came to the place, they sat down. Yahyáhaäs didn't offer them meat, but he said: "Let us smoke," and he gave his pipe to the elder brother. With the first whiff, the pipe broke. "Let me smoke your pipe," said Yahyáhaäs. When he couldn't break the pipe by drawing on it, he tried in every other way. At last the boy said: "You sha'n't break my pipe; it is the only one I have." He snatched it away from Yahyáhaäs, put it in his pouch, and started to go.

"Stop and wrestle with me," said the spirit. "Did you meet a man who lives straight west on this road? He is a bad man; he kills every man that passes his house."

The boy didn't listen; he hurried on. The spirit pretended to turn back, but only went aside till they were out of sight, then followed them.

They traveled a good many days. The little boy was used to walking now; he didn't get tired or hungry, so they traveled day and night. One day, when they were near a river, they saw the spirit of Yahyáhaäs again.

He stopped them, and asked: "Have you a pipe?"

"No," said the boy.

"Every man has one when he travels," said the spirit.

"I have no time to smoke. I am looking for a place to cross this river. Do you know of one?" asked the boy.

"Yes, above here there is a place where the river is shallow.

How did you pass the one-legged man's house? He lives on the road you came over. His house is under the rocks; all you can see of it is the smoke that comes out."

"We are going to Sun's house," said the elder boy. "We must hurry on; we've no time to talk."

They left the spirit at the crossing. There was a big stump in the middle of the river; it was Yahyáhaäs' crossing-place. He leaped from the bank to the rock and from there to the other bank. The elder boy took his little brother under his arm and jumped across the river.

"Stop! stop!" called Yahyáhaäs' spirit. "Give me your pipe."

The brothers paid no heed; they went on, and at the end of two days came to a house covered with deerskins. Some of the skins were dry; others were fresh. Around the house there was a great deal of deer meat.

"Let us go to that house and get something to eat," said the little boy.

"Don't go there," answered his brother. "That is the one-legged man's house."

Yahyáhaäs was watching; when he saw the boys pass he came out, and going around them, came up driving a deer that looked tired and ready to fall. As the spirit met the boys, the deer ran off.

"You have made me lose my deer!" screamed the spirit. "Now give me your pipe to smoke."

"We have no pipe."

"Travelers always have a pipe."

"I have traveled long," said the boy. "When I had traveled two summers, my tobacco was gone."

They left Yahyáhaäs and went on. That night they crossed two mountains, and the next day the elder brother said: "We are near the end of our journey." Just then Yahyáhaäs came to them; on his back were two deer. The elder brother saw him first. "That is the spirit of the one-legged man," said he to the little boy. "Don't be deceived."

The brothers turned to black coals, and a strong wind, like a whirlwind, carried them along. Sometimes they rolled and sometimes they went through the air. When they were over two high mountains, they took their own forms. Again Yahyáhaäs came to them. This time his face and body were painted white. "We have no time to talk with you," said the elder brother, and they hurried on.

When they reached the top of the third mountain, the spirit of the one-legged man was there. That time his face and body were painted red, and long bright hair floated behind him. He called out: "Who are you that can never be caught?"

The moment he spoke, the brothers again turned to black coals, and a whirlwind carried them away. The whirlwind stopped on the bank of a dried up stream, and the boys took their own forms, and traveled on. Many times Yahyáhaäs' spirit met them, always in a different dress, and painted differently, but the brothers knew him.

At last the boys reached the eastern ocean, where nothing stood between the water and the sky. There were lots of rocks there. The brothers sat down and the elder took out his pipe to smoke.

That minute Yahyáhaäs was there, and said: "Let me smoke." That time the boy gave him his pipe. (He was going to destroy the spirit.) Yahyáhaäs tried to break the pipe, but couldn't; then the boy said: "Give me your pipe." With the first whiff he broke it to pieces.

"You must wrestle with me," said Yahyáhaäs. He built a fire and fastened his leg to the rocks.

"You must stand by the fire with your back toward us," said the elder boy to his little brother. "When you hear us wrestling shut your eyes and run as fast as you can. Don't look back. Run straight east. Run on the water; and don't stop till I call to you. We have left the house where our father and mother were killed. We are leaving the world, but each year we shall see our father's country."

When the boy had killed Yahyáhaäs, he threw him into the water, and said: "You will never be a person again. You will only be something to entice and fool people. You will think that you can kill people, but you will have no strength.

You will wander around on the mountains and appear (in dreams) to doctors, and they will be your servants."

As the boy ran off, the spirit called: "When I appear, you will appear, but you will have no power. You and your brother will no longer be persons; you will be stars, and between summer and winter your people will fight over you."

The younger boy was at the edge of the sky when the old man's spirit said: "You will be a star." Right away he was one. As soon as the elder boy reached the edge of the sky, he became a star, too.

NOTE. — Those two stars appear early in the morning toward the end of winter. They are the heralds of spring.

THE RAINMAKER

CHARACTERS

Gáhga	Heron (Small Green Heron)
Kāhkaas	Stork

GÁHGA and his brother lived together. They were so small that people called them "the two little Gáhga brothers." The elder brother was blind, but he was a great doctor; he could see everything, by the help of his medicines.

One day a man came to the Gáhga brothers, and said: "A great many people are going to snare deer. They have made bark ropes and tied them between trees; now they are ready to drive the deer in. They want you to come and help them."

The elder brother was married. He had a nice-looking wife and a little boy. He said to his wife: "You must pound seed and get ready to go with my brother. I don't want to take my medicines there; I will stay here by the fire with our boy. I can't look out of my eyes. Maybe the deer would kill me."

The woman pounded seed; she left some for her husband and little boy to eat, and took a bagful for herself and her brother-in-law. Gáhga got out his medicine and watched his wife and brother. He sat by the fire, but he followed them all the way to where the people were driving in deer. As he watched them, he got jealous and mad, for he saw that his wife and brother were fond of each other. When they came home, they brought a fawn. The woman cut it up, roasted the meat, and gave some of it to her husband; he kicked it away. She gave him some wûdjûk (weed like mustard), to eat; he tasted of it, spat it out, and threw the rest in the fire.

She said: "The people were kind to me to-day; they gave me the fawn and asked me to come to-morrow," and she began to pound seed and get ready to go.

The next day when the woman and her brother-in-law were starting off, Gáhga said: " I know what kind of stuff you are feeding me! I know you are making sport of me. You don't fool me. You can do what you like; I don't care for you any longer, but I will make you feel sorry." They didn't answer, didn't say a word to him.

That day Gáhga's sister came to see her little nephew. Gáhga said: " I want you to get me a straw plate."

" Why do you want a straw plate? " asked his sister.

" Get it for me, I want it."

She wouldn't get him the plate till he told her what he was going to do with it, and he wouldn't tell. She was afraid of him; she knew he was mad about something.

After a while old man Kāhkaas came; he was kin of Gáhga. Gáhga asked him for the plate and he gave it to him, and said: " Your brother is stealing your wife. All the people at the deer hunt say so. But you must keep quiet; you mustn't get mad. You are old and blind; your brother is young, and your wife is nice-looking."

Gáhga screamed, he was so mad. He called his sister and said: " Lead me to the hunt! "

She was so scared that she had to do as he told her. He took the straw plate, and the three started. When they got to the place, his sister said: " Sit down here, away from the snares; then you will be safe."

" No," said Gáhga, " I am going where my wife is."

" Don't be a fool," said his sister. " She doesn't want you; she has another man."

Gáhga took the plate from under his arm, and sat down on it.

About midnight his sister asked: " What are you doing? Why don't you lie down and go to sleep? Why are you sitting on that plate and keeping awake all night? "

" Keep still and let me alone," said Gáhga. " Stay here by me; I am going to punish those people." Then he got up and began to dance on the plate and to call out: " Ho! ho! ho! "

Right away rain came down, but Gáhga didn't get wet.

He kept shaking himself and calling: "Ho! ho! ho!" Each time that he called, it rained harder. There was deep water everywhere, but the plate was dry and the ground around it was dry. The people got as wet as though they had been swimming.

Gáhga's sister said: "You shouldn't get mad and act in this way; you will kill everybody."

He didn't listen to what she said; he called, "Ho! ho! ho!" and danced faster and faster. The people were almost drowned; the water was up to their arms. Still Gáhga kept shaking himself and dancing and calling: "Ho! ho! ho!"

When the people saw that Gáhga and his sister were dry, they said to his brother: "You have done this. You have made Gáhga mad. You have taken your brother's wife," and they threatened to kill him.

He said: "I don't want her. I am going to die; I am freezing."

The people caught hold of the woman, dragged her along in the water, and threw her down in front of her husband. He stopped dancing, and right away it stopped raining.

The people said: "You shouldn't be mad at us. We didn't do this. We don't want to die; we want to go home. You should feel sorry for us and dry up the water."

Gáhga was sorry for them. He danced on the plate, but he didn't call: "Ho! ho! ho!" The water began to go away, and soon the ground was as dry as it had been before the rain, and every one went home except Gáhga and his wife and his brother.

Gáhga sat on his plate; he wouldn't get up or he wouldn't speak. His wife got mad. She pushed him, and asked: "Why don't you get ready to go home?" He didn't answer: then she took hold of his arm, jerked him up, threw him on top of the load of meat on her back, and went home.

His brother went off on the mountains; he was afraid of Gáhga, and afraid of the people; for they hated him, and the woman didn't care for him any longer.

Gáhga was so jealous and cross that he drove his wife away. His sister took the little boy, and Gáhga stayed alone. Maybe he is dead and maybe he is living. Doctors who have him for their medicine can make rain whenever they want to. It is a good medicine. When any one has it, they can look through a man's body just as we look through a window.

OLD MAN LULUS-DEWIEAS OR EARTHQUAKE OLD MAN

CHARACTER

Lulus-Dewieas . . . . A Sweet Root; Dewieas means a Great Eater, a Glutton

Old man Lulus-Dewieas and his son and daughter-in-law lived in the country where the lava beds are now. They ate a great deal of sweet lulus; it was the old man's medicine. Always when the son went to hunt for deer, he told his wife to take good care of his father, and be sure to give him food before she ate herself, or gave any food to the children. If she didn't, she would bring misfortune on herself and the children. The woman remembered what her husband said, and she always gave the old man food first; he was glad and fed his grandchildren.

One day, early in winter, the son said to his wife: "There is plenty of game now. I want to kill a good many deer before deep snow comes. While I am gone, you mustn't forget to feed my father before any one else." The old man was white as snow; he was very old and was almost blind.

The next morning, when the young man was starting off, he said: "I had a bad dream last night. I don't want to go, but the children are always crying for fat meat. I dreamed that I came home and found only a deep hole where our house is now. You must keep the children away from their grandfather. Don't let them bother him; he might get mad. As long as you treat him well, he won't harm them."

When the young man got to the top of the mountain, he looked back; he could see his house, but somehow he felt lonesome and scared. He kept listening, as if he expected to hear something. It was the first time that he had felt that way. He found a deer and drove it on to a hill, and shot at it.

Right where it stood, it disappeared. Then he knew that something was going to happen to him. He said: "This is the first time I have lost a deer after shooting it." When he got tired of looking for the deer, he sat down to rest.

After her husband was gone, the young woman got a heavy stone and began to pound seeds. While she was pounding, she made up her mind to find out what her father-in-law would do if she put the seed away without giving him any. When the seed was fine enough, she put up the mortar without saying a word. When the old man saw her do that, he crept out and sat down on the south side of the house. As he sat there, he began to swell up. He took black paint and painted himself in stripes. Right away he began to turn and turn, and to throw up dirt. His hair grew as red as fire, and when the hole he made was large enough, he sank into it.

When the little girl saw her grandfather going down in the ground she screamed: "Oh, grandfather, come back!"

The woman heard the child cry, and she ran out to see what the matter was. When she saw what had happened, she called: "Oh, father, come back. I'll give you lots of seeds to eat! Come back!"

But the old man had gone too far, and was too mad; the house, the woman, and the children all sank into the hole.

The old man went on, boring as he went. Everywhere he broke and threw out the earth. Once in a while he raised himself up a little. At such places the earth would be level for a short distance, then it would sink down in a deep hole and leave a wide opening in the ground.

The son heard a terrible roar and he knew that his wife had made his father mad. People living a long way off heard the roar. They knew what kind of an old man that was; they stayed in their houses and fastened up their doors. As the old man traveled, he kept calling his own name: "Lulus-Dewieas, Lulus-Dewieas!" When the young man came to where his house had been, he found only a wide gap in the earth. He followed the sound of his father's traveling and called to him; but the old man didn't hear him.

He traveled under the ground till he got beyond Mount

Shasta and came to where there was water. He stopped there, but stayed under ground. The son stood above the place and spoke to his father.

The old man said: "You must not feel badly; my spirit belongs to this earth. You must go away from me; you must not try to follow me. I shall live forever under the earth."

Lulus-Dewieas could hardly speak when he said this. The son left him, and ever after wandered around in the world. He felt sorry and lonesome.

MÁIDIKDAK'S DAUGHTERS

CHARACTERS

Máidikdak	Snowbird
Wus	Fox

MÁIDIKDAK and her two daughters lived in the south. The old woman knew that five chiefs lived in the north, with their father, who was a chief, too. She wanted her daughters to marry those five brothers, so she made them ready for the road. To one daughter she gave a basket of food; to the other beads, nice shells, and porcupine quills.

When the girls were ready to start, she said: "If you see a man coming from the east, you will know he is Wus. Don't stop to talk to him. He is a powerful man; he can do anything he likes. If he gets mad, he will turn you into an animal or a bird. Don't go on the west side of the lake. Follow the trail on the east side."

When the girls came to the lake, the west side looked nicer, the trail was brighter. The elder sister wanted to follow it, but the younger sister said: "Our mother told us not to go on that side."

The elder sister said: "You can follow the other trail if you want to. I am going on this trail; it is nicer."

The younger girl didn't want to be alone, so she went with her sister. When they passed Wus' house she was frightened. She said: "I feel as if somebody were looking at me."

"I feel that way too," said the elder sister. Presently they saw a young man coming toward them.

"What nice girls those are," thought Wus. When he came up to them, the younger sister said to the elder: "Don't stop. Go right on. This is the man our mother told us about. Don't speak to him."

But the elder girl stopped. Wus made her stop. The younger went on a little way, then she turned back; she was afraid to go on alone.

"Where are you going?" asked Wus.

"To the chief's house," said the elder sister.

"What chief is there out this way? I am the only chief here. I am the chief of this world."

"You are not the chief we are going to. That chief never travels around. Our mother told us there was a bad man on this side of the lake. His name is Wus; he doesn't smell good."

"I know that man," said Wus. "He is not bad. He has power and can do anything he wants to."

"We are not going to stop here," said the elder sister. "We are going to the chief who lives in the north, and has five sons."

"Go on, if you want to," said Wus.

When the girls started, Wus watched them till they went out of sight; he was saying things in his mind. As they traveled, they became old women, with humps on their backs; their bodies shriveled up, there was no flesh on their bones, they could scarcely move; their hair turned white, and their teeth fell out. Their beautiful clothes turned to dirty straw; their strings of beads were twisted bark; their baskets looked old and broken and the roots in them turned to moldy skins; the shells and porcupine quills were bits of bark.

The younger sister said: "We didn't go the way our mother told us to. That man was Wus; he has done this. If we had gone on the east side of the lake, we shouldn't have met him. We should have done as our mother told us; she is old, and she knows more than we do." After a long time, they got to the chief's house. The five brothers were out hunting. The chief didn't know what to give the women to eat; he thought they were too old to eat roasted liver (old people's food). When he gave them some, they pushed it away. They lay down to sleep, and while they were sleeping the five brothers came. They knew Máidikdak's daughters and knew who had made them old.

The youngest brother asked: " Did you give these women anything to eat? "

" I gave them liver," said the old man, " but they couldn't eat it; they haven't any teeth."

The young man was glad they had come; he sat down and watched them. About midnight they turned to beautiful girls. In the morning, when they woke up, they were old women again.

The chief said to himself: " What kind of a man is my son? Why does he stay by those dirty old women? "

The young women heard his thoughts and they felt badly. At last they crawled up and went out to wash in the river. The elder sister said: " If we swim, maybe it will make us young again."

They took off their dirty, ragged clothes and old torn moccasins and began to swim. Right away they turned to beautiful girls; their long hair floated on the top of the water. As they swam, they talked and laughed, for they were glad to be young again. They made sport of their father-in-law, and said: " That big chief thought we were old women; he fed us liver! "

The young man heard this and said to his father: " You fed those girls dirty liver. Did you think they were old women? "

The girls kept diving down in the water and coming up, and soon they began to change. They became green-headed ducks, and floated off toward home. The young man felt badly; he didn't want them to go.

Old Máidikdak heard them coming, and when they were near the house, she said: " My daughters, you didn't do as I told you. I told you about that bad man. If I hadn't this would be my fault; now it is yours." She tried to catch them, but couldn't. At last she went under the water and caught hold of their legs. She pulled off their feathers and they were girls again.

The next morning the young man said to his father: " I am going to carry my wives' clothes and beads and porcupine quills to their mother."

When he got to Máidikdak's house the two sisters were off gathering wood. The old woman saw him sitting on top of the house and she asked: "Who are you?"

"I am one of the five brothers who live in the north."

"Are you the youngest?"

"Yes, I have brought back your shells and porcupine quills. Wus changed your daughters to ducks."

"Come in, son-in-law, my daughters have gone for wood."

The young man was glad. When the girls came, he said: "I have left my father and brothers. I will live here now."

Ningádaniak.[1]

[1] The edge or rim; meaning the end of the story.

WUS KUMUSH AND TSMUK

CHARACTERS

Kaiutois	Wolf	Wus Kumush	
Nátcaktcókaskĭt		Wusweléḳgăs	Wus' Old Woman
Tsmuk	Darkness		

OLD man Tsmuk and his wife had three sons and one daughter. The daughter was always thinking about Wus and singing about him.

Wus heard her, but he didn't know how to get to her, for everywhere around Tsmuk's place it was dark. He tried in all directions, but couldn't get there. He listened to the girl's song. At last he thought: " I can do anything I want to; I am Wus. I will make a place where that girl will come, and I can see her." He burned over ground and made it ready for ges.[1] Then he thought of ges, and it grew there right away.

One day, when the three sons of old man Tsmuk were starting off to hunt deer, they asked their sister: " What will you eat while we are gone? "

" I have nothing to eat," said the girl.

" Not far from here," said the brothers, " there is ges growing; you can dig that." And they told her where the place was.

Wus saw her digging roots and singing, and he thought: " How can I get near her without frightening her? " He turned himself into an old woman, put his bow and arrows and quiver into a basket, tied bark around his legs and head, just as an old woman does, and went to the girl. He talked like a woman, spoke kindly, asked her who she was, and where her home was.

The girl was tired; she complained because she had to come so far for roots.

" Are you very far from home? " asked Wus.

[1] A certain root. English name unknown.

"I have to camp one night on the way back," said the girl. When she started for home, Wus hurried the sun down, made night come quickly, then he said: "Let us sit down and sing songs."

While they were singing, Wus wished her to sleep. She went to sleep right away. Then he built a brush house over her; he worked all night, and in the morning the house was finished. When the girl woke up, she was in a bright, many-colored house, and she wondered where she was. When she remembered, and looked around for the old woman, she saw a handsome young man; his clothes were covered with beads.

The next day Tsmuk's daughter had a child. It was like any child, except that it had fox ears. The mother cried.

"Why do you cry?" asked Wus. "Are you sorry to be here? For a long time I have listened to you. When I have been out hunting, I have heard you singing about me. If you don't like me, why did you sing that song?"

"I am not crying about you, I am crying about my baby; I think my father or brothers will kill it."

"They will not kill the baby. I have power; I can do anything; I am Wus," said the young man.

Wus pushed the sun and made it go down quickly. As soon as the woman was asleep, he fixed the baby's ears, made them like the ears of a person. He did this by thinking hard and wishing them to be that way.

Old Tsmuk and his wife were looking for their daughter. They knew that Wus had been trying to find her and they thought he had caught her. They called to her, and listened for her song, but didn't hear it.

Tsmuk's daughter wanted to go home; she wanted to see her father and mother. Wus knew her thoughts, and he asked: "Why do you think of such things? What I wish for will be. To-morrow you will go home."

The next morning Wus wrapped up the baby and tied it on a board. The child was bright and beautiful. It looked like a rainbow.

Old man Tsmuk sent his youngest son to hunt for his sister. When the young man saw her coming, he didn't know her, she was so beautiful; she was different from what she had been before. He ran into the house, and said: "There is a beautiful woman coming." When the second brother saw her, he said: "That is our sister." The woman was alone, except for the baby on her back. When she went into the house, her father asked: "What man have you found? If Wus is your husband, you can't stay here!"

Wus was a long way off, but he heard what the old man said and he was angry. He thought: "I will find out if old Tsmuk is mad at his daughter." Then he wished the baby to turn to a little fox. When the young woman took the baby off her back, it was like a baby fox. It was covered with hair.

"That child smells like a fox!" cried the old man. He snatched it and threw it out of the house. The mother screamed. Wus heard her, and said: "Now I will torment Tsmuk." That moment Wus' wife was an old woman. Her youngest brother was so frightened that he lay down and cried. The baby was crying itself to death, but the mother couldn't do anything; she was bent over and helpless, too old to go out of the house.

Wus thought: "Bring in that child!" That minute the young man got up, went out, and brought in the baby and put it by its mother. He said to his sister: "Lie down, and I will cover you up."

Wus thought: "My brother-in-law is going to like me," and he was glad. He gave his own feelings to the young man.

The brother watched his sister, and after a while he saw that she was getting younger; then he said: "Go to the river and swim. Maybe you will be young again. I don't care if you are old, I love you just the same; but I am sorry for the baby." He kept the child covered, and it went to sleep. He went to sleep himself, and slept till the middle of the night, then he woke up, but he slept again, and when he woke up the second time it was almost morning. He looked at the baby; it was like a person. He didn't go to sleep again; he was afraid to; he thought if he did the child would turn into a fox.

"Do you know what Wus can do?" asked his sister. "He

can do anything. He can make people old in a minute; he can turn them to anything; he can move a house or tear it down by wishing. When I saw Wus, he looked as I do; he was a woman and carried a basket on his back. While I was asleep, he turned to a man and built a house. The house is so bright and has so many colors that it hurts my eyes to look at it. If anything happens to Wus' child, I think we shall die. When it was thrown out, I got old; now that it is in the house, I am growing young again."

"What are you talking about?" asked Tsmuk. "Old Wus is listening to everything. He listens while he catches mice to eat."

When the brother and sister started to go to Wus' house, they didn't tell their father where they were going. Soon they heard Wus blowing on reeds, making music. It was nice and it sounded far off. They followed the music till they came to the house. The brother stood outside; he was afraid to go in.

Wus said to the woman: "Why do you let your brother stand outside? Tell him to come and sit here by me."

When the young man went into the house, he couldn't see, it glittered so; the light was so bright that it hurt his eyes; he had to hold his head down. Wus said: "I know that you like me," and he called the young man brother-in-law. "Take off your clothes and put on these I give you; then you can look around."

The sister asked: "When do you want to go back to our father and mother?"

"In two days I will go," said the brother.

"Will you take blankets and beads with you?"

"No," said the young man, "I shall come back; I don't like to stay there."

Wus wanted to go to Tsmuk's house. His brother-in-law said: "I will show you the way; you will get there if I am with you."

They all started; when near the house the young man went ahead. Old Tsmuk spoke cross to him; asked: "Have you been in Wus' house?" and he called Wus bad names.

At last the young man said: " Don't say such bad things of Wus; if you do, harm will come to you."

" How can Wus harm me? " asked the old man. " I have lived a long time, and nobody has been able to harm me," and he kept abusing Wus.

Old woman Tsmuk cried; she thought Wus was a nice-looking man, and she didn't want to hear him abused. She spread around mats and blankets, and Wus and his wife went in and sat down.

" Why does your mother cry? " asked Wus.

Tsmuk heard this and it made him mad. He screamed to his wife: " Put that man off by himself! He smells badly; he will spoil all our seeds and roots! "

Wus didn't listen to his father-in-law. He said: " I wonder if I could find any game if I went hunting? "

" My brothers hunt," said his wife, " but they never catch anything."

Wus didn't want to hunt; he wanted to torment his father-in-law. As soon as he was a little way from the house, he turned into a fox. One of his brothers-in-law was outside; he saw the fox, and called: " Look! a fox is coming."

Old Tsmuk said: " That is not a fox; that is your brother-in-law. You see what kind of a man he is! " And he scolded the son who had been at Wus' house.

Wus caught a sackful of mice, carried them to the house, and sent his mother-in-law outside to roast them.

" What smells so badly? " asked old Tsmuk.

" Mother is roasting mice," said the youngest son.

" Are you going to eat mice? " the second brother asked the youngest.

" Yes. Are you going to stay with father? "

" No," said the second brother. " I don't like his way."

" Then you must eat some of those mice."

They ate together. Wus spoke to his father-in-law, but the old man didn't answer.

" Are you going to be mad all the time? " asked Wus.

" Yes," said old Tsmuk. " I don't want you for a son-in-law. I think you are bad; that you are dirty."

"Why do you think so?"

"Because you are not a person; you are not a man."

Wus asked again: "Are you going to be mad all the time?"

"Yes. You have no sense. I don't like you; you smell badly."

Wus asked the third time: "Are you going to be mad all the time?"

"Yes. I want you to go to your own place; I hate you."

"In which direction can you see farthest?" asked Wus.

"I can see far off in any direction I like."

"What do you see when you look straight east?" asked Wus.

Old Tsmuk looked toward the east. That moment Wus made a great wind come from the west. The old man's body melted like snow, and right away he turned into a black cloud, and the wind blew him off toward the east. Wus said: "Hereafter, old man, you will have no sense. You will no longer be a person. You will be darkness, and people will sleep when you come; but I shall never sleep when you are here. I shall sleep in the daytime and travel when you come. People will call you Tsmuk, and will do evil when you are around. They will steal, and will kill one another, for you are bad, and will give them bad thoughts. I asked you three times if you were mad, asked you not to be mad."

The son said to his father: "From quarreling with my brother-in-law you are no longer a person. I thought you had power, but you hadn't. You were calling Wus what you were yourself. I don't care for you any longer. I like Wus."

Wus said to his brothers-in-law: "You will come to my country and live with me always." To his wife he said: "I am taking you from Darkness; now you will change feelings. I will give you the water of life. When we get to the house, you must go in first, drink the water you find there, and give some to each one of your brothers and to your mother; it will change your minds. As you travel, go straight ahead; don't look back. If the wind comes from the east, you must go around it. Old Tsmuk has tried to beat me in many ways; maybe he will try again."

When they got to Wus' house, the young woman went in and gave water to her mother and to her brothers. As they drank, they seemed to open their eyes, they had good feelings, felt light.

Wus said to his wife: "Off on a high mountain I have an old grandmother; her name is Wuswelékgăs; I am going to see her." When he started, he began to sing. The old woman heard his song, and said: "My grandson is coming."

Wus traveled fast; he went like a spirit, and right away he was there. He thought: "I will cheat her." Then he said: "Grandmother, I have lost my mind; this world has made me lose it. When I slept, Gäk woke me up, and I hadn't my mind."

His grandmother said: "I was afraid Tsmuk would kill you."

"No," said Wus. "I have turned Tsmuk to a cloud and driven him away. But he may try to beat me yet; that is why I came to tell you to take care of yourself."

"How can I take care of myself? I shall be hungry," said the old woman.

"I will show you where there are mice," said Wus, and he took her to a field where there were lots of them. She was glad, for she would always have plenty to eat.

When Wus started home, he began to sing. His wife said: "Wus is coming," and she pounded roots for him to eat.

When Wus got to the house, his brother-in-law asked: "Will you go with me to hunt deer on the mountain?"

Wus said: "I always hunt on the flats; I never go to the mountain."

The brother-in-law went to the top of a high mountain, and when night came he camped there. Wus hunted on the flat and came back with plenty of mice. When he got home, his wife had another child. Wus kept awake for five days and five nights; his brother-in-law didn't come home.

Wus' wife said: "I feel badly. I am afraid something has happened to my brother."

Wus said: "I know which way he went; I will track him."

He started out and soon found his brother-in-law lying under a tree. "What is the matter?" asked Wus. "Why don't you come home? Your sister feels badly; she thinks that you are lost."

"My toe nails have fallen out," said the young man; "I was going to stay longer, but I will go with you."

Wus knew that he had been thinking about his father, and he felt sorry for him. When they got home, Wus said to his wife: "I am going to a swimming pond on the mountain; maybe I will have a good dream about my brother-in-law. Maybe I will find out what is going to happen."

Wus couldn't forget his brother-in-law; he felt lonesome. He sang all the way up the mountain, then he piled stones and worked till morning. At daylight he fixed a bed of dry grass and lay down and slept. He dreamed that he heard his brother-in-law say: "I am going away from you; I shall never come back. I am going to stay lost."

When Wus woke up, he was crying. He was sorry that he had come to the mountain to dream. When he got home, his wife was painted. She said: "We can eat now; the baby is five days old. You must put red paint on your face."

Wus painted his face, then he sat down and ate. When he got up, he said to his brother-in-law: "While I was on the mountain, I had a dream. I heard you say that you were going away, that you would be a person no longer."

The young man was angry; he scolded Wus for going to the mountain.

Wus said: "I will go away myself, then you can stay here; I will change to an animal, but I will keep a little of my mind." Wus left his wife and children and wandered off, — a fox.

The wife cried; the brother-in-law felt ashamed; he scolded her, and said: "Throw the children out; I don't want them around here." The mother said: "Wus told me to keep the children."

"I won't have them here," said her brother, and he threw them out. The mother screamed. Wus heard her and put his head to the ground to listen. Soon he heard his children coming — they were little foxes. He waited for them, and asked: "What is the trouble?"

"Our uncle threw us out."

Wus didn't know what to do; he thought a while then said: "You must live with my grandmother, old Wuswelékgăs; she will take care of you. I am going to the end of the world. You mustn't tell her where I am." He took the children part way, then pointed out the old woman's house and left them.

Old Wuswelékgăs was glad to have the boys, for she was lonesome. "Where is your father?" asked she.

"We don't know," said the elder boy.

She didn't believe him and she kept asking the same question till at last he said: "My father has lost his mind and gone off. He said that we would never see him again." Then the boy told her how his father went to a swimming pond on the mountain and had a bad dream, and their uncle threw them out.

The old woman felt badly; she asked the earth to give her grandson his mind. She roasted mice for the boys and showed them how to play with bows and arrows. One day, when the younger boy was eating, and was crying for his mother, he got choked with a mouse bone. The grandmother tried to get it out of his throat, but she couldn't, and the child died.

The next day old Wuswelékgăs buried the body and covered it with ashes and stones. That night she begged the earth to give her grandson his mind again. She said: "He is off on a mountain at the edge of the world. You used to have power and strength; now bring back my grandson's mind."

Wus heard his grandmother's voice and it gave him some strength. He was only bones; there was no flesh on his body. He started, went a little way, then sat down and rested. He was too weak to go far.

Every evening old Wuswelékgăs called: "My grandson, my grandson! where are you now?" And she kept asking the earth to give back his mind. She talked to Wus, and said: "When you were a child you went to the great mountain and it gave you power. Now you must go again, and you will get strength. The mountain will give you your mind."

Wus heard this and grew strong. He went to the top of

Wewékeni, and lay there five days and five nights. He thought: " I shall get my mind back here. I am lying on the head of Wewékeni. I am lying where all living things get their mind. I shall get my mind from the head of this mountain." He was glad. He talked loud, and as he talked he looked toward the west, then toward the east, and told how he suffered. He looked north and then south; he talked all the time, asked for power. His mind came back to him a little at a time. Then he asked in the same way for flesh to come on his body. He heard his grandmother say: " Your little boy is dead. You must come and see the only boy you have." Before he started, Wus spoke to the mountain, and said: " You are my mountain. I thank you for giving me back my mind."

When the boy saw his father, he felt lonesome.

The grandmother asked: " Why are you lonesome? "

" I am thinking of my little brother."

" Don't think of him; think of your father," said the old woman.

The next day Wus remembered his first cousin, Kaiutois. He wanted to see him. His grandmother didn't want him to go; she said: " Why do you leave me? I thought you would stay here always."

Wus said: " I must go; I don't feel well here."

" There will be many bad places along the road," said the old woman. " You will meet Wekómpmas. He carries great stones on his back; he has dug deep holes around his house, and when a man falls into one of them, he throws stones on to him and kills him."

Wus wouldn't stay; he wasn't afraid. He started off and soon he met Wekómpmas, a big, old man. In his house he had five yans [1] hung up; they were his medicine, and he didn't let any one touch or go near them. Just as Wus met him, Wekómpmas turned and ran home; he felt that some one had touched his medicine.

Two men went to Wekómpmas' house; one was a fool. He talked smart and felt smart, but always did foolish things. Those men saw the yans, and the foolish one said: " Let's

[1] A vegetable like an onion.

eat them. Old Wekómpmas says they are medicine. I don't believe it. If we eat them and they make us vomit blood, we shall know."

Wekómpmas' sister tried to stop them, but couldn't. As soon as they had eaten one yan, she climbed a tree near the house and drew up her child. Then she listened for her brother.

When he came he called out: "Where are my yans? Where are my yans?" He killed the two men, then he scratched his arms with his nails and sucked his own blood. Right away he was a man-eater. He killed all the people around and ate them. Then he started off to find others to kill and eat. As he traveled he looked in at every smoke hole, but he found only empty houses, for everybody had heard of him and had run away. In only one house did he find a living person. In the house at the edge of a village was a woman with but one leg. She sat inside making a basket. When Wekómpmas looked down the smoke hole, he was glad, and said: "She doesn't see me! Now I will have something to eat!"

But Nátcaktcókaskĭt had seen him, for she had an eye on the top of her head. Just as he was going to throw a stone down and kill her, she took her cane, and, with one hop, went far away, turned into a bug as small as a louse, and crawled under the rocks.

Wekómpmas tried to get her; he punched the ground with a stick, turned everything over; but Nátcaktcókaskĭt was a medicine woman, and he couldn't find her.

As Wus traveled around, he came to a village where all the people were crying. "Why are you crying?" asked Wus.

"There is a terrible man-eater in this country; he destroys whole villages. He will kill and eat us."

"I will meet him," said Wus. "Give me strings to tie back my hair, and don't make any noise."

Women gave him bark strings; as he tied his hair back with them, they turned into beaded bands.

Old Wekómpmas was coming along through a low place at the foot of a hill. Wus took off his own skin, filled it with grass, and put his mind in the end of the nose. He left his body in a damp place where it wouldn't dry up, then his skin and mind ran off to meet Wekómpmas. As he got near, the old man put down his stone, and asked: " Where are you going? "

" I am just traveling around," said Wus. " Where are you going? "

" I am going around the world," said the old man, and he began sucking the blood out of his arms, he was so glad that he was going to have something to eat.

Wus asked: " What are you doing? "

" Come and lie down on this hole," said Wekómpmas.

" Why should I do that? " asked Wus.

" It's a game."

" Will you lie down when I get up? " asked Wus.

" Yes."

Wus stretched himself across the hole, and said: " I think you will hit me! "

" No, this is the way we are going to play." The old man raised his stone and struck Wus on the back, but it didn't hurt him, for his body wasn't there. He jumped up, and said: " Now lie down here, old man. I am in a hurry; I want to go."

Wekómpmas lay down and Wus struck him a terrible blow, smashed him to pieces, then he said: " Hereafter people will pound roots and dried meat with you. You will no longer be a person; you will be a stone pounder (pestle)."

Wus went to his body, sprinkled his skin with water, got it moist and soft, and put it on; then he went to the house of the one-legged woman. He sat on one side of the fire, she sat on the other side. Wus and Nátcaktcókaskĭt were the only people left in that village. She fed him roots and seeds. While he was eating, he cried, for he had no home, and he was thinking where he could go. While he was crying, he fell asleep.

The woman fixed him a nice place, then she woke him up and said: " You must sleep here where I have fixed you a place. Why do you think about leaving me? Whoever comes to me can never go away."

Wus said: " When I came here I didn't think I would find anybody alive."

"What do you think now?" asked the woman.

"I think that I shall have to stay here." Nátcaktcókaskĭt was glad; she said: "We will raise many children."

The next morning Wus said: "I will go to the mountain and bring home some dried deer meat I left there."

"I will go with you," said the woman.

Wus looked at her leg, and asked: "How can you go?"

That made her laugh. She said: "I have traveled all my life on one leg. You must go ahead; I always travel alone. As soon as you are on the mountain and ready to pick up the meat, I will be there."

Wus ran all the way. When Nátcaktcókaskĭt thought he was there, she took her cane, and with one hop came down at his side. Wus was scared, but right away he thought: "How shall we carry all this meat?"

Nátcaktcókaskĭt knew his thoughts; she said: "You must make a big bundle of the meat, then go home as fast as you can. I will take care of the bundle."

She put the bundle on her back and with one hop was at home.

The next morning Wus killed a deer and made himself a cap out of the skin of its head. He looked far off around the country, but he couldn't see any one. The world seemed empty, and he felt lonesome. He went home, and lay down by the fire.

His wife said: "I told you not to think of anything, not to be lonesome. You have been feeling sorry for the world because so many are dead. You are lonesome."

The next day Wus killed five deer and brought them all home on his back. Nátcaktcókaskĭt had made them light. He thought: "Where shall I put them; there is no room in the house."

The woman said: "Put them down; there will be plenty of room." And there was.

That day Nátcaktcókaskĭt had two children, a boy and a girl. She washed them, then took ashes from the fire, and rubbed them. While she rubbed the children they grew fast. In a few days they were running around.

Wus made the boy a bow and arrows out of big blades of dried grass. The mother said: "That is not right; there are bad thoughts in those things."

The next day the woman had two more children, and not long after two more. She had children every few days, and always two at a time. Soon the house was full of children. They played together and were happy, but the mother was sorry that their father had made them arrows for playthings. She knew that trouble would come from them; that the children would get to quarreling and fighting.

The house was crowded. Wus had to hunt all the time to get meat enough. He scolded, but his wife said: "I told you that we would have many children. If there are too many, you must build another house."

The mother took no care of the children; they grew up by themselves, and grew very fast. Soon they began to quarrel and fight with one another. Wus was unhappy; he wanted to go away from a house where there was nothing but fighting.

The woman knew his thoughts; she said: "Why don't you try to find other people?"

Wus was glad to go. When he started, he said: "Hereafter one half of the people in this world will fight with the other half. There will be no peace."

After traveling a long time, Wus came to a village. A fool lived in that village; as soon as he saw Wus, he called out: "There is the father of many children! Look at him!" He followed Wus, and wouldn't leave him; he kept calling out: "Look at him! Look at him!" At last Wus got mad and slashed him with his knife. The fool screamed and ran around. Every man kept his house closed, no one would let him in. At last he died.

Wus said: "I didn't want to hurt you, but you made me mad." He was sorry and he sent for Gäk to come and step over the body.

Gäk came, stepped five times over the body, and the man stood up. He had a good mind now, and was thankful for what Wus had done.

When Wus went home, he found his children quarreling. He lay down without eating. His wife said: "We won't have any more children; they are bad."

Wus divided the country between his children, gave each twelve of them a place by themselves. To the first twelve he said: "You will stay here, you will be called Modocs." To the second twelve he said: "You will be near the big mountain and will be called Klamaths." So he divided his children into tribes, and made each tribe speak a different language. Most of the tribes of the west come from that division of Wus' family, and Wus named each tribe. To the first twelve children, the Modocs, he said: "You will be the strongest of all the tribes and the greatest warriors."

Wus kept five of the youngest children.

He felt badly about his children, he blamed himself. He said: "Somebody must have given me the thought to make those arrows; I did wrong."

Now Wus and Nátcaktcókaskĭt and their five youngest children traveled north toward the end of the world. When they came to a large river Wus saw little fish in the water. "I am hungry," said he. "I don't want little fish; I want salmon." That moment the river was full of salmon. He caught a good many and took their heads off. Then he said to his wife: "Cook these fish a long time, for if we eat them raw, we shall get sick and die. So it will be hereafter; people who eat this kind of fish raw will get thin and die."

Nátcaktcókaskĭt said: "I saw deer tracks near the river; I want some deer meat to eat." The next morning Wus went to Pakol Keni to hunt deer. Soon he saw a big stag. As he got near it, the stag hallooed like a person. Wus thought: "Who can be ahead of me?" The stag hallooed again. That time Wus heard the words, and he said: "I know who you are; I know all about you. I used to kill your people to get sinews out of their backs and strings out of their legs."

Wus killed the stag and carried it to his camp. When he told his wife that the stag had hallooed at him, she said: "Something bad is going to happen to you." She was angry at him for killing the deer.

Wus wanted her to eat some of the meat, but she wouldn't and they began to quarrel.

Wus said: " Give me one of the children and I will go away."

" No! " screamed the woman, " I will keep them all! " And jumping up, she said: " Hereafter you will be a black crow! You will no longer be a person. You will only be good to tell people where dead things are! "

Wus said: " You are like the wind that never stops blowing; you are always talking. Hereafter you will be a Dó-dő-la and sing all the time. You will watch for daylight so you can begin to sing, and you will sing till night comes, and your children will be like you! " And so it was.

FROST AND THUNDER

CHARACTERS

Blaiwas	Eagle	Wâhŭtus	
Gowwá	Swallow	Wus	Fox
Lok	Bear	Yahyáhaäs	(Always represented as a one-legged man)
Tsasgips	Frost That Breaks Trees		

Gowwá and Wâhŭtus were married to the same woman; she was kin to Gowwá.

One day the two men went hunting and left their wife at home. While they were gone Wus came along, and said to her: " Come to my house and be my wife. I have a big house and lots of nice blankets and beads. Why do you stay with these men? They are poor."

" I don't want to go with you," said the woman. " Gowwá and Wâhŭtus will come right away. If you stay here, they will kill you."

" I am not afraid of those men," said Wus. " I am stronger than they are; I can kill them." She couldn't make him go away.

When the men came, each had a deer on his back. " Cook some deer meat," they said to the woman. " We are hungry." They didn't see Wus.

She said: " A man is holding me; I can't get up."

" You are fooling us; nobody is holding you. Hurry up and cook for us."

When the woman didn't move Gowwá got mad and went toward her to jerk her up; then he saw Wus holding her down.

The fire had gone out, and it was dark in the house. Gowwá punched the fire and said to Wâhŭtus: " There is somebody over there with a nice skin on. We'll kill him and make a blanket." They caught Wus and pulled his skin off, then they threw him out.

The next morning, when Gowwá's mother went for water, she saw Wus and she felt sorry for him; she went to a swamp, and got cattails and wrapped them around him. Right away the cattails turned to nice fur. Wus was cured; he went home.

That day, while the two men were off hunting, Lok came and stole their wife. She was afraid of him and had to go. There were five Lok brothers, living in a house under the rocks.

When Gowwá and Wâhŭtus came home and found their wife gone, their old mother-in-law said: "Lok, a big, nice-looking man, came and carried her off."

The next morning Gowwá and Wâhŭtus started for Lok's house. As they went along they practiced killing each other to see how they were going to kill Lok. Gowwá killed Wâhŭtus and went on a little way alone. Wâhŭtus came to life and overtook Gowwá. Then Wâhŭtus killed Gowwá and went on. Gowwá came to life and caught up with Wâhŭtus. So they kept on till they got to Lok's house.

Gowwá climbed to the top of the house. Wáhŭtus went in at a hole on one side.

The five brothers were lying by the fire; one jumped up, tore Wâhŭtus into little pieces and threw the pieces out. Wâhŭtus grew together, came to life, and ran into the house. Five times Lok killed Wâhŭtus, tore him to pieces, and threw the pieces out; each time Wâhŭtus ran in again.

Gowwá stood on the top of the house and waited. When they had killed Wâhŭtus five times, he crept down and began throwing flint at the brothers. He was a great doctor, and right away all five of the brothers were dead. Then Wâhŭtus and Gowwá took their wife and went home.

The next day while they were off hunting Yahyáhaäs came and stole their wife, and carried her off to his house. Whenever Yahyáhaâs saw a nice woman, he took her; he stole everybody's wife. Five great rocks were around his house, and he lived underground, in the middle. The name of the house was

Hwălis; nobody but Yahyáhaäs could get into it. There were many women there; he carried them in on his shoulders.

Wâhŭtus and Gowwá didn't know how to get their wife back. At last they sent to all the people in the world and asked them to come and help break the rocks around Yahyáhaäs' house. Everybody came, and each man tried, but no one could break off even a small piece of a rock.

Then Tsasgips (Frost) came. He was such a small man they had forgotten to ask him. He said: " I can break those rocks."

The people didn't listen to him; they kept on trying to break them. Then somebody asked: " What does that little fellow say? He talks all the time! "

" He says that he can break these rocks," said Blaiwas.

Then men began to talk about Tsasgips, and to say: " Maybe he had better try. Maybe he is a kiuks [1] and can do something."

The people got him ready, sprinkled him with white paint, so he was all white spots in front. He made, with his mouth, a noise like blowing; the first rock crumbled to pieces. He made the same noise with his mouth and struck against the second rock; the rock fell into small pieces. He broke all five rocks in the same way. Then the people killed Yahyáhaäs with arrows, but his spirit went up in the air and became Thunder. They shot a great many times at the spirit as it flew up, for they saw it rising, but they couldn't hit it; they missed it every time.[1]

[1] A " medicine man."

YAHYÁHAÄS

CHARACTERS

Gäk	Crow	Tcûskai	Weasel
Skóŭks . . .	Woodtick. (In every story Tick is a Shasta woman.)	Tskel	Mink
		Yahyáhaäs	

SOUTHEAST of the Modoc country there was a large village. The people of that village lived on seeds and roots. One day a man came from the south, and said: "Seeds are ripe. It is time to gather them."

The people were glad. All went; only four persons were left at home. In one house there was a sick woman, the chief's wife. She had a little girl and a baby. In another house was a very old woman.

The chief's wife was afraid of Yahyáhaäs. She said to the little girl: "There is a Yahyáhaäs around. I have often seen him near the river. When he travels, he hops with his one leg and keeps calling his own name. He has a great bushy head. He is awful tall and is always naked. He comes from the rocks and mountains off in the north. You must watch for him, and if he comes here, we will run away."

One day the little girl saw a man coming. She called to her mother to come and see him. The mother said: "That is Yahyáhaäs! Take the baby on your back and run as fast as you can to where the men are. Tell them to come home and save me."

The little girl put the baby in the water basket, but Yahyáhaäs was in the house before she could start. She said: "I am going for water." She took the basket and went to the creek, then she ran off as fast as she could; she couldn't go very fast, for the baby was heavy.

The old woman knew that Yahyáhaäs was in the sick woman's house, but she didn't go there; she took her grass blankets and hid herself in the bushes. When Yahyáhaäs went into the house, the sun began to go down fast; he made it go.

The sick woman thought: "If I am good to him, maybe he will let me live." She gave him salmon, and said: "Eat this."

"Eat this," repeated the man.

She gave him an eel; he kicked it away. She gave him white roots, and said: "Eat these."

"Eat these," said he, and kicked them away.

She gave him dry manzanita berries, and said: "Eat these; they are good."

"Eat these, they are good," said the man, and he threw them in her face.

She gave him a blanket; he threw it at her, and said: "Use it yourself." She was frightened. She thought: "I will say I am going for wood, then I will run away."

"I am going for wood," said Yahyáhaäs. He was right behind her.

She went for water; he was there by the creek. She stayed out of doors; he did, too. Every time she said: "Go away!" he said: "Go away!" When she cried; he cried. She went to the bushes where the old woman was; he followed.

When the sun was down, Yahyáhaäs rubbed his forehead with his hand and made the woman sleep as if dead. At daylight he began to tickle her; she laughed till the sun was high, laughed till she died. Yahyáhaäs cut off her little finger and put it on a string of fingers he wore around his neck; then he went off to the mountain, where he lived under a great flat rock. He had children under the rocks, but he had no wife.

When the little girl found the men and told them that Yahyáhaäs was going to kill her mother, they left their seeds and went home. They found the woman dead and they began to hunt for Yahyáhaäs to kill him.

Two brothers, Tcûskai and Tskel, lived near a swimming-place on the top of a high mountain. Skóûks, a Shasta woman, was Tskel's wife. She went to visit her kin in Shasta, and took her baby with her. Tcûskai was lonesome; he missed the baby. One day when he was out on the rocks, he heard people mourning. He wanted to go where they were, but Tskel said: "Stay in the house. Don't run around everywhere."

Tcûskai said: "I am watching for Skóŭks; I want to see if she is coming."

He went high up on the rocks and listened; then he went in and said to his brother: "There are lots of people crying in the village down at the foot of the mountain."

"Stay in the house," said Tskel.

"I am going to sit by the smoke hole and watch for Skóŭks," said Tcûskai. After a while Tskel asked: "Are you there?"

"I'm right here," said Tcûskai's voice. Tcûskai was at the foot of the mountain, but the next minute he was in the house and teasing to go and see why people were crying.

Tskel said: "Well, go and find out what the trouble is; then come back. Don't let them hire you to do anything."

Tskel dressed his brother up in the clothes he had worn himself when he was a boy, and he started. As soon as he was outside of the house, he was in the village.

The people were ready to burn the dead woman; men were piling up nice things to burn with her, — beads and shells and blankets. When they saw Tcûskai, some of the men asked: "Who is that nice-looking young man?" Others said: "There is Tcûskai; maybe he can make this woman alive again. His brother is strong; he can do anything he likes."

They talked to Tcûskai, promised him many wives and nice shells and beads. At last he said: "I can bring the woman to life if I can find Yahyáhaäs and kill him. Then you will give me the chief's daughter."

He began to hunt for Yahyáhaäs. He went to the edge of the world, then traveled in circles, working in all the time. He ran on every mountain, every hill, and every tree. He ran under the ground and under rocks and into holes. In one day he went all over the world, but he didn't find Yahyáhaäs.

The next day Tcûskai listened at every hole, as one would listen at a door to hear people talk or snore. Under a great flat rock on the top of a high mountain he heard Yahyáhaäs snore. He crept under and saw him; then he went to the village, and said: "I have found him under a rock. Bring lots of wood and dry grass and pile up around the rock; when the rock is out of sight, set fire to the wood. Then stand around and throw in every stick and coal that falls out."

They did this, and soon there was a terrible noise under the rock. The hills and rocks and the whole country shook. Yahyáhaäs burst; the rock blew into little pieces, and a big bird flew up to the sky. It was Yahyáhaäs' spirit. The people went back to the village. Tcûskai stepped five times over the dead woman, and she got up. She was glad to be alive. The chief gave Tcûskai nice things, and gave him his daughter.

The next day Tcûskai went home. Soon he saw Skóŭks coming. She had on a Shasta dress, and had Shasta things in a bundle on her back, and on top of the bundle was the baby. Tcûskai went to meet her. He took the baby and ran around with it; he was glad.

Tskel said: "Don't be silly. Act like a man!" Skóŭks laughed, for she liked Tcûskai.

Tcûskai told Skóŭks: "The chief's daughter is my wife. Maybe they will come here to-day."

Tskel was glad; he said: "My little brother is going to be a strong man; he will be stronger than I am."

"Our house is too small," said Skóŭks.

"Go out and walk around it in a big circle," said Tcûskai. "Each time you take a step, put your foot down hard." Skóŭks did so, and when she got around there was a large house instead of the small one.

Skóŭks cooked plenty of deer meat. Tcûskai lay down on one side of the house and wrapped himself in a panther skin blanket.

When the people came, the girl stopped a good way from the house. Skóŭks brought her in and seated her by Tcûskai. The girl's mother had two small bones; she tied one in each side of Tcûskai's hair. Skóŭks fed the people deer meat, then she put a Shasta cap on each woman's head, and said to Tskel: "Tcûskai must give these people nice things."

Tskel took a buckskin shirt and pounded it to powder, rolled the powder in a deer skin, and wet the skin. Then he thought hard, and said: " I want many buckskin shirts," and he drew out of the skin a buckskin shirt for each man. Now they all had a plenty of nice things to carry home. The mother-in-law's sister was the last one to go, and she said to her niece, " I haven't enough to carry home. I am ashamed of you; you gave yourself away for nothing."

Tcûskai was mad; he began to break off little bits of the bones his mother-in-law had tied in his hair; soon he had a great pile of beautiful beads. Then he took five bites out of his panther skin blanket, and he had five beautiful blankets. He gave the beads and the blankets to the aunt, and she went home.

After a day or two, Tcûskai's wife said: " I'm lonesome here; I wasn't made to live in the mountains. I want to go home."

Tcûskai and Tskel were mad. Tcûskai said: " Go home and never think of me again. I hope our women won't be like you and get tired of their husbands so soon."

Skóŭks asked: " Is she going to stay always? "

" She will not live long," said Tcûskai, " and I will not live always; I don't want a wife."

Skóŭks took a handful of dirt, threw it into the air, and said: " Let her be a bird! " She threw a second handful toward the woman, and she flew off to the mountains, a bird.

Then Skóŭks asked Tskel: " Is there anybody who can go to that woman's village and turn all the people into birds? "

" Yes," said Tskel. " Old man Gäk can do it. He lives on a mountain in the east. He is a great doctor."

Tcûskai went to old Gäk's house and told him how his wife had treated him. Gäk flew to the village, in the form of a crow.

When the people saw him, they called out: " See that great black bird. Maybe he has come to eat dead fish."

Gäk said: " I didn't come to eat dead fish; I always eat deer meat." Then he shouted: " Let all these people be birds and creeping things, not be persons any longer." And so it was.

YAHYÁHAÄS

CHARACTERS

Blaiwas . . . . Eagle
Tusasás . . . . Joker (Skunk)

FIVE Blaiwas brothers started off to hunt for deer. When they got to the top of the first high mountain, they took out their fire-drill to make a fire. As they turned the drill they talked to the mountains, to the trees, to the rocks and the bushes, and asked for good luck, but they forgot to ask the drill to keep Yahyáhaäs away. They made a fire, cooked their meat, and then got ready to hunt. When they were leaving the camp, they hung their dry meat and their seeds on a tree where they could get them when they came back in the evening.

After they had gone some distance, one of the brothers said: "That is the place where Yahyáhaäs comes. He starts from the east; when he sees any one he walks slowly, but he can go around and come up in front of a person. He can disappear like a flash. Sometimes his face is painted red, and he carries a red cane with red feathers on the end of it. Maybe he will come while we are gone and will eat our meat and seeds."

The men were sorry that they had forgotten to tell the drill to keep Yahyáhaäs away.

Just then one of them looked east, and said: "There he is; he is coming now!"

The men were scared; they didn't dare to run away, so they sat down and waited. When Yahyáhaäs came to them, he said:

"Well, well, I thought I would never see people again, but I see them now. I am glad you are here. Why don't you start a fire?"

"We forgot our drill."

"I thought people never forgot their drills. What are you here for?"

"We came to hunt for deer and rabbits."

"I have looked around all the morning," said Yahyáhaäs; "I have been everywhere, but I haven't seen a deer track."

"We may as well give up hunting and go home," said one man to another.

"Can't you feed me smoke?" asked Yahyáhaäs.

"We have no tobacco."

"This earth will make people trouble if they don't carry a fire-drill and tobacco," said Yahyáhaäs. "If you can't feed me with smoke, you must wrestle with me."

"We have no pipe or fire-drill to make smoke with," said the eldest Blaiwas brother. "How can we feed you with smoke when we can't start a fire? We are in a hurry. We didn't come here to wrestle or play games, we came to hunt."

"This is my way," said Yahyáhaäs. "If people don't feed me smoke and make me glad, I wrestle with them and throw them; then I am glad. Will you feed me smoke?"

"We can't," said Blaiwas. "We have no tobacco."

"Then we will wrestle," said Yahyáhaäs.

The men didn't want to wrestle; they said they didn't know how. But Yahyáhaäs kept talking about wrestling, talked till half a day was gone.

Yahyáhaäs was red from head to foot. His red cane was sharp at both ends, and on his back was a red quiver full of red, sharp-pointed arrows.

At last Blaiwas said to his brothers: "We had better wrestle with him. It is just as well for us all to die here. If we start for home, he will kill us."

Yahyáhaäs fixed a place for his leg and piled up stones on a cliff above the lake. The eldest brother was chief; he was the first man to wrestle. He said: "Be strong, my brothers, you can't save yourselves. If he throws me over the cliff into the lake, don't get weak. Be strong and all die together." Then he sent a young boy to the village to tell the people that Yahyáhaäs was going to kill him and his brothers.

Right away Yahyáhaäs threw Blaiwas over the cliff. As he sank in the lake, his bones boiled up to the top of the water, washed against the rocks, and rattled terribly.

Yahyáhaäs threw over one man after another. As each man sank, he turned to bones and the bones floated against the rocks, struck hard and made a great noise.

In Blaiwas' house there was an old medicine woman. She woke up, and said: "I dreamed that I saw people crying and putting ashes on their heads. Our men have been killed. At noon to-morrow we shall get word of it."

"Women always have bad dreams," said Tusasás. "There is nobody in the world strong enough to kill the five brothers." At noon the next day a boy came along the trail; he was crying and screaming. When he got to Blaiwas' house, he said: "The five brothers are killed. By this time not one of them is alive." He went to the next village and told the same news.

Tusasás threw dirt on his head and rolled in the ashes. The people cut off their hair and mourned. The next morning they said: "Let us go and see the place where our men were killed."

Blaiwas' little boy was sleeping by the fire; his sister shook him, and said: "Wake up and wash your face; we are going to see the place where Yahyáhaäs killed our people."

When his face was washed, the boy said: "Fix my feet; I want to go too."

"You are too small," said his mother. "Why do you want to go?"

"I want to die with my uncles. I am lonesome; I don't want to live any longer."

"You are too small to go. Yahyáhaäs could take you up with one finger and throw you over the cliff."

"I am going where my uncles were killed," said the boy. "Paint me with red paint right in the center of my head, where my thoughts come in and teach me."

They painted him and got him ready to go. Tusasás cut a long cedar tree, tied it on his head, and went with the others. He started off as if going to gamble; he laughed, jumped, and whooped. The people said: "Yahyáhaäs will hear you and he will kill us all."

"It won't be hard for me to kill Yahyáhaäs," boasted Tusasás. "I will throw him over the cliff quickly." Then he said to the boy: "Why are you here? I sha'n't need your help. You are too small to go to the mountains; you had better go home."

The boy didn't look at Tusasás; he said to his mother: "You must stop crying. I want all the people to stop crying and follow me." He went ahead.

The people looked at him and stopped crying. When they got to the lake, Yahyáhaäs was not there, but he was not far off. The people hunted for the place where the men had been killed, but they couldn't find it. Then the little boy said: "Here it is! Yahyáhaäs is coming. You can't see him, but I can. He will soon show himself in the east."

Tusasás said: "I will be the first man to wrestle with him; I will throw him into the lake."

The people said: "It is bad to make fun of our chief and the men that were killed here. You will make trouble for us."

Right away they saw Yahyáhaäs coming from the east. He had on a pale yellow coat that rattled as he hopped along. He had a yellow cane, and his face was painted yellow. When he came to the people, he said: "I like to see men and women. I don't like to walk around and see no one; it makes me lonesome. Will you feed me smoke?"

"We have nothing to make smoke with," said one of the men.

"Did you come to play with me?" asked Yahyáhaäs. "I like to wrestle. The last man I saw threw me, and went away somewhere."

The little boy sat on the edge of the cliff; he didn't say anything, just looked at the water. At last he began to see men swimming around under the surface; then he saw the five brothers and lots of other men, — his own people. He felt strong and glad when he saw them.

Tusasás said: "You want to fight, don't you? You think you can kill Yahyáhaäs, don't you?"

“Let the boy alone,” said his mother. “Don’t make fun of him; maybe he can teach us things.”

Yahyáhaäs kept asking the men to wrestle with him. At last they said: “We may as well get killed here. If we start for home, he will follow us.” And they began to wrestle. Soon every man was over the cliff, except Tusasás. One man was very strong; he nearly broke Yahyáhaäs’ leg. Yahyáhaäs screamed out: “That is not the way to wrestle. You shouldn’t twist my leg!”

“It is right for me to throw you any way I can,” said the man. “You have killed a great many of my people.” Yahyáhaäs laughed, threw the man, — took him up with one hand, and flung him over the cliff.

When Tusasás began to wrestle, he held tight to Yahyáhaäs.

“Look out! Don’t hold me so tight,” said Yahyáhaäs.

“I have always seen men hold tight,” said Tusasás, and he clung tighter. But Yahyáhaäs loosened his hold and threw him into the lake.

The little boy told the women to go home, then he sat there alone.

“Why do you sit there so long?” asked Yahyáhaäs. “I wonder if such a little fellow can wrestle. Come and try.” Yahyáhaäs caught hold of the boy and began to throw him up and play with him.

“Why do you make fun of me?” asked the boy. “Wait till you get through.” He caught hold of Yahyáhaäs, twisted his leg, broke it off, and pushed him into the lake.

Then the boy called: “Come out, my people. Come out of the water!”

There was a great noise, then all the men came out of the lake. The boy called to them: “Don’t look back! Don’t look back! If any man looks back, he will die.” As they climbed up the cliff, the boy stood on the edge and said to each one: “Don’t look back. If you do, you will die.” When all were up he followed them and kept calling out: “Don’t look back! Don’t look back!”

Yahyáhaäs came out of the water and screamed to the

people, " You haven't thrown me yet! I am standing in the same place. Why do you run away? Come back and throw me! "

The boy said: " Yahyáhaäs is dead; that is his spirit. It will kill us if we look back." They were far off, but still they heard the call: " Come back and wrestle! Look back and see me! The boy lies; he didn't throw me. Men don't run away. Come back! "

The boy said: " Don't look back! " He talked to the spirit without turning his face toward it. He said: " You will not treat my people in this way again; but you will always live. You will always be on the mountains and by the water; you will walk around by the lakes and rivers; but you will never be a person again."

Then the boy said to his people: " It is hard work to live in this world; we will be birds and live in the air." That moment they all became birds. The boy is a medicine bird. Doctors often see him, and he helps them cure sick people.

Yahyáhaäs is a great medicine; if a doctor has him for a medicine, he can cure a dying man.

YAHYÁHAÄS AND THE KÚJA SISTERS

CHARACTERS

Blaiwas	. .	Eagle
Galaíwa	. .	Mouse
Kaiutois	. .	Wolf
Kĕlaiwa	. .	House Mouse
Kúja	. . . .	Rat
Kûlta	. . .	Otter
Wŏn	. . . .	Elk
Yahyáhaäs	.	The One-legged Man

OLD Kúja and his five daughters lived in the mountains east of Tula Lake. The old man never went hunting, or went out of the house. His five daughters were hunters. When getting ready to hunt, they took off their clothes and became red from the waist up; then they put on breech clouts and went out as men. One of the sisters built a ring of fires around the mountain they wished to hunt on. The fire and smoke drove the deer toward the top of the mountain. The other sisters shot the deer with arrows; an arrow always went through a deer and came out.

Whenever the Kújas were hunting deer, people knew by the smoke which sister built the fire. The smoke from the fire built by the youngest sister went highest and straightest, for she was the strongest. The smoke from the fire built by the fourth sister was not as straight or as high; and so on. The eldest sister's fire smoked the least, and the smoke spread everywhere, for she was the weakest.

The Kújas had always hunted on those mountains. Nobody else could hunt there, for when the sisters knew that a man was on one of their mountains they built fires around it, drove him toward the top, and killed him.

In old Kúja's house there were many sacks of dried meat and of white roots. When the sisters went to dig roots, each one carried a basket on her back and had a long digging stick; they looked like old women.

On a mountain southwest of where the Kújas hunted there was a large village. Blaiwas had a house there; he was chief of the village. One morning the Kúja sisters went to hunt deer on a mountain west of the one they lived on. In Blaiwas' village men called to the women: " Come out and look at that mountain over there! The Kúja sisters are driving in deer! "

Some of the men said: " Let us go over there and see how those sisters look! " Others said: " Those sisters are wise; they can turn us or themselves into anything they want to. Let them alone! "

Blaiwas said: " Keep away from the Kúja sisters. From the waist up they are as red as blood. I have tried to get near them, but I couldn't. Their fire was far away, but I was burning up."

Old man Yahyáhaäs was visiting in Blaiwas' village. He heard the men talking and he asked: " What are you talking about? "

" About the Kúja sisters," said Blaiwas. " They don't want to marry, and nobody can get near enough to see how they live. They are young girls, but when they are out hunting they look like men, and when they are digging roots, they are ugly, old women."

" What are you afraid of? " asked Yahyáhaäs. " I came here for a wife; maybe I had better take one of those sisters; they would give me plenty of deer meat."

" You'll not get a wife here," said Blaiwas. " My people have soft blankets and nice beads. Your blanket is stiff and so hard that it sticks out like a dry elk skin. The girls don't like you."

The next morning the sisters built a fire around Lokúmsis, a mountain in the west. Men called to Yahyáhaäs and said: " Look over there! That is what we were talking about yesterday. The Kúja sisters are out hunting."

" I can go there and see how they look," said Yahyáhaäs.

" Nobody can get near enough to see them," said Blaiwas.

" I can go there and take their bows and arrows from them. They can't hurt me, unless they throw me down."

"You had better stay away from those girls," said Blaiwas, but Yahyáhaäs didn't listen to what he said; he started off. He took a mountain at a step, but before he could get there, the sisters put out their fire and went home. They had heard everything the men said. Yahyáhaäs hunted for them all day, then he went back to Blaiwas' village.

The next morning the sisters hunted on another mountain. Yahyáhaäs started again, but before he got there, they put their fire out and went home. Each time they saw Yahyáhaäs coming, they said to the mountain: "You are our friend; draw him away from us." And it did.

Old woman Galaíwa lived in Blaiwas' house; she was kin of the Kúja sisters. Now Blaiwas was mad at Yahyáhaäs. He was chief, and he didn't want Yahyáhaäs to bother the Kúja girls. He knew they had power to do anything they wanted to. He was afraid they would get angry at his people. He said to Galaíwa: "I want you to try and go to old Kúja's house. If you get there, ask the Kúja sisters if Yahyáhaäs bothers them. Tell them he says they are only common women, and he can do what he likes with them. Tell them how he talks."

When Galaíwa got to Kúja's house, the sisters were out digging roots. Old man Kúja said: "My daughters can't hunt any more. A one-legged man, with a big head and bushy red hair, is always trying to get near them. They see his head first. He has a straw quiver on his back and carries a cane sharp at both ends; the feathers of a red-headed woodpecker are tied around it in two places." (The feathers were Yahyáhaäs' medicine.) "With one step he crosses a high mountain. Do you know anything about that man?"

Galaíwa told him all that Blaiwas had said about Yahyáhaäs.

When the girls came, their father said: "The one-legged man boasts that he can come where you are and take your arrows away from you."

Each of the five sisters cried out: "I will not run away from him again. I will stay and see if he can get my arrows!"

Old Kúja said: " I am afraid Blaiwas will get mad if you do anything to Yahyáhaäs."

" No," said Galaíwa, " the chief and his sons hate Yahyáhaäs. They don't want him to stay in their village."

" Are the chief's sons like us? " asked the sisters.

Galaíwa didn't answer; she said: " It is late, I must go home."

The Kúja sisters said: " We will fix your eyes so no matter how dark it is, you will see the trail and get home. We will open our eyes wide, and give you some of our light." The youngest sister opened her eyes wide and looked into Galaíwa's eyes. Right away a little black spot came inside each of the old woman's eyes. Then everywhere it seemed bright and light to her; she traveled fast; she didn't have to look for the trail. Since then all of her kin can see as well at night as in the daytime.

Early the next morning the Kúja sisters went to hunt for deer. The youngest sister started the fires around a mountain, then they sat down on flat rocks and waited for Yahyáhaäs to come. While they were sitting there, they asked one another: " Which of us will try first? " The eldest sister said: " I will." The youngest sister said: " You must fix your mind on what you are going to do, then think of nothing else." She got red all over; her arms and legs and eyes were as red as fire.

They saw Yahyáhaäs coming. He started in the southwest, went toward the north, then turned west, and came to their mountain. They watched him all the time. When he saw them, he squatted down and began to creep toward them. He crept behind every tree and stone and every blade of grass. Every step he took he thrust his cane down under the earth.

Each sister had a bunch of woodpecker's feathers in a hole in her nose. As Yahyáhaäs came along, the eldest sister took a feather out of her nose and stuck it under the ground. It came up a streak of fire in Yahyáhaäs' cane; he was so scared he almost lost his mind. When he got near, she took out a second feather, put it under the ground, and it also came out a streak of fire in Yahyáhaäs' cane. That time he was so scared that he dropped his cane and called out: "What are you doing? This is my cane!"

"What do you think now?" asked the eldest sister. "You boasted that we had no power, that you could take our bows and arrows away from us."

"You must wrestle with me," said Yahyáhaäs. "That is the way I find out how strong people are."

"You must make a fire first," said the sisters.

Yahyáhaäs took his fire-drill out of his quiver and tried to start a fire.

The sisters laughed, and said: "You must make it with your own power, not with a drill; anybody can use a drill."

"How can I do it?" asked Yahyáhaäs.

"Do as I do," said the eldest sister. She pulled up a spear of grass and threw it into the air. It came down blazing. Then she said to a big rock: "Stand apart far enough for a leg to go between you." Right away the rock opened. Then the sisters said to Yahyáhaäs: "Put your leg in there and get ready to wrestle."

Yahyáhaäs painted his face straight up through the middle; then he asked: "Which sister is going to wrestle with me first?"

"I am," said the eldest. "I will wrestle a while for fun, and then in earnest." As she spoke a bunch of red-headed woodpecker's feathers came out of her head. She began to wrestle with Yahyáhaäs. Soon he said: "That is enough. Let the next one try."

The eldest said to the second sister: "Put your foot in where his leg is." Then she said to Yahyáhaäs: "Hurry, now! It is getting late!"

All the time the sisters were gathering wood and putting it on the fire. Yahyáhaäs tried four of the sisters. He couldn't do anything with them; only the eldest moved a little, three of them stood as firm as a rock.

The youngest sister said to the others: "It is my turn now. Make the fire blaze up high! Put on more wood, then stand with your backs toward me." She said to Yahyáhaäs,

"I'm ready!" That minute she put her arms around him. She broke his leg off and threw him into the fire. They punched the fire around him, made it blaze up high — it was a great pile — then they ran away as fast as they could.

Yahyáhaäs' spirit called: "Come back, old Kúja's daughters, come back! You haven't killed me. Come back and wrestle with me."

"You are killed," said the sisters. "You will never be a person again, but your spirit will always roam around on high mountains."

He called till they got back to the house.

Old Kúja asked: "Where are my deer entrails?" — He never ate any other part of the deer.

"We didn't hunt for deer to-day," said the youngest daughter. "We are going to swim and then dig roots."

After that the sisters hunted deer for five days. On the fifth day, Blaiwas and his sons sent old woman Galaíwa to ask if they had seen Yahyáhaäs. When she got to the house, she said: "Blaiwas and his five sons want to know if Yahyáhaäs has been here to bother you. He has gone away, and they don't know where he is."

"We haven't seen him," said the sisters. "Maybe he ran into our fire and got burned up. Why does Blaiwas send you to ask us questions? Do those young chiefs want to marry us?"

Galaíwa didn't answer. She knew now that they had killed Yahyáhaäs.

Old Kúja said to his daughters: "I feel lonesome. I am hungry all the time. You don't kill deer enough. Why don't you marry some of those men in Blaiwas' village? They would hunt for me, and I would have plenty to eat."

The sisters said: "There are many men in that village; which shall we go to?"

"The eldest must go to Blaiwas' son; the second to Kaiutois' son; the third to Wûlkûtska's son; the fourth to Wŏn's son." To his youngest daughter he said: "You must get Kûlta's son, for he can make a road under the ground, and can go under the water and get different kinds of fish. He can make a road to the ocean and drive fish into the river. I want to eat such fish as he catches."

The girls started early; when they got near Blaiwas' village they met old Galaíwa and she told them which houses to go to. The first house was Kûlta's. The youngest sister stopped there; the others went on.

Tusasás lived in that village. When he saw the sisters coming, he began to make fun of them and tell lies about them. "Why do you let those girls come into your houses?" asked he. "They don't smell good; you should drive them away." He made such a fuss that young Blaiwas and Kaiutois and Wûlkûtska and Wŏn ran off and hid.

The next morning all the people gathered in Lok's house to talk and make up their minds what to do.

Old Galaíwa asked Blaiwas' son: "Why didn't you stay with your wife? She will get mad and kill you. Those sisters have great power. They can do anything."

Lok said: "I am afraid of those sisters. My home was on a high mountain; I never lived where the land was flat. Those sisters took my mountain and drove me away. You should have let them alone; you shouldn't have sent Galaíwa to ask questions."

The people talked a long time; they didn't know what to do.

The next morning the eldest sister went to the second and together they went to the third and the fourth sister. They found that each sister had stayed alone; then they went to Kûlta's house to see their youngest sister. Her husband had stayed with her; he liked her, and she was glad. She didn't want to go home with her sisters, but they said: "Our father will feel lonesome if we come home without you," so she went.

As soon as they left Blaiwas' village, Tusasás got on top of a house and called out: "Old Kúja's daughters came to hunt for husbands, but they have gone home without them." He called the girls names and made sport of them. He kept screaming: "Look at them! See them go home!"

Some of the people said: "Old Tusasás ought to be killed;

he will get us into trouble." At last Blaiwas made him stop screaming and talking.

The sisters turned back; they looked like men. They made a circle around Blaiwas' house and danced a war dance. The people were terribly scared; they ran into their houses and looked through the cracks. When the dance was over, the sisters started for home. All the way they made a great noise. When they went into the house, they pounded their father on the head and back with their fists, and said: "Old man, to please you we have tried to get husbands. They ran away from us!" They pounded him again, almost killed him.

When Kûlta's son found that his wife was gone, he felt badly and cried.

"Why didn't you catch her when she went out?" asked his father. "She is a good daughter-in-law; I like her."

"I didn't know that she was going," said the young man.

Kûlta was frightened; he was afraid of the sisters. He went to old man Witkátkis, and said: "You must come and talk to my son." — Witkátkis was a great kiuks.

When Witkátkis looked at the young man, blood came out of his own mouth, and he said: "You are going to die. You will follow your wife, and when you get where those sisters live your blood will spread over the ground."

The next morning the sisters told their father to make them bark sticks. He made five, and gave one to each girl. "Why didn't you talk to them over the fire?" asked the youngest sister.

"You can talk to them yourself," said the old man.

They built fires around the mountain, then they put the sticks on one of the fires, and said: "Draw to us those men who made fun of us." The eldest sister said to her stick: "I want Blaiwas' son to be here before me." Each sister, except the youngest, talked to her stick in the same way; then they asked the youngest sister: "Why don't you talk to your stick?"

"I have nothing to tell it," said she. While they were hunting, her bowstring broke. She felt lonesome; she knew something was going to happen.

Kûlta's father tied a stone knife on his son's arm, and said:

"Don't let old Kúja have this unless he will take you for his son-in-law."

When the young man got to the house, the old woman hurried off to tell her daughters that he had come. The youngest sister began to cry; the eldest sister said: "We will kill him and throw him out." The old woman screamed: "Let him alone! He isn't one of the men who made fun of you." But they ran in, caught hold of Kûlta, pounded him hard; pounded him till he died, then they threw him out.

The youngest sister put ashes on her head and tied a blanket around herself, as a woman does when she mourns for her husband. She told her mother to take Kûlta's body off and put sticks over it.

Down in Blaiwas' village, old Witkátkis said: "In a dream I saw fresh blood spread on the ground. Kûlta is dead!"

Blaiwas said to Galaíwa: "You must go to old Kúja's and find out what they have done to Kûlta."

When Galaíwa was near the house, she saw Kûlta's wife mourning, and she asked: "Have you killed Kûlta?"

"My sisters have killed him," said the young woman. "You must make his father think he is alive. I want the other men to come here. Then I will show my sisters what I can do."

When Galaíwa got home, the people asked: "Is Kûlta alive?"

She said: "I didn't see him; he was off hunting for deer."

Blaiwas didn't want his son to go to Kúja's house, but the young man was drawn there; he couldn't help going.

That day the eldest sister's bow broke. She sat down with it in her hand; she felt lonesome. The youngest sister asked: "Why do you feel lonesome? Why don't you mend your bow?"

"How can I? It is broken."

The sister took it, and right away it was whole. She threw it into her sister's lap, and said: "You think you have as much power as I have. You have killed Kûlta. Wait a while; you will find out what I can do."

When they got home, young Blaiwas was there. The eldest

sister went in and sat down by him. The next day Kaiutois came, and then Wûlkûtska's son, and Wŏn's son. The four sisters wanted to stay with their husbands, but the youngest sister made them go with her to hunt for deer.

That night Galaíwa came again.

" Why do you come here so often? " asked Kûlta's wife.

" Blaiwas sends me to see if his people are alive yet."

" They are people yet," said the young woman, " but I feel worse and worse all the time."

Galaíwa said: " You have power; why don't you bring Kûlta to life? "

" His body is spoiled," said the woman. But she told her mother to uncover the body and put it in water.

Old woman Kúja said: " You always tell me if anybody kills you to put your body in water, but that won't bring Kûlta to life." She put the body in water, washed it, then stretched it out and stepped over it a good many times. At last it moved. She washed it and stepped over it again. Then Kûlta stood up. He was glad to be alive, and to see his wife.

Kûlta's wife said: " Hereafter, my sisters and their husbands will not be persons. They will be spirits and will roam around on the mountains."

TSMUK AND GŌSHGOISE

CHARACTERS

Góshgoise	. Rabbit (small)	Skóla . . .	Meadow Lark
Juljulcus . .	Cricket	Tsmuk . . .	Darkness
Kaudokis . .	Worm	Yaukûl . . .	Stone People
Lóluk . . .	Fire		

FIVE brothers lived together on the east side of Tula Lake; all had the same name, Yaukûl; the youngest was chief. Not far away lived the five Tcpun brothers, kin of the Yaukûls; each brother had one child. The wives of those men had been captured by the Yaukûl brothers, and made servants.

Each day old woman Yaukûl went to the top of her house and watched the trail. Whenever she saw people coming, she called to her sons, who sat by the fire, with long spears stuck in the ground around them. They went out, killed the men, and brought the women home. The brothers never left the house except when they went to kill people.

Each morning old Yaukûl went to every house in the village and sent the women to dig roots; then she watched them from the top of the house, and if a woman ate even one little root, she had her punished.

One morning, the old woman said to her sons: " There is snow on the ground."

The youngest son said: " Tell the Tcpun brothers to go for rabbits."

She went to the house of the five brothers, and said: " Go and hunt rabbits; my sons are hungry for meat."

Four of the Tcpun brothers had been worked so hard that they were only skin and bones. The fifth brother was able to hunt, for while hunting he always stole and ate a rabbit. The brothers had only ragged bark blankets; the old woman took away the rabbit skins.

The youngest brother got ready and started; as he went along, he picked up pieces of bark to tie on his feet to keep them from freezing. While hunting he kept saying: "I am hunting as though I were going to eat, but I never eat."

Each day for three days an orphan boy heard those words. When he got home, the third night, he said: "Grandmother, in the woods I hear a man talking and crying. I thought no one lived around here."

"What does he say?"

When the boy told, the old woman said: "That is my brother," and she began to cry. Then she told Góshgoise, the boy, about the Yaukûl brothers. "To-morrow I am going to see that man," thought Góshgoise. The grandmother knew his thoughts; she knew he would try to kill the Yaukûls.

The next morning old Yaukûl said to her sons: "There is snow on the ground."

The youngest son said: "Tell the Tcpun brothers to go for rabbits."

She went to their house and said: "This is a good day to hunt rabbits; my sons are hungry for meat."

The youngest brother started off. He killed rabbits by calling them to him and dropping large stones on them. That day the boy was watching; he saw the man a long way off, saw him kill a rabbit, skin it, and then build a fire. He went toward him, and when near hid behind bushes. When the man turned to pick up sticks, he saw the boy and was scared. He said: "I never saw you before; I didn't know there was any one like you living around here."

"My grandmother and I live among the rocks," said the boy. "I came to see you; I often hear you cry. Why can't you eat what you kill? I wouldn't kill, if I couldn't eat."

"Where I live, nobody can eat," said the man; "the Yaukûls would kill them. They have killed your father and all your people. I am sorry you heard me crying. I don't want them to find you; I want you to grow to be a man. That is why I never looked for you."

"Why don't you cook another rabbit?"

"They will kill me if I carry home only a few. The old woman never has enough."

The boy had his belt full of rabbits; he gave them to the man, and said: "Stay here and cook these; don't go home till it is dark, don't go till you are sure the old woman can't see you. Then feed your brothers and the children. To-morrow I will come and see you."

"It is a bad place; don't come," said the man. "The Yaukûls will kill you. You must stay away and grow up."

When the boy got home, his grandmother said: "You are late, but you haven't any rabbits."

"I met my uncle and gave him my rabbits. I have found out why he cries so. He has to hunt rabbits for the Yaukûl brothers, but if they knew that he ate even one little rabbit they would kill him. To-morrow I am going to see my uncles."

The grandmother said: "If you go, you will not come back; the Yaukûl people will kill you."

"I am going," said the boy. "Get my things ready."

His grandmother gave him a spear like the spears used by the Yaukûl brothers.

"I don't want that spear," said the boy, "it will break."

She gave him a thick axe, and he said: "That is too heavy." She gave him a knife, made of wood and covered with pitch, and he said: "That is not strong enough; it will break."

That night, while the boy was asleep, the old woman made a quiver out of her own hair. The quiver was blue and bright. Then she made a spear that would last always and never get old or break. At daylight she said to him: "Now, my grandson, it is time to get ready. Wash and eat, then I will tell you what to do."

He washed in the brook and ate pounded seeds. Then she gave him the spear, and said: "Go to the rock out there and try this spear. Stand on the right side of the rock and strike it five times." He struck four times, and each time great pieces of rock fell; the fifth time the rock split in the center. Every time he struck, the spear looked like a flash of lightning.

His grandmother said: "Look at your spear and see if it is hurt."

"No," said the boy, "it is as good as ever."

"Well, put it in its quiver; then stand up straight."

He stood up straight. She made him tall and covered his body with five kinds of rock. The outside cover was of granite.

Then the boy asked: "How many places are there where people kill folks?"

"The Yaukûl place is the worst of all," said his grandmother, "but between that place and the end of the world in the north there are three bad places."

"Don't get frightened if I am gone a long time," said the boy. "I am going to all those bad places." And he started.

Old woman Yaukûl, from the top of her house, saw him coming. Her sons were lying on their backs and looking at her through the smoke hole; they thought she saw some one, and the chief called out: "Whom do you see?"

"I see a man who is just big enough to bring water. He has a rabbit-skin blanket, and he has something on his back, something that is nice and bright."

"Go and get him," said the chief, "and the thing he is carrying. I wonder who it is that has never heard of me!"

When the old woman got to Góshgoise, she said: "Give me your blanket and quiver."

The boy walked along; he didn't say a word.

She went back to her sons, and said: "He looks like a bad man; he won't say a word, and he won't give me what he has on his back." She called him names; she was mad.

Her son said: "Go again!"

When she came to Góshgoise the second time, she said: "Give those things to me, quick; my son is mad."

Góshgoise was lying on the ground with his head on his hands. He didn't say a word, didn't notice her. She talked and talked, but couldn't get the things. She went and told her sons that the man wouldn't give her his blanket and quiver, and wouldn't speak to her.

The youngest son said: "Who can that man be? Has he

never heard of me? I thought every one knew about me. Go again, and this time be sure to get the things."

The old woman ran to Góshgoise, and screamed: "Give me your blanket and quiver! This is the last time I'm going to ask for them! My sons are as strong as you are. You'll give up your things when they come!" She was mad, she looked ready to fight. The Tcpun brothers were watching; they were scared. Still the boy didn't say a word. When she couldn't make him speak, she went back to the house.

Her son screamed: "Where are the things?"

"He won't give them up."

"I'll go and kill him," said the eldest brother. When he stood up, he was so tall and heavy that he shook the house. He thought he could kill the boy easily, so he didn't put on his stone cover. With one step he reached Góshgoise. "Give me those things!" shouted he.

Góshgoise stood up. With his right hand he held his spear under his left arm, but his head was covered with his blanket, as if he didn't hear or see the man.

When Góshgoise didn't answer, Yaukûl screamed: "Don't you hear?" and he raised his spear to strike. That minute Góshgoise's spear flashed out and took Yaukûl's head off with one blow.

Góshgoise threw the head over the house, and the body after it. The old woman cried out: "What is that? It looks like my son's head!" and she ran around the house to see what had fallen.

Góshgoise went into his uncle's house, and said: "Cut a hole through the wall, so that I can see out."

When the Yaukûls saw that Góshgoise had killed their brother, they got ready to fight. They had a sister, who had never been out of the house, and had never spoken to any one. When the brothers were putting on their stone bodies, the sister said: "You will find that you are not the strongest people in this world," and she began to cry. The brothers were frightened. They had never heard their sister's voice before.

Góshgoise gave a spear to each of the five Tcpun brothers

and said: "If the last Yaukûl comes, you must help me fight him."

When the second brother was half-way to the house Góshgoise met him, and the two began to fight. At the first blow the boy struck Yaukûl with his spear; the first kind of rock flew off. When Yaukûl struck the boy, only dust flew. The boy hit Yaukûl five blows. At each blow a different kind of rock was broken. When the fifth cover broke, Yaukûl died. Each blow of the boy's spear was a flash of lightning. The third and fourth brother came out to fight. Every time they struck Góshgoise a blow, he said: "In another place," so they never hit him twice in the same place. Góshgoise struck their covers off and killed them.

When the fifth brother came, he struck first, and raised a flash of fire that went through three of the boy's stone covers. Góshgoise struck off two of Yaukûl's stone covers, then told his uncles to strike right where he had struck. They broke all the covers and killed theman. As he died, the boy said to him: "Hereafter, you and your brothers will be nothing but water fowls, you will eat only dead fish. People will laugh at you, for you will always sit by the water, whichever way the wind blows."

Góshgoise killed old woman Yaukûl and threw her body off; she became the same kind of bird as her sons. The daughter he took for a wife. Among the captives in Yaukûl's house he found his mother and aunts.

"I am going away," said Góshgoise to his uncles. "You mustn't stay here; you and all these women must go to my grandmother's place." He knew that his grandmother would have a big house ready for them.

He asked his mother how many people there were at the next bad place.

"There are five brothers," said she. "The eldest brother has a beautiful wife. Those brothers have killed all the men and children in that country. The women are captives and have to dig roots for the five brothers. The eldest brother's wife goes with them to watch them while they dig."

Góshgoise traveled on. He went to the top of a high mountain, looked down on the other side, and saw, on the flat below, women digging roots. The first woman was his father's sister; her head was covered with pitch, for she was mourning for her husband. When Góshgoise got near, he crept along quietly till he stood behind his aunt. She saw a second shadow and turned around to see what made it. The minute she saw Góshgoise, she knew he was her nephew; she cried out: "Go away! Why did you come here? This is a bad place!" Góshgoise didn't answer. "How did you pass the Yaukûl brothers?" asked his aunt.

"I killed them."

"The five Kaudokis brothers live here," said the woman. "We have to work for them. If we didn't work, they would cut our legs or ears off and make us eat them. The eldest brother has a beautiful wife — that bright woman over there — she looks like the moon."

"I have come here for a wife," said Góshgoise. "Have those men sisters?"

"Oh, my nephew," said his aunt, "go away, you will be killed. We are all captives. There is no woman here for you."

"I want that bright woman," said Góshgoise, "and I'm going to fight for her."

He ran to the woman, caught hold of her, and made her sit down; then he put his head on her knees.

"Who are you?" cried the woman. "Go away! The five brothers will see you and they will kill you. Go away!"

She cried, and all the women cried and begged Góshgoise to go away; but he stayed there; he wouldn't get up, and he wouldn't let the woman get up.

The Kaudokis brothers wore blankets made of untanned elk-skin. Góshgoise heard the noise of some one running and at the same time pounding a dry, stiff hide. The eldest brother was coming.

The women cried: "Run away; he will kill you!"

"No, he won't," said Góshgoise, and he covered his head with his blanket. Mole was Góshgoise's medicine, and was always with him. He said to Mole: "Make holes around here!"

Mole made a great many holes. When Kaudokis came rushing along with a spear in his hand, he fell into one of the holes, and Góshgoise cut his head off. The second brother came and was killed in the same way. The women were watching; they were glad. Each time they called out: "Another is coming!"

As the third brother came near, he called out: "Where did you come from? What do you want here? Nobody can beat me!"

That minute he fell into a hole, and Góshgoise cut his head off. Each time Góshgoise killed a Kaudokis, he pulled off his elk-skin blanket, and put it on himself.

The women said: "Now the youngest brother is coming! He is stronger than the others."

The fifth brother came in a terrible whirlwind. Góshgoise thought: "Maybe he will kill me," and he cried to Mole: "Dig deeper holes!" Just as Kaudokis raised his spear to strike, he stumbled and fell into a hole. Góshgoise cut his head off, put on his elk-skin blanket, and said: "Hereafter, you and your brothers will be nothing but creeping things." That minute the souls of the Kaudokis brothers flew out and became worms.

Góshgoise took the eldest brother's wife for his own wife; then he freed all the captives and sent them, with his wife and his aunt, to stay with his grandmother, while he went farther.

His aunt said: "As you travel, you will come to a high mountain; from the top of the mountain you will see a large village. Old man Juljulcus lives there. He has one son and one daughter, and if any man falls in love with the girl, her brother kills him."

Góshgoise traveled very fast; that night he camped on a high mountain, and the next morning he looked down into the valley. There was a river in the valley, and many women were walking along the bank; they were hunting for roots. Behind them all, Góshgoise saw Skóla, one of his aunts. As he went down the mountain, he stopped often to listen, for all those women were singing. He could hear his aunt's voice. She was cleaning roots and throwing them into a basket that she had on her back. When Góshgoise came behind her, she saw two shadows. She turned around and looked up; when she saw who it was, she cried out: "Why did you come here? This is a bad place."

"Do you know me?" asked Góshgoise.

"You are my nephew. How did you pass the house of the five Kaudokis brothers?"

"I killed them."

When Góshgoise saw the daughter of old Juljulcus, he told his aunt he was going to her.

"What are you going to her for?" asked Skóla. "Don't go there; you will get killed. Don't you see that great pile of bones there by the house? Those are the bones of men who have come for old Juljulcus' daughter." That minute the wind began to blow, and Skóla said: "They know that you are here. They know everything. The brother is coming to kill you."

"Who is 'Two-Tongued' talking to?" asked one woman of another. (They called Skóla two-tongued, because she could talk two ways.) "He is a nice-looking man, but Juljulcus will kill him."

Góshgoise ran to old Juljulcus' daughter, caught hold of her, drew her down, and put his head on her knees.

She was scared and tried to get away. "Let me go!" said she. "No man can fall in love with me; if he does, my brother will kill him."

The brother was coming in the middle of a whirlwind. His blanket, made of the dried skin of people, rattled terribly.

The sister bent over Góshgoise to save him. He said: "You mustn't do that; you might kill me." He told Mole to dig a great hole right there near him. The wind blew so hard that the women fell down and were blown along over the flat, but Góshgoise held himself and the girl to the ground.

Just as Juljulcus' son lifted his spear to strike, he fell into the hole Mole had made, and Góshgoise killed him. "Hereafter," said Góshgoise, "you will be small and weak; nothing but a cricket. You will lie near roots, and wherever people put their seeds and dried roots under the ground, there you will be."

Juljulcus' spirit came out and was a cricket. When the girl stepped over her brother's body, the cricket jumped on Góshgoise; it seemed to like him.

Góshgoise spent the night at old Juljulcus' house; in the morning he asked his wife: " Are all the great fighters dead? "

She asked her father, and he said: " My son-in-law, bad people live near the ocean. As you travel, you will come to a high mountain; from the top of that mountain, if you look toward the ocean, you will see a village, with smoke rising from each house. You must get to that village after dark. Don't go there in daylight."

Góshgoise told his father-in-law and all the women to go to his grandmother's place and stay there till he came.

" How far away is your grandmother's house? " asked the old man.

" It is on the other side of the world, in the south," said Góshgoise.

Old Juljulcus' spear was the little lightning that flashes all around the sky. Góshgoise gave his spear, long lightning, to his father-in-law, and took the old man's spear. His wife gave him seed to eat on the road, and they started. Old Juljulcus looked back, and said: " Son-in-law, don't forget what I have told you."

It took Góshgoise two days to reach the mountain, but his wife and his father-in-law camped a good many times before they got to his grandmother's house.

When Góshgoise reached the top of the mountain, he found a spring; he talked to the spring, and to the earth, and to the trees, and to the rocks; asked them not to hurt him. When he looked toward the ocean he saw many houses and smoke coming out of each house; then he remembered what his father-in-law had told him. As soon as he saw the smoke, the sun went down.

The village was full of people; they looked like lightning bugs, throwing fire, for each person had a lighted torch. When Góshgoise got to the village, he found the people killing one another. He crept up carefully, and with his short lightning spear began to cut off heads. All night he killed people and burned houses. At daybreak, when there was no one left to kill, Góshgoise went to the mountain, and standing on the top, looked down. Only one house was left; that was the house of old Tsmuk. (The people he had killed were Lóluks.) Góshgoise stayed all day on the mountain, and when night came he went to Tsmuk's house. (Day was night for the people who lived with Tsmuk and night was day.)

In Tsmuk's house there was a great ball of light; the light was so strong that no one could look at it. Góshgoise held his lightning spear in front of the ball, and said: " My spear is as bright as this ball; my long spear would be stronger and brighter than the ball."

Tsmuk's daughter was near the door. She had the bright ball right there at her side. Góshgoise sat down by her and turned his spear over. It frightened those in the house, and one man called out: " What is that? I saw something flash." Góshgoise held the spear near his head, and they didn't see it again.

There were six persons in the house, — the old grandmother, Tsmuk, his wife, his two sons, and his daughter. When the elder son was going to make a fire, Góshgoise held out his spear. The young man saw it and was scared. In the morning it was night for him, and he could see Góshgoise. He pushed his brother, and said: " That is what came in here last night." He pushed his father, and said: " That is what came in here last night! "

Old Tsmuk and his family were terribly scared, for lightning was darting among them, and it was red like fire. The three men ran out of the house, for they were afraid the thing would kill them.

Gushwean, an orphan, who had run away when Góshgoise was killing the Lóluk people, came to the old man's house. " Something strange got into our house last night," said old Tsmuk; " we didn't know it was there. It is bright and nice, but it scares us." Then the old man asked: " Where did you come from? "

" I live near here. Some one has killed all my people."

" Maybe this thing killed them," said the old man; " it is bloody. Look in and see it."

" No," said the boy. " It will kill me."

Old Tsmuk and his sons were afraid to look in. The mother and daughter were in the house. The girl was crying; she was sorry for her father and brothers. When she cried, Góshgoise asked: " Why do you cry? "

" This is the first time my father and brothers have ever been out of the house."

" Tell them to come in," said Góshgoise. She told them, but they wouldn't come; they were afraid.

Old Tsmuk asked: " Can I live if I come in? " His voice trembled. " If you will put that thing away, I will come." Old woman Tsmuk told him that the stranger had put his spear under his arm. Then Tsmuk said: " Ask the stranger if he has come for my daughter."

" I have come for her," said Góshgoise.

Then the old woman asked: " Where will you stay? "

" I won't stay here; my old grandmother is far away in the north. I will take my wife to that place."

When old man Tsmuk came in, Góshgoise put lightning above his head, and it shot through the house and up to the sky. He did this to let his grandmother know that he was at the end of his journey. Then he gave the spear to his father-in-law to pay him for his daughter. Since that time old Tsmuk has had short lightning.

Tsmuk took hold of Góshgoise's hand, called him son-in-law, and began to cry because he had nothing to give him. Tsmuk and his family were naked; they had no beads or blankets.

" Why do you cry? " asked his wife. (She was a powerful old woman; she could do anything.) When he told her, she said: " There is an island off in the water; my brother lives there. You can go to that island and get shells for our son-in-law. I will make you an elk-skin canoe." She cut an elk-skin into four pieces; one piece was for the bottom of the canoe, one for the top and one for each side. " This canoe is strong," said she. " Don't be afraid, and don't think of anything bad. If a storm comes, it will go around the canoe."

Tsmuk and his younger son got into the canoe; the old woman raised a strong wind behind it, and the canoe flew over the water. When it was going very fast, old Tsmuk thought: " What would happen if a storm came? " That minute a terrible whirlwind struck the canoe and drove it back to the shore.

Then the water was calm. The old woman felt badly; she knew Tsmuk had thought of a storm. She told him again not to think of anything, not to be afraid, then she made a strong wind behind the canoe, and that time it reached the island.

" What did you come for? " asked the brother-in-law.

" A man has come for my sister," said Tsmuk's son. " My father has nothing to give him."

The uncle brought beautiful shells and beads. As he loaded them into the canoe, the canoe grew larger and larger, till Tsmuk had as many shells and beads as he wanted.

The day that Tsmuk started for the island, his daughter had a little girl. After fasting, Góshgoise wanted to go to his own home, for he was hungry. He was a great hunter, but he couldn't hunt in Tsmuk's country, and he couldn't eat what the Tsmuk people ate.

" You mustn't go," said his mother-in-law; " you must wait for the canoe."

He went to the top of the high mountain, and looking off, saw on the water something as big as a hill. " That must be an island," thought he. When he went back to Tsmuk's house, he said to his mother-in-law: " In the water there is an island as big as a hill."

" That must be the canoe," said the mother-in-law, and she went out to see.

As soon as Tsmuk and his son left the island, they fell asleep, and they slept till they were near land. Old Tsmuk woke up first. He wanted to talk; he shook his son, and asked: " What do you think of your brother-in-law? "

" I like him," said the son.

That moment the canoe stopped; it was sinking, but the old woman spoke to it, called: "Come farther! Come farther!" The canoe stopped sinking. She made a rope of deerskin, threw one end of it to Tsmuk, and began to pull the canoe toward land. Under her arm she had her daughter's baby.

When Tsmuk saw the baby, he was glad; he wanted to get ashore quickly. He went to the end of the canoe and ran forward to jump, but he hit the canoe and pushed it away. The old woman had to talk a long time and make the wind blow in every direction, before she could get it back again. Old Tsmuk was so scared that he couldn't speak, and he couldn't hear.

His wife was scared and mad; she screamed to him: "You have made lots of trouble. You will no longer be a person; you will be darkness, to be used when people want to sleep!" And so it was.

Góshgoise and his wife went to his grandmother's house, and old woman Tsmuk and her sons went with them. The daughter kept the ball of light by her side, and when people saw them coming they were scared, and said: "Those people are coming to kill us." But as soon as the grandmother saw them, she said: "That man is my grandson!" Then every one was glad.

After that, Góshgoise lived in his own country, with his wives, his grandmother, and all his kin.

KAIUTOIS FOOLS WUS

CHARACTERS

Kaiutois	Wolf
Wus	Fox

KAIUTOIS was sick for a long time, and he was alone in his house. One day Wus went to see him and Kaiutois said: "I want you to find me something to eat; I am hungry."

Wus killed some mice, put them in a basket, and carried them to Kaiutois. Kaiutois ate them at one mouthful and said: "I feel better, but I am weak, for I am hungry. You must call deer and try to kill one. Call loud so they can hear, and say: 'Come and dance. Big-ribs is going to die.' When they come, you must kill a white-faced one; they are the fattest."

Wus called: "All those who live in the mountains, come! The man who has killed so many people is dying. I am going to have a dance. I am glad."

The deer didn't hear, so Wus called again: "Big-ribs, the man who drives you around and kills you, is dying. Come and dance!"

That time Big deer heard, and said: "Get ready; Wus wants us to dance with him. Big-ribs is dying."

When they started, Wus saw them and called to Kaiutois: "They are coming! they are coming!"

Kaiutois lay down and Wus wrapped him up so no one could see him. When deer crowded into the house, Wus took a club and began to dance; every time he came to Kaiutois, he struck him with the club. The deer danced and raised a terrible dust.

At last Big deer said: "That is enough; we have a long way to go before dark."

Wus said: " If this man doesn't die to-night, I will call you again to-morrow."

The white-faced deer went first. They looked so big that Wus was scared; he didn't touch them. The last to go was a fawn. Wus told him to wait, and when the big ones were out of sight, Wus killed the little one.

Kaiutois ate him and complained that he hadn't enough. He said: " It is just as if I hadn't eaten a mouthful. I didn't tell you to catch that little lean fawn; I told you to kill a big, white-faced deer. To-morrow you must call to the wŭyĕs (mountain sheep). Maybe it will be easier to kill one of them. They live among the rocks."

The next morning Wus called: " Those who always live among the rocks, come and dance. The man who runs after you and kills you is going to die, and I am glad. When he killed a deer, he drove me off; he never gave me a bite. Come and dance with me! "

Wus watched, and when he saw them coming, he told Kaiutois.

Kaiutois said: " Wrap me up tight. When they are through dancing, kill one that has never had young; they are the best."

When the wŭyĕs were in the house, Wus took up a club, and they all began to dance. They danced a long time and raised a terrible dust. When they were ready to go, they looked so big that Wus was afraid; he let them all go but the last one, a little fellow. He held him back, and said: " Wait, wait a minute, you will get pushed down if you go in that crowd."

When the large ones were out of sight, Wus killed the little one and told Kaiutois to get up and eat.

Kaiutois couldn't stand up; he was too sick; so Wus fed him. Kaiutois said: " This meat is too soft, and there isn't enough of it. I shall never get well if I don't have plenty to eat. You must kill something that is fat and old."

Wus said: " Maybe I could, if you would help me."

Kaiutois found him a heavier club and told him to call the antelopes. Wus called: " Antelopes, come and dance with me. The man who has eaten so many of your people is almost dead. He will die quickly if we dance."

When Wus saw them coming, Kaiutois said: "Cover me with something thin; maybe I'll catch one."

Wus stood on the top of the house and danced, and sang: "I'm glad Kaiutois is going to die. He always drove me away when he had anything to eat." When the antelopes were all in the house, Wus told them to stand around and see him dance on Kaiutois. He jumped up and down on Kaiutois, while Kaiutois looked at the antelopes and picked out the one he wanted, — the fattest one. When they were through dancing, and ready to go, Wus caught hold of the fat antelope. It came near carrying him off, but Kaiutois jumped up and killed it.

Kaiutois ate the meat and fat and gave the intestines to Wus. He felt stronger then, and said: "Maybe I will get well if I can get out in the woods. Maybe I can kill big game again."

Wus helped him out, and after a while Kaiutois told him to call deer. He said: "I'll go into the house and wrap up in a blanket, and when they are almost through dancing, you must say: 'This man is dead. Throw him out!' When they throw me out, I will run at them and kill as many as I can."

Wus called: "I want everybody who lives on the mountains and among the rocks to come. Kaiutois is almost dead. This is his last day, we must all dance!"

Everybody came, for everybody was glad. When they had danced enough, they threw Kaiutois out and started for home. Kaiutois ran after them and killed a great many. Wus helped him all he could. Kaiutois told him he should have as much as he wanted to eat, but when the deer were piled up in the house, Kaiutois drove Wus away, told him to go and hunt mice for himself.

Kaiutois stayed in the house till he had eaten all the deer meat. Then he turned to a wolf and went off to the mountains. He never had a home again.

BLAIWAS AND THE HEAD

CHARACTERS

Blaiwas	Eagle	Tcûskai	Weasel
Dásläts	Panther	Wûlkûtska	Marten
Ndúkis	Hawk		

BLAIWAS, Dásläts, Wûlkûtska, and other strong men, lived in a house on a high mountain. They were head men, and all the people around brought them meat. One day, Blaiwas said: "We had better let old man Ndúkis divide our meat." They called Tcûskai, a fast runner, and sent him for Ndúkis.

Ndúkis had four brothers and a mother, and he lived in a brush house — just as we did long ago. Ndúkis went to Blaiwas' house and divided the meat; he ate some, but he didn't carry any to his mother or his brothers.

The next morning, when the head men were starting off to hunt, Ndúkis went with them. He hunted all day, but caught only one mouse. He ate the mouse and went home. Blaiwas sent again for Ndúkis to come and divide the meat; when he had divided it the men began to make fun of him for being such a poor hunter. They made him open his mouth and then they threw meat into it. When he had swallowed all the meat he could, they sent him home.

Old woman Wûlkûtska and her two daughters lived at the foot of the mountain. There was no one to kill game for them, and sometimes the mother was almost starved. One day she said to her daughters: "Great hunters live on the top of the mountain; they always have lots of deer meat. You must go there and get husbands."

One of the girls asked: "How can we go; we don't know where their house is?"

The mother said: "There is only one big house. You

will know Blaiwas when you see him, for he flies without moving his wings."

When the girls came to the top of the mountain, they sat down to rest and watch for Blaiwas. They hadn't been there long when they saw Ndúkis coming.

He was out of breath, for it was hard for him to fly high.

The elder sister said: "There is Blaiwas; he flies just as mother said he did."

The younger sister said: "No, that isn't Blaiwas." They watched him till he flew down among the rocks; then the elder sister said: "His house is down there; we must follow him."

When Ndúkis got home, he was so nearly dead that he fell into the house. His mother jumped on him, and asked: "What is the matter?" (He knew that the girls were watching him and he had tried to fly as Blaiwas did.) The old woman kept asking what had happened, but Ndúkis wouldn't tell.

When the sisters came in sight of the house, the elder said: "That is Blaiwas' house."

The younger said: "Mother told us that Blaiwas' house was large; that one is small. It isn't Blaiwas' house." The elder sister scolded her and pulled her along.

When Ndúkis saw the girls coming, he told his mother to hurry and fix a good place for them to sit.

"What shall I fix it with?" asked the old woman. They had no mats or blankets.

"Oh, anything," said Ndúkis. "You must watch, and if the girls sit down near the house, you must bring them in. They are sisters; they saw me flying and they followed me."

When the girls came to the top of the house, the old woman told Ndúkis. He turned his eyes up, as Blaiwas did, and sent her to bring them in. The girls saw him turn his eyes, and the elder said: "Yes, that is Blaiwas. See what big eyes he has." She went in and sat down by him.

When Blaiwas and the head men came home, they sent Tcûskai to tell Ndúkis to come and divide the meat. Ndúkis said: "Why do they always send for the chief to divide their meat? I am tired of it." He didn't want to leave the girls.

When the meat was divided, the head men told Ndúkis to open his mouth. Then they amused themselves by throwing pieces of meat at him. They fed him the livers and intestines, parts which they didn't like. When he had eaten all he could, he started for home; on the way he thought: "What shall I feed those girls with?"

When he couldn't think of anything else, he said: "I will cut some of the meat off from my legs," and he did so. When he gave the pieces to his mother to cook, she asked: "Why didn't you bring more? Here isn't half enough for the girls to eat."

The younger sister tasted of the meat, and said: "This isn't deer meat. This tastes badly." The elder sister scolded her. The younger said: "You think this man is Blaiwas, but I know he isn't."

Ndúkis acted as much like Blaiwas as he could.

The next morning Blaiwas and the head men went to hunt for deer. Ndúkis didn't go; he wanted to stay with the girls. At night the hunters came back with deer hanging in their belts, as men hang squirrels in their belts now.

Blaiwas said: "Old man Ndúkis is getting lazy. Tell him to come and divide this meat." Ndúkis held back, scolded, and said: "Why do they always send for the chief? I won't go." But he wanted to go and have plenty to eat.

After he had been gone a while, the younger sister said: "Let us go and see how that man divides meat." They followed his trail till they came to a big house. They crept up carefully and looked in. Ndúkis was sitting by the ladder, and men were throwing meat into his mouth. The sisters saw Blaiwas and then they knew that it was his house.

The elder sister was ashamed, and they both started for home.

Ndúkis knew what had happened, and so did Blaiwas; and they followed the girls. Blaiwas caught up with them first, and when Ndúkis came, the two men began to quarrel. Blaiwas' four brothers came and so did Ndúkis' brothers, and there was a big fight.

The eldest Blaiwas said to the sisters: "I am going to cut

off Ndúkis' head and carry it above the sky. You mustn't look up. If you do, the head will fall and kill my brothers."

The five Blaiwas brothers killed the five Ndúkis brothers: then the eldest brother cut off Ndúkis' head and flew away with it. He was almost to the sky when the sisters looked up; they couldn't help it. That minute the head fell to the ground. It flew at the four Blaiwas brothers and killed them all.

The head was the husband of the two sisters. The younger sister was afraid of the head; she wouldn't stay where it was. The elder sister put it in her basket and carried it on her back; she cried all the time.

After a while, the head asked: " What do you see? "

" I see a deer," said the woman.

" Climb up as high as you can, then take me out of the basket, and put me down, looking toward the deer."

The woman got as high as she could and put the head down. " Now look," said the head. It flew straight at the deer and killed it. The woman put the head back in her basket, then camped.

The head said: " Put me where I can watch you."

She made a sort of scaffold and put the head on it. Then she cut up the deer and hung the meat on a tree to dry. When the meat was dry and the woman was ready to go home, the head said: " You must put meat in the basket; then put me in, and put meat on top of me."

The woman thought she would go and see Kumush, for maybe he could do something for her husband. On the road she wouldn't speak; she was afraid that if she saw a deer the head would kill it, and she would have to dry the meat.

When Kumush saw the woman, he said: " I must have that woman for my daughter," and he asked her: " Have you anything to eat?

She put down the basket, and when Kumush looked at the meat, she said: " Don't take much.

Kumush thought: " Why does she say that? Maybe she is hiding something," and he began to pull the meat out of the basket.

The woman went into the house, for she was afraid. The

head had great eyes and long hair, and when Kumush came to it he was scared; he threw down the meat and ran into the house.

The head called out: " What are you doing? Take me into the house, I don't want to stay out here." (The head could fly when it got mad or wanted to kill something, but not at other times.)

Kumush said to the woman: " This head is your husband; we must bring it in." He fixed a place for it and carried it in. The next morning, Kumush said: " I am going to make a sweat house for this man. I like him; I will make a body for him." (He wanted to kill the head.)

Kumush made a sweat house and covered it with five kinds of stones. He heated rocks red hot and put them inside, and carried the head in and put it down by the rocks; then he went out and fastened up the place with stones.

Soon the head called out: " I've sweat enough. Take me out!" Nobody came. It screamed louder: " Take me out quick! If you don't, I will get out and kill you both!" When nobody came, the head flew up and struck the stones on top of the house. It broke four of them, then its strength gave out, and it died.

Kumush said: " I don't hear any noise; maybe your husband is dead."

The woman said: " Wait a little; don't open the place yet. If he is alive, he will kill us."

When Kumush opened the sweat house, he saw a beautiful young man lying on the ground; but he was dead. Kumush felt sorry. The woman felt sorry, too. Kumush took the body out of the sweat house; then he piled up logs and burned it. When it was burning, he said: " Hereafter, people will do this way: When their friends die, they will burn them as I am burning this man." And that is the way we did till white men came.

WUS AND HIS TROUBLES

CHARACTERS

Kuyas	Red Ants	Tálwas	Hot-Water Baskets
Pshagéknik	Gopher	Wus	Fox
Slikwis	Fire-drill		

TEN Tálwas brothers lived in two houses, five in one house, and five in the other; near by, in two other houses, lived the ten Slikwis brothers. One day Wus came from the west and went into the house of five of the Slikwis brothers.

"Oh," said Wus, "what are these nice long sticks here around the fire for? They would make good gambling sticks. I will take them. If I meet people, I can gamble with them and beat them with such nice sticks."

He took all five of the Slikwis brothers in one hand.

As soon as he had them, they blazed up high. They were mad at him for picking them up.

He threw them down and ran out screaming: "What can those things be? Are they people?" He cried, for his hand was burned.

When he came to the second house, he looked in and said: "Those look like the same kind of sticks, but I will try to pick them up. I could beat everybody if I had such nice gambling sticks." As soon as he took the sticks up, he screamed, threw them down, and ran out of the house. His hands were burned and his hair was singed. "Oh," said he, "I never heard that such kind of people lived around here. I don't like them; they are bad people."

He went farther and came to the house of the five Tálwas brothers. When he went in, he saw water baskets standing near the fire,

"Oh," said he, "I am glad to see water; I am dry. Everybody is gone; the water is left to cook with when they come back." Wus looked for something to eat, and when he couldn't find anything, he said: "I will wash my hands in one of these baskets, and I will drink out of another." He put his hands into one of the baskets; the water boiled up and scalded him. He screamed, then all the baskets boiled up and threw water. Wus was terribly scalded. He ran out of the house, then looked back, and said: "What can that be? I am almost dead!"

He went on till he came to the second house. He looked in, and when he saw five other baskets, he said: "They would kill me; I won't touch them." He hunted inside and outside of the house for something to eat, but couldn't find anything. He was so dry that he crept up to one of the baskets and put his little finger into the water; it was cold water. He thought: "Now I will have a good drink. This is just water; that over there is something else. This is such water as I drink when I am traveling." He began to drink out of the smallest basket.

That was the youngest brother, and he didn't get mad. He knew how his brothers had scalded Wus and he felt sorry for him. He thought: "Let him drink of me if he wants to; I will be cold for him." But the other brothers began to jerk and gurgle and bubble up; they were mad at Wus. Wus got scared and ran out.

He stood at the door and looked in. The four brothers boiled up and threw water over the house. Wus was terribly scared; he ran as fast as he could till he came to two other houses. Those were the houses of the ten Kuyas brothers. He went into the first house; there was a big fire burning. He looked around and wondered where the people were who built the fire. He thought: "I will wait till they come; maybe they will give me something to eat, since they are going to cook."

Wus waited till the middle of the day, then he said: "I am tired of waiting; I'll hunt around and maybe I can find something to eat." He couldn't find anything, then he said: "I will stay till night; they will come when it gets dark," and he lay down by the fire.

The five brothers were sitting around the fire, but Wus didn't see them. When he lay down, one brother bit him. He jumped up and screamed: "What bit me?" Another brother bit his leg, a third one bit his hand. Wus screamed: "What can it be that bites so?" And he threw burning coals around the house to kill what had bitten him. The five brothers were mad, and they all bit him.

Wus ran out of the house, came to the second house, looked in and saw a fire burning. Five brothers were sitting around the fire, but Wus couldn't see them. Those five brothers jumped on him and bit him; the other five came in and helped them. Wus screamed with pain, but they didn't stop biting. They killed him and had almost eaten him up when Pshagék-nik came in.

He saw Wus, and asked: "Old man, why are you sleeping so long?"

That minute Wus jumped up, and said: "Oh, I'm sleepy!" He went out of the house and traveled on toward the north.

CEDAR BIRD'S DAUGHTERS MARRY BULL SNAKE

CHARACTERS

Kéis	Rattlesnake	Wámanik	Bull Snake
Kékina	Lizard	Wískäk	Cedar-bird
Kéwe	Eel	Witkátkis	A Hawk
Kûlta	Otter	Ygiak	A Bird "that never sleeps." (English name unknown.)
Moi	Squirrel		
Ndúkis	Duck-hawk		
Tcoóks	Crane		
Tusasás	Joker (Skunk)		

NDÚKIS' house was on the bank of Klamath Lake and near it was the house of old man Tcoóks. On the south side of the lake lived Wískäk and her two daughters. The daughters liked the Shasta people; they went often to see them and carry them presents. Once, on the way home, the girls stopped to dig roots west of where Ndúkis and Tcoóks lived. Ndúkis saw them. He thought: "Those are nice-looking girls. They dig roots fast. I like those girls."

Now Witkátkis came to visit Ndúkis and his son; they were kin. Ndúkis' wife said: "I'm glad you have come, there are nice-looking girls living right south of here. They are good workers; they dig roots summer and winter, you should get one of those girls for a wife."

"I am afraid they wouldn't like me," said Witkátkis.

"Where do they live?" asked Ndúkis' son.

"You have traveled all around," said his mother. "You ought to know where they live. When you are on the mountain, look toward the south, and you will see a big house; they live in that house."

The next time the sisters came from Shasta, they camped

on the way, and in the night one said to the other: " I can't sleep; I feel that somebody is looking at me."

" I feel that way, too," said her sister. They got up and started for home.

Ndúkis' mother said: " If you want to see those girls, you must go to the mountain and watch for them. After a while you will see them digging roots. Don't go to their house. Wait a little while and watch them, then go down the mountain till you come to a small house. An old man lives in that house. He is kin of old man Tcoóks. Go in and talk to him."

Ndúkis went to the mountain and soon he heard the girls singing. They always sang when they worked. He watched them and saw how quickly they dug roots; then he went to Tcoóks' house.

Tcoóks had been fishing. He was cooking fish when Ndúkis got there. " What did you come for? " asked the old man. " You never thought of me before — young men should travel around and see people; that is the way to be strong. Do you want some fish? "

Tcoók's wife said: " Ndúkis never eats our kind of food; he eats ducks."

" Cook him a duck," said Tcoóks, but he thought in his head: " Why doesn't he eat fish? "

The old woman cooked a duck and gave it to the young man. He ate all around the neck, but didn't eat the rest of the duck.

" Why don't you eat? " asked Tcoóks. " My old woman is kin to you; you should eat lots. In a strange house it would be right not to eat much; here it's different."

" He never eats much," said the old woman. Ndúkis didn't say anything.

" You are a young man, you should have a wife," said Tcoóks. " There are nice-looking young women in the next house; they are great workers."

" They wouldn't like me," said Ndúkis.

" Once Kûlta tried to buy those girls," said Tcoóks. " They wouldn't go with him. They said they didn't belong to the water and they wouldn't marry a man who lived in the water.

Maybe they will go with you; you live on land. Every time a rain is over, they bring out nice things, — beautiful shells, and beads."

"I want you to go and buy them for me," said Ndúkis. "I am kind of scared."

Tcoóks went to old woman Wískäk's, and Ndúkis went home.

Tcoóks said: "Don't you get tired of your girls sometimes? They are old enough to get a man. They have lived single a long time."

"Kûlta wanted them but I couldn't make them go with him," said Wískäk.

"My nephew wants them," said Tcoóks. "He told me to ask you for them. He will give you nice things."

The girls were digging roots; when they started for home, and were near the house, the elder said: "I hear somebody talking. Some man is in our house. Let us sit down outside."

"No," said the younger. "It is better to go in." They went in, sat by the fire, and held their heads down. The elder whispered: "I wonder what Tcoóks is here for?"

Their mother asked: "Will you marry this man's nephew?"

The elder sister asked the younger: "What will you do?"

"Ndúkis lives on high rocks," she said. "Maybe we would fall off. I don't like high rocks."

Wískäk said: "I knew you would say something bad." Then she asked the elder sister: "Will you go with him?"

"No. Why do you ask a second time? Ndúkis is not like us. He doesn't live the way we do. I wish you would let us alone."

Tcoóks said: "I am afraid of Ndúkis. He can beat everybody by getting up early. That is the kind he is. If you go around digging roots, he will be watching you. He won't want you, but he will be mad. That is his way."

The next morning, when the girls started off, they said: "We are going to Mlaiksi." [1]

"Why do you go there so often?" asked their mother. "You had better not go to-day, you might meet Ndúkis."

[1] Mount Shasta.

"We will go where we like," said the elder sister. "We are not afraid; Ndúkis can't hurt us."

They started early, but Ndúkis was on the mountain, watching for them. The elder sister walked ahead. Every step she took she stumbled, as if the step were telling her that she was going to meet somebody. At last she said to her sister: "My steps stumble. That means something."

"Tcoóks told us Ndúkis was a bad man when he got mad. It is your fault if we meet trouble," said the younger girl.

They looked around as they climbed the mountain, but Ndúkis was sitting on the highest rocks and they didn't look high enough to see him. When they were on the other side of the mountain, the younger sister looked back. She saw Ndúkis and screamed. She ran one way, and her sister ran another. They were frightened. They went into thick bushes and stayed there a long time. Ndúkis sat on the rocks and laughed to see how frightened they were. He sat there till midday, then went home.

That day young man Moi was out hunting for deer. He was fine-looking. He wore a beaded buckskin band around his head. All at once he came upon the Wískäk girls hiding in the bushes. "Who are you?" asked he. "You scared me."

The elder sister said: "I know you; you are the little chief who lives by the river. You are our kin."

"Come out of the bushes," said Moi. "Who frightened you?"

"We saw Ndúkis watching us," the elder sister said.

"He is a nice young man," said Moi. "He won't hurt you, but you can go with me if you are afraid of him."

"No," said the elder sister, "we are going to Mlaiksi." And they traveled on.

When Ndúkis passed Tcoóks' house, the old man asked: "Where have you been?"

"I have just been walking around," said Ndúkis. "I met the two sisters. They were scared and ran into the bushes. I don't like them."

When Tcoóks told Wískäk that Ndúkis was mad at her daughters, she cried; she thought maybe he had killed them.

On the way home from Mlaiksi, the girls saw people digging roots in places where they had always dug.

When they told their mother, she said: " Stay in the house. I will go and see why they are digging around here."

She took five steps and was there. The people were scared. They had never seen Wískäk, for she always stayed at home and sent her daughters to dig. When she found that they were getting all the roots, she went home, and said: "Come and help me; we must dig fast and get as many roots as we can."

Those people lived near Shasta River. When they started, they sent word to all their kin that they were going off to dig roots, but they forgot to tell young man Wámanik, who lived on the north side of the digging place, so he started off alone.

The elder Wískäk girl said to her mother: " You go straight ahead: we will go on the north side, where there are nice long roots." When they got there, the ground was turned up and all the roots were gone.

Wámanik was there. When he found that the roots had been dug, he was mad. He stood up tall and looked bright. The elder sister didn't see him. The younger one saw him and ran.

Wámanik fell in love with her right away. He thought she was so nice-looking that he would like her for a wife, and in some way he took hold of her heart, so she wouldn't get frightened. He followed her to the spring where she went to get water to drink.

Her sister was there. The younger asked: " Did you pass anybody? "

" No."

" Then your eyes are poor, for I saw a nice-looking young man."

The elder sister took her cap and was going to drink. Just then Wámanik stood up in the form of a snake, She screamed, dropped her cap, and ran off, when she came to where her mother was digging, she was so scared that her eyes were sticking out, and she couldn't speak.

Her mother asked: "Why don't you talk?"

After a while she said: "There is a big snake in the spring."

"Well, well," said her mother, "what kind of a man do you want? You can't live single all your life."

When the elder sister ran away, Wámanik turned to a nice-looking man. He came up to the younger girl and said: "I can be a great many different things. I am a spirit of this earth; I have seen you often, but I didn't want to show myself to your sister; I wanted to frighten her. I don't like her as well as I do you. I have heard you talk, and I want you for a wife, for I like you. I can turn to a snake, but I am a man, and I have lots of nice clothes." Then he turned to a snake again, for he saw the old woman and her daughter coming.

On the way home the younger girl said to her mother: "Make a bed for us and put on our panther-skin blankets."

Wámanik was under the ground just where the girls were sitting. In the night when they woke up, they felt somebody between them. At daylight Wámanik went down in the ground right where the bed was. Every night after that the girls changed. If a person saw them one day they didn't know them the next. Wámanik came each night. In the daytime he was under the ground near where they were digging roots.

There was a Tusasás among the people digging roots, and he said: "I am going to marry those nice-looking girls. They are great workers; they will get me lots to eat."

People knew now that Wámanik was the husband of old Wískäk's daughters, and that that was why they looked different each morning, so they said to Tusasás: "If you make Wámanik mad, you won't be a person long. He is a strong man; he can do anything."

Tusasás said: "I am stronger than Wámanik. I am not afraid of him."

Wámanik heard him talk about his wives and right away he was mad. He made Tusasás itch till he scratched the skin and flesh off from his body. People laughed at him, and said: "Maybe Wámanik will kill you; he is a great doctor."

Wámanik said to Kéwe: "Go and tell Tusasás to stop making fun of my wives and stop talking about me. If he doesn't, he'll no longer be a person."

Wámanik was bright like the sun, and both his wives were bright. He was so bright that people couldn't go into old woman Wískäk's house. He was a man at night and when he went to hunt for deer, but if he got mad, or didn't want people to see him, he turned to a snake and went under the ground. He was a great hunter. There was lots of deer meat in the old woman's house.

Wískäk's brother had such a large family that his children were always hungry. Wámanik told his mother-in-law to send for him to come and get meat. The old woman sent a man for him, but the man came back alone, and said: "He won't come." That made the old woman cry; she said: "My kin hate us."

The man said: "They are afraid of your son-in-law; that is why they don't come here. They don't want to see him."

"I won't hurt them," said Wámanik; "they are my wives' kin. I have no people; I belong to the Earth. I live under the mountains and under the water. Go and tell them not to be afraid of me; tell them to come. I am a person. Maybe they don't know that."

The man went back and talked nice, but they wouldn't come. Then he said: "If you don't come, you will make Wámanik mad."

They all came. Wámanik gave nice things to the youngest boy. "Are you afraid of me now?" asked Wámanik. "I heard what you said. I can hear what people say when they are far away. I like you and I want you to like me." The children ate lots. They felt glad.

One day old Wískäk said: "My girls are tired of digging roots, I want to dig sometimes."

"They'll never get tired," said Wámanik, "they'll always work. You are old and you must rest; you'll die soon."

Kékina said to Wámanik: "Your wives don't love you. There is a young man after them all the time. They wanted to marry Ndúkis."

That made Wámanik feel badly. In the evening, when he went to his mother-in-law's house, he asked the elder sister: "Is any one in love with you and your sister?"

"No," said the woman. "Why do you ask that?"

"I don't like the way you talk. You don't tell me the truth," said Wámanik. "The first time I saw you, your eyes stuck out, as if you had seen somebody; you looked scared. I won't keep you if somebody else wants you."

Old Wískäk had been after red bark to color roots; when she came home she found her younger daughter crying. The girl told her what Wámanik had said. The old woman was angry, but she didn't know what to do.

Kékina went to Ndúkis, and said: "Wámanik is saying bad things about you."

Ndúkis listened and heard what Wámanik said to his wife. The next morning he went early, before anybody was up in the world, and sat on a rock where he could see old Wískäk's house; he looked awful ugly. Ygiak, a man who never slept, was out hunting for sticks; when he saw Ndúkis, he was so scared that he dropped his sticks and ran home.

At midday Ndúkis came down from the rocks. Somebody ran into Lok's house, and said: "There is going to be a great fight. Ndúkis is mad at Wámanik and he will kill him."

Lok said: "Ndúkis has a big spirit. Wámanik is strong, too. They will scare each other, but they won't fight."

Old Wískäk was willing Ndúkis should kill her son-in-law, for she didn't like him. She said to her daughters: "I am going to leave you; I have lived with you long enough. I don't like your husband. When he wanted you, why didn't you say that you couldn't live under the ground, that you would smother? You should have taken Ndúkis; he is your kind." As she talked, she turned to a bird, and when she was through talking, she flew off to the mountains. She did it herself; she didn't want to be a person any longer. But each day she came back and talked to her daughters; she wanted to make them willing to turn to birds and go with her to the mountains, for she could not go far away while they were persons.

People heard Wískäk talk as she flew around. The youngest daughter said: "I wouldn't talk so much. You wanted us to marry. Wámanik is as good as Ndúkis."

"Ndúkis doesn't turn to a snake every time he goes out of the house," said the old woman.

The elder daughter cried all the time, and didn't eat anything. She didn't want to go to the mountains; she didn't want to stay with Wámanik, and she didn't want to marry Ndúkis. She said to her mother: "You mustn't come around where people live; you must hide among the brush and trees."

Wískäk didn't like that. She said: "I will turn you into a snake, and when you cross the road in front of people they will throw dirt in your face. You will deceive people; you will pretend to be kind, then you will bite them."

She turned her daughters into snakes, and then flew off toward the east. As she started, she called out to her son-in-law: "You will never be a man again; you will be a snake, with a body like your panther-skin blanket."

The old woman kept going east till she came to a place where there were low cedar trees; she made her home there. She talks like a person yet, and that place is full of her kin.

LOK AND HER CHILDREN

CHARACTER

Lok . . . . Bear

Lok was a widow with two children; she lived with her mother. The old woman took care of the roots. She put them in a hole and slept with her head near it. When her daughter brought roots home and poured them into the hole, the children wanted some of them to eat, but the old woman said: " First I must give roots to the fire, to the mountains, the trees, the house, and the springs." (This is the custom.)

The daughter said: " My children are hungry; you must give them some of the roots."

Lok said: " You don't know about these things. If they get sick, you will blame me."

The old woman took roots and talked to the mountains; she said: " You must give us wood that won't burn us." To the springs she said: " Old grandmother, you always have water under your care; give us plenty of good water." To the house she said: " You know us, our house that we built." She talked to each part of the house. (If people didn't talk to the posts of the house they would fall. The woman who told this myth said she had known of such cases.) To the posts she said: " Hold up this house; be good to us."

She packed away all the roots they dug, ten large basketfuls, then she and her daughter brought in wood enough to last till spring.

The old woman said: " Grandchildren, I want you to bring me gum from the cedar trees." When they brought it, she covered her face with it and stopped up her eyes. Then she lay down with her head over the hole and didn't go out of the house again all winter. Some mornings she woke up and gave a handful of roots to the children. In the night, when the children were asleep, she ate plenty of roots herself.

One morning her daughter asked: "How is it that rats are always gnawing; why don't you kill them?"

"I wish you wouldn't listen to everything," said the old woman.

One morning she said to the little girl: "I wish you wouldn't cry in the night."

The mother said: "You don't give the children enough to eat; they are hungry."

"You don't know about the winter," said the old woman. "It's going to be long, and our roots won't last: the snow will be deep yet."

The children were hungry, but their mother said: "You mustn't cry, it makes your grandmother worse."

The boy said: "Let us kill her; she has no eyes."

"If we tried to kill her, she would kill us; you are small and I couldn't run fast enough to get away from her."

"What are you whispering about?" asked the grandmother.

"The children talk low because thev are weak· you are starving them to death."

One morning old Lok asked: "Which way does the snow come?"

The boy looked out, and said: "It comes from the north."

"That shows it will be good weather to-morrow." She gave the children a few roots.

The next day the old woman said: "I wish I had some meat to eat."

"Stop!" said her daughter. "Don't talk like that." She was afraid that her mother wanted to kill the children and eat them.

The next morning the grandmother asked: "How does the sky look?"

The little boy said: "There are clouds."

"Where are the clouds?"

"They are around Omisna."

"That means rain," said the old woman. "It won't be long till spring comes." She took out plenty of roots and pounded them for the children. (They were fooling her.)

The next day she sent the little girl to look at Mlaiksi.

The girl said: " Smoke is rising from the top of the mountain, as if someone had made a fire up there."

The old woman was taking out a few roots, but she poured them back, and said: " There is going to be a great storm."

The storm came. It put out their fire, and for four days old Lok didn't move. Five days the children were without anything to eat; then she asked the little boy: " How does it look now? "

" It is raining."

The old woman said: " If it rains, you can go and dig roots."

The daughter cried and told her the children were starving. She gave them a few roots. The little boy said to his mother: " Why can't we dig a hole near the roots and steal some of them? "

" I know what you are talking about," said the old woman. " I know that it is winter yet."

One morning she asked: " Is it spring? "

Her daughter said: " I don't know," and she told the children not to tell their grandmother anything about the weather. It rained and hailed. Every night the mother and children cried. Each morning they stamped on the ground to find out if it were soft. One day the mother went off, and when she came back she brought a few roots. The children were sitting out of doors, and she heard the old woman ask them: " Where is your mother? "

" She has gone for wood," said the boy.

The mother put away some of the roots and gave the rest to the children.

The old woman asked: " Does it snow yet? "

The little boy said: " There is so much snow that I can't see the tops of the trees."

The grandmother put more gum on her eyes, rolled herself up tight, and lay still.

The mother made two pairs of straw moccasins, and the next morning started for roots. It was spring now, and she found plenty for her children to eat. While she was gone, the old woman asked: "Which way is the wind?"

"From the southwest," said the boy. His mother had told him to fool his grandmother, and let her lie there all summer. The mother could make the wind blow — the wind was her medicine. Every time she found a fly in the house, she killed it with a porcupine quill, so the old woman wouldn't know it was spring.

There were a good many of the Lok people around the place where the mother dug roots; she left some roots for them to take care of, and said: "In two days I will come back and bring my children."

When she got home, she made moccasins for the children, and in the morning, when she was ready to start, she said to her mother: "It snows. I am tired of packing wood; I am going to take the children to the woods and keep a fire there; you never stay by the fire."

The mother worked all day and dug a great many roots; she had a big basketful to put away. She wondered where she could put them so the old woman couldn't find them. Then she thought of Keŏnise, a hill where Lok didn't go. It was a long way off, but she carried the roots there and hid them.

When the children didn't come back, the grandmother scratched around in the ashes, found live coals and melted the gum out of her eyes; then she tracked her daughter.

As soon as the daughter knew that her mother was coming, she went to the house, took the roots out of the hole, and threw them around everywhere.

When the old woman came back, the daughter said: "We won't be persons any longer. In later times people will kill and eat us."

The old woman said: "It is better so."

They wandered off to the mountains, and from that time only a male bear and female bear live together, and they never have more than two children.

GÄK AND THE KAIUTOIS BROTHERS

CHARACTERS

Gäk	Crow	Skóůks	Woodtick
Kaiutois	Wolf	Tcûskai	Weasel
Kaltsik	Spider	Tciwididik	Road Runner
Kéwe	Eel	Tskel	Mink
Pakol	Deer		

THE eldest of the five Kaiutois brothers was a great man. The brothers were all good hunters; they had plenty to eat and to wear. Gäk lived near them, and when they went to hunt, he followed to find the game that ran off and died.

One day the brothers asked Gäk to go with them to visit Tskel and Tcûskai. They made deerskin moccasins to wear on the journey and told Gäk to make himself a pair out of antelope skin. They wanted to start before daylight. Gäk woke early and called the brothers.

They said: " We are up already," but they were not.

Gäk said: " That isn't true; nobody in the world can beat me in getting up."

The brothers told Gäk to walk behind them. They traveled all day, then camped. That night Gäk's medicine, slikwis (the fire-drill), woke him, and said: " Swallow me! " The youngest of the Kaiutois brothers thought: " How can Gäk swallow his fire-drill? " That minute the drill stuck in Gäk's throat and choked him.

The eldest brother said: " Whoever thought this must unthink it, then Gäk will unchoke. If he dies, people will say we killed him. Who thought about his swallowing his slikwis? "

The youngest brother said: " I thought: ' He can't swallow such a long stick,' but I don't know how to unthink it, or how to talk the slikwis out of his throat."

For a minute Kaiutois held his head in his hands — Gäk was almost dead — then he said to Gäk: " Since that is your medicine, it must come out of your throat." The drill came out right away.

Gäk's mother knew that he was choking, for the little fire-drill, that he had hung up in the smoke hole at home, fell.

The next day they got to Tskel's house. Tskel was glad to see them; he told Tcûskai not to play tricks with the Kaiutois brothers or Gäk, for they were his kin.

Tskel and Tcûskai got deer meat for their visitors and Skóŭks, Tskel's wife, cooked it. Tcûskai watched the men.

Gäk was ashamed of his moccasins; he took down Tcûskai's quiver and his own, and said: " Let's go and hunt."

Tcûskai wouldn't go; he looked at Gäk's feet, and began to bother him. Gäk tried to hide his feet, then Tcûskai asked one of the five brothers: " Why don't that old fellow sit still? "

Gäk got mad and wanted to go home. The eldest Kaiutois told him not to feel badly, but to stay; for those men were his kin.

Tskel said: " I am glad you came. My brother is so full of mischief that I can't go visiting. I hunt, but many deer get away from me and die in the woods."

" Gäk can track deer," said Kaiutois; "he always finds ours."

Tskel said: " I will go and tell him where I killed a deer yesterday; maybe he can find it."

Tcûskai wanted to go, but Tskel told him to stay at home, that they would come back as soon as they found the deer.

Gäk tracked the deer and found it among brush and fallen trees. He called to Tskel: " Here it is! "

They skinned the deer. It was as fresh as if just killed. They made a fire and cooked some of the meat, then they started for home.

Tskel asked Kaiutois if he would let Gäk stay with him a while.

Kaiutois said: " Your brother is bad; he would tease him. My brothers never meddle with him; your brother might make him mad and he would kill you."

Tcûskai ran out to meet them. He asked: " Did old Gäk find that deer? "

Tskel scolded him, told him not to talk so much.

At that time people softened deerskins by soaking them in water and then chewing them. Old man Kéwe lived near Tskel's, and he always chewed skins for him. Tskel gave Gäk the skin for finding the deer, and Kéwe chewed it for him.

The next day Kaiutois said: " We must go home now." While they were getting ready, Tcûskai stole Gäk's fire-drill. He took it to a muddy place, stuck it in the ground, and tried to break it.

Gäk fell backwards, blood came out of his mouth, and he died.

The Kaiutois brothers were scared, they didn't know what to do. They didn't know what had made Gäk die.

Tskel looked in Gäk's quiver and saw that the fire-drill was gone; then he went to look for Tcûskai. He found him at the spring, trying to catch fish with Gäk's fire-drill. Tskel caught hold of his brother, dragged him along, threw him into the house and pounded him till he killed him. Then he asked the brothers how Gäk could be brought to life. They didn't know.

Tskel said: " If Gäk comes back to life, my brother will live again; but if he stays dead, my brother will stay dead. I never taught him to treat people this way."

Tskel had red paint that was boiled; he gave it to the youngest brother and told him to paint Gäk's fire-drill over, make it nice and red. When that was done, he laid the fire-drill on Gäk's head.

After a long time, the drill brought Gäk to life; then he sang to the earth and wind, and tried to cure himself. When Tskel saw that Gäk was alive, he stepped five times over Tcûskai's body. Then Tcûskai jumped up, and said: " Oh, I've slept a long time."

The five brothers and Gäk went home, and Tskel took a deerskin to old man Kéwe, to have him chew it soft. When he came back, he said to Tcûskai: " Stay in the house. Don't go to old man Kéwe and bother him."

Tcûskai thought: "I wonder why Tskel don't want me to go to Kéwe's house." As soon as he had a chance, he slipped out and went there.

Kéwe was chewing the skin; he had all of it in his mouth except one little end. Tcûskai took hold of that end and pulled the whole skin out of the old man's mouth. At the same time he pulled out all of Kéwe's teeth but two.

Kéwe was so mad that he said: "As long as people live, deerskins will be good as far as I have chewed this one, but the end I haven't chewed will be hard and rough." And as Kéwe said, so it is. And since that time Kéwe people have but two teeth.

Tcûskai carried the skin home, and said: "I found old Kéwe eating up our deerskin; I got it away from him." Tskel was mad; he scolded Tcûskai and struck him with a stick.

When the five brothers got home, Gäk's mother was crying. She said to Gäk: "You must never go away again; I have always told you that some one would find it easy to kill you."

Old man Wus chewed deerskins for the Kaiutois brothers. One day when a skin was stretched out to dry, a coal fell on it and burned a hole. Wus was scared; he didn't know what the brothers would do.

When they came home, they found him crying. The elder brother asked: "What are you crying for?"

"A coal fell on the deerskin, and burned it."

The brothers laughed and made fun of Wus, said: "A man shouldn't cry for such a thing; you will never be of much account. You will be poor and always be hunting for something to eat. Take the skin and make moccasins for yourself."

Wus was glad to get the skin, for the brothers didn't give him much. The next day he said: "I left my mother a long time ago, I must go and see her."

The brothers gave him dried meat to carry to her, and told him to come back soon, and chew skins for them.

On the way home, Wus forgot about the Kaiutois brothers. His mother was almost starved; the dried meat didn't last long; Wus and his mother were soon poor and hungry. Wus hunted mice, but he gave only the smallest ones to his mother; sometimes he gave her only the heads.

One day, when Wus was hunting, a Pakol girl came to the house to borrow grass to make a cap.

Old woman Wus said to the house: " Grow small! "

The girl asked: " Why is the house getting small? "

The old woman said: " That is always the way it does when a stranger comes; you can creep out backwards." She made the awl over the door grow long. It stuck in the girl's head and killed her. The old woman cut up the body; then she thought: " I will pay my son for feeding me mouse heads." She took a dry old piece of an intestine and talked to it; said: " Go out there on the flat and when it is dark burn like a camp fire, and talk as if there were a lot of people sitting by a fire. When you see Wus coming, go farther and farther, draw him away as far as the great water."

The old woman cleaned up the blood, so Wus wouldn't see that anything had been killed in the house; then she cooked a piece of meat and hid it under her blanket.

When Wus came with mice his mother cooked them for him. He ate the bodies and gave her the heads. While she crunched the heads, she ate meat, too.

Wus listened; he thought that his mother was eating something besides mouse heads. Right away he jumped up and asked: " What are you eating? "

" I am eating mouse heads. How could I get anything else to eat? " Again she ate heads and meat.

Wus searched till he found the piece of cooked meat.

" Where did you get this? " asked he.

" Your uncles were here a little while ago, they have plenty of deer meat."

" Why didn't they give you more? "

" They are near here now. If you look out, you will see their camp. They couldn't go far, for they had a heavy load."

Wus looked out; he saw the fire and heard people talking. " I am going over there! " said he, and he started off on a run. When he thought he was almost there, the fire and the talking were farther off. He ran very fast, but couldn't get to the fire; it was always a little ahead of him. Each time he said: "Now I shall jump right down by it," but he never got any nearer than he was when he started.

Wus was a fast runner; from a flat, with one jump, he reached the top of a high mountain. When he wanted to run very fast, he called: "Wich! wich!" When he wanted to go slow, he said: "Hach! hach!" In one night he got near the great water. When the sun came up, he was on a high mountain. Looking down, he saw a fire, and men roasting meat and talking, and throwing knives at one another. Wus said: "Now I shall be there!" He called: "Wich! wich!" and made a running leap. He came down where he thought the camp was, but he found only sand; the fire was far off on the water. He turned back, but he was too weak to walk; he lay down on the ground, and began to cry.

Tciwididik heard him; she was his aunt. She came, pushed him with her foot, and said: "Your mother fooled you; she wanted to kill you. You shouldn't always do what people tell you to." She put Wus in her basket and took him to her house. When he was almost well, she carried him part way home. He traveled many days, camping each night. He spent the last night in Kaltsik's house.

Wus' mother had cut her hair off and covered her head with pitch; she was mourning. When she saw Wus, she screamed, she was so glad. She rubbed deer marrow on his body and cured him; he got fat. They moved to a new place where there were lots of black crickets. Sometimes Wus killed a basketful in a day, and he and his mother had plenty to eat.

WAR BETWEEN BEASTS AND BIRDS

ONCE there was a war between beasts and birds. Bat was on birds' side. In the first battle, the birds were badly beaten. As soon as Bat saw that the battle was going against them, he crept away, hid under a log, and stayed there till the fight was over.

When the animals were going home, Bat slipped in among them.

After they had gone some distance, they saw him, and asked one another: "How is this? Bat is one of the men who fought against us?"

Bat heard them, and he said: "Oh, no! I am one of you; I don't belong to the bird people. Did you ever see one of those people who had double teeth? Go and look in their mouths, and see if they have. If you find one bird with double teeth, you can say that I belong to the bird people. But I don't; I am one of your own people."

They didn't say anything more; they let Bat stay with them.

Soon after, there was another battle; in that battle birds won. As Bat's side was getting beaten, he slipped away and hid under a log. When the battle was over, and birds were going home, Bat went in among them.

When they noticed him, they said: "You are our enemy, we saw you fighting against us."

"Oh, no," said Bat, "I am one of you; I don't belong to those beasts. Did you ever see one of those people who had wings?"

They didn't say anything more; they let him stay with them.

So Bat went back and forth as long as the war lasted. At the end of the war, birds and beasts held a council to see what to do with him. At last they said to Bat: "Hereafter, you will fly around alone at night, and will never have any friends, either among those that fly, or those that walk."

WUS WANTS TO MARRY A BUTTERFLY

CHARACTERS

Djáudjau	Flying Squirrel
Wálwilégas	Butterfly
Wus	Fox

Wus and his mother lived at Wusnésee. Wus was a middle-aged man. There was a spring of water right by their house, at the foot of a high mountain. It was a nice place to live, and Wus and his mother had been there a long time.

One day Wus asked his mother: "Is there a swimming pond on any of the mountains around here?"

"Why do you want to know?" asked his mother.

"I want to go and swim."

"You are too old to go; only young men, who want to be great gamblers or doctors, go to those swimming places."

Wus had fallen in love with a Wálwilégas girl that he had seen near the spring, but his mother didn't know that.

He kept asking the old woman to tell him where the swimming ponds were, and which were the best ones. She wouldn't tell him; she always said: "It is too late for you to go to such places. You are too old. You should have gone when you were young. There are no swimming ponds near here."

"I don't care how far away they are," said Wus. "I'm going. You must send for old Djáudjau to come and make holes in my ears and nose."

"There is no use in making holes in your ears and nose," said the old woman. "You are too old to go to the swimming ponds. The earth and the mountains won't listen to what you say."

When she told old Djáudjau what her son wanted, he said: "It is too late, but let him try; maybe he can get something out of this earth. If the earth pushes him away, he will come home. But I think he is after some woman, and is trying to fool you." The old man made holes in Wus' ears and nose, and tied a deerskin blanket around him.

When Wus was ready to start, he asked: "Where are the most powerful swimming places?"

"The first swimming place is on the top of Mlaiksi, the other one is on Mlaiksi's brother," said the old man. "But I don't think you will get to either place."

"No matter how far away they are," said Wus, "I can get there."

"I don't think you will go far," said the old man. "I think you are in love with some woman. But if you go, you must do right; don't stop on the road, except at night, and don't touch anything. When you get there, you must pile stones and talk to the mountains and the earth. When I was a young man I went to all the swimming places. I talked to the mountains, to the earth, to the trees, and to the rocks. They gave me power and made me strong, but I did just what old people told me to do. If you do your own way, the earth will push you away. I wouldn't have thought of these things, but you have wakened me out of old age. These things were told to us when the world was made. After you leave here, you mustn't think of yourself. You must lose yourself. You mustn't think of what you have in your heart. I can see your heart. I know that you are trying to fool us. After you have been on the mountains and done your work, there will be time enough to get a wife. You must sing on the way and sing as you go around on the mountains; say: "My father, I have come to you; I want to be your son. I want you to give me all you can; I want you to put good thoughts in my head."

When Wus started, old Djáudjau walked behind him and called to the mountains: "Wake up! wake up! Wus is coming for you to see him and take care of him. You have ears to hear with. I want you to listen to him, and give him all that is in this world."

When Wus got to the foot of the mountain, he saw that the mountain was covered with snow. It looked so high and cold that he almost turned back. He didn't think he could live to get to the top, but he kept on walking. He camped ten nights. As he traveled, he sang the song the old man had taught him. All the way the words of old Djáudjau pushed him along. At first he didn't mean to go, he was fooling his mother. When he was near the top of the mountain, he was so weak that he fell and rolled back — that was because he was too old — but he got up and went on. At dark he was at the top; he piled up stones and talked to the mountain, to the earth, to the sky, to the clouds, to the trees, and to the rocks. Then he lay down and went to sleep.

Wus dreamed that the mountain was a white-headed old man who asked: "What are you doing here? I am the biggest of all the mountains," said he. "I shall live always. I shall never grow old or die. Is that the kind you want to be? I will give you your life because you have called me father, but you must live where the sun goes down, for other people are coming to live where you are living now."

When Wus woke up, he started for home. He had been gone a long time, and his mother thought he was lost, but old Djáudjau said: "I know where he is. He has made no mistake."

When Wus was on the way home, his mother saw a big fire on the top of the mountain. It looked as if it went way up to the sky. Wus didn't build that fire; the mountain built it to show his mother that Wus had been there. She thought he had gone off somewhere else.

When old Djáudjau knew that Wus was near home, he heated stones and sweated; then he went to meet him. He said: "If you dreamed anything bad, you must tell it; but if you dreamed of the mountain talking to you, you mustn't tell the dream. The mountain talked to me when I was young. It said that I should never die, that my spirit would live always, that I should live among the mountains — but I shall not have this form much longer."

Wus was changed. He didn't look as he did when he went away; he looked better and stronger.

The old man said: "You mustn't eat meat for ten days.

If medicines appeared to you in your dream, you mustn't eat meat for twenty days."

"I don't know about any of the medicines that travel around on this earth," said Wus.

The old man said: "After ten days 1 want you to try and get one of those nice-looking Wálwilégas girls for a wife."

When the ten days were over, Wus sweated, then Djáudjau painted his face and body red and gave him nice clothes. The old man was glad that Wus was the Mountain's son. He said: "Take your bow and arrows and shoot birds. Don't pick up the first one you shoot; don't pull the arrow out; leave the bird right there, as if you threw it away."

Wus killed a yellow-footed duck and left it on the ground; then he killed other ducks and took them home. The old man had deer meat ready and Wus ate. He was glad to eat; he hadn't eaten anything since he started to go to the mountain.

When he had eaten enough, he said: "I want to go and see people." He started out but hadn't gone far, when he saw a crowd of Wálwilégas girls; they were washing roots in the creek. He watched the girls a long time, then he said: "How beautiful those girls are. They are too small, but they are beautiful. I don't know which one I like best."

The girls were on each side of the creek; some of them saw Wus and called out: "There is Wus. He is coming here!" Others said: "No, that isn't Wus." The nicest-looking one of all the girls said: "No, that isn't Wus." Another girl said: "Yes, it is the same old Wus, but he has been on the mountains; that is why he looks differently."

Wus went to the bank of the creek and sat down among the girls. That minute all the youngest and nicest-looking girls got up and went away. One of the largest and oldest called out: "Why do you go away? Why don't you stay here and finish washing your roots?" But they had scattered and gone.

Wus was mad in his heart; he got up and started for home. On the road he came to a house and went in to see who lived there. He found Gíuwas and his wife. They were glad to see him. The woman was kind. She asked: "Have you had anything to eat?"

"No," said Wus, "I haven't been hunting. I have been down by the creek where there was a crowd of girls."

"Those are bad girls," said the woman. "They act proud, as if they thought every man must fall in love with them; they never feed anybody. How did they treat you?"

"They got up and flew off," said Wus. "Hereafter, they will travel in that way, but they will be people no longer."

All the old Wálwilégas women were crying, for their daughters were no longer people. The girls had lost their minds. They had become common butterflies.

After Wus had eaten enough, he said: "I am going now."

The woman was afraid he would turn them all to animals; she told her husband to hurry to the river where their son was fishing and tell him to get out of the way.

Wus knew their thoughts; he could hear them as if they talked aloud, and he said: "I won't hurt you or your son."

When the young man saw Wus coming he hid and Wus went by, didn't see him.

When Wus got home, his mother asked: "Did you see those nice-looking girls? Did they give you roots to eat?"

"No, they treated me meanly. They are nothing now. They have no minds."

Wus and his mother moved away from the foot of the mountain, but Djáudjau wouldn't go. He said: "I am named for the mountains and I will never leave them."

Old Djáudjau is hunting on those mountains yet. People who travel on high mountains often hear him calling his own name. Wus and his mother went to Klamath Lake, and people say that they live there now.

LOK SNEWÉDJAS

CHARACTERS

Blaiwas . . . . Eagle	Lok . . . . . Bear
Kai . . . . . . Rabbit	Snewédjas . . Married woman
Kaiutois . . . . Wolf (Gray)	Tskel . . . . Mink
Kékina . . . . . Lizard	Tusasás . . . Skunk
Kískina . . . . Beetle	

LOK SNEWÉDJAS was a woman in the daytime and a bear at night. She lived under the ground on the top of a high mountain; nobody could see her either when she was a bear, or a woman.

A big chief lived in the lava bed country between that mountain and Lake Klamath.

One day his son came home without game. The chief was mad and he scolded. The young man felt badly. His mind told him to go to the mountain and forget his troubles. As soon as he started, a great snow-storm came and the wind blew so terribly, that he could hardly walk. When he got to the foot of the mountain, he sat down under a cedar tree and waited.

Once in a while the clouds went away and it stopped snowing; he could see everywhere. Then it snowed again.

Once, when it was bright, the young man looked up and saw, on the mountain, something hanging on a pole. Lok Snewédjas made him see it. She had seen him when he was hunting and had heard him talk to himself and say he had no friends and no place to go. That made her feel sorry for him. She liked him; she wanted him to come to her.

When the young man saw the pole, he said: "I didn't know that people lived up there. I have been on this mountain many times, but I have never met anybody or seen any house.

I will go and find out who lives there." As he started, it stopped snowing; he could see everywhere.

When he got to the pole, he found a deer hide on it, and right there by the pole was something that looked like the smoke hole of a house. He stood around a while, then he went in. He found a beautiful house with nice things everywhere. On the north side of the house sat Lok Snewédjas. She was a good-looking woman; she had long black hair and bright eyes. The young man sat down on the south side of the house.

Lok Snewédjas got up, took a pinch of yĕlalwek, a sweet seed that nobody else in the world had, put it in the center of a straw plate, and set the plate down by the young man. He thought: "I wonder what I am going to do with that little bit of seed?" He took up one seed and put it in his mouth. It melted and was nice and sweet; he thought it was the best thing he had ever eaten. He kept eating, ate fast, but the same amount of seed was always on the plate. He was afraid to be in a strange house with such a powerful woman.

Lok Snewédjas knew his thoughts; she could hear them as well as if he spoke. She gave him pounded deer meat, and he thought: "Where does she get this meat?" She laughed, for she heard him think.

When the young man couldn't eat any more, he rested his elbow on the ground and put his head on his hand. Right away he was asleep. Lok Snewédjas thought: "I wonder why he is sorry that he came here;" she waited to see if he would wake up and go home. When he woke up, he reached to get a deerskin to put under his head for a pillow. Lok Snewédjas said: "I have made a bed for you, you must lie on it." He was scared, but he lay where she told him to; then she made him go to sleep. She was afraid if she went to sleep first, he would see her when she was a bear.

In the night the young man woke up. The fire was burning. He looked over to where the woman was sleeping and saw a big black bear; its mouth was open and its long teeth were sticking out. He was terribly frightened; he wanted to run away but he couldn't move.

Lok Snewédjas woke up; she knew what the young man

thought and she felt sorry. She said: " I am this kind; I am a woman in the daytime and a bear at night. I belong to the mountain. The earth is my mother, the mountain is my father. They give me my food and keep me alive. I have always seen you traveling around on the mountain. I saw your heart; I was sorry for you. You felt lonesome; you said you had no kin who cared for you. I liked you and wanted you to come and live with me."

The young man didn't speak, but he wasn't afraid any longer. Just at daylight Lok Snewédjas became a young woman; she was bright and nice to look at. She gave him water to wash his face; she stirred the water with her finger and it rose up like foam. She had everything ready to eat. She never cooked; the mountain and the earth gave her food.

When the young man wanted to track deer, Lok Snewédjas said: " Don't go far; stay near the house." Right away he saw a big deer. He killed it and carried it to Lok Snewédjas. After that she only let him hunt once in a long time. She was afraid he would go off and leave her.

" I never stayed at home; I hunted every day," said the man.

" I know that," said Snewédjas; " I saw you. You had to kill deer then, but when we have plenty to eat, it's not right to hunt. The mountain and the earth feed us."

Blaiwas, Kaiutois, Tskel, Kai, Kískina, Kékina, and all the people who lived in the young man's village, were out looking for him. They went everywhere on the mountain, but they couldn't find him. Sometimes they were walking on top of Lok Snewédjas' house, but they didn't see it.

One day the woman said: " I hear people crying. Your mother and sisters are mourning for you. Do you want to go and see them? "

" No," said the young man, " my father abused me. I don't care for him any longer. I want to stay here with you."

Lok Snewédjas was glad. She said: " If you are going to stay here, I will tell you about my father and mother. When you walk on the mountain, you are walking on my mother. Don't harm a tree, or a bush, or a leaf, or anything. Put your mind on the deer you are tracking, and don't listen to anything. When a deer leads you to the other side of the mountain, you must not touch a plant or even a leaf there. If you do, it will cut your body. On the trail you will see a little animal; then right away you will see a great many of them. If you turn your head to look at them, you will lose your mind; you will wander off on the mountain and get lost. Don't think of those animals; follow the deer. The animals are there because the mountain doesn't want you to go where they are. My father doesn't know you yet, but he knows that you are here with me."

Once, when the young man was out hunting, he heard a great noise, then he saw a deer standing on the edge of a high rock. He shot at it. The deer reached out its head. The arrow hit one of its horns and bounded back to the bow. The young man said: "Lok Snewédjas forgot to tell me about you." He didn't shoot again; he went home. When he got there, he said: "I didn't kill a deer to-day. I shot at one, but the arrow came back to the bow. The deer stood in the same place, but I didn't shoot again. I thought I knew the place well, but I never saw that kind of a deer before."

Lok Snewédjas said: "You saw it because the mountain didn't want you to kill deer where that deer was. The mountain always whoops and makes a great noise if a stranger goes there. If you had shot a second time, the mountain would have twisted your mouth and body. You must not go there again."

The young man was afraid now; he said: "My mother and sisters are lonesome; that is why they cry all the time."

"Why don't you go and see them?" asked Lok Snewédjas.

"I don't want to, but I'm going to stay in the house with you." He stayed in the house a whole year. Lok Snewédjas had a little boy. As soon as he was born, she rubbed him with red paint; after that she rubbed him three times each day; in the morning, in the middle of the day and just as the sun went down. It made the child grow fast.

One night, when the boy was crying, his father said: "I

will take him off the board and let him sleep on the mat."

"We might roll over and kill him," said the mother.

"No," said the father, "I will take care of him." And he took the baby off the board and put it on the mat with its face up against his own face. In the night he woke up and looked at the baby. It was a little bear. The father was frightened. He thought: "Maybe some time my wife or child will kill me, and eat me." He wondered if his son would be a bear when he was grown up. He was sorry that the child was like its mother.

The mother bear knew what he was thinking about; she turned over, and said: "Uh! uh!" in her sleep. The next morning she asked: "What did you think about in the night?"

"I thought how nice our boy looked when he was a bear. In the daytime he is like both of us, but in the night he is like you."

The child grew fast. Soon he was walking around. One day the woman asked: "Why don't you go and see your father and mother?"

"How can I? The boy is too little to go with me."

"He won't cry," said the woman. "When you are half-way he will forget me."

"If we go to-day, will you go with us?" asked the man.

"I will go to-morrow. I am going to look over my beads to-day," said the woman. "You can go to-day, but when evening comes don't let anybody touch our boy, and don't let him play with the children. At two different times he will turn to a bear, — in his sleep, and toward night, when he plays. There is a Tusasás in that place. In the evening he may play with the child and tease him. If he should, the boy would turn to a bear; then somebody might kill him."

"I will take care of him," said the father.

Lok Snewédjas put a handful of yĕlalwek seed in a piece of deerskin, and said: "When you get home put five deerskins on the ground; then, with three of your fingers, take five pinches of the seed and put on each one of the five skins. You will have plenty to feed your father and mother and all the people in the village, but don't let them carry any of the seed away. If they do, it will spoil this food; we can never use it again."

The man took the little boy on his back and started. As soon as he was away from the house, he forgot all that his wife had told him. When he got to the village he stood around a good while; then his youngest sister saw him and called out: "My brother has come!" She cried, she was so glad to see him. He left the little bundle of seed on top of the house and went in.

When Tusasás saw the man and child, he said: "That is just what I thought!"

The women pounded Tusasás; told him to keep still, and not make the young man feel badly.

The young man said to his sister: "Go out and get what my little boy brought."

Then he told his mother to put down five white skins. As soon as they were spread out, he put five pinches of seed on each skin, and right away the skin was covered with nice, white seed. Tusasás put a whole handful in his mouth. It increased and spread, till it came out of his ears and his eyes and his mouth. It made his stomach so big that he thought he was going to die.

The young man said: "You thought nothing of me when I was here; now you see what kind of a wife I have. She has all kinds of roots and seeds and meat, but she never digs or hunts."

When the sun was going down, the children wanted to play with the little boy. He was pretty, they liked him and tried to be nice to him, but the boy didn't want to play.

Blaiwas said: "Let the child alone. He is a little fellow; he might get hurt, and then he would cry for his mother."

The children were playing and shouting, but the child paid no attention to them. His aunt carried him around; she liked him, she wanted to keep him in her arms all the time.

The mother didn't feel happy. She knew what was happening at her father-in-law's house. She wanted her husband to take care of the child himself, as she had told him. When she heard the children whooping and running, she got frightened and started off to save her child.

The young sister began to play with the children. She put the boy down, and he ran around, too, but he began to run the way a bear runs. He slapped one child, then another. He pushed them down and drove them around. The children screamed, they thought he was a real bear.

When the mother was half-way, she began to cry. She knew harm would come to the boy before she could get to him.

There was a great noise among the children. Tusasás screamed. "People! People! A bear is eating your children!" The boy was just playing as a little bear plays. Tusasás got his bow and arrow and shot the child under the arm. That minute he was a little boy again. The father thought his sister had the child in her arms. When he heard the noise he knew what had happened. He called to the people: "That is my child! That is my child!" but he was too late; the boy was dead.

The mother came with a terrible roar. The earth trembled. When she shook herself, it was as if the earth was turning over. She tore up the ground, pulled up trees; tore big rocks from under the earth and threw them around like little stones. When she got near, she shook herself; the earth moved and the houses fell. A terrible storm of dirt and wind came with her. She was in the middle of the whirlwind. It was dark and nobody could see her.[1]

There were two orphans, a boy and girl, in the village. They were little people; they didn't grow any, but the girl was strong and she knew things. She always carried a long stick, sharp at both ends. When the people thought they were going to be killed, the girl told her grandmother to paint her stick red. Then she painted red lines across her forehead, breast, and stomach, and on the top of her arms, and went and sat down in front of where Lok Snewéjdas was coming, twisting and tearing up the earth. Lok Snewédjas turned and

[1] The relator of this story said that after telling it there would be heavy wind, for the story always brought a wind-storm.

passed on the right side. Just then the girl punched her stick into the middle of the whirlwind. The storm stopped that minute, and there on the ground lay a beautiful young woman in a dress covered with beads and porcupine quills.

The young man cried. He knew that he had killed his wife and child by not doing as she had told him to. He got Gäk's medicine basket and put it on the boy, then he stepped over him and the child came to life. But he couldn't bring Lok Snewédjas to life in that way. Everybody felt sorry. They didn't know who lived in the world that could make the woman alive again.

The young man said: " If we can bring her to life, she will never be a bear again."

Blaiwas said: " I will give nice things, deerskins, shells, and porcupine quills to anybody who will bring this woman to life."

The young man stepped over her five times, then ten times, and twenty times; she only moved a little.

Some of the people said: " There is an old woman among the rocks by the lake, Skoks is her medicine, maybe she could make the woman alive again."

They sent a man after her; when she came, she said: " I want somebody to scream for me. This woman's spirit has got near where the sun goes down; but maybe we can make it hear."

Skoks went into a man and screamed loud.

Then the old woman said: " Her spirit has turned around. It is coming back! " Soon she said: " The spirit is here! It is going into its body."

Right away the young woman stood up. She was beautiful and bright and well. When she saw the orphan girl, she said: " You don't look strong or powerful. If I hadn't had that storm with me, you couldn't have killed me."

She stayed three days at her father-in-law's house, then she went back to the mountain with her husband and child.

Before they started, the young man said to his mother and his sister: " You will never see me again. I will stay with my wife always. I don't want to kill her spirit by coming back here where I forget all she tells me."

They left and nobody ever saw them again.

The young man's friends hunted for them and got other people to help, but they could never find their home or see them.

Lok Snewédjas took back all her seeds; she didn't leave one of them, so no one has ever tasted of that kind of food.

To this day people can hear voices on that mountain. They are the voices of Lok Snewédjas and her children, but nobody ever sees them.

SNAKE TRIES TO MARRY SQUIRREL'S DAUGHTERS

CHARACTERS

Djáudjau	Flying Squirrel	Tcoóks	Crane
Gäk	Crow	Tusasás	Joker (Skunk)
Gapni	Louse	Wálwilégas	Butterfly
Juljulcus	Cricket	Wámanik	Bull Snake
Kāhkaas	Stork	Weketas	Frog (small, green)
Kai	Rabbit	Wekwek	Magpie
Káwhas	Blackbird	Wískäk	Cedar-bird
Kékina	Lizard	Wisnik	Garter Snake
Kískina	Beetle	Wûlkûtska	Marten (black)
Leméis	Thunder	Wus	Fox
Lóluk	Fire		

WÁMANIK lived at Wiwĕnsi, in a hollow between two mountains. There was a creek near the place, with lots of fish in it. Wámanik caught fish and ate them. That was the way he lived.

East of Wiwĕnsi lived a great hunter who had four children, three daughters and a son. This man and his son each had a song that they sang while they were hunting.

Wámanik was a good hunter, too. One day, he went, with two other men, to hunt deer. When he was on the south side of a mountain looking for tracks, he heard a man singing. He thought: "It must be a beautiful man who has that nice song. This is the first time I have heard any one sing on this mountain. I would like to see that man, but maybe I'd scare him." He went up a little higher; he looked around everywhere, then waited. At last he saw a young man coming along the trail with a deer on his back. He passed near where Wámanik was hidden in the grass, but Wámanik didn't see his face. He ran ahead to get where he could turn and look back at the man, but even then he couldn't see his face.

The young man thought: " I feel scared, as if somebody were looking at me. I never felt this way before."

When Wámanik got back to his party, each man had killed a deer; and they were roasting meat. They asked: " Didn't you find a deer? "

" No," said Wámanik, " I didn't see a track."

Just then the men saw Tusasás coming along with a fawn. They said: " There is the young man who always talks smart."

Tusasás came up and threw the fawn on the ground. " Here is meat," said he. " Cook it for yourselves." He felt proud.

Wámanik said: " Go home and get something cooked for us." (Wámanik was chief).

When they started for home, Wámanik asked Wisnik, one of his kin, to go with him by another trail; then he asked: " Have you ever seen, on the mountain, a young man who sings all the time he is hunting? "

" I have seen him a good many times," said Wisnik. " It is strange you have never seen him; you often travel around near where he lives. His father is old man Djáudjau. He belongs to this mountain; he has lots of power. The young man has three sisters, nice-looking girls."

" I have never seen him," said Wámanik, " but his song is nice; I like it. You must go and get those girls for me."

" They wouldn't like such a big man as you are," said Wisnik.

" I can turn to a small man, if I want to."

" Maybe they have men," said Wisnik.

" We will go and find out," said Wámanik. " I must have those girls."

" You stay at home," said Wisnik, " and I will go. Maybe you would frighten them."

Wisnik always sang as he traveled. On the road to the old man's house he sang all the time, sang loud.

When the second sister went to the spring for water, she heard some one singing, far off; when she got back to the house, she said: " Some one on the mountain is singing. I like the song: it sounds nice." The eldest sister said: " Maybe the chief of the mountain is out hunting. Wámanik always sings when he is tracking deer."

They looked toward the mountain and listened. Soon they saw Wisnik coming. He had a bow and arrows. He was playing on the bowstring and singing.

The youngest sister always worked, dug roots and helped her mother. The two older sisters were lazy; they sat around, they wouldn't work. Their hair touched the ground; they wore bead-covered dresses, and white caps made of deer fat.

When old Djáudjau saw Wisnik, he asked: "Where did you come from?"

"From home," said Wisnik.

Djáudjau could always talk with people's thoughts without their knowing it, and right away he knew why Wisnik had come. Old woman Djáudjau got the young man something to eat.

The eldest sister said: "I am hungry. I am going to get something to eat."

The second sister said: "I am hungry, too," and they started off.

Their food was the inside bark of pine trees. Their mother had told them to always begin at the bottom of the tree and work up, for if they began at the top the bark would fall, and kill them.

While the girls were gone, old woman Djáudjau said to Wisnik: "You have never been here before, and I have never seen you traveling around."

"I am on the mountains all the time," said Wisnik. "I often see you. I came here because my chief sent me. He wants to know what you think about your daughters; he wants to marry them."

Old man Djáudjau said: "My son has gone somewhere; he takes care of those girls." In his heart he was afraid of Wisnik. "My son wants to get good men for his sisters. He doesn't want them to be abused. You must stay till he comes; then he will tell you what he thinks."

At midday the young man came with a large deer on his

back. He was frightened when he saw Wisnik. Wisnik looked at him hard; he thought he was nice.

Old Djáudjau said to his son's mind: "What do you think about it? That chief over in Wiwĕnsi wants your sisters." The young man was so frightened that he didn't know what to do. The old woman went outside and cried. Everybody knew that Wámanik was a bad man when he got mad, and that he got mad easily. The young man thought: "I sha'n't live long if Wámanik marries my sisters."

Old man Djáudjau said: "I don't know how Wámanik found out about us. I am sorry he wants my daughters. It is easy for him to get mad. He kills a great many people. I don't care for myself, but I am afraid something will happen to my son."

When Djáudjau's daughters came home and saw their mother crying, they asked: "What are you crying about?"

She told them, and said: "My daughters, you must say something. Your brother never harms anybody. All he knows is how to be happy. If you don't marry Wámanik, trouble will come to us."

"Why doesn't Wámanik marry a woman of his own people, one that lives in the ground?" asked the eldest sister. "We are not of his people; we wouldn't be happy in his house." Then she began to make fun of Wisnik.

When Wisnik got home, he said: "Those girls won't marry you. They say they can't live with our people. They told me to ask you why you didn't marry a woman of your own kind. They are afraid of you; you get mad so easily."

"Those girls needn't be so proud," said Wámanik. "I was only trying them; I don't want to marry them."

The next day Wámanik and Wisnik went to hunt for deer. They killed one and stopped at the foot of the mountain to roast some of the meat. Wisnik wanted to go home, but Wámanik said: "We will camp and stay here all night."

The next morning young man Djáudjau went to hunt. He didn't kill anything; he couldn't even find a track. Wámanik and Wisnik stayed in their camp for five days. Wisnik was singing all the time, but Djáudjau didn't hear him. After five days Wámanik sent Wisnik home; he said: "You needn't come again; I am going to stay here for ten days and hunt deer."

"Why do you do that?" asked Wisnik. "Old Djáudjau said you had no home; that you made it anywhere. You had better come back with me." Wámanik wouldn't go and he wouldn't listen to anything Wisnik said.

The young man hunted deer for five days, but couldn't find even a track. Then he said to his father: "I can't call deer; they don't come when I sing. What can I do to get them?"

The old man heated rocks and had his son steam himself; then he gave him some of the sweet-smelling stuff that comes out of the corners of a deer's eyes, and said: "Swallow this; if you are going to kill a deer the smell of this stuff will come out of your mouth." No smell came from the young man's mouth, but he went to hunt. He tried to sing, but Wámanik drew his song from him; he couldn't sing any longer. He went home and lay down.

His mother asked: "What is the matter?"

"I feel as if I couldn't walk any longer. I feel as if I had to fly."

They steamed him again, and gave him sweet roots to eat. His mother said: "If deer are to come to you, the roots will smell out of your nose." She held her nose to his, but there was no odor. Then she said: "My son, I don't know how you are to be cured."

"I will try once more," said the young man. He went out to hunt, but didn't see any game. That night he dreamed that he was lying against something hard, that something heavy lay across his body and crushed him down on stones. When he told his dream, his mother cried. To hide his dream she got an old panther-skin, burned it in the fire, and rubbed his face with the ashes.

Old Djáudjau's nephew, a little bit of a man, came from the East to visit his uncle. The girls were glad to see him; their brother was off trying to find a deer. The little man asked: "How far is it to Wûlkûtska's house?"

" It is very far," said his uncle; " you must stay here to-night."

When the young man came, he was glad to see his cousin; they talked a long time. When he went to sleep, he dreamed that the little man choked him to death, and then went far off on the mountain. He thought he saw his mother and sisters crying.

The next morning, after the little man had gone, the young man asked his father to go and show him where he used to hunt when he was young. They went, but when they got to the place, they didn't find any deer.

The young man said: " I feel as if I were dead." The next morning he said to his father: " I am going away. I want you to stay at home and not to feel lonesome in the world. I shall die to-day. I feel as if somebody had tied me up and was going to kill me."

He went to Wámanik's mountain. Wámanik was singing to draw him there; he couldn't help going. When the young man got to the mountain, Wámanik began to stretch. He stretched out far from the foot of the mountain. Then he stretched around the mountain and began to crush it. The young man heard a terrible roar. Trees were breaking, and stones and rocks were cracking. A great storm of wind and stones came. The young man lay down and tried to hold to the earth. But Wámanik pressed the mountain still harder. His body looked like the sun. He kept stretching till his head was right there by the young man; then he asked: " Are you afraid? "

" No," said the young man, " I am not afraid of you. I have never done you any harm. I feel like a little child."

" I feel badly for you," said Wámanik, " but I want to punish your sisters. I want to show them what I can do when I am mad. I caught you in this way, so I could talk to you."

That night Wisnik dreamed that he saw the young man's head and Wámanik's head. He was scared. The next morning he started early and walked till he got to where Wámanik was pressing the mountain, then he said: " Now I know why you wanted to stay here. You wanted to kill this man. He is not to blame for what his sisters did." He felt sorry for the young man.

"Go home," said Wámanik. "I don't want you around here."

"One of those girls said that if you married them you would kill all of their family. You are making those words true!" said Wisnik. He was mad at Wámanik. He pretended to go home, but he went to old man Djáudjau's house. The youngest sister was crying. "When did your brother go away?" asked Wisnik.

"More than two days ago."

"Wámanik has caught him," said Wisnik. "He has him on the mountain and is crushing him. You must make up with that man, or he will kill you all. He has lots of power."

"We won't talk to him or see him," said the eldest sister.

"Then your brother will die soon. Wámanik has pressed him to the mountain for two days. He feeds him. He wishes food and drink to be in his mouth, and right away it is there. He keeps him alive to torment him as long as he can."

When the little sister heard this, she ran off to the mountain to find her brother; she was crying. When she came where he was, she said: "I want you to tell Wámanik that I will be his wife as soon as I am old enough."

"No," said her brother, "I don't want you to pay for me; I shall die soon."

Wámanik heard what they said and he didn't like it. "I won't have her," said he; "she is too young. I want your other sisters."

Wisnik listened to what Wámanik said; then he told old Djáudjau: "Your son is alive yet, but his heart is almost dead; it feels flat. Wámanik wants your daughters."

"We won't go," said the girls. "He has our brother; let him keep him. We won't change our minds." They laughed at their mother because she cried all the time.

Wisnik went back to Wámanik, and said: "No matter what you do, those girls won't have you; they hate you worse than ever."

"Go home and stay there," said Wámanik. "I know what I will do."

"You will kill that man for nothing," thought Wisnik, but he didn't say anything, he went home.

Wámanik said to the young man, "I won't take your little sister. I don't want her; I want your two older sisters, but I will let you get up and go home."

Wámanik drew himself in, loosened the young man, and let him go home; then he went home himself. The girls laughed and were glad. They thought that Wámanik hadn't much power. They didn't feel afraid of him; they talked about him and made fun of him.

Wámanik stayed at home and laughed and sang. He didn't talk about the girls, but he had made up his mind that when seed time came he would get them.

When seeds were ripe, the sisters went, each day, off toward the lake, to gather them. Then Wámanik sent Wisnik to tell Wus he wanted to see him. When the old man came, Wámanik said: "I want you to go to Djáudjau's house and get his two oldest girls for me. I don't want the little one. Tell the old man I shan't ask for those girls again."

In the evening Wus got to Djáudjau's house. The old man asked: "What do you want? Why do you come here?"

"The chief sent me to say that he must have your two daughters. If you don't send them to him, he will get mad and kill all of your children."

"I like Wámanik," said the old man. "He let my son live. I am glad, for he is all the boy I have." Then he shook the girls, and woke them up.

"Come and talk to this man," said he. "Wámanik is mad. He let your brother live, but if you don't go to him he will kill us all. You must say right away what you will do. This man won't wait long; he wants to go back. You were not made to live single, you didn't come up from the earth."

The eldest sister pushed her father away, and said: "Go off and leave us alone; we want to sleep."

The brother said: "Don't talk to them. Don't try to make them go to Wámanik, if they hate him. He is just as good as any man. He has a clean skin, and it is bright and beautiful; I like him." Then he said to Wus: "Tell Wámanik that I have done what I could for him. If he wants to kill me, he can. I am not afraid to die, but I can't make these girls go to him. If he wants them, he must come and talk to them himself."

Wus said to the girls: "You must do as I tell you; I love everybody in this world. I love you, but no one can save you from that man if you make him mad." Wus talked all night, talked nice, but the girls didn't listen to him. At daylight he went back to Wámanik.

While Wus was gone, Wámanik made two flutes with many holes in them. When he saw Wus coming, he went to meet him. He asked: "What did they say? Are they coming?"

"I wouldn't walk so slowly," said Wus, "if they had said they would come. The father and brother are willing, but those girls hate you."

"I wonder why they hate me. I can be a man. See."

He pulled off two blankets and became a nice-looking man.

"I am a man. I shall never stay old; each year I shall be young again. They will grow old and die, but I shall always be young." He stuck his flutes up in the ground and hung on them the blankets he had taken off.

Wus said in his heart: "He is awful mad. It is too bad to kill such nice-looking girls. I am sorry for them."

The girls grew sleepy; they wanted to sleep all the time. Old Djáudjau said to them: "You haven't done as your brother asked you to. Now trouble is coming to us. Go off and sleep in the bushes. Stay by yourselves."

When the girls were asleep, Wus made lots of Wámanik's kin and hung them on the bushes where the girls were sleeping. He had power and he did this by wishing hard. The eldest sister dreamed of snakes; when she woke up and saw them, she screamed.

Her brother called out: "Why don't you keep still? What do you make such a noise for? You don't let us sleep. If dreams frighten you, go off into the woods and jump around and scream. You have had your own way; now when trouble comes you must show us what you can do."

Every time the sisters fell asleep, they dreamed of snakes, and when they woke up there were snakes all around them. They were terribly scared.

The next morning the young man said to his father: "I want to go and see my cousin, Wûlkûtska. I don't want to stay where my sisters are. I don't like them any longer."

"I will go, too," said the old man. And they started.

The younger of the two sisters asked: "Where have my father and brother gone?"

"They have gone far off," said the mother. "They don't like to be here. You scream and keep them awake nights, and you won't do as they say. They know that trouble is coming."

Now from the different villages, people were moving toward the lava bed country. There was to be a great council. Word had gone out that a new people was coming, that the present people were to be turned to other things. The council was called to give the present people a chance to decide what they would be, where they would live, and which would be the nicest-looking.

Old Djáudjau and his son went to the council. Wámanik was there, and Wisnik, and Wus, and Wálwilégas and Wekwek, and Weketas, and Wískäk and Gapni, and Gäk, and Kískina and Káwhas, and Tcoóks, and Kāhkaas and Kai, and Kékina, and Lóluk, and Leméis, and Juljulcus. All the people in the world were at that council.

The two Djáudjau girls were there. Their brother wouldn't let the little sister be with them, so they wandered around alone.

The people talked about how every one would be, about who should be chosen to be the nicest-looking, and if there was any one among them powerful enough to turn to something that would never get old, that would live after they were all dead. As they looked around, they said: "Those Djáudjau sisters are nice-looking, but they are pale; they look sick."

Wûlkûtska's daughter said: "It is that man over there, the man with such a bright blanket, that makes them look that way. He is mad because they won't marry him." The different people told what they wanted to do. Lok said: "I will live in the mountains. I will raise children and have many kin."

Wískäk said: "I and my kin will be birds; we will stay a little while in one place and then go to another. We will never harm anybody."

Some said: "When we change, we will go east to where the sun comes up." Others said: "This is our country; we will stay around here." When the council was over all the people went home.

Djáudjau's daughters were scared. They felt sick, felt that Wámanik was killing them. They told their father to send word to the chief that they would go to him. The old man sent Kékina to tell Wámanik.

Wámanik laughed, and said: "Didn't I tell you that I wouldn't let them go a second time? I don't want those girls. I am going to kill them; they won't be persons much longer."

Midikdak's daughter was sorry for the sisters. She cried and said to them: "I am afraid Wámanik will kill you. He has killed people in this way before. It's his way."

When Kékina came back, he said: "Wámanik doesn't want your daughters. He says that he is going to change them; that they will be people no longer."

The girls said: "We haven't much longer to live, anyway. We don't care to stay in this world. Even Wámanik won't live always. He won't care so much for his bright skin when he comes to die. He may change his skin and look young, but he will have to die." Then they said to their father: "We are going away. We will live in the woods and have good things to eat. Wámanik will no longer be a person; he will not have good things to eat. People will abuse him, and he will live under rocks and in little stony hills."

The girls changed to flying squirrels and went toward the east. As they flew, snakes dropped from their mouths and hearts, — the snakes that Wámanik had put there. As the snakes fell out, they ran off in every direction, and that is why there are so many snakes now.

When the little girl saw her sisters turn into common djáudjaus and heard their call, she felt sorry for them. She cried, and said: "Let us go with my sisters."

The whole family turned to djáudjaus and flew away to the woods.

WON AND DÛNWA

CHARACTERS

Dûnwa	Stone Woman
Tcoóks	Crane
Wŏn	Elk

An old woman and her granddaughter lived together. When the girl was grown, the grandmother urged her to get a husband, but she didn't want one. The old woman teased till the girl got mad, struck her with a club, killed her, and said: "Now the crows can eat you!"

The girl took a basket on her back and started off. The body of the old woman called out: "You won't get there!"

The girl saw a crow carrying off a piece of her grandmother. She felt sorry; she thought: "She used to be my grandmother; now black crows are eating her."

When the girl got near the place she wanted to go to, the ground grew soft and she sank in it; the old woman made it so.

Wŏn, the husband of Dûnwa, was on the top of a high mountain. He saw the girl, and said: "She was coming fast; now she is standing still. I will go and see what the trouble is." He found that the ground had dried up and fastened the girl's legs down. He thought, "What shall I do to help her?" That minute there was a noise like a heavy clap of thunder. Wŏn said to the girl: "That is my wife. She is mad, but I am going to get you out of the ground."

He ran to a pile of bones that he had on the mountain, took a leg bone out of the pile, went back and rubbed the girl's legs with the bone; right away the dirt loosened, and she pulled her legs out.

Wŏn said: "Now you are my wife. I will have two wives. Dûnwa won't care. You must be careful what you think. If you talk right out Dûnwa won't know what you say, but what you think she will know. She is a great eater; she eats three deer at a time. I am afraid of her. In the daytime she is like a rock with big eyes, but at night she is a nice-looking woman."

Dûnwa knew that her husband and the girl were coming; she kept striking rocks and making a terrible noise. When they went into the house, the man thought: "This girl is my wife."

The rock woman knew what he thought. She was like a pounding stone, but she could move around and work. She cooked a whole deer for Wŏn and the girl.

Wŏn said aloud to the girl: "You must eat this meat or she will get mad."

The girl thought: "I can't eat so much."

Dûnwa jumped up and down and raised a terrible dust. The man said: "I told you not to think anything about this woman." They were both frightened.

When night came, Dûnwa was a woman. The three slept in the house. Just at daylight Dûnwa was a rock again. She said to Wŏn: "To-night your new wife must sleep in the bushes; I will sleep in the house."

That night Wŏn said aloud to the girl: "Will you stay around here, or shall we go off to a new place?"

The girl said: "Get ready; we will go away from here. I am afraid of Dûnwa."

The next day Dûnwa was busy eating; she didn't miss Wŏn till almost night. Then she began to track him. Wŏn and the girl had got to a big river when they heard her coming a long way off. She was mad; she made a noise like heavy thunder.

Wŏn was scared. He asked: "What can we do? If she overtakes us she will kill us. If we could cross the river, maybe we could get away."

There was a house on the other bank of the river, and near it old man Tcoóks was fishing.

Wŏn called out: "Uncle, help us across?"

Tcoóks said: "Don't you see that I have no canoe?"

The man begged so hard that at last Tcoóks lay down and stretched one of his legs across the river. When Wŏn and the girl were over, he told them to go into the house; he went back to fish.

Dûnwa came like a great stone ball; she hit rocks and trees. Sometimes she rolled along on the ground, sometimes she flew through the air. When she got to the river, she called out: "Old man, take me across!"

"I have no canoe. How can I take you across?"

"Did you see my husband?"

"I haven't seen any one."

"His tracks are here; you put him across. How did you do it?"

Dûnwa scolded and threatened till Tcoóks stretched his leg across the river. When she came down hard on it, Tcoóks said: "Be careful, I am not a canoe." He was mad; he turned his leg and shook her off. She sprang on again. He turned his leg a second time, and a second time she sprang on. The third time he shook her off she fell where the water was deep. Tcoóks drew away his leg and she was drowned.

Wŏn didn't go back to his old home; he and the girl stayed with Tcoóks.

WUS AND TSMUK'S DAUGHTER

CHARACTERS

Blaiwas . . .	Eagle	Pap	Gray Fox (a short name for fox)
Iúnika	Dusk or Twilight	Tsmuk . .	Darkness
Kaiutois . . .	Wolf	Wus . . .	Fox
Lok	Bear		

LOK and other people lived on a flat where there were wild cherry trees and plum trees. Wus was in love with Lok's daughter. When she went with the other women to get cherries, he turned into a nice-looking young man and tried to get near her. Sometimes he braided his hair and put a big feather in it, but Lok's daughter always knew him, for she could see hair between his toes, no matter how he was dressed. (Wus had toes like a man's toes, but between the toes were long hairs. He could never hide his feet.)

One day, when Wus had on a blanket and leggings covered with beads and porcupine quills, and looked like a rich young man, he tried to talk with Blaiwas' sister, but she saw his feet and knew he was Wus. When he caught hold of her, she pulled away, and said: " I know you. You are Wus."

" How do you know that I am Wus? "

" I can see the hair between your toes."

Wus was mad; he left her and went back to the mountain, to Piéamtcir, where he and his mother lived.

Wus never bothered Kaiutois' daughter, for he called Kaiutois brother. One day she said to him: " You should go away from here. The girls don't like you; they always see the hair between your toes."

That night Wus' mother said: " If you don't stay at home, you will get into trouble with the chief. He doesn't want you to bother those girls."

" I want Blaiwas' sister for a wife," said Wus.

" Don't think about her," said his mother. " Blaiwas has given her to a man who lives in the lake."

" I don't care if he has; I will have her."

His mother told him to let the girl alone, but he was so mad he wouldn't listen to her. The next morning he said: " I am going to catch Blaiwas' sister to-day. After I have caught her, I will go to Blaiwas' house. If he don't like me, he can throw me out."

His mother said: " That young man has taken her away."

" If he hasn't more power than I have, I will get her," said Wus.

When he came to the flat where the girls were picking cherries, he asked: " Where is Blaiwas' sister? "

" She has a man now," said Kaiutois' daughter. " She has gone away with him."

" Who is he? "

" He is the youngest of the five Kûlta brothers. He lives in the East, far from here."

The next day Wus told his mother he was going to travel around to see people, and he started off.

As Wus traveled, he sang his love song. One day a Kûlta girl heard him and told her father that some man was coming. " You must stay in the house," said the father. " That is Wus. He feels badly because my nephew has taken Blaiwas' sister."

Old Kûlta was fishing. He called to the fish, and said: " I want to feed that young man." Then he put his basket at the edge of the water, and said: " Come now, come into my basket! " Right away his basket was full of fish. When Wus came to the river, Kûlta said: " This is the first time you have visited me. You feel badly because my nephew has taken Blaiwas' sister away from you."

Wus was mad, but he didn't say a word.

Kûlta said: " Women have sharp eyes; they can tell if a man is smart. They don't want to marry a common man."

Wus didn't speak. He ate a few fish, washed his hands, and started off.

"Why didn't he say good-by?" asked Kûlta.

"You made him mad," said his daughter. "He never eats much; he travels all the time."

On the way home, Wus met Kaiutois' daughter, and she told him that Blaiwas' daughter had come back to see her father, and Kûlta was with her.

"Will they go home soon?" asked Wus.

"Yes, but you mustn't harm them."

"I never harm people," said Wus. "You shouldn't think that way of me."

When he got home, his mother asked: "Where have you been?"

Wus said: "I don't want you to ask me things all the time. If you bother me, I will go off and not come back."

The next day Blaiwas' sister and Kûlta started for home. The woman walked, but the man traveled in the lake. Wus watched him. Once, when Kûlta put his head up out of the water, Wus was right there.

"Oh, you scared me!" said Kûlta.

"Why should I scare you?" asked Wus. "I am a living person like yourself."

"You are in my way," said Kûlta.

"How can I be in your way? I came here to get a drink."

Kûlta went off under the water; he felt badly, felt lonesome. When the woman came to the bank, he got out of the water and walked along on dry land.

Kûlta said: "Somebody is coming." He stubbed his toe and fell; Wus made him. That minute Wus was there. His clothes were covered with beads, and he looked nice.

Kûlta was afraid; he asked: "Why do you bother me? I didn't know that you wanted this woman. I know you; you are Wus."

Wus said: "I don't want her. I never saw her before. I am not Wus. Does Wus look like me? Does he dress in beads? I never saw Wus. My house is over there where you have been."

Kûlta didn't want to talk. He started on, but Wus got ahead and walked in front of him.

Kûlta said: "You can have this woman."

When she wasn't willing to go with Wus, he said to her, "I don't want to give my life for you. You must go with him."

"He will never pay for me; why should I go with him?" asked the woman.

Kûlta had a piece of soft, white stone that he could paint with. Wus asked for half of it.

Kûlta said: "No, I can't give it to you; my father told me never to part with it. I had rather give you the woman."

"Can the paint do anything? Has your father any power? I have power, I can do anything. See, off there is where Blaiwas lives."

The woman looked, and right away she turned to a common eagle. As she flew off, Wus said: "You will no longer be a person. You will be a bird. The people to come will use your tail feathers to doctor with and to wear for an ornament." Then he said to Kûlta: "You will no longer be a person. You will be an animal that even a woman can kill. I am Wus; I can do anything."

When Wus got home, he said to his mother: "When I travel around, I hear Tsmuk's daughter singing. I am going to find out why she always sings about me. She lives off by the great water. Those people always live by the great water. I shall be gone a long time."

It took Wus a good many days to make the journey. At last he came to the top of a high mountain, and looking down, he saw Tsmuk's house. Tsmuk's daughter saw him, though she was in the house. She said: "Momáltciks (Big Eyes) is coming, — the man who is always after some girl."

Daytime was night for those people. There were people living near Tsmuk's house, and when it was growing dark, Wus saw that they were getting ready to dance. He fixed himself up, put blue shells in his hair, and put on a blanket covered with nice beads, then he went down to the flat.

When the people saw him coming, they stopped dancing and asked one another: " What strange man is that? "

Pap was there. He knew Wus; he was his cousin. Pap asked: " Why did you come here? "

" I wanted to look around; I got tired of staying at home," said Wus.

Pap said: " These people will give you one of their young women."

" I don't want one. Where is Tsmuk's house? I came to get his daughter."

" What could you do with Iúnika? " asked Pap. " You can see her only a little while just before dark. No one can see her in the night or in the daytime. That is why she doesn't get a man. I don't think you can go into Tsmuk's house. You must dance with us."

" What kind of a dance is this? " asked Wus. " Where is the hair you are dancing over? "

" This isn't that kind of a dance. We dance to stay at home and be glad." (When they had a war dance they danced over a hair out of an enemy's scalp.)

Wus danced better than Pap or any of the other men. The people liked him and wanted to give him one of their young women.

Pap said: " Iúnika won't have anything to say to you. I have listened to her, and she always sings against you. When she gets angry, she can do almost anything. She knows a great many things that we don't know."

" I know as much as she does," said Wus. " Maybe I can't take her home, but I will try. You must go with me. If we can't get into the house, we will come back."

That night Wus danced better than he had before. Pap's wife asked: " What does that young man live on? He hasn't eaten since he came here."

" I don't know," said Pap; " he travels around all the time. No matter how far away a place is, he goes there."

Toward night Wus went off to a green spot, and, looking toward the sun, he saw lots of black spiders in the air. He caught the spiders in his mouth and ate them. After he had eaten a great many, he went back to Pap's house and said to his cousin: " You promised to go with me to Tsmuk's house."

" I am afraid to go," said Pap. " They may make our eyes dark, so we can't see in the daytime. Iúnika will know you."

" If you are afraid, I will go alone," said Wus.

" No, if you go I will go, too."

It was just dark when they got to Tsmuk's house. Wus made his eyes bright and told Pap not to look at him.

" What can you do? " asked Pap.

Wus turned his body dark blue, and Pap couldn't see him. " Where are you? " he asked.

" I am right here," said Wus. " Now do you think I can do things? You can go home. I will go into the house. If I get into trouble, I will come back to you."

Wus went into Tsmuk's house and sat down by Iúnika. He was as dark as she was. When he touched her she screamed; she knew Wus was there.

Wus was scared; he ran out of the house and back to Pap's.

Pap was afraid that old man Tsmuk would blame him, so he left his wife and went home with Wus (that is why there are Paps in Oregon; there were none there till that man went home with Wus).

They didn't camp on the road; they traveled day and night.

Old woman Wus was glad to see her son. She said: " Blaiwas is angry about his sister."

" Why does he blame me? " asked Wus. " I have traveled over a great many mountains. I have not been around here. I started long ago. What does he say? "

" He says that you killed Kûlta and his wife."

" I am not going to stay here," said Wus. " I am going to travel around."

After that he and Pap wandered from place to place. The old woman stayed at home.

FROG STEALS DEER'S BABY

CHARACTERS

Blaiwas	Eagle	Tokwa	Mole
Kāhkaas	Stork	Tsiwididik	Road Runner
Kówe	Frog	Tskel	Mink
Lok	Bear	Tusasás	Joker (Skunk)
Swaiä	Deer	Wámanik	Bull Snake
Tcíkas	Wren	Wekwek	Magpie
Tcûskai	Weasel		

SWAIÄ and her husband lived at the head of Sprague River, near a flat where there were many roots. Swaiä had a baby, which she carried around strapped on a board. One day when she was digging roots, Kówe came along, and said: " Let me take care of your baby; then you can dig faster."

Swaiä's husband had told her not to let Kówe touch the baby, but Swaiä thought: " I will not go far; I can watch Kówe all the time."

Kówe took the baby on her back and sat in a spring that was right there where the mother was digging. After a while Swaiä said: " You needn't sit so long in one place; you can walk around a little."

" I never dig roots. I will stay right here. I am afraid if I move around, the baby will cry." She held the baby all day, and Swaiä dug a great many roots.

That night Swaiä's husband told her to always keep her eyes on Kówe; if she didn't they might lose their baby. Kówe might steal it.

The next day Kówe said: " You can go as far as you like. You needn't watch. If the baby cries, I will take him to you."

Kówe took such good care of the child that Swaiä began to feel easy, so she went farther and farther. Once in a while she called: " Is the baby crying? "

"No," said Kówe, "the baby is good," and she began to carry it around.

Swaiä said: "Don't go near the spring again. If the baby drank water, it might make him sick."

"I won't go there," said Kówe. "I will just carry him around till he goes to sleep."

Swaiä was off near the hill. Kówe kept going nearer the spring; she was waiting for a chance to steal the baby. At last Swaiä got so busy digging that she forgot to watch Kówe. Then Kówe ran to the spring, jumped in, went down under the water, and out of sight.

Just then Swaiä called, "Bring the baby here!" Kówe didn't answer, and Swaiä ran around calling: "Kówe! Kówe!" She nearly lost her mind; she didn't know which way she was going.

When her husband came, he said: "You must go one way, and I will go another. We will look everywhere. We will turn to common deer, so that we can look in the brush and among the rocks."

Kówe traveled a long way, going underground from one spring to another. At last she came to her own place. There were lots of people there. Kówe had three babies, but she didn't care for them; she spent all of her time taking care of the baby she had stolen. She hid the child and nobody knew that she had it till it began to walk. Then people asked one another: "Whose child is that?" When they asked Kówe, she said: "It is mine." They didn't believe her; some said: "No, that isn't your child. Look at your children. They are different; they are not like this boy. Whose child is it?"

"It is mine," said Kówe.

"No, it isn't," said one old woman. "Your children look just like you; this one is nice-looking."

"He is nice-looking because I carry him around all the time," said Kówe.

"Take up one of your own babies and carry it. Let us see if it will look like this one."

They talked till Kówe took up one of her children and carried it around on her back. When she put it down, they said: "It hasn't changed a bit. We knew that it wouldn't. This nice-looking boy is not yours; you stole him."

"I didn't carry my baby far enough; that is why it didn't change."

They made her carry it again, but it didn't change. Then they said: "We know that this boy isn't yours. If we can find his mother, we will give him back to her."

Kówe was scared, and she kept the boy out of sight as much as she could. When he began to run about and play, she said to him: "You must never play with any of the children around here. You must play with your sisters."

He thought Kówe's girls were his sisters. The girls didn't like him, for their mother was kind to him and she scolded them. When he cried she whipped them; she said that they abused him. Once, when one of the girls was angry at him, she said: "You are not our brother. Our mother isn't your mother. What makes you call her mother?"

When the boy told Kówe what his sister said, she whipped the girl and wouldn't let her play with him again.

One day, when the boy was playing near the river, he found a mud-hole and sat down by it and made balls to throw at birds. That night he said to Kówe: "If I had a bow and arrow, I could shoot birds." She gave them to him, and the next morning he went to the mud-hole and watched for birds. After a while he saw one with long legs, — a Tsiwididik; he shot at it and hit it in the leg.

"Don't shoot again!" called out Tsiwididik. "If you will take the arrow out of my leg, I will tell you a story."

Swaiä took the arrow out, then Tsiwididik said: "You think that Kówe is your mother, but she isn't; she stole you when you were a little baby. Your father and mother mourned for you and hunted everywhere for you."

The boy began to cry.

"Don't cry," said Tsiwididik. "Grow fast and get strong. You must stay with Kówe till you are a big boy. If you ever see two deer together, you mustn't kill them or shoot at them. Maybe they are your father and mother. This is all I have to tell you."

Tsiwididik flew away and the boy went home. He could hardly see, his eyes were so swollen from crying.

"What have you been crying about?" asked Kówe.

"I have lost my arrow."

"You shouldn't cry about that. I can make you all the arrows you want."

The next morning, when the boy was going off to play, Kówe said: "You must not go far, or stay long; I am lonesome when you are gone."

The boy didn't like Kówe now. He felt sorry for his father and mother; he didn't want to play. He went where the Kówe people were gambling with sticks and watched them. He grew fast. After a while men taught him to gamble; then he wanted to gamble all the time.

Kówe said: "You should stay at home. It isn't right to gamble every day."

But the boy wouldn't listen to her; he was thinking: "When I win enough, I will go away from here."

Kówe sat by and boasted: "You can't beat my son; you can't beat my son! He is the best gambler in the world!"

Soon Swaiä won all the beads and shells the people had; then he stole away in the night, left the Kówe people. While he was going along the river, he saw Tcoóks. The old man sat by the water trying to catch fish with a flint-pointed spear. Swaiä shouted to him; called him "Uncle." Just as he shouted, a big fish got away from the spear.

"You are not my nephew," said Tcoóks. He was cross, for he had lost the fish. He wouldn't talk with Swaiä; he got up and went off toward the hill.

Swaiä traveled on till he came to the edge of a village, then he turned himself into an old man, and his shells and beads into dirty old trinkets, and sat down by the trail.

Ndukis' daughter saw the old man and right away she knew he was young. She took him home and pounded seeds for him. Her sisters were angry at her for bringing such a dirty old man into the house.

He made a pillow of his pack and lay down. He looked

old and wretched. The Ndukis people were nice-looking, and each one of them had a duckskin blanket.

As soon as it was dark in Ndukis' house, the old man became young and bright and beautiful, and his bundle began to shine. The house was full of light from Swaiä and his bundle.

When the people heard that the old man had changed, that he was young and fine-looking, they came to see him. They asked him to run a race with them. Blaiwas, Tcûskai, Tskel, Lok, Wekwek, Tokwa, Wấmanik, Tcíkas, Kāhkaas, Tusasás, were at the race; everybody was there.

When Swaiä began to run, he made himself old. As the runners passed him, they laughed, and called out: " We can beat you easily! We can beat you easily! " They ran around a hill. The first time around the old man was behind. Then he became a young, fine-looking man and won the race each time. He beat Tskel, a great runner, and Lok (whose name was Kĭc — to look far off), for Swaiä could run faster than eyes could look.

Swaiä liked the Ndukis people. He stayed with them always.

HOW KALASLÁKKAS WON HIS WIFE

CHARACTERS

Blaiwas	Eagle	Kumal	Pelican
Kalaslákkas . . .		Leméis	Thunder
Kletcowas	" He Goes Fast "	Lok	Bear
Komúchass . . .	Old Age	Ndukis	Duck-hawk
Kówe	Frog	Peltoquas . . .	
Ktsítco or Nän'ih-las	Bat	Súbbas	Sun
		Tusasás	Joker (Skunk)

KLETCOWAS and his wife had a daughter and two sons. The mother loved her sons but didn't love her daughter; she abused the girl till at last she made up her mind to go and ask Blaiwas to take care of her. Blaiwas was chief of the village where Kletcowas lived. The girl was so beautiful that Blaiwas put her in a basket and put the basket under the ground.

An old woman and her grandson lived in a hut at the edge of the village. The boy's name was Kalaslákkas. He was a little fellow whose father and mother had been killed.

Blaiwas had a big house and many people lived in it; among them was Tusasás. Tusasás went often to see Kalaslákkas' grandmother, for he liked to tease the boy. One day he said to him: " If you will do as I tell you, maybe you can get that nice-looking girl that Blaiwas keeps in a basket under the ground."

" I don't like that," said the old woman. " You shouldn't say such things to my grandson." Other people scolded him for talking that way to a little boy.

Tusasás said: " The old woman needn't be so proud of her grandson; he isn't of much account."

When the grandmother told Ktsítco what Tusasás had done, he said: " Don't feel badly. If my nephew will do as

I tell him, he will get power. On a mountain in the East there is an underground swimming place. If Kalaslákkas goes there and piles up stones and swims, he will get wisdom. He will grow quickly and will get that girl for a wife."

The grandmother cried; she didn't want the boy to go, but old Ktsítco said to him: "If you do as I tell you, you will be a young man right away. Rub your body with ashes and go."

The grandmother felt badly; she thought the boy was too small to go off alone, but she rubbed his body with ashes and gave him a rabbit-skin blanket. And he started.

When Kalaslákkas got to the top of the mountain, he piled up stones; then he went down in a hole where there was water and came out in a pond that the hole led to. He swam around for a long time; then he lay on the stones. He went to sleep and dreamed that somebody said: "Look at that beautiful woman in the South; would you like her for a wife?" When he woke up, he was tall and had beautiful long hair.

As soon as he got home, his grandmother said: "If you had a dream, you mustn't tell it; keep it in your head. If it was a good dream, you must stay out of doors and not talk to any one."

The next morning his grandmother said: "Now you must go to Yomaka, a swimming pond that is always covered with thick ice. If the pond likes the person who comes to it, it will open a place for him to swim."

Kalaslákkas took his rabbit-skin blanket and started. When he was climbing the mountain, he heard men singing and gambling. He followed the sound till he came to the swimming place; then he listened and heard the singing down under the water and under the ground. That was because the pond was glad to see him. The ice melted, and there was water for swimming. When the boy went into the water, he heard a great noise, like many men shouting. That was because the pond was glad he had come. He looked down in the water, but he saw only stones.

When Kalaslákkas was through swimming, he got out of the water and lay down on the rocks. After a while he fell asleep and he dreamed that he saw a man with a long white feather standing up in his hair and heard him say: "I am the chief of gamblers!"

When Kalaslákkas told his grandmother what he had dreamed, she said: "The earth and mountains have taught you many things. You will be a strong man and a great gambler." Then she told him of another swimming place and said: "When you start from here, don't look back or look around; look straight at the mountain. If you don't feel lazy, you will get to the swimming place about dark. When you get there, sit down by the pond and listen; listen till words come to you out of the water. Somebody lives there."

When the boy got to the pond, he piled up stones and then sat down to listen. Soon he heard some one in the water say: "Why do you feel lonesome? What do you want me to give you? Don't wait for somebody to put you in; come and swim."

Kalaslákkas went into the water and began to swim around. Right away he felt something drawing him under. He went down till he came to a beautiful bright house; then he saw that a man was with him. The house was full of all kinds of bright shells. The man opened a skin door, and asked: "Do you want to see a beautiful woman?"

As Kalaslákkas looked at the woman, he felt himself going up to the top of the water again.

The man said: "When you get to the top, dive five times and then go home."

When Kalaslákkas was near his grandmother's house, he sat down to rest. She washed herself and went to meet him. She asked: "Was the earth glad to see you, and to have you walk on her? Do you think the earth is satisfied with you?"

"I think the earth is good to me," said Kalaslákkas.

"Do you want to go to another swimming place?"

"If it is right to go around more, I will go," said the boy.

"There are more places and you will get strength from them," said the old woman.

"How shall I do at the next swimming place? One day I wanted to drink some water."

"You must dive in the pond, and when you are down deep, take five big swallows of water. If you see water in any other place, you mustn't touch it."

"What if I should choke?"

"You won't choke. You must do what I tell you. This earth is my mother; she has given everything for us to eat and drink. She is your grandmother and the sun is your grandfather. You won't die if you do right. If you listen to the earth, the mountains, and the swimming places, they will teach you what to do when you are a man. They will make you strong, and you will live to be old."

When Kalaslákkas went into the pond, he felt something under him. It was a bear that lived in the water. As soon as he felt it, it was gone. He swam around for a long time, then got out of the water and lay on the rocks. Soon he heard a bird call; the bird belonged to that swimming place. It was the strongest bird in the world. Kalaslákkas fell asleep and dreamed that he heard a bear roar. The roar was like heavy thunder, and Kalaslákkas was scared. He jumped up and ran home.

His grandmother pounded seeds and white roots for him to eat; then she said: "Now you will climb that mountain in the south, and as you go down on the other side, you must pile stones till you come to a lake. If the lake doesn't like a person to swim in it, great bumps of water will come up on top, as if somebody under the water was angry. If the wind blows from the south, it is a sign that you must go in and swim." The old woman made holes in her grandson's ears and put little black sticks through them and through his nose. When he started off, she put her hand over her eyes, looked after him, and talked to the earth.

As Kalaslákkas went toward the mountain, he heard a girl singing and dancing, and he said to himself: "I didn't know that there were people on this mountain. Some one must be camping here, and that girl is dancing her maturity dance." He was afraid to go along the trail, for if she saw him it would spoil all he had done. He turned and followed another trail.

When he got to the pond, he went into the water. While

he was swimming, he heard a noise like the dragging along of a dry elk-skin. It was made by the water against a rock that looked like a man wearing an elk-skin coat. While Kalaslákkas listened, the water began to roar and roll, and there was a great noise. He was afraid, but he said: "I must do as my grandmother told me. I mustn't give up."

Then he saw a mass of long black hair floating toward him. He followed the hair till he came to a second rock standing up in the lake like a big man wearing an elk-skin coat. Then he came to a third and a fourth. The fifth was lying down in the water near the bank, and his coat was just behind him. Those were the five Peltoquas brothers who had been turned to stone by Komúchass. The fifth and youngest brother had just thrown off his coat when Komúchass overtook him.

Kalaslákkas came out of the water and lay down on a rock. He fell asleep and dreamed that a man with long black hair came to him, and said: "I was a man once; I was a strong man, nobody ever beat me at gambling." When Kalaslákkas woke up, the waves were washing over him.

The old woman steamed and bathed herself, and watched for her grandson to come. When he came, he was a young man; she hardly knew him. She gave him pounded seeds to eat and went with him to a place where she had a fire and hot stones. After he had steamed and sweated, she put red sticks in his ears and nose, and said: "This is the last time you will go to the mountains. You are working for yourself and for the earth; you must be glad to do the work," and she told him where to go.

When he started she spoke to the earth, screamed out, as if calling to somebody, said: "You know my grandchild. He walks on you every day. He wants to be strong. I am not selfish, I give my grandson to you; you must teach him." She talked to the mountains, to the trees, to the rocks, and to everything, said: "You know my grandson. He wants to learn from you."

When Kalaslákkas got to the mountain, he piled up stones till they stood around the swimming place like people. He went back and forth at work till after dark; then he sat down by the pond. He saw stars way down in the water and he thought: " People are under there with torches."

In that pond were five Kai brothers turned to rock; each rock was like a tall man. When those brothers lived they were great gamblers.

Kalaslákkas went into the water and rubbed against each one of the five rocks ; then he came out and lay down to sleep. In his dream he saw the brothers; they were dressed in buckskin. Each one had a long feather in his hair and a gambling plate in his hands. The eldest said to him: " If you want to be our brother, and be like us, we will give you what we have." He thought they threw him a long feather and a gambling plate.

Kalaslákkas woke up and went home. His grandmother made a sweat-house and heated rocks, and he bathed and sweated, then she dressed him. He was tall and beautiful; she told him he must not touch food for five days. "You must give yourself to the earth," said she. " If you do, you will live long in this world; but if you eat meat or fish now, you will die soon. You must remember Tusasás and try to be strong."

Kalaslákkas had forgotten Tusasás.

Tusasás came again to the grandmother's house, which was dirty and old in the daytime, but beautiful at night. When he saw Kalaslákkas, he said: " I wouldn't travel over the mountains and try to grow up just to get a woman! " and he laughed.

The grandmother said: " You think you can do what my grandson has done. You never can. You think you can do everything. You can do nothing but talk and boast, you will always be called Tusasás."

Old man Kletcowas and his sons used to gamble with the chief and his people. Sometimes, when gambling, Blaiwas would have the basket taken out of the ground and Kletcowas' daughter put on a gambling plate where he could see her.

Blaiwas and his people gambled with Kletcowas and his sons and old Kumal till they had nothing left, were naked. All their blankets and skins were gone, and they had only grass to wrap around themselves at night. Then Blaiwas told Ndukis to go and ask the old woman's grandson to come and gamble for him.

When Kalaslákkas' grandmother told him that his kinfolks wanted him to play for them, she said: " Your uncle is naked. He has lost everything."

Kalaslákkas thought in his heart: " Why does Blaiwas send for me now? He has never taken any notice of me. I didn't know he was my uncle."

His grandmother asked: " Why don't you speak out, not think all the time? You must tell me if you will go."

" Where is Tusasás? " asked the young man. " Why doesn't he play for Blaiwas' people? I won't go there."

The next day Blaiwas' people and old Kumal and his friends began to quarrel. The old woman fixed up her house tight, with her grandson inside; she didn't want him to see the fight. After a while they made up, stopped fighting, and began to gamble. Ndukis came to the old woman's, and said to the young man: " Your uncle has a bead shirt, made when he was a young man; he will give it to you if you will come and gamble for him."

Kalaslákkas didn't speak. His grandmother said: " You must say whether you will go or not. How do you feel? "

He didn't speak. Ndukis went back and told Blaiwas that the young man wouldn't come.

" What ails him? " asked Tusasás. " Is he proud? Does he think that he is chief? I will go and bring him here by the hair."

Blaiwas scolded Tusasás, told him to stop talking.

Ndukis said: " What is the use in sending me all the time? Kalaslákkas won't come and he won't speak to me. You chiefs speak right out and talk, but he won't. He isn't willing to talk to everybody. You must go to him."

The next day Blaiwas went to the young man and said: " My nephew, I have lost everything; will you come and play for me? "

" When I was small," said Kalaslákkas, " you never looked after me or were sorry for me. You didn't call me nephew.

It is no use for you to try and hire me now; but I will g play."

Blaiwas said to the grandmother: "Kalaslákkas is g to play for me to-morrow. Give him a nice feather and a shirt."

"No," said the young man, "my body will do as well naked as dressed. I will go as I am. But you must make an opening in the ground where the men are sitting; I won't go in by the smoke hole."

When the people saw Kalaslákkas, they began to talk and whisper and to ask one another where such a beautiful young man came from.

Tusasás said to the old woman: "Your grandson wouldn't come in at the smoke hole; he thinks that he is the biggest chief in the world, that he is made out of something nice. He has a body just like mine; he needn't be so proud."

"Keep still!" said the old woman, and she told Blaiwas that Tusasás was abusing her grandson.

"Go and help the women cook meat," said Blaiwas.

"I won't do it," said Tusasás; "I wouldn't do it if Leméis or Súbbas told me to."

"Throw him out!" cried Blaiwas.

Men took hold of Tusasás by his thick hair and pulled him out of the house. His hair was as long as he was himself. It was all of the same length; not one hair was sticking up. It was black and glossy and stood out around him.

Kalaslákkas won the first game. Kumal was frightened; he said: "Some great gambler has come; maybe we shall get beaten."

Tusasás put his mouth against a crack, and called out: "That game wasn't hard to win; I could have won it myself."

"Go and bring water for the women," screamed Blaiwas. "Keep away from here!"

The women pounded Tusasás, pulled him away and told him not to make Kalaslákkas mad.

The young man began to sing the song he had heard the gamblers sing at the swimming place. The song made every one happy. It sounded like many persons singing. It was beautiful, but nobody could learn it. Blaiwas had the girl brought on a gambling plate and put down with her face turned to the wall. When she looked over her shoulder at the gamblers, she saw Kalaslákkas and looked at him so long that her eyes ached.

Before midday he had won back half of all Blaiwas and his men had lost. When they stopped to rest, he said: "No one on either side can eat meat or fish till we are through gambling."

While the gamblers were resting, the young man went home. His grandmother said: "Take some good smelling leaves and put in your nose, so you won't smell what the women are cooking, for it isn't long since you were at the swimming places and traveling on the mountains. Every morning, while you are gambling, you must go, before the sun is up, and swim in the lake."

When they began to gamble again, Ndukis said to the chief: "You should drive Tusasás away. If he makes Kalaslákkas mad, we shall be naked again. You don't know what kind of a man he is. He has been to all the swimming places on the mountains."

They gambled all night. Kalaslákkas won every game. The next day he said to Blaiwas: "My swimming place said that just before midday you must say to me: 'Now be strong. Be like the chief of gamblers'!"

At midday the chief said: "My nephew, you must be strong; you must be like the chief of gamblers at the swimming place."

Those words frightened Kumal's people. Tusasás looked through an opening, and called out: "He can't do more than I can!" Men ran after him, drove him away, and said: "You will lose your life if you meddle with that man. His grandmother can do anything."

At dark they stopped playing. Kumal's people were naked; they had lost everything they had.

Old Kletcowas and his five sons were ashamed. The eldest said: "I don't want any one to have our nice things; we will bet our sister. If Kalaslákkas wins her, we will get everything back."

The old man said: "That is what our girls are for;" then he said to Blaiwas: "I want that young man to play for my daughter. If he wins her he can have her for a wife."

"Will you play for the girl?" asked Blaiwas.

Kalaslákkas didn't speak; he hung down his head. He was ashamed. Blaiwas asked him a second time. He didn't answer. Then Blaiwas asked for the last time: "Well, what will you do?"

"I will play for her," said the young man, "but if I win I will stop playing; I will never gamble again."

"If you win her, I shall be glad," said his grandmother. "My body is worn out; she will take care of me."

"How many games must I play to get her?" asked Kalaslákkas.

"You must win ten games from us," said old Kletcowas.

Kalaslákkas played the ten games and won the girl.

Tusasás said: "I could have won the girl long ago, if they had let me play."

"Keep still," said Dúduois, "or you will no longer be a living person."

"Let him say all he wants to," said the old woman. "This earth will punish him. This earth hears every word he says, and when a man says bad things, she throws them back to him."

The next day Tusasás was sick. He begged of Blaiwas not to let him die. "I have no power to save you," said Blaiwas.

Kalaslákkas gave old man Kletcowas and his sons all the things he had won from them, and they went home. He took the girl to his grandmother's house; she was his wife.

The next day Kalaslákkas went with Blaiwas and his people to hunt deer. "Can you call deer to the mountains?" asked Kalaslákkas.

"There is no way to call them," said Blaiwas.

"I will call them," said the young man. He tied his hair up in a bunch on the top of his head, then he whistled like an elk.

Down where the elks were they talked to one another. Kalaslákkas heard them ask: " Are any of our people gone? Somebody, our brother or sister, is calling us. We must go and see who it is."

All the elks went in a crowd toward the place where they heard the whistle; when they saw Kalaslákkas they ran off. As the last one was getting out of sight, the young man shot at him and killed the whole line; only two were left.

All night Blaiwas' people were cutting up meat. In the morning, Kalaslákkas told his wife to carry some deer meat to her father and brothers. When the youngest brother saw his sister coming with something on her back, he called out: " Our sister is coming! "

The brothers were glad, and the father said: " That is what daughters and sisters are for, to feed us from whatever family they marry into."

They got ready and went back with her. When the old man saw the meat and skins, he said: " My son-in-law is the strongest man in the world," and he began to boast.

Blaiwas' people made elk-skin coats, then they made sharp arrows to see which man could send an arrow through the skins. Soon they got mad at one another and began to fight.

Now Kalaslákkas' wife had a little boy. The father, to keep awake five days and five nights, went off to the mountains to roam around. When the grandmother came, she asked: " Is the baby a boy or a girl? "

" A boy," said the mother.

" Oh, my poor grandson," cried the old woman, " he will lose his life. For a girl, it is right to go to the mountains, but for a boy he should have stayed here. What mountain did he go to? "

" To Sláptcatcak."

" Oh, my grandson, my poor grandson," cried the old woman, " he is lost."

That night the mother shut her eyes and nodded; she thought some one said to her: " Look this way." She looked and saw men in elk-skin coats fighting, and the man who talked to her said: " This will grow and grow. Hereafter people will always fight." When she woke up, she cried: "Grandmother, I couldn't keep awake; I nodded and dreamed," and she told the dream.

"You have brought great misfortune on your people," said the old woman.

The mother couldn't help closing her eyes again. This time she saw the elk-skin coats lying piled up; their wearers were dead.

Kalaslákkas walked around the swimming place on the mountain; he piled up stones and then sat down to rest. He couldn't keep his eyes open; he fell asleep and dreamed that the great bear of the swimming place was angry with him, and said: "If your child had been a girl, you could have come here, but it is wrong to come here when a boy is born." The bear roared at him terribly, then the young man saw his grandmother there by him. The bear sprang at her and tore her to pieces.

When Kalaslákkas woke up, he knew that he had done wrong. He sat on the mountain all day, afraid to go anywhere. He thought: "My grandmother told me that whenever I dreamed of my kin it meant me." Toward dark he got up and started for home; when he got to the house, he found his wife and grandmother crying.

The grandmother said: "I am sorry that I raised you and tried to teach you our laws. It was wrong for you to go to the mountain without asking me. I have been long in this world. You will die soon unless the child dies. If he dies he will take the dream back. You must build a fire on top of the mountain and talk to the mountain, tell it everything, tell it how sorry you are. If you make a big fire in the evening and it burns bright and fast, it is a sign that your dream will soon come to pass. But if you have to work a long time to get the fire lighted, it is a sign that the drill delays the dream, and the earth wants you to live a little longer."

Kalaslákkas took his drill out of his quiver and started. At sundown he got to the top of the mountain and began to build a fire. The drill worked hard and the fire was long in kindling. Then he said to the mountain: "My mountain where I traveled when I was a boy, be good to me. Fire, you can burn up everything; I want you to burn up my dream and my wife's dream. My earth and wind, I want you to let me live a little longer." He talked to everything, talked a long time. Then he started for home. He had gone to the mountain slowly, for he was sorry to die, but he went home quickly, for he felt stronger.

Blaiwas and his people had moved away, scattered to different places. Kalaslákkas camped by a spring. "Who owns this spring?" asked he. "The one who made it," said his grandmother. "Old Kówe lives way down under the water; she is in every spring in the world. She is our grandmother. If she gets mad at anybody, she can dry up the deepest water."

"There are many roots around here," said Kalaslákkas; "we had better stay and dig them."

"I am afraid here," said the old woman. "Nobody can stop a dream. This is a dangerous place."

"What can I do?" asked the young man. "We must have something to eat." He went to a small lake, not far away, to hunt for duck eggs. He found all he could carry.

"Don't go on the south side of the lake," said his grandmother; "that is the side that Lok always comes on."

That day Kalaslákkas' wife broke her digging stick. Kalaslákkas said: "I will go to the mountain and get you another."

"You mustn't go," said his grandmother, "I will go."

But the young man went. His wife and grandmother cried: they were afraid. He went to the top of the mountain, where there were large pine trees. He cut two long sticks, then started for home. There were trees and brush on the side of the mountain. As Kalaslákkas was coming out of a clump of brush, he heard something following him. He looked and saw a great bear right there near him. He ran to a tree, caught hold of a limb, and was pulling himself up, but the bear sprang at him, pulled him down, and tore him to pieces.

When he didn't come home, the grandmother knew that the dream had come to pass. As soon as it was daylight, they tracked him to the tree where he cut the digging sticks. Not far away the old woman saw crows and she screamed: "There is where my grandson is!" They found only bones. The old woman said to the bones, "You see what this earth can do when she gets mad with us. She has large eyes, she can always see us. You didn't do as I told you."

They gathered up the bones and put them in their basket. As they went down the mountain, they built fires to let old Kletcowas know that they were in trouble.

Kalaslákkas couldn't be brought to life while his child lived. The mother wanted to have the child killed, but Blaiwas said: "He is too old to kill."

When the boy heard people talk about killing him, he laughed, and said: "Do you think my father would come to life if I died? No, he will never come to life. I will not die, but I will turn to something else, and I will live on the mountains. I killed my father and I shall kill many people. My life will last always in this world."

Right away he lost his mind and went off to the mountains. Every evening he ran around the place where his grandmother lived and called out to her, but he wouldn't go into the house.

Kalaslákkas' son is on tne mountains yet, a little person, so small that he can scarcely be seen, but he often appears to doctors. He can throw an arrow into a person's body. The arrow is so small that a man cannot see it, but it hits his life and kills him.

If Kalaslákkas' son meets a man, he turns him to a bird or a creeping thing.

THE SLOA BROTHERS

CHARACTERS

Blaiwas	Eagle	Tskel	Mink
Gäk	Crow	Wámanik	Bull Snake
Kéis	Rattlesnake	Wûlkûtska . . .	Marten
Sloä	Wildcat		

FIVE Sloä brothers and their two sisters lived together. All the brothers were married, except the youngest. That one was beautiful; he had long blue hair, and his face was white and bright. His father and mother kept him in a basket under the ground. Every night his mother brought him out, washed his face, combed his hair, and gave him nice things to eat; then put him back before his brothers and sisters were awake.

The sisters hadn't seen him since he was a little baby, but the elder sister liked him so well that she wouldn't marry anybody else. Each night she lay on the ground near the hole where his basket was. The eldest brother didn't like that. He said: " Our sister has no sense. She acts as if she were no kin of ours."

There were many people in the Sloä village. One day all those people went off to hunt deer. When they came together to roast meat, Wûlkûtska said to Blaiwas: " Why doesn't your son marry Sloä's sister? "

" My son isn't old enough yet; he hasn't much sense. She is a nice-looking girl; you should marry her yourself."

" I will try," said Wûlkûtska. He told old man Yaukûl to ask Sloä's mother if he could have her daughter.

That evening Yaukûl said to old woman Sloä: " You must be tired of keeping your daughter after she is old enough to marry. The chief's youngest brother wants her. He will give you nice things for her."

The old woman told her daughter that Yaukûl said Wûlkûtska wanted her. Her father said: " You are growing old; the chief's son is a nice-looking young man; you should marry him."

The girl was mad; she said to her mother: " If you want him in the house, you can marry him yourself; I don't want him." The girl was cross. She wanted to make everybody do as she liked.

The next morning, after the brothers had started off to hunt, and the sisters had gone to swim in the river, the father and mother took their youngest son out of the basket to bathe him and give him roots to eat.

He said: " My sister uncovers my basket and talks to me. I want you to hide me in some other place."

Out in the ocean there was a little island as big as a house; the eldest brother made a place there to keep his blue-haired brother. While he was making the place nice, he pretended to be off hunting; when it was finished, he carried his brother there and hid him under the ground. One day, when he took roots to the island, his little sister went with him to watch that her older sister didn't follow them. They went home after dark, for they didn't want their sister to see which way they came.

The elder sister spent all of her time out of doors, swimming and gathering wood. The third time the brother went to the island, he left his little sister there to take care of her brother and keep the elder sister away.

For five days the sister hunted for her brother. She hunted everywhere, — over the mountains, under the rocks, and out on the flats. Then she said: " I wonder where my little sister has gone. If I find her, maybe I will find my brother, too."

When she asked her mother, the old woman said: " Your sister is in the south, with your brother."

" Why did you stop bathing my brother and why have you carried him away? " asked the girl. " Some day I will kill you all."

When she had hunted everywhere else, she went to the island

and there she found tracks, then she knew that her brother and sister were somewhere on the island. She pulled up the tula grass and looked under each blade of it, but she couldn't find them.

When the little girl saw her sister coming straight toward the island, she took a spear of tula grass and scraped it out with her finger nail, made it like a canoe; then she put her brother in it and they went under the water, went home.

When the elder sister couldn't find them, she knew that they had seen her and had gone away. That made her mad. She said: "We will see who is the most powerful!" When she got back to dry land, she lay down, and rolled over and over on the sand, and cried "Wah-ha-ha! Wah-ha-ha!" Then she sat up on her knees and began to travel fast; all the time calling out "Wah-ha-ha." Right where she had rolled and along the trail she traveled, fire roared and blazed up to the sky. She went around the village where her father and mother lived and each minute she called: "Wah-ha-ha! Wah-ha-ha!"

The whole place began to burn. The people were terribly scared. Gäk turned to a crow and flew up to the sky; Blaiwas became an eagle; Witkatkis turned himself to a hawk and flew away. Tskel and Wámanik and Kéis and their kin went deep under the ground and were saved. All the other people, and the girl's own family, except her little sister, were burned up.

The little girl was like her sister; she was powerful, could do anything she wanted to, and she got outside the ring of fire.

The elder sister took her brothers' hearts, put them on a string and tied the string around her neck; then she swam back to the island. She was glad now.

The little sister wandered around and cried, she felt so lonesome. At last she stopped crying and began to watch her sister when she swam in the lake. The sister would call in different ways, sometimes like a duck or a water bird, sometimes like an animal, but she always looked like a woman. Once, when she had been all day swimming and dancing in the water, she went to the island and right away fell asleep. The little sister made her sleep.

Then the girl took a spear of tula grass, changed it into a canoe, and went to the island; she cut the string of hearts from her sister's neck and put it in her bosom: then she cut her sister's head off and went back to land.

The head went back to the body, and the young woman was alive again. She made a mournful noise, like an animal crying.

The little sister heard her, and said: " Cry all you want to; you can't kill me! " She took up a handful of ashes, threw them toward the island, and said: " You can never burn people up again. You will always live in the water. When the coming people taste of you, they will say: 'This meat doesn't taste good,' and they will spit it out."

The young woman heard what her sister said. She was mad; she made a motion up and down with her hands; they were turning to wings. Right away she became a large, spotted sea bird and swam off on the lake.

The little sister got dry grass from the mountain and spread it down on the ground where each house had been. In one day there were as many houses as there had been before the fire. She gathered all the bones she could find and put them in a basket of boiling water; then she said to herself: " I mustn't get up when they call me. No matter what they say, I must lie still and not answer." She rolled herself up tight in a mat and lay down.

At sunset the people began to come out of the basket. Each person went to his own house and soon the houses were full again. The five brothers came back to life. Their father was the last one to get out of the basket; he stepped on the little girl's feet, and then she got up. Her brothers and father and mother were lying by the fire. She saw smoke coming out of all the houses and knew that everybody was alive. Then she was glad, and all the people were glad.

COLTZ AND WUS

CHARACTERS

Coltz	Porcupine
Wŏn	Elk
Wus	Fox

COLTZ started to travel. On his journey he came to a deep river; he followed it up, and then followed it down, but couldn't find a crossing place. Then he sat down on the bank, and looking at the water, wondered what made it so deep. He sat there three days, then some of the Wŏn people came to the river to cross. One of them, an old man, traveled slower than the others. He waited, and when the rest had crossed, he said to Coltz: "Why do you sit there looking at the water? Why don't you cross?"

"I can't," said Coltz.

"Why don't you swim, as we do?"

"The water is deep. I feel scared."

"Get on my back," said Wŏn, "I will take you over."

"I am afraid that I would get washed off."

"Sit behind my head."

"You might turn your head around and drop me off."

"Creep into my ear."

"You might shake your head, and I would fall out."

"Take hold of my neck and hang on tight."

"I couldn't hold on long enough; I should get tired and drop off. Then I would get drowned."

"I don't want to leave you here looking at the water. It makes me feel sorry. You must come. Hurry, now, my people have left me; they are far off by this time. Creep into my mouth; I won't chew you."

Coltz crept in, then went down and sat right by Wŏn's heart.

When Wŏn got across the river, he felt sharp things sticking into his heart; he forgot that he had let Coltz creep into his mouth. The sharp things hurt worse and worse. He lay down on the ground and died.

Coltz crept out of Wŏn's mouth and went to hunt for a piece of sharp rock (obsidian) to cut up the body. As he hunted, he talked to himself, said: "I wish I could find something to skin Wŏn with. I've nothing to scrape my arrows on." He said different things, so if any one heard him, they wouldn't know what he was talking about.

Wus was near by; he heard Coltz talking and he listened. He thought: "I wonder what that old man is saying." He waited, heard Coltz say the same words again, then he said: "Hach! hach! hach!" and ran a little nearer. He heard the same words a third time, then he scratched his head and thought hard. "I believe that old man has killed an elk," said he. Then he called out: "Hach! hach! hach!" ran right up in front of Coltz, and asked: "Old man, what did you say?"

"I didn't say anything; I'm hunting for a stone to sharpen my arrows with."

Coltz was terribly scared.

"No," said Wus, "you said you had nothing to skin Wŏn with. I'll lend you my knife, if you will tell me where your elk is."

"I haven't any elk. I was just talking to myself, and making believe I had one."

"You have killed an elk. Tell me where it is, and I'll help you cut it up. You are an old man, but I am young; I will skin the elk for you."

"I haven't any elk. How could I kill a big elk? I have no bow or arrows."

"You are wise," said Wus. "You have power; you can do anything. You are a big man."

Coltz began to feel proud. At last he said: "Come and see what a big elk I have killed."

When Wus saw the elk, he said: "Now, Coltz, let's play a game. We'll run and try to jump over the elk. The one that jumps best and farthest will have him." Wus had made Coltz think he could do anything.

"How far shall we jump?" asked Coltz.

"Not far," said Wus.

Coltz said "Chi! Chi! Chi!" and ran. He jumped and fell on top of the elk. Wus tried; he hit the elk and fell back. (He was fooling Coltz.)

Wus said: "We'll try again; I'm sure you will beat."

"It is mine, anyhow," said Coltz.

Wus ran first, hit the elk, and fell back. Coltz landed on top of the elk.

"You'll beat," said Wus.

"What will you bet?" asked Coltz.

"I'll bet my knife; then the elk and knife will be yours, and you will have something to skin the elk with."

Coltz was glad. He wanted the knife. "This is the last time," said Wus. "If neither of us get over, we will divide."

Wus ran hard this time, jumped, and went over. Coltz came down on the elk. "The elk is mine!" said Wus.

"Let's try again," said Coltz. Wus jumped over six times, then he said: "I am through jumping. The elk is mine."

"Won't you give me a piece?" asked Coltz. "Give me the heart."

"Go away," said Wus. "If you make me mad, I'll kill you. This is my elk. I want it all."

"Give me a little piece of the fat," begged Coltz.

Wus drove him away, but he came back. Wus jumped on him, took a stone and pounded him till he thought he was dead. Then he divided the meat, said: "This is for my mother; this is for my children; this is for myself."

Coltz began to move. Wus jumped on him and pounded him till he was dead. He made a great pack of some of the meat, and when he was ready to put it on his back, he took off his cap (it was full of holes, like a little round sieve), put it down by the elk, and said: "My cap, if Coltz moves, shout for me." He put the load on his back and started.

Coltz moved a little. Cap called out: "He's alive! He's alive!" Wus went back, pounded Coltz, smashed him all up.

Then he said: " My cap, shout if Coltz moves! " He put the pack on and started again.

Cap called: " He's moving! He's alive! " Wus dropped his pack, ran back, and smashed Coltz up again. But he hadn't gone far when Cap called: " He's alive! "

Wus was mad. He said: " I wonder what kind of old man that is. Why can't he die? " He pounded him a long time, broke him all up, then he threw the pieces away. " He is dead now! " thought Wus, and he ran off as fast as he could, got beyond the mountain. Coltz came to life, but he didn't move for a long time: he was watching Cap.

At last he said: " I'll kill you, old Cap." He sprang at it, and before Cap could shout, he tore it to pieces, and said: " I never heard a cap talk before. This kind of person has no mind. You'll never talk again, you'll never be alive again! "

When Wus got home, he fed his children. They were glad to eat meat; they were almost starved. Then he said to his mother: " You must get up early in the morning and help me pack all the meat home. We will dry it. There will be lots to eat."

When Cap was dead, Coltz carried to the top of a high tree, all the meat Wus had left; he built a fire, and began cooking.

When Wus and his mother and children came, the meat was gone. Wus tracked Coltz to the tree; he called him " brother," and teased him to give him some of the meat. At last he said: " Brother, drop us down just a little piece. We are hungry."

" Stand in a row and shut your eyes," said Coltz. " I'll throw you a piece." When they were in a row, he threw down the backbone of the elk and killed Wus and his children and his mother.

Then Coltz said to Wus: " As long as this world stands, you will live by stealing." Wus' spirit answered: " Hereafter you will not be a person. You will never have an easy time again; you will live on grass and not kill game."

THE BAD BROTHER

CHARACTERS

Blaiwas	Eagle	Tcakonŭs	Duck (gray-headed)
Dásläts	California Lion	Tcûskai	Weasel
Djáudjau	Flying Squirrel	Tohós	Duck
Ķai	Jack Rabbit	Tskel	Mink
Kékina	Lizard	Wámanik	Bull Snake
Kúja	Rat	Wisnik	Garter Snake
Kujasûp	Rat's Mother	Wéwenkee	Whip Snake
Kówe	Frog	Wŏn	Elk
Lok	Bear	Wûlkûtska	Marten
Pakol	Deer		
Sloä	Wildcat		

A WOMAN had two children, a boy and a girl. She lived with them at Yáni.

The mother gave the boy dry red roots to eat, but she always fed the little girl fresh white roots; for herself she pounded seeds. The boy was jealous. One day, when his mother was digging roots, he said to his sister: "Let us go and play. I am lonesome here."

While they were playing, he kept saying to the little girl: "Our mother loves you better than she does me."

His sister said: "No, she doesn't; but I am little." The boy wouldn't give up; he kept saying: "Our mother loves you better than she does me."

At last the girl said: "I don't want to play any longer; I want to go back to the house."

"All right," said the boy, "but we will stay where we can see mother."

When they got to the house, he told his sister to sit where she could look out, then he began to sing: "Nénûm, nénûm!" (Up, up!) After a while he asked: "What is our mother doing?"

The girl said: "She is down by the pond digging roots and putting them in her basket."

Again the boy sang: "Nénûm, nénûm!" then he said: "Look again. What is our mother doing now?"

"She is putting the basket on her back."

"Nénûm, nénûm!" sang the boy. "Look now."

"She is starting for home."

"Nénûm, nénûm! What is she doing now?"

"Oh! the pond is coming up!" screamed the girl. "Mother's feet are in the water! Rain is coming down just where she is!"

"Nénûm, nénûm!" sang the boy. "What is she doing now?"

"The water is up to her ankles."

"Nénûm, nénûm! Look again, sister."

"The water is up to her knees; she can't walk!"

"Nénûm, nénûm! Look now."

"Oh, the water is half-way to her body!" cried the little girl.

"Nénûm, nénûm! Look out again, sister."

"The water is up to her arms."

"Nénûm, nénûm! Look now."

"Oh, it is up to her neck!" He kept singing.

"The water is rising fast now; I can only see mother's eyes!" cried the girl.

"Nénûm, nénûm! How is it now?"

"Our mother has gone down in the water; I can't see her!" cried the little girl, and she fell on the ground and screamed. She cried all day, cried herself to sleep.

The boy was singing and fixing his arrows. He was glad that his mother was dead.

The next morning, while his sister was sleeping, the boy shot an arrow into her leg. When she cried, he said: "Get up! You are a young woman now. You must go and hire somebody to sing for you, so you can dance your maturity dance. You must dance five nights without sleeping." He gave her rattles, and said: "When you get to a spring, stand there till Kówe comes for water. She will see you and take you home with her. When the five nights are over, you can come back here. I will stay on the mountains while you are gone."

The girl started; with each step she took she grew a little taller. When she got to the spring, she was a young woman. She was covered with red bark. She drank water from the spring, then stood in the low grass and waited

Soon Kówe came to get water. As she was starting away, she saw a shadow in the water and stopped to look at it. "Oh," said she, "I didn't know I was so nice! I'm glad!" She looked a long time, then turned to go away, but she came back and looked a second time. She looked a third time, then she saw a beautiful girl dressed in red. She jumped at her, caught hold of her arm, and said: "Oh, my grandchild, where did you come from?"

She wrapped her blanket around the girl, took her under her arm, and carried her home.

That night she called to Tohós and all the Kówe people to come and sing for her grandchild to dance. — She called the girl grandchild, but she was no kin to her. — When they came and began to sing, Kówe danced with the girl to show her how.

Not far from old Kówe's house there was a village where all kinds of people lived. They heard Tohós and the Kówes singing and came to see what young girl was dancing. Kówe hid the girl under her dress, wouldn't let them see her. Wámanik tried to peek at her; Kówe scolded him and drove him away. Other men came, but they couldn't see the girl. Kówe hid her under her clothes, and Tohós and the Kówes stopped singing as soon as they knew that some one was around.

The third night the Wámanik people tried hard to see the girl, but Kówe hid her in the straw of the house and put the fire out.

Kówe always knew when people were near. She heard Blaiwas as he went up high in the air and looked down. Right away the singing stopped, and the fire went out.

Tskel tried to steal up and look at the girl, but Kówe heard him and hid her. Gäk said: " I shall see that girl! " But he talked so loud that Kówe heard him as soon as he started from home. When he got to her house, nobody was singing, and it was dark all around.

The fourth night Wisnik went to Kówe's house. He went under the ground and stuck out his head near her fireplace. It was early, and the Kówes hadn't begun to sing. He saw the girl and looked at her till his eyes got dim. He couldn't look enough. When he went home, he said: " There is a beautiful girl in old Kówe's house; I have spoiled my eyes looking at her."

Kówe knew that somebody had been in her house. The girl said: " I saw a man, but I thought that you knew he was here."

That morning they held a council in Wámanik's village, to decide who should go to Kówe's house and get the girl for a wife.

Kówe knew of the council and she said to the girl: " Many men are coming here to get you for a wife. You mustn't have anything to say to the men from that village over there. They are not the kind of people for you. The Wámanik people and the Wéwenkee and Wisnik people live there. Tcûskai and Tskel and Wŏn and Wus live there, too. You don't want any of those men. Far away from here there are five brothers; each one is a chief and has great power. If they come, you mustn't look at them, unless you are willing to marry them."

That evening all the men in the village went to Kówe's house. When the first one came, the house was a little grass hut, but right away it began to grow big and nice-looking. As the people came, each man had plenty of room. The largest and most important men came first: Wŏn, Lok, Kaiutois, Blaiwas and Wámanik. The girl made fun of them all; she said to Dásläts: " I don't like you; you are too proud of your spotted blanket."

She told Tcûskai his mouth was too sharp! She laughed at Tskel, told him his eyes were jumping out of his head; to Pakol she said: " You are proud of your warm blanket." She told Lok his hands and feet were too big, and he ate too much. To Tcakonŭs she said: "You are proud of your white hair." When Wâmanik came, she said: "You are proud of your spotted blanket and your big mouth." She told Wisnik that his eyes were small and dim. When she saw Kékina, she laughed, and asked: "How could a woman like your big flat feet and rough skin?"

When the five Wûlkûtska brothers came, they stood outside. The youngest brother said: "Why should we go into this house? There is no woman there that we want." The eldest brother said: "I will go in and see her; you can stay here." When he went in, the girl looked up, but right away she looked down again. She looked at four of the brothers in the same way. The youngest brother stayed outside a good while, and when he went in he sat down near the wall, but the girl looked at him; she was glad to see him.

All the people from the village went away; then the five brothers went. The eldest went first, then the second and the third and the fourth; the youngest was the last one to go.

Kówe loosened the girl's hair, took off her red bark dress, and put on one covered with beads, then told her to follow Wûlkûtska. When the girl overtook the young man, he said: "I don't travel on the ground or under it. You should have taken some other man. We were visiting Wus; we didn't go there to get a wife. Our home is a long way off; I don't think you can go there. We travel on the tops of trees; you will have to look up all the time. You should have taken Kai or Sloä or Wâmanik."

The girl cried, and said: "I followed you because Kówe told me that I belonged to you."

The girl was beautiful. Her hair touched the ground and it was black and glossy. The young man was sorry for her. He said: "You can come if you can track us." Then the brothers sprang up and began to travel from one tree to another. The girl had to hurry; she stumbled often, for she had to look up to see which way the brothers went. When they camped, they waited a long time for her to come up. The girl followed them for ten days; she was only skin and bones. The brothers never hunted and never ate anything.

The tenth time they camped, the youngest brother said: " I feel badly. I have a nice wife, and she is starving." The elder brother said: " You shouldn't have gone to old Kówe's. You knew that the girl didn't live as we do."

The younger brother cried, but he said to his wife: " You can't follow us any longer. You are skin and bones; you will die soon. We are only half-way home. Djáudjau is our cousin; he lives near here. You must go to him; he is a great hunter, and will get you plenty to eat. He is as good-looking as I am. You will forget me."

The young man felt lonesome; he liked the girl and didn't want to leave her.

The eldest brother said: " Djáudjau's mother wears a cap made of deer fat. She is digging roots. You will see her a long way off, for her cap is white and bright. But the Kújas live around there, and maybe old woman Kúja will be out digging roots, too. She is thin, and wears an old cap. When she sees you, she will jump and be afraid; she will think you are the ugliest thing she has ever seen. But Djáudjau's mother will take hold of your hand and lead you to her house."

When the brothers started off, the youngest one was crying; he turned back and called to his wife: " You mustn't care for that man; he eats only horns. But his mother will be good to you and feed you."

When the girl looked far off she saw two houses, one was covered with deer meat, the other was made of sticks and dry grass. The first woman she saw was Kúja's mother; she walked up behind her. When the old woman saw her shadow she jumped and ran away. Then the girl saw Djáudjau's mother; she knew her by her white cap. Djáudjausûp took her by the hand and was glad to see her. She took off her cap, turned it inside out, and rubbed the girl's body with it; then she took her to the house and fed her deer marrow.

Kujasûp stood a little way off and watched; when she saw the marrow, she said: " That belongs to me! "

Kúja went to the house, and said: " That girl is for me; she didn't come here to get your son."

The old woman said: "You are a thief. You come here every night to steal our deer meat," and she drove him away.

When Djáudjau came, he lay down in the house. The girl saw that he was white and nice-looking, and had long black hair; she liked him.

Old Kujasûp began to quarrel with Djáudjau's mother; she said: "That girl must go with me; she is my son's wife."

Djáudjausûp said: "You have lived here always. Nobody ever came to see you or your son. My nephews sent this girl to us. She followed them, but they travel on the tops of trees. She couldn't live as they do, and they sent her to my son." The Kújas called the old woman names, said she didn't tell the truth, said the girl belonged to them.

Djáudjausûp got so mad she called her son and told him to kill Kúja. The young man shot Kúja in the breast, and said: "You will no longer be a person; you will be a rat, and you will be a thief, as you have always been. You will make little houses of sticks, and people will call them Stcäkaltis (stick houses)."

Kúja and his mother and all their kin became common rats and ran off to the mountains.

Not long after that, the young woman had a baby. Her husband asked her if she had a father or a mother. She told him how her brother got jealous and killed her mother. Djáudjau said: "I want to see my brother-in-law."

His mother gave them a bundle of dried deer meat and they started. When they came to the pond where her mother was drowned, the young woman cried; she felt badly. Her brother was living in the house where they had lived with their mother. He was married and had two children. When they got to the house, he was off on the mountain hunting deer.

The woman said: "He hunts all the time, but he never kills a deer; sometimes he gets a rabbit or a squirrel."

The sister put her bundle of dried meat on the ground. It got big; there was a great pile, plenty for everybody to eat. Soon the brother came; he was old and thin. He didn't say much to his sister or his brother-in-law.

The next morning Djáudjau went to hunt deer. The brother

asked: “ Why does he go? He won’t kill a deer. I am a good hunter, but I never find a deer.”

That evening Djáudjau came home with ten deer in his belt. He carried them as other men carried rabbits. The brother looked mad. He didn’t like his brother in-law.

The sister said to Djáudjau: “ We must go home. I want to start now. My brother doesn’t like you: I am afraid to stay here.”

They started in the night, and early the next morning they came to a swimming place on top of a high mountain. Djáudjau got some green twigs, rubbed himself all over with them, then he rubbed the twigs on the ground, and said: “ I have been to see my bad brother-in-law; I have brought away some of his bad thoughts. Now, earth, take them all.” Then he swam in the pond and talked to the mountain. The mountain talked to him like a living person, and he forgot his brother-in-law.

When they got home, the five Wûlkûtska brothers were there. They all claimed the child.

Old woman Djáudjau said: “ It isn’t right for you to take my daughter-in-law’s child away from her.”

The young woman said: “ You didn’t care for me. You thought you were better than I was, because you could travel on trees and I had to travel on the ground. Now you want my baby. Hereafter you will travel slow, and it will make you sweat; you will no longer be persons.”

The brothers said: “ Hereafter you and your husband and his kin will be Djáudjaus and roam around in the mountains.”

And so it was.

KOWAM AND GAHGA

CHARACTERS

Gáhga . . . . Heron
Kówam . . . . Red-billed Duck
Lok . . . . Bear

KÓWAM and his little brother lived on the south side of Klamath Lake. The little boy's name was Gáhga.

Kówam had a nice-looking wife, and when he went to fish in the lake, he always told her that if any one came to bother her she must send Gáhga to tell him.

One morning, when Kówam had gone to the lake, and his old mother-in-law was out gathering wood, Kówam's wife sat down by the fire and began to make a reed basket for Kówam to put fish in. After a while the old woman ran in and cried: " The big-footed people are coming! "

Soon the five Lok brothers came in and sat down by the fire. The eldest brother put his head on the young woman's lap.

Gágha began to cry, and Lok said: " Why do you cry, little boy? Are you sorry for me because I haven't a wife? This woman is my wife."

Gágha kept crying. At midday his eyes were so swollen that he could hardly open them. " Stop crying," said his sister-in-law. " Go and find your brother and tell him that the big-footed men are here. Maybe nothing has happened, and he doesn't know there is trouble at home."

Gágha cried all the time he was going to the lake. When he found his brother Kówam asked: " What's the matter? What makes you cry? Did you hurt yourself? "

" No," said Gágha, " five of the big-footed people from the north side of the lake are in our house, and one of them has his head on my sister-in-law's knees."

"Is she crying?" asked Kówam.

"No, but I've cried all the time, I'm so sorry they have taken my sister-in-law away from me."

"If she isn't crying, she doesn't care for us, and there is no use in crying. If they had made her cry, I should kill those men."

Kówam sat still a long time; he was thinking what he could do. Then he said to Gágha: "Stop crying and get some wood; we will cook fish to eat. You must hurry, so we can go home before it's dark."

Little Gágha could hardly stand; he had cried so long that he was dizzy.

Kówam said: "Don't cry any longer. I know what I will do to those big-footed people."

They built a fire and cooked fish. Gágha's tears were dropping all the time he was eating.

"Stop crying and finish eating!" said his brother. "Whenever a man has a nice wife he is bothered. It will always be that way."

Kówam filled an old basket with fish, picked it up, put it on his back, and said: "Now we will go home."

"How can we go home while those big-footed people are there?" asked Gágha. He was crying again.

"I am not afraid of those men," said Kówam. "That is my house; I will drive them out of it or I will kill them."

When they were part of the way home, Kówam said: "Little brother, take my bow and arrow and shoot me in the heart."

"How can I do that? You are my brother."

"It won't hurt me. I want you to practise shooting."

"You are my own brother, all the one I have. I won't do it," said Gágha.

"You must," said Kówam. "It won't hurt me."

"It will kill you; then I shall be all alone," said Gágha.

Kówam talked a long time, asked in every way, but Gágha always said: "You are my brother; I won't kill you." At last Kówam said: "If you don't shoot me and make me strong, I will let the big-footed people have your sister-in-law; I won't try to kill them. You can't kill me. Nobody can kill me; I shall live always."

At last Gáhga took the bow and arrow and shot Kówam in the heart, killed him; then he ran, for he felt scared. Right away Kówam overtook him, and said: "Now shoot me in the heart and tear my body to pieces." Gáhga did as Kówam told him to and then ran away. Again Kówam overtook him. That time he said: "Kill me and pound my body to pieces; then mix the pieces with dirt and stones." Gáhga did as he was told. Soon his brother caught up with him, and said: "Kill me, then pound my body up and throw the pieces away." Gágha did that, and went on; he didn't run that time, he just walked; he didn't feel scared any longer. Kówam came up behind him, and said: "Now, little brother, try again. Kill me, then build a big fire and burn up my body and let the wind carry the ashes away." Gáhga did that. His brother overtook him again.

"What kind of a man are you?" asked Gáhga. "Is there any way to kill you?"

"I wasn't made to die," said Gáhga, "I shall live always. Now kill me and cut off my feet and hands and carry them away. Hold them tight."

Gáhga shot Kówam in the heart, cut off his hands and feet, held them tight in his own hands, and traveled on, went fast. Right away his brother called to him. Gáhga's hands were shut, but the feet and hands that he had been carrying were gone, and Kówam was by his side. Then he cut Kówam's head off and threw it away. At once the head and body came together.

The brothers were almost home now and Kówam said: "You must take my bow and quiver and wait on top of the house; I will go in alone. Don't be scared when they throw me out; they can't hurt me."

Kówam went in, pulled Lok's head off from the woman's knees, and threw him out of the house. Lok came in, caught Kówam, killed him, and threw the pieces on the fire.

Right away Kówam had Lok by the throat. He choked him and threw him out.

When Kówam was killed and thrown out, his mother-in-law screamed: "I am glad you are dead, old Black Legs!" When Lok was thrown out, she screamed, "Now you are killed, old Big Feet, my son-in-law is a great man!"

The fight lasted all night. Just as daylight came, Lok tore Kówam's head off; he kicked the body out and held tight to the head. That moment Kówam said to his brother: "Now I am ready to fight. I was just waiting for another sun to come up."

He took his bow and arrows and shot at the Loks through the smoke hole, and killed them all. Then he covered the house with dry grass, piled up wood around it, and set it on fire.

Gáhga screamed and cried; he wanted his sister-in-law saved. Kówam wouldn't listen to him and wouldn't let his wife out. Then Gáhga got mad at his brother, and said: "Hereafter you won't have a person for a wife. You will be an animal. People will call you by different names, and you will always live in the woods and make a great noise talking."

Kówam said: "Punch a stick in where your sister-in-law was sitting." She was dead, but a voice spoke out of the fire and said to Kówam: "You will always stick your bill up in the sun and look off on the water. And you, my little boy, will be like your brother." — Ningádaniak.

MINK AND WEASEL

CHARACTERS

Blaiwas	Eagle	Lok	Bear
Gäk	Crow	Moi	Squirrel
Gapni	Louse	Nänı́hläs	Bat
Kāhkaas	Stork	Skóŭks	Woodtick
Kaiutois	Wolf	Súbbas	Sun
Kaltsik	Spider	Sukas	
Kéis	Rattlesnake	Tcûskai	Weasel
Kékina	Lizard	Tskel	Mink
Kówe	Frog	Tusasás	Skunk
Kûlta	Otter	Wŏn	Elk
Leméis	Thunder		

Two brothers, Tskel and Tcûskai, lived together not far from Klamath Lake. Tskel's wife was Skóŭks. Tcûskai was a little fellow. One day when Skóŭks was outside cooking deer meat and was blowing the fire to make it burn, she saw Tcûskai watching her; that made her mad and she threw the meat into the fire. Tskel hit Tcûskai and told him to stay in the house when Skóŭks was cooking; then he said to Skóŭks: "Cook more meat; Tcûskai and I are going to the mountain to hunt for deer. If I kill a big deer, we will camp and stay all night." Tskel never killed a deer; no matter how many he saw, he always let them get away.

When they got to the mountain, they saw a large deer; Tcûskai killed it, and they camped in sight of a big hole between the rocks. Tskel wouldn't camp very near the hole, for he was afraid his brother would go into it and get hurt. Tcûskai would go anywhere, he wasn't afraid of anything.

Tskel cut up the deer; then he and Tcûskai lay down, one on each side of the fire. As soon as Tcûskai was asleep, Gopher came and ran across him, just to tease him. Tcûskai woke up and called his brother: " Come here! Come and see this little fellow! I will give him a piece of our meat, and we will catch him."

Tskel didn't move; he was asleep. Tcûskai gave Gopher a small piece of meat. He took it and ran off to the rocks, then came back for more, carried that off and came back again. Each time he came Tcûskai gave him a larger piece. At last all the deer meat was gone; then Tcûskai went to Tskel, shook him, and said: " Get up! Get up! This little fellow has carried off all of our meat."

Tskel didn't move or say a word. Tcûskai gave Gopher all the roots Tskel had brought from home; then he took off Tskel's belt and gave it to him. Gopher carried it under the rocks. He gave him Tskel's deerskin cap and his rabbit-skin blanket.

In the morning when Tskel woke up, the north wind was blowing and he was almost frozen. He asked Tcûskai where the blanket was. Tcûskai said: " Gopher took it."

" Then you gave it to him," said Tskel; " Gopher couldn't unwrap me."

Tcûskai began to feel cold; he wanted to get into Tskel's ear, but Tskel was mad, and threw him out. Then he tried to get under Tskel's arm, but Tskel pushed him away and sat with his arms folded across his breast, for he had no blanket and he was cold.

" Why are you so mad? " asked Tcûskai. " I will get those things back; they are over there under the rocks."

It was near daylight; Tcûskai was freezing to death. Tskel made a fire and told him to lie down near it and get warm. Then he made himself a bark blanket. When Tcûskai was warm, his brother said: " Now you must get back the things you gave to Gopher."

Tcûskai ran to the rock and looked into the hole; he thought it was awful deep, but he ran back, and said: " The hole isn't deep; we can build a fire and drive Gopher out."

" I want my blanket," said Tskel; " maybe you can crawl in and get it."

The mountain was Gopher's house. The rocks were only

the roof of it. Tcûskai saw his brother's belt, but he was afraid to go and get it. Tskel said: " Make a fire and blow the smoke into the hole. How long can you fan the fire without getting tired? "

" I can fan it till Gopher comes out," said Tcûskai.

" But there are many holes," said his brother. " You will have lots of trouble. Do you think you can fill the holes with stones? "

" I can fill them quickly," said Tskel. He ran around, threw stones into the holes, then came back and blew the fire. But the smoke came out through other holes, and Tskel said: " Go and stop up every hole you can find."

Tskel, to make Tcûskai sorry for what he had done, hid all the water in a hole where he couldn't find it. Little Tcûskai got very thirsty. He ran from one spring to another but couldn't find water; then he knew that his brother had hidden it and he said: " I want some water."

" You can't have any until you have killed Gopher," said Tskel. " When he is dead, I will give you some."

Tcûskai filled all the little holes and fanned smoke into the big hole. At midday he said to his brother: " I am stronger than you are; you never could have filled all these holes." He went again to hunt for water. At last he found the place where Tskel had hidden it; then he drank and drank, drank nearly all the water there was in the hole.

Tskel wondered why Tcûskai didn't come back. At last he thought: " Maybe he has found the water; I will go and see." Tcûskai was still drinking, and only a little water was left. If Tskel hadn't thought of the water and gone to look for his brother, he would have drunk it all and there would have been no water in the world.

Tskel caught hold of Tcûskai and threw him against the rocks so hard that he killed him; then he scattered the water. There was only a little left, but it spread fast, spread until there were rivers and lakes. Then Tskel went to his brother, took off the string of rattles he wore around his neck, and struck him five times with it. Tcûskai came to life. Tskel said: " The holes are stopped up; now I will help you kill Gopher.

He is terrible to look at when he is mad. You must keep your eyes closed; if you see him, you will die."

Tskel had two stone knives. He gave one to Tcûskai, then he built a fire and blew the smoke into the big hole. Tcûskai listened; there was a noise of some one moving around in the hole. He was so scared that he died. Tskel brought him to life, and said: "You mustn't get scared. That was only a young Gopher; old Gopher hasn't moved yet."

Tskel blew more smoke into the hole. There was a roar as though the mountain was going to burst open. Tcûskai died again. Tskel brought him to life, and said: "You have played with these people and made all this trouble; now you must stay here till it is over. Don't get scared every time you hear a noise."

Just then old Gopher moved and the earth shook. Tcûskai was dreadfully frightened. (He was on one side of the hole and Tskel was on the other.) There was a shaking and roar, then a great, red, fiery head came out of the hole. Tskel cut the head off with his long knife, skinned it, and made a cap of the skin; then he buried the head under great flat rocks. Right away the rocks were as red as blood. (They are red to this day.)

Tskel said to Gopher: "Hereafter you will be of no account. You will dig in the ground and people will make fun of you."

If Tskel hadn't killed Gopher, there would be no one living in the world now.

In the hole where Gopher was it is always hot, no matter how cold it is outside. Gopher's body, turned to stone, is still in the hole.

After Tskel killed Gopher, he and Tcûskai went home, but Tskel didn't want to stay there. He thought about his cousin, Kaiutois. One day he said to Skóŭks: "I am going to see my cousin," and he sent Tcûskai to ask Gäk if he would go with them. Gäk was willing and the three started off. As they traveled, people told them they mustn't go near the Leméis family, that they were killing everybody, that each day they carried off men to eat. Tskel said: "I am traveling around the world to see people; I'm not afraid of Leméis."

When they got near Leméis' house, Tskel put on his gopher-skin cap and put little Tcûskai under his arm, where he couldn't do any mischief. Then he gave Gäk a sharp bone, and said: "When they give you dead men's meat to eat, make a hole in your throat and let it out; don't swallow it."

The five Kaiutois brothers and old man Leméis with his wife and five boys lived in one house. The five Kaiutois lived on one side of the house and old Leméis on the other. When Tskel went to the house, the Kaiutois brothers and Leméis boys were off hunting for deer.

Old Leméis and his wife saw Tskel's gopher-skin cap and they were so scared that they ran out of the house. They built a fire and began cooking; they were afraid to go inside. The wives and children of the Kaiutois brothers were frightened, too.

Tskel sat in the house with his head down. Tcûskai teased him to let him put the cap on and run out and scare the old man, but Tskel pinched him and told him to keep still where he was, under his arm. Gäk was lying on the ground and looking at Tskel.

Soon old Leméis' eldest son came home. When he saw his father and mother outside, he asked: "What are you doing out here?"

The old man said: "There is something strange in our house. We can't stay there. We have never seen anything like it before. It is terrible!"

"What is there stronger than I am?" asked the son. "I have been off killing men. I am not afraid of this thing."

"You haven't seen it," said old Leméis. "You can't go into the house."

The young man went to the house. He took one step down the ladder, saw Tskel's cap, and turned back, screaming so loud that the ground shook. He said to his father, "There is something there stronger than I am; I can't go in."

The second brother came home. He saw his father outside and asked: "Why are you out here?"

"There is something in our house stronger than we are. We can't go in," said the father.

The young man laughed, and asked: "What is there stronger than I am? There is nothing I can't kill." He was down two steps of the ladder when he saw the cap; he screamed and ran out.

One after another the five brothers came home. Each brother got one step farther into the house; each one screamed and ran out. The fourth brother said: "I am stronger than anybody. If this man had ever heard of me, he wouldn't have come here." He took four steps into the house, roared with fright, and ran away. The fifth brother was the strongest of all the brothers. There were five steps down into the house; he was on the last step when he saw Tskel's cap. He roared and with one step was out.

The five Kaiutois brothers came home just at sundown. When Tskel saw them, he looked up and they knew him. He took off his cap, put it behind him, and they all went in. Then they called their wives, and asked: "Why didn't you cook for this man? He is hungry. Come in and cook deer meat for him."

Tskel said: "Tell Leméis and his sons to come in. It is cold outside." They were glad; they went in, and right away they began to cook dead men.

Kaiutois' meat was done first, and Gäk and Tskel ate deer meat. Little Tcûskai said: "Let me down, brother; I want to eat. I am hungry." Tcûskai pinched him and told him to keep still, but Tcûskai said: "I can't, you don't give me enough to eat"

When Leméis' meat was done, the eldest son gave some of it to Gäk. Gäk put it in his mouth, but it came out of the hole in his throat and dropped on the ground.

Tskel put some strong sticks in Gäk's arms, for he knew that the Leméis brothers would try to kill him. They sat down by the fire and asked Gäk to come and sit near them. Then they said to one another: "Let's twist arms," and the eldest brother said: "Come and play with us, Gäk."

Gäk said: "I never play that way." After they had teased him a long time, Tskel said: "Play with them; I won't let them hurt you."

The eldest brother took hold of Gäk, twisted his arm hard, but couldn't break it; it was soft. " Stiffen your arm," said Leméis. Gäk stiffened his arm, but Leméis couldn't break it. Then Gäk took hold of Leméis' arm, twisted it hard, and broke it. Leméis ran out of the house and died.

The second brother was ashamed. He said: " That is the way my brother always does. If he gets beaten, he runs away. Try me." He twisted Gäk's arm, but no matter how he twisted he couldn't break it. Then Gäk twisted his arm and broke it, and he ran outside and died.

Gäk killed four of the brothers; then the youngest and strongest wanted to try. Gäk didn't want to twist arms with him, but Tskel said: " Don't be afraid, he can't kill you." Gäk held out his arm and Leméis twisted it terribly. Gäk screamed; he couldn't help it, it hurt so.

Then Tskel said to Leméis: " Let me twist your arm." He took hold of Leméis' hand with a tight grip and broke every bone in it; then he twisted his arm and broke it.

When all five of the old man's sons were dead, Tskel said: " Hereafter you will be of no use in this world. You will be persons no longer. You will go up to the sky and all you will do there will be to frighten people by making a big noise."

He told the five Kaiutois brothers not to live in the house with old Leméis and his wife. " Their house is dirty," said he. " It smells of dead people. The juice of dead people runs on to your meat; you have the taste of it now, and in after times you will try to kill people."

The Kaiutois brothers moved away. Old Leméis and his wife felt badly; they were lonesome for their children. Tskel said: " You can go to your sons; you are of no use in this world," and he sent them to the sky

Now Tskel and Tcûskai went home. Skóūks was mourning; she thought they were dead.

The next day Tskel went to hunt. He killed five deer and was home at midday. He was dry and he sent his brother to bring him some water. Tcûskai ran to the spring, and there, sitting in the spring, was an old, white-haired man.

" What are you here for? " asked Tcûskai. " We don't

want old men in our spring. My brother is dry. I am after water for him. Get out of our spring!" He told him two or three times to get out. The old man didn't move, but at last he said: "Go and tell your brother to come and wrestle with me." Tcûskai ran back to the house.

"Why didn't you bring me some water?" asked Tskel.

"There is an old man sitting in the spring," said Tcûskai. "He won't let me get a drop of water."

"Go back and get me some water!" said Tskel.

Tcûskai went back and screamed: "Get out of there, old man! You are all dirt; you'll spoil our water!"

The old man didn't move, but he said: "Tell your brother to come and wrestle with me. I hear that he has killed all the Leméis people. I am their kin. I have come to wrestle with him."

Tcûskai said: "Let my brother have some water to drink; then he will come."

The old man turned around and let Tcûskai take a little water out of the spring. Tcûskai carried it to his brother, and said: "That old man has come to fight you for killing the Leméis people. He wants you to come to the spring and wrestle with him."

Tskel drank the water and ate pounded seed. Then he went to the spring and wrestled with the old man. They wrestled till dark, then the old man threw Tskel, rolled him up in a skin blanket, took his own form, — an animal with great horns, — put Tskel on his horns, and carried him down in the water and off under the ground. He carried him a long distance, then came out near a large lake. He took Tskel off his horns, unrolled him, and said: "Look around, before I kill you."

Tskel saw that they were on a narrow ridge of rock that ran, like a little trail, to the middle of the lake.

The old man said: "When I get to the end of this trail, I will cut you into small pieces and throw you to my children. They are hungry for your flesh. As I throw the pieces, I will say: 'Here is a piece of Tskel. Eat it.' They will be glad, and all my kin will be glad that you are dead."

When he was through talking, he rolled Tskel up again, put him on his horns, and started. Tskel moved a little.

"What are you doing?" asked the old man.

"I am scratching myself."

"You needn't scratch; you will die soon."

"I itch; I can scratch while I live," said Tskel. He moved again.

"What are you doing now?" asked the old man.

"I don't lie easy."

"Why bother about that? you will die soon."

"I don't want to suffer while I live," said Tskel. He was getting his stone knife out. It was tied up in his hair and the old man hadn't seen it. With the knife Tskel cut holes in the skin blanket for his eyes and his hands, and just as he got to the end of the trail, he stuck the knife into the old man and killed him. Then he cut the body up and threw it piece by piece into the lake. As he threw the pieces, he called out: "Here is Tskel's shoulder! Here are Tskel's ribs! Here are his legs! Here are his arms!" As fast as he threw the pieces, the old man's children caught and ate them. At last he threw the head. It was an awful-looking thing, enough to scare any one.

When the children saw it and knew that they had eaten their father, they were so mad that they sent everything they had to find Tskel and kill him. They sent what they thought he would like, — knives, hatchets, beads, shells, blankets — to lie in his path. If he took up any one of them, he would die.

Tskel passed them all till he came to the last, a stone knife sharp on both edges, that looked so nice that he picked it up. Right away the ends of his fingers were burned off. He dropped the knife, rubbed his fingers with his own stone knife, and they were well again. Then he went on till he reached home. Skóŭks and little Tcûskai had covered their hair with deer fat and pounded coal; they were mourning for him.

When Tskel saw Tcûskai, he asked: "What are you doing? Why are you so dirty?"

Tcûskai said: "I was just going to look for you."

Skóŭks said: "He should be whipped for telling lies. He

has been everywhere in the world hunting for you. Just now he came home and put coal on his head, for when he couldn't find you he thought you were dead."

Tskel was chief in the Klamath country. He was the strongest person living. No other man could have killed the old man of the lake.

Now Tskel stayed at home for a long time. He killed deer and dried the meat and told his brother many things about the people in the world.

One day when he was out hunting, he heard somebody singing a beautiful song; he listened and wondered who it was. Then he followed the sound. It drew him along till he came to a big cedar tree. A woman was sitting on a bough of the tree and throwing cedar berries on to a blanket spread under the tree. When she saw Tskel, she called out: "Come and sit on the blanket!" He knew she was the old man's daughter, and he wouldn't go near her; he went home.

The next day he heard the song again, but he didn't follow it. He went home and told Skóŭks that the old man's daughter had come to kill him. He didn't hunt again. One day the woman came and sat in a clump of bushes near Tskel's house and told the crows to fly over her. Little Tcûskai saw the crows and said to his brother: "The crows are eating something. You had better go and see what it is."

"Don't go near that place," said Tskel.

Tcûskai thought: "Why does my brother tell me not to go to those bushes? I am going." He went around the house, out of Tskel's sight, and crept toward the bushes. He found a woman sitting on a low stump; as he went up to her she spat out beautiful beads. The second time she spat, Tcûskai picked up some of the beads. Each time she spat the beads were more beautiful than before.

"What kind of a woman are you?" asked Tcûskai. She didn't answer.

Tcûskai went home, and said: "Oh, brother, there is a beautiful woman over there in the bushes. You must have her for a wife. Send Skóŭks off and take her." Tskel said: "Why don't you get her for a wife; she must have come for you." He was sleepy. He had been in a half dream since the first day he heard the woman's song.

Tcûskai went three or four times to see the woman and each time she spat beads. When she found that Tskel wouldn't come to her, she went to the house. Skóŭks saw her coming and she fixed herself up. She had power and could do things. Tskel was lying on the ground. When the woman came in, she sat down by him and began spitting beads. Then Skóŭks spat, and her beads were nice. The woman was frightened a little; she spat long white beads; Skóŭks spat more beautiful beads. They kept spitting beads till, just as the sun went down, the woman by her power made sleep come over Tskel and Tcûskai, and made Skóŭks grow so sleepy she could scarcely see. When darkness came the woman began to wrap Tskel in a skin blanket to carry him off.

Right away Skóŭks was wide awake. She jumped on the woman and fought with her. They fought all night. First one would have Tskel and then the other. He was sound asleep all the time. There was such a dust from their fighting that Tcûskai was covered with it. Just at daylight Skóŭks gave out; she couldn't fight any longer.

The woman snatched up Tskel and carried him off. She went under the ground, and as she went she made a furrow on the surface. Skóŭks followed for a long time, but she couldn't get at the woman, for she couldn't travel underground. At last she went home, struck Tcûskai with his neck rattles, and said: "You had better get up and follow your brother. You found him a nice wife, nicer than I am. Now you can go and live with them!"

Tcûskai woke up and went off to look for his brother. The trail had disappeared; he couldn't find even one track.

When the woman went into the ground, she was just such an animal as her father had been. She carried Tskel on her horns till she came out at the lake, then she put him down and said: "I will let you rest twice before I kill you. How do you like this place?"

"I like it. I have been here before," said Tskel.

She carried him to the middle of the trail in the lake, then she put him down, and asked: "What did you do when you were here before?"

"Nothing."

"Do you think you will ever go home?"

"No."

"What do you think you will do when you die? Will you come to life, or will you stay dead?"

"I don't know," said Tskel.

She took him up to carry him to the end of the trail where she could throw him into the lake. He got his knife out, a little at a time, and just as she was going to put him down again, he cut her head off. From each side of the ridge the water rushed up; the ridge shook and made a terrible noise. Tskel cut the woman's body up, and threw the pieces into the water. As he threw them, he called out, "Here are Tskel's ribs! Here is Tskel's arm!" He threw the head; then ran with all his might. When the old man's sons saw the head and knew that they had eaten their sister, they were so mad that they sent stone knives, beaded blankets and skins of all kinds to lie on the trail in front of Tskel. He had hard work to jump over them without getting burned, but he didn't touch or hit even one. When he got home Skóŭks and little Tcûskai were mourning. Their hair was cut and pitch was running over their faces. They sat with their heads down and didn't look up.

Tskel sat down by Tcûskai, and asked: "Why are you so dirty?"

Tcûskai jumped up, and cried out: "Are you here? I was just going to look for you."

Tskel said: "Heat some water. I am going to wash Skóŭks' head, and yours, too."

After he had washed their heads, he wrapped a skin blanket around them, and the next morning Skóŭks and Tcûskai had nice long hair.

Now Tskel moved off a little way from his old home. He made arrow points and killed deer.

Kāhkaas was kin of Tskel and one day she came to visit him. Soon Tcûskai ran in, and said: "I see lots of little tracks around here. Twist me some strings, Kāhkaas, so I can trap the things that make the tracks."

Tskel said to Kāhkaas: "Maybe they are the tracks of your children. Where did you leave them?"

"I left them high on a tree off in the middle of the great water. My children are safe."

Kāhkaas twisted strings for Tcûskai and he set his trap. Soon he came back bringing the five Kāhkaas boys in his trap. Kāhkaas was terribly angry and sorry; she said: "Give them to me; I will go off in the woods and roast and eat them." (She went to bury them.) Tcûskai watched Kāhkaas. Tskel knew that trouble would come, that Kāhkaas would try and kill them. He lay down, he felt sorry.

Soon Tcûskai cried: "Get up, brother! A great elk is coming. I'll go and kill it."

"Don't go in front of it," said Tskel. "Shoot it from behind!"

Tcûskai shot three times at the elk; each time he hit its horns. Then the elk turned, caught him on her horns, and ran off to the mountains. She ran a long way, then changed into Kāhkaas and flew, with Tcûskai, to the tree on the island in the middle of the ocean.

When the elk ran off with Tcûskai, Tskel fell on the ground and cried. Then he jumped up and started off to find him. He went everywhere, stopped at every house, and asked every person he met if they had seen little Tcûskai. But nobody had seen him. At last he came to a house where a sick woman lived; she was covered with sores. When she saw Tskel, she called out, "Don't come in here!" Tskel asked: "Have you seen my brother?" "I haven't seen anybody, I never go anywhere, and nobody ever comes here. You can ask at the next house."

Tskel went on till he came to a rock house right on the trail. He couldn't see a door. He walked around the house, but couldn't find an opening. Then he called out: "Who lives here?" The rock answered, "I live here!" — The house was a person. — Tskel asked: "Have you seen my brother? Kāhkaas has carried him off." "I go nowhere, and nobody comes here. I have no eyes, I can't see. You can ask at the next house. The people there see a great deal; maybe they can tell you where your brother is."

When Tskel got to the house, there were five persons inside and one said to another: "Make room for that man to come in and sit down." "I can't," said that one. "I'm just finishing my work. You can make room for him." "I can't, I'm just beginning my work." — Some of the men were braiding threads and others were twisting them. — When each man had refused to make room for Tskel, it was just sunset. He went into the house, gave the fire a kick, and sent it everywhere. It burned up all the threads and ropes the men were making.

"I feel lonesome," said he. "I can't listen to your words; they make me mad. I have lost my little brother; Kāhkaas has carried him off. Do you know anything about him? — Sprinkle your threads with water and roll them up; they will be whole again. — I have been everywhere in the world, but I can't find Tcûskai. I want to ask Súbbas if he can tell me where he is. I can do everything, but I can't find my brother. I want you to go up to Súbbas' house and ask him if he has seen Tcûskai."

Old man Kaltsik said: "We never go to Súbbas' house. No one ever goes there."

Tskel said: "I will give you anything you want if you will go." Tskel teased a long time, and at last Kaltsik said: "I will go."

He started just at daybreak. He traveled fast, going up all the time. He reached Súbbas' house in the middle of the sky before Súbbas got there. He turned himself into a little clump of bushes, right on Súbbas' trail. When Súbbas came hurrying along, he stumbled against the bushes, and said: "What is here? I never saw anything on this trail before."

Kaltsik took his own form, jumped up, and said, "I am here."

"What are you here for?" asked Súbbas.

"Tskel has lost his brother, little Tcûskai, and he wants you to tell him where he is."

"I can't wait to talk," said Súbbas. "I am always hurrying along; I only stop here at midday. I'm afraid Lok will catch me."

"Oh," said Kaltsik, "you should tell Tskel where his brother is. I'm sorry for him; he feels lonesome."

"Come to-morrow," said Súbbas, and he hurried along. It was night when Kaltsik got down to the ground. The next morning he started and before midday he turned himself into weeds and lay on Súbbas' path. When Súbbas came rushing along, he said: "What is this? I never saw anything on my trail before." Kaltsik sprang up. "Why have you come here?" asked Súbbas. "I have no time to spend talking."

Kaltsik said: "Tskel will give you anything you want if you will tell him where Tcûskai is. He has all kinds of things; beautiful beads — "

"I am brighter than beads. I don't want beads!" said Súbbas, "but I want a ring and a string of green shells to hang on my ears, and a white blanket to cover me on bright days. Tell Tskel to send you up to-morrow, if he has those things to give me."

Súbbas went on and Kaltsik got back to earth just before dark. He told Tskel what Súbbas wanted, and Tskel began to make the things. He worked all night; in the morning they were ready, and Kaltsik took them up to Súbbas. Súbbas was glad.—He still wears the ring. People can see it just before a storm. (Circle around the sun. It is called Wänämsäkät-saliyis.) They can see his green shells and his white blanket, too.— When he had them all, he said: "This morning when I was over that mountain in the east, I heard a man chopping wood and off on an island I caught the smell of burning flesh. That old man on the mountains has Tcûskai."

When Tskel found out where his brother was, he turned himself into an old woman, with a hump on her back, and went to the mountain.

When the man saw him, he said: "I think you are Tskel."

Tskel said: "I'm not a man, I'm an old woman. I heard that you had caught Tskel's brother and were going to kill him; I want to see him."

"I have him on an island; he'll die soon. He killed all of my sons. Now I am going to kill him. Help me with this wood."

Tskel helped pack up a load of wood, then the old man bent over and Tskel put the load on his back and gave him a cane to help himself up by. "Bend," said he to the cane. "Break and go into the old man's heart."

The cane broke and one half of it struck the old man in the heart and killed him. Tskel put the pieces together and the cane was whole again.

The old man had told Tskel that he was so glad to have Tcûskai that he danced all the time he was carrying wood to smoke him. Tskel strapped the pack of wood on his own back and danced along with it till he came to the canoe; then he danced in the canoe.

Old Kāhkaas had two servants, Kéis and Lok. Kéis guarded the landing. When Tskel got out of the canoe, Kéis wanted to spring at him, but Tskel said: "Don't touch me. I am your master!" He said the same to Lok, who was sitting by the smoke hole on top of the house, and Lok let him go down the ladder into the house. As soon as he was at the foot of the ladder, he saw Tcûskai hanging over the fire. Old woman Kāhkaas was smoking him. He cut Tcûskai down and put him under his arm. Then he caught Kāhkaas and tore her to pieces. He threw the pieces off in different directions, and they became hills and mountains. He took Tcûskai home and cured him.

After a time Tskel said to his brother: "We will go and hunt for Wŏn." — Wŏn was so large that he had to bend down to cut off the branches of trees. — When Skóŭks gave them seeds to eat, Tskel said: "If we don't come back soon, you will know that we have killed Wŏn."

They hadn't gone far when Tcûskai cried out: "I see a big deer!"

"Keep still," said Tskel, "and go on till we see Wŏn." In a little while Tskel saw Wŏn, and, not far from him, a deer. He called to Tcûskai: "Keep still! You mustn't eat seed; if you do Wŏn will get away."

Tcûskai thought: "I wonder what Tskel is doing. I hope he will kill the deer, too." Tskel went between the two. Just as he was ready to shoot Tcûskai thought: "I'm hungry, I'm going to eat a few of our seeds. Tskel won't miss them."

That moment Tskel's bow and bowstring broke. He knew that Tcûskai had eaten seeds. Tcûskai was scared; he ran to a spring and washed out his mouth, then came back to his brother. Tskel scolded. Tcûskai said: "What makes you so mad? I didn't eat any seed. Look in my mouth," and he opened it.

Tskel struck his brother. He had a deer's head on; he took it off, put it on Tcûskai's head, and said: "Now go and hunt for Wŏn."

"I can kill him easily," said Tcûskai.

Tskel said: "You think that Wŏn runs on the ground. So he does, but he runs in the air, too. He goes on all kinds of trees and he goes back and forth in the sky. You will have to follow him around the world before he will stop running." When Tcûskai was ready to go, Tskel said: "Take some seeds," but it was too late. Tcûskai had started.

Before Tcûskai had gone very far, he saw Wŏn and began to follow him. He ran across rocky places, ran five times over the tops of pine trees, and five times over the top of high grass, five times across mole-hills, five times across the sky, and five times around the world, then he ran east on the sky till he came near a village where Blaiwas was chief.

Kékina and Gapni were Blaiwas' servants; they were on top of the house sunning themselves. Kékina said: "It sounds as if my cousin were coming;" again he said: "It sounds like my brother, blowing on his medicine stick. Tell the people to come out and look."

When Gapni told them, Gäk said: "You can't see much with your little eyes; you are not like me. I can see all over the world."

Blaiwas said: "Little Kékina never tells a lie; somebody must be coming. Go and see who it is. Tell old man Moi to look; he can see everything under the sky and in the whole world."

Moi said: " Somebody is coming. Tell the people to be ready to shoot when I call out."

The people made a ring, and when Wŏn came, he rushed inside of it. Then every one shot at him; Kéis hit him in the foot, Nänīhläs hit him on the horns, Blaiwas hit him in the shoulder. At last they killed him. When Wŏn was on the ground, Kéis jumped on one of his legs; he wanted to get meat from the middle of it. (Tcûskai hadn't come yet.) People said to Kéis: " Get off; don't make Tcûskai mad. He has been following Wŏn for a long time."

Tcûskai came slowly, for he was tired. When he got to the place, he told Kéis to get off Wŏn and help to skin him. Kéis wouldn't move. Tcûskai pushed him away, but he jumped back; then Tcûskai threw him off and told him he was in a hurry, for he had far to go. The third time Kéis got on to Wŏn, Tcûskai threw him over a mountain, but he was back in a minute. Tcûskai was so mad that he pounded Kéis' head till he made it flat. That is why rattlesnakes have flat heads. He cut off Wŏn's foot that Kéis had hit with an arrow and threw it after Kéis.

Gäk had shot Wŏn in the leg, and Tcûskai gave that leg to Gäk. And so he divided Wŏn's body among the people; then he took a large piece on his back and started for home. When it was dark, he camped in a woodpecker's hole, in a tall tree.

Kéis was a great doctor. He was mad and he made it snow all night; he thought he could kill Tcûskai in that way. But Tcûskai made a fire in the woodpecker's hole, and kept himself warm. He put a round stone in the fire and heated it, and in the morning, when he started for home, he rolled the hot stone along on the ground in front of him. Where the stone went, the trail was dry. Everywhere else the snow was so deep that only the tops of trees could be seen.

When Tcûskai got to the house, he went in quietly, didn't make any noise. Tskel and Skóŭks were mourning for him; they didn't see him, or hear him. He asked: " Why are you mourning? Did you think that I was lost? Your heads don't look nice; they don't smell nice. Go and wash them."

They were glad now. Skóŭks went out to get the meat Tcûskai had brought; she couldn't move it. Then Tskel went; he couldn't raise it from the ground.

"What is the matter?" asked Tcûskai. "I didn't bring that meat with the head strap; I used the chest strap." He carried it into the house with one hand; then he blew on it and made it small, but there was meat enough to last all winter.

Tskel cut the meat in strips to dry; he worked all night, and finished just as the sun came up. Then he took a piece of the fat, fastened it on the top of Tcûskai's head, and said, "This will always stay as it is now; it is small, but all the people in the world could feed on it." Then he said: "You have lived long enough without a wife; you must look for one."

"Where can I find a wife?" asked Tcûskai.

"If you go to the place where they killed Wŏn, you will find a clearing where women are digging roots. When you get to the edge of the clearing, shoot an arrow. It will come down near a spring. You must be at the spring by midday."

Tcûskai walked and walked. After a while he came to the clearing and saw women digging roots. Then he shot an arrow. When he got to the spring his arrow was sticking up in the ground there. He sat down, put his elbows on his knees, and his head on his hands. The women went towards the spring, digging as they went.

Kówe saw Tcûskai first; she took off her cap and wanted to give him water. He didn't look up or move. She ran to the other women, and said: "There is a nice-looking young man sitting by the spring. I gave him some water, but he wouldn't take it; maybe he will take it from you." The women crowded around Tcûskai; each offered him water, but he wouldn't take it. The chief's daughter offered it but he didn't take it. Kaiu-tois' daughter tried, but he wouldn't look at her. Blaiwas' daughter said to a woman: "Go and tell those Maidikdak girls to come and try." When the woman got to the girls, she said: "A nice-looking young man is there by the spring. We have all offered him water, but he won't take it. Maybe he will take it from you."

They went to the spring. The elder sister took off her cap,

filled it with water, and gave it to Tcûskai; he drank half of the water. The younger sister offered him the cap; he drank the other half of the water. Blaiwas' daughter saw the arrow; she tried to pull it up, but couldn't. Then each woman tried in turn. Some watered the ground to soften it, but nobody could pull the arrow out. Then Blaiwas' daughter said: " Let Maidikdak's daughters try."

The elder sister pulled the arrow half-way out; the younger pulled it all the way out and put it in her basket. Then she went to dig roots.

Kówe saw the fat on Tcûskai's head and wanted to loosen it, but she couldn't. She bit at the knots, but the women drove her away. Blaiwas' daughter said: " You mustn't use your teeth. Whoever loosens fat with their teeth will be Tusasás' wife." All the women tried to take the fat off from Tcûskai's head, but no one could do it. They sent for Maidikdak's daughters again. The elder one loosened it; the younger took it off.

The women went home and Tcûskai was left alone. Kówe ran with all her might, jumped, fell, puffed, at last got home. Then she said to her mother: " Tcûskai drank from my cap; make a good place for him! " Old Kówe was glad. She made ready a nice place for her son-in-law.

Each young woman told her mother the same thing, except Maidikdak's daughters; they didn't say anything. Tusasás made ready a place for his son-in-law.

He was so glad that he ran around and boasted, said: " Tcûskai drank from my daughter's cap; he is my son-in-law."

When Tcûskai got to the village he stood in the middle of the road. Blaiwas wanted to lead him into his house; so did all the other chiefs; but he wouldn't go. At last old Maidikdak asked him to come to her house, and he went.

The next morning Blaiwas asked Tcûskai to run a foot race. All the men were mad at Tcûskai and wanted to kill him. Every man in the village ran against him. When Tcûskai started, he went under the ground. He ran faster than anybody and got to the goal first. One after another the runners came till all were there; then they turned and looked back to see where Tcûskai was. Tusasás said: "I wonder when he will get here?" and he made fun of him. Then they saw that Tcûskai was ahead of them.

When they were ready for the race back, Tcûskai said: "Go on! You needn't wait for me." He ran under the ground. He came to the goal first and won the race. The second man to come was Blaiwas, the third was Wus. When Kûlta overtook Tusasás, he said: "Little brother, stop and pull this sliver out of my foot with your teeth." Tusasás stopped, but he couldn't get the sliver out; men had to come and carry Kûlta home.

Blaiwas said: "Now we will hunt deer." They drove the deer to the mountain and left Tcûskai alone there. He sent one arrow and killed all the deer on the mountain.

The next morning Maidikdak's daughter had a little boy; he grew fast and soon was running around.

After a time Tcûskai wanted to see his brother. When he got to Tskel's house he found that Tskel had a boy larger than his own. The two little boys were like brothers. Tskel asked Tcûskai to go to the lake and get him reeds for arrows. "Get the kind of reeds that have tear-drops on them," said he. "Those are the best to make arrows."

Tcûskai went, and looked in every place; when he couldn't find reeds with tear-drops on them, he put his fingers in his eyes and made tears come; then he dropped them on the reeds. He shed so many tears that his eyelids got swollen; he could hardly see.

When Tcûskai went to the lake, he went along the south side, for old Sukas, a man-eater, who drew people in with his breath and swallowed them, lived on the west side. Going home he made a mistake; he thought the west was the south side, — he couldn't see well. Soon he met old Sukas.

Sukas said: "Come and wrestle with me, then you can go home."

Tcûskai had to wrestle. About the middle of the afternoon he threw the old man, but as he went down Tcûskai slipped and fell on him. Sukas' stomach was so big and flabby that it covered Tcûskai up; he couldn't get out and he could scarcely breathe. He didn't know what to do. Then he heard Skóla say: "Somebody must scratch and kick hard; that will kill the old man."

Tcûskai began to kick and scratch, and in a little while he broke the skin; the old man's stomach shrank up. Tcûskai got up and ran home.

Tskel asked: "Where are the reeds? Why were you gone so long?"

Tcûskai said: "I met old Sukas and wrestled with him."

"I told you not to go that way," said Tskel. He was cross and scolded. That made Tcûskai mad.

The next morning Tcûskai made arrows for his boy and told him to shoot Tskel's boy while they were playing. He did, and Tskel's boy was two days getting well. Then Tcûskai put poison in an arrow and told his son to shoot Tskel's boy again. Tskel knew what his brother was doing; he put poison in his son's arrow and told him even if he were dying, to kill Tcûskai's boy.

The next day both boys were dead. Tcûskai and Tskel felt lonesome. Tskel said: "I will go to Lamsewe and swim." — When people lose their friends and feel badly about it, they go and swim till they feel better. — He told Tcûskai to go to another mountain, but he didn't go; he followed his brother.

When Tskel saw him, he was mad and he said: "You will be a person no longer. You will look funny to people and they will laugh at you when you run in and out of holes. They will think there are five or six of you, but there will be only one."

Tcûskai said: "You will no longer be a person, you will have no power. In winter, when the water freezes, people will hunt for you in the tula grass and will kill you."

All this took place. Those two great powers turned into common little minks and weasels, such as live now and are killed by hunters.

Tcûskai was always full of tricks. He taught his son to kill his cousin; and that is why people of kin sometimes kill one another now.

GÄK KILLS PAKOL

CHARACTERS

Gäk	Crow	Ndukis	Hawk
Kiuks . . .	An Indian Doctor	Pakol	Deer
Kumal . . .	Pelican	Wíle	A Fawn
Moi	Squirrel	Wus	Fox

GÄK was an old man and he was a doctor; his wife was young.

Off in the mountains there was a platform of rocks. Gäk lay on the platform; he was sick. His medicines were the earth and the wind, and he sang to them all the time, trying to get well.

One morning Gäk told his wife (Wíle) that he was going to die, and asked her to call to her mother and father and aunts and uncles and cousins, and tell them to come and see him for the last time.

Wíle stood on the rocks and called: "My mother, my father, my aunts and uncles and cousins, come and see Gäk; he is going to die."

Her father was away on the mountain, but he heard her and said: "That sounds like my child's voice."

Right off Wíle saw hundreds of her people gathering and she called to Gäk: "They are coming! They are coming!"

Gäk got up, turned around, and lay down so there was just room enough for one person to sit on the edge of the rock. Then he said to Wíle: "When they get here, have the fattest one, the one with the black spot on his forehead, sit here by me. I am going to leave him everything I have."

When they were all standing around Gäk, he said to the one with the spot on his forehead: "I want you to be the last man to bid me good-by." Then he covered up his head and made a sound like groaning. The Pakols waited a long time to see him die. At last they began to say good-by. There was such a crowd that it was sundown when they were through. Then Gäk told the fat Pakol, the one with the spot on his forehead, to say good-by.

Just as Pakol was getting up to go, Gäk kicked him off the rock; he fell over the precipice and was killed. Wíle and all the Pakols were so scared that they ran away. Gäk went down among the rocks and began to eat Pakol's body.

The Pakols said: "The greatest one of us has been killed," and they mourned for him. (The Gäk people can never get enough to eat; they feed themselves with both hands.)

Wus was no longer a person, but he could still talk. He came to the ledge of rocks, looking for something to eat. He saw Gäk eating and called out to him: "My brother, how did you get so much meat? How did you get down there among the rocks?"

"I shut my eyes and jumped. Come down and eat with me."

"I am afraid."

"Go back a little way, shut your eyes, run to the edge, and jump."

Wus said, "Eg! Eg!" and ran, but just as he got to the edge of the rocks he opened his eyes and stopped. He did that three times.

Gäk scolded, and said: "You must do as I tell you. If you open your eyes when you jump, you will get killed."

Wus tried again, then he said: "Oh, my brother, throw me a piece of meat."

Gäk said: "If you want to eat, you must come down here."

"Well, this time I will come!"

Wus jumped, but he caught on the bushes, and climbed back.

Gäk said: "It is getting dark. If you don't come, you will have nothing to eat."

"I will come this time."

Wus went over the rock like a feather, but when he was half-way down, he opened his eyes; then he fell and was torn to pieces. His head, alive and with open eyes, was far away from the body.

Gäk felt badly; he and Wus had always been good friends. He said to the head: "Wus, I thought you were the strongest person in the world; now you are torn to pieces. You didn't do as I told you to; you opened your eyes."

Gäk talked to his medicines, the earth and the wind, then he got his red medicine basket,[1] picked up the pieces of Wus, joined them together and stepped over the body three times. He covered the body with the basket and told Wus to lie still, that the basket would cure him, but he mustn't get up till he came and took it off. Gäk went back to eating.

At sundown Wus began to kick and to call: "I am well; come and take the basket off!" He called many times. Each time Gäk said: "Lie still a while longer; you needn't be afraid. There is plenty of meat; we can't eat it in all night." At last Gäk took the basket off.

After that Wus and Gäk lived together. The Pakols wanted to kill Gäk, because he had killed their best man. All kinds of people hated him, and wanted to kill him, but when any one got near him he wasn't Gäk; he turned into something and got away. One morning two small men started to hunt for him; when he knew they were coming, he turned himself into a bird and flew away.

Gäk had a blanket of bright rock (obsidian); he put the blanket around him, turned into a man just like Ndukis, and sat down on a high rock in sight of his enemies. He painted his face white, to make them believe he was Ndukis. His enemies came and looked at him, — a long line of people. All the people that walk, or crawl, or fly in the world were there, and all had good eyes. Each man gave his opinion, and each thought it was Ndukis.

Blaiwas said: "Nobody in the world can see plainer than I can; that is Ndukis." Old man Moi knew the man was Gäk, but he didn't want to say so. When they asked him what he

[1] A medicine basket is made of tckula, a kind of willow, and is painted red. When the basket is not a medicine, it is used as a sieve. The old Indian woman who related this Gäk myth said: "The basket is a good medicine. If a man is wounded, and the basket is put over him, he gets well."

thought, he said: "You have a wise old man here" (he meant Kumal); "if he doesn't tell you who that man is, I will."

Gäk sat perfectly still on the rock. He knew that Kumal was wise, and that he had a blanket made of five kinds of stone. Gäk's blanket was made of four kinds of stone.

When Kumal came up, the people gave him a place where he could stand and look at the man on the rock. He looked a long time, then said: "How could you be fooled? That is Gäk, the man who killed Pakol. He has painted his face white and made himself look like Ndukis, but don't you see his large mouth?"

Gäk came down from the rock, took his own form, and began to fight with the crowd. He killed every one who fought with him; some wouldn't fight, they ran away.

Gäk struck at Kumal's throat, cut through the old man's stone blanket, and killed him; he tore his body to pieces, threw the pieces in the water, and said: "You will no longer be a person. You will be a fisher, and live in the water." The other bodies Gäk turned to rocks, then he went off to the mountains. Wus had been eating the bodies of the men Gäk killed. When the bodies turned to stone, he followed Gäk to the mountains.

THE STONE PEOPLE

CHARACTERS

Heûwûs	The stone that pounders are made of
Wûspahlákls	Hairless Fox (Lakl is hair)
Nkok	Bird (English name unknown)
Lŭ'luphlainik	Name of a hill (Lulup is eye)

A GREAT many of the Heûwûs people lived near Tula Lake. They were smooth, round people. They had no faces, but they could talk to one another. Every morning and evening a young woman passed their place on her way to the lake to catch fish. They knew when she was coming, for she sang as she traveled. They could hear her far off. Her song said: "I am a great hunter of fish and of seeds."

The young men of the Heûwûs people listened for the girl's song and were glad when they heard it; they thought she was nice-looking, and they wanted to marry her. Some said: "We can't talk to her;" others said: "Maybe she isn't good; she might break us up." "Why should we be afraid?" asked others. "If she broke us to pieces, we wouldn't die; we shall never die." The chief said: "Let that girl alone. I like her; every morning her song wakes me up." One man said: "I don't want her to pass so often; the next time she goes by here I will say something to her."

That evening when the girl passed, nobody spoke to her; some of the men wanted to, but others wouldn't let them.

Early the next morning the Heûwûs people heard the girl's song and said to one another: "She is coming!" "She doesn't hurt us," said one young man. "Don't bother her." "Why does she come here so often?" asked another. "Maybe she belongs to this place." One big Heûwûs said: "I am stronger than any of you. I will have this good-looking girl for a wife." "Maybe she will break you to pieces," said one of the young men. "I am not afraid; she can't kill me. If she hurts my body, I will hurt her in some way."

The girl listened to the Heûwûs people: when she was a long way off, she could hear them talking.

Some of the young men sent their spirits to the lake to turn to fish and jump up in the water and paddle around where the girl was.

"Why do you come here?" asked the girl. "You can't fool me. You may turn to anything you like, but I will know you. I have heard you talking about me; I don't like you. You needn't be jealous because I go around here. This is my place. Maybe I shall live here as long as you do."

The young men were ashamed; their spirits went back to their bodies, became Heûwûs again.

That evening, when the girl went home, there was a nice-looking bow lying on the path she always traveled. She said: "I wonder what man is trying to fool me now?"

When she got near the creek, she met a number of the Nkok people. They asked: "Did you see a bow?"

"It is back there on the trail," said the girl. "What are you doing around here? Why do you bother me? What kind do you think I am? I belong to this earth. I was made when this earth was made. The place around here is mine. I know when anybody is trying to fool me. What could I use you for? Don't you see that I travel as wind and air travel? I have no use for you. You will no longer be living persons; you will be hunters of fish in lakes and creeks." Right away the men turned to birds and flew off over the water.

The next morning, when the Heûwûs people heard the girl's song, the chief said to the young men who had sent their spirits to be fish and bother her: "You have made trouble for us all. You shouldn't have meddled with that girl. She is powerful; she will be mad now and will do us harm."

When the girl came along the trail, she saw Wûspahlákls sitting in front of her. He looked sleepy.

She said: "Who are you? No living person looks as ugly as you do. Go away!"

Wûspahlákls lay down on the trail; he didn't listen to her. She went around him on the north side.

When she came to the Heûwûs' place, she sat down and looked at them. She said: "Why, you nice little Heûwûs, you are as smooth as you can be."

She picked up one and struck the ground with him; he didn't break. She said: "Oh it is not easy to break you, is it?"

The Heûwûs screamed: "Oh! Oh! you hurt me! You think that I am not a living being, but I am."

"You are talking to me; I am glad," said the girl. "That is what I want. You haven't spoken to me before, but I have heard you talk about me. I don't hate you. You belong here, and so do I. I thought we should be here always and be friends, but you don't want it that way." She put the Heûwûs down and went on. Soon she saw Wûspahlákls again; he sat on the trail in front of her. She called to him: "Get out of my way!" When he didn't move, she took off a bone scratcher she wore around her neck, went up to him, scratched off all of his flesh, and pounded him to death. Then she went on.

The next morning Wûspahlákls crossed the trail in front of her and went into the bushes. The girl stopped; she was scared. She went home, painted her body and her hair red, and started off in another direction; she traveled around everywhere and asked every one she met: "Who owns you?" She asked the rocks, the trees, the leaves. At last she asked a little hill: "Who are you?"

"I am Lŭl′uphlainik," said the hill.

"Whose eye are you?" asked the girl.

"I am this earth's eye."

The girl camped by the hill, and said to it: "I want you to tell me about yourself."

The hill said: "All these things around here belong to the earth; they were made at the same time. This is not a good place for you. Over on the lake, where two little air boys live, is a nice place for you."

The girl was short and thin, and after she was painted she was red all over. She started for the lake. As she was passing a mountain, a voice spoke out of it, and asked: " Where are you going? " Right away she was gone; she sank into the earth; only one eye looked out of the ground.

" Where have you gone now? " asked the voice.

" I am looking at you," said the girl. " You are bad. I want you to be something else."

She came out of the ground, rubbed black paint on her hands, and on her face, from her chin to the top of her forehead. Then she asked: " Who are you who talk so much and make such a noise? I want you to go far off on the mountain, where you can't bother people who are traveling around. Go where you won't be seen often."

He couldn't go unless he looked at her. She knew this, so she said: " Look at me; I want to be friends with you."

He had to look at her; he couldn't help it.

That moment he became as red as she was. She said: " I am a spirit and hereafter you will be a spirit. Sometimes we will help each other." As soon as he looked at her, he went off to the mountain. Each spirit went its way and both will live always.

PITOÍOIS

CHARACTERS

Kāhkaas	Stork	Tskel	Mink
Kûlta	Otter	Wûlkûtska	Marten
Pitoíois			

Pitoíois and her two brothers lived together; their father and mother were dead.

Pitoíois was beautiful; she had a long neck, and her hair was black and so long that it touched the ground. She was the fastest worker in the world. She was always digging roots. With one dig she could bring up a whole basketful. In a day she dug over a large plain as though it had been ploughed. She piled up the roots, thought "I want them in my basket," and they were there.

Pitoíois' brothers were great hunters; while she was digging roots, they were hunting for deer, but they never got out of sight of their sister, for they thought Wus might come and bother her.

Wus was always watching Pitoíois, but he didn't go near her; he was afraid of her brothers.

One day Pitoíois' brothers asked: "Are you through digging roots in the places we found for you?"

"Yes, I am ready for another place. Are there many places around here?"

"There are a few more. Are you tired?" asked the elder brother.

"I am not tired, but I'm afraid; I always feel that somebody is looking at me."

"Who are you afraid of?" asked her brother.

"Of Wus. I know that he is watching me all the time."

"Though we are off on the mountains we always see you,"

said her brother. "Nobody has been near you. There are two more plains to dig over; then we will go away from here. Sometimes I see a smoke on a mountain, but it is far off."

Pitoíois dug all the roots and pounded them up. Then the brothers moved to a new place. They made a brush house and went to look for a deer.

The next morning Pitoíois began to dig roots in a place where her brothers could watch her. The elder brother had such powerful eyes that he could count all the trees, all the brush, and all the plants; he could count everything. He looked far off in the east and saw somebody dodge behind a tree. It was Wus. When he saw him, though the sun wasn't in the middle of the sky, he went to his sister and took her home.

"I don't know why I am so afraid," said Pitoíois. "I feel worse every day, but I never see anybody."

"To-day I saw somebody off on the mountain," said her brother.

"That's what I thought!" said Pitoíois. "Every day I feel that somebody is looking at me; to-day I was frightened."

Wus camped on the top of the mountain. He thought: "I wonder why those men never leave their sister? I can do anything I like; I am Wus. I will make them forget her." He began singing, sang a beautiful song. All day and all night he sang, to draw their minds out of them, and make them forget Pitoíois.

The girl was uneasy; she wanted to finish her work. In two days all the fields were dug up. She packed the roots without waiting to clean them, and her brothers moved to a place not far from where the five Wûlkûtska brothers lived. The father of those brothers was a great eater; he could never get enough to satisfy him.

Wus followed Pitoíois. He said to himself: "This time they will forget her." The girl went to dig roots and her brothers started off to hunt. The flat was square, but Wus made it long, and he multiplied the roots. It took Pitoíois all day to dig them. Wus talked and sang; the brothers couldn't hear the song, but they felt it and forgot all about their sister.

"I am losing my mind," said the elder brother. "I feel as I did when I was a little child."

"I feel that way, too," said the younger brother.

When they got to the house, their sister was there; she had her roots in the creek, washing off the mud. When they told her how they felt, and that they almost forgot her, she said: "I am not afraid now; I don't feel as I did in those other places."

The next day the brothers said to Pitoíois: "We are going to hunt; you had better stay in the house and pound the roots. Don't lie down; if you do, you will go to sleep and harm will come to you."

Pitoíois pounded her roots, worked with her beads, and then straightened out her hair to see how long it had grown; it dragged on the ground.

The brothers went in different directions to look for deer; when they met, the younger brother said: "Off in the east from where I was I heard a man singing a beautiful song."

"Perhaps it was Wus," said the elder brother; "he is always trying to deceive people."

When they were home and were through eating, the younger brother said: "I wish I had something to amuse myself with."

"What do you want?" asked his brother. He thought it was wisdom or nice beads.

"I want a wife." (Wus had put that thought into his mind.)

"There are no women near here," said his brother.

"We can go far off and hunt for one."

"I am willing to go," said the elder brother.

The next morning they said to Pitoíois: "We are going away; you must stay in the house and pound roots."

"I shall get tired of staying here; I shall want to dig roots, but I will stay near the house."

The brothers went toward the north. The first house they came to was Kāhkaas'. "What are you traveling around here for?" asked the old man.

"We travel around to see people, but we have traveled a good many days and we haven't seen anyone."

“ Are you looking for a young woman? ” asked Kāhkaas.

“ Yes, we want a wife. Do you know where there are any women? ”

“ I know the daughter of old man Kûlta.”

“ We don’t want her; she dives under the water. We can’t dive. We want some woman who goes on dry land as we do.”

“ There is nobody around here,” said Kāhkaas. “ As long as I have lived I’ve seen no woman but Kûlta’s daughter. You had better go toward the west; you may find people in that direction.”

The brothers started off. They were gone a long time.

Pitoíois got tired of staying in the house and she went to dig roots.

Going east, in lines from north to south, she left the land in furrows. Wus had made the flat wide and full of roots. When she got to the east end of the flat, she turned and started for home.

Wus changed himself into a nice-looking young man, with long black hair. His clothes were covered with beads and he wore beautiful moccasins. He overtook Pitoíois, pulled her down on the ground, and put his head on her lap.

She cried and begged him to let go of her. Her cry sounded like sad singing; she cried her own name: “ Pitoíois, Pitoíois.”

The five Wûlkûtska brothers were hunting. The youngest brother heard Pitoíois’ cry, but it sounded far off. At first he thought it was a bird singing. He heard it again and stopped to listen; then he thought: “ That must be the sister of the two hunters.” He heard it five times, and the fifth time the cry sounded so sad and pitiful that he went toward it. He traveled till night: still the song was far away, then he went home. He had no game. Each one of his brothers had a large deer.

Those brothers had had many wives, but their father had killed and eaten them. When the young man told his brothers what he had heard, they said: “ It must be the sister of the hunters,” and they wondered why she cried. “ Perhaps Wus has caught her,” said one of them; “ he is always tormenting women.”

"Her brothers watch her; nobody can go near her," said the youngest brother.

"Perhaps they have gone far off," said the eldest brother.

Pitoíois was sitting on the ground and crying. Her eyes were so swollen they could scarcely be seen. Wus kept teasing her to go to his house, but she wouldn't go, no matter what he promised.

The next morning, when the five brothers went to hunt, they kept near together. They killed a deer and built a fire and roasted some of the meat. What they didn't roast, they hung on a tree. All the bones were left on the ground. While they were eating, the youngest brother heard something and he listened. His brothers noticed that he stopped eating.

"What is the matter?" asked the eldest brother.

"I've bitten my tongue."

"No, it's not that; you hear something."

Then he told them that he heard the cry that he had heard before. They didn't hear it, but they said: "We will find out what it is." As they followed the youngest brother, they all heard the cry. When they came to the top of the mountain, where Wus was when he was singing, they looked down into the valley and saw a beautiful girl sitting on the ground, crying. They knew who she was but they were afraid to go to her; they were afraid of her brothers. Then they saw that a man was lying with his head on her lap, and they knew it was Wus.

"If we save her," said one of the brothers, "which of us will have her?"

"I don't want a wife," said the eldest brother; "our youngest brother can have her."

The youngest brother shot an arrow. It went under the ground and came out near Wus. He jumped. The brothers went down the mountain, the youngest in front. When he got to where the girl was sitting, he snatched her away from Wus. Wus turned into a fox and ran off. Then the young man took Pitoíois by the hand and sprang with her over five mountains, a spring for each mountain.

His brothers said: "What shall we do to keep the old man

from eating this girl? She is too nice to be eaten up. We must watch him all the time and kill him if he tries to get her."

Tskel was the servant of the old man and his five sons. He stayed at home with the old man and watched for the sons to come. He was on the top of the house looking for them when he saw them coming with Pitoíois. He ran in and said to the old man: "They are coming with a beautiful woman."

"Where are they?" asked the old man. He was pounding people's bones.

"You needn't think that you are going to eat her; she is too beautiful," said Tskel, and he snatched the old man's mortar and threw it away.

The old man went out and found the mortar. "Don't you do that again," said he. "I can't do without my cap" (he always called the mortar his cap), and he put it under his arm.

When the brothers came, they told Tskel to watch their father and not let him hurt Pitoíois. The old man didn't look at the girl while his sons were around, but as soon as they went to hunt he got up and began to move around.

"Why do you get up?" asked Tskel. "You always move around when you have a daughter-in-law; you want to eat her. Sit down!" When he didn't sit down, Tskel jumped on him and pushed him down. Tskel liked the old man and didn't want him to do wrong.

When Tskel told the brothers how their father acted, they were frightened. They said: "We had better take the girl back to her brothers. In two days we will start."

The next day Pitoíois wanted to dig roots. The eldest brother asked his father if he would let her alone if she dug roots for him to eat.

"Yes," said the old man. They told little Tskel to watch him; then they went off to hunt for deer.

Pitoíois dug a great many roots. As fast as she dug them, the old man pounded them in his mortar and ate them. He ate till midday, then he was satisfied. He praised Pitoíois, called her daughter-in-law, and told her he would never hurt her.

"Don't believe him," said Tskel; "he always talks that way, but he never tells the truth."

Pitoíois dug roots till night, then took home a basketful and put them around the house, a handful in a place. Each handful became a big pile. At the end of two days she had a great many roots dug. When the brothers got ready to go home with her, the old man pounded dried meat for them to take; there were five large piles of it. As each brother reached down to take his load, it became so light and small that he felt that he had nothing to carry.

The old man began to move around again. "Keep still, old man," said Tskel. "As soon as they get away, you can pound your roots." When he wouldn't keep still, Tskel snatched his mortar and threw it out. The old man went quickly and brought it back.

Pitoíois and the brothers traveled till midday; then the youngest brother put a small piece of dried meat in a basket. Right away the basket was full of meat. He put the basket on Pitoíois' back and told her to go to her brothers' house; they would be there by night.

When Pitoíois' brothers came home and found the arrow sticking up in the ground, and saw Wus' tracks, they knew that he had been tormenting their sister, and that the five brothers, the great arrow men, had taken her away. They felt badly; they hung out the clothes she used to wear and began to cry.

When Pitoíois was near home, she heard her brothers crying and it made her feel sad. They were glad when they saw her. When they asked where she had been, she said: "The five Wûlkûtska brothers saved me from Wus; I am the wife of the youngest brother."

"Where are they now?" asked her brothers.

"On the mountain near here."

"You must get ready something for them to eat."

Pitoíois pounded roots, and her elder brother made a place for the men to sit. When they came in, he called the youngest man brother-in-law.

The Wûlkûtska brothers felt badly; they were afraid that the old man would kill Tskel and then follow them.

Old Wûlkûtska made Tskel sleep; then he tracked his sons. Soon he was on top of the last mountain. He was the fastest traveler in the world. He peeped over the top of the mountain and looked around in the valley.

When the Wûlkûtska brothers and Pitoíois were ready to start for home, her brother said to the youngest Wûlkûtska: " She is all the sister we have; you must be good to her. She will work and help you feed your father."

When the brothers looked toward the mountain, they saw their father looking over the top of it. The eldest brother went around the mountain, came up behind the old man, and snatched the mortar from under his arm, just as he was taking it out to throw at Pitoíois.

" Why are you here? " asked the son. " We told you to stay with Tskel. You are not safe when you are away from home."

" I wanted to see the brothers of my daughter-in-law."

" You can't see them. Go home! " said the son, and he was so angry that he threw his father's mortar over four mountains. It came down in front of their house.

Old Wûlkûtska could do nothing without his mortar; he hurried after it.

When Tskel woke up and didn't see the old man, he was terribly scared. He went out to hunt for him just in time to see the mortar coming and dodge it. When it fell, he picked it up, took it to the creek, and buried it in mud; only the rim of the mortar could be seen. Tskel had to hurry, for the old man was coming fast, like a cloud.

When he got to the house, he called to Tskel: " Where is my cap? Where is my cap? "

" I don't know where your cap is."

" Tell me quickly. I am almost dead."

" I don't know; you always take it with you. What have you done with it? "

" I shall die. I want it now. Hurry and find it! I am sleepy." That minute he dropped on the ground, dead. The mortar was his medicine, his life.

Tskel tried to make him get up. He pushed him, and said:

"Get up, old man, your sons are coming. Don't sleep so long." When he didn't move, Tskel was frightened and sorry. He ran to the creek, got the mortar and put it in the sun to dry. As soon as it was dry, he ran to the old man, and said: "Get up, grandfather; I have found your cap!" Tskel was crying.

Wûlkûtska didn't move; he was cold and stiff. Tskel pushed him ever so many times, but he didn't stir. Then Tskel took his own medicine, a stick that he carried behind his ear, and hit Wûlkûtska with it; he moved a little. Tskel hit him again, kept hitting him, and saying: "Get up, grandfather, get up, grandfather! Here is your cap."

At last the old man came to life. Then Tskel said: "I hid your cap to see how I could kill you. You must never tease your daughter-in-law, for I know where your life is. If you kill her, I shall hide your cap and not get it for you."

The old man was frightened, but his mind wasn't changed. When he saw his sons coming, he went into the house and watched them through the cracks. When they were near, Pitoíois put down her basket. As soon as they were in the house, the old man went out to see if they had brought roots; he hunted everywhere, but couldn't find the basket.

"Why don't you stay in the house?" asked his son.

"I am hungry. I am hunting for what you brought. I haven't eaten anything for two days. The first day I ate all you left in the house."

Pitoíois told him where the basket was. He was going to jump at it and swallow all the roots at once, but she called to him: "Put down a large skin and pour the roots on to it, then take up a pinch of them with the ends of your fingers; that pinch will be so big that you can't eat all of it."

"There isn't a mouthful in the whole basket," said the old man, and he was going to swallow all of them. When his son ran toward him, he snatched a handful of the roots and ate them. That moment he was so full that roots ran out of his mouth, and on to the ground; he fell down, rolled over, and choked to death.

Pitoíois gathered up the roots that were on the ground, made them small, put them in the basket, and covered the basket up. The sons were glad that their father was dead, but Pitoíois felt badly; she liked her father-in-law, and didn't want to kill him. She hit the old man two blows on the back and two on the head. The roots came out of him, only enough were left to satisfy his appetite, and he was alive again.

Tskel said: "See what you got by doing what your daughter-in-law told you not to do. Don't do that way again. Next time no one will save you; you will die and stay dead."

The old man didn't listen to Tskel's words; his mind wasn't changed. The next morning, when the brothers were starting off to hunt deer, they said to Tskel: "Watch the old man; don't let him torment Pitoíois. She has power and knows what she can do to him if he makes her angry."

Old Wûlkûtska slept till afternoon; when he woke up, Pitoíois had gone for water. He looked through the cracks and watched for her to come; he meant to kill her. When Pitoíois was near the house, he raised his mortar ready to throw it.

Tskel was watching him; he crept up, snatched the mortar, and said: "Old man, what are you doing? What did your sons tell you? They will kill you if you harm your daughter-in-law. They didn't care for their other wives, — they were common women and could do nothing; but this woman has power."

The old man was helpless, for Tskel had his mortar. He promised not to harm Pitoíois.

When the brothers came home, Tskel didn't tell them what Wûlkûtska had tried to do, but when Pitoíois wouldn't eat they asked her what the trouble was, and she said: "Your father came near killing me." The youngest son was so mad that he snatched his father's mortar and broke it into bits.

That minute the old man turned as red as fire and every little bit of the mortar was as red as fire. He ran and gathered up the bits, held them tight up to himself; and right away the mortar was there.

The brothers were scared; they thought: "He can't be killed, but he has the power to kill us." Tskel said: "Don't feel badly, there is one way to kill him. If you bury his mortar in the ground under water, he will die. I tried it one day."

Now the five brothers started off for a long hunt and Pitoíois went with them. They said to Tskel: "If the old man gets hungry, you can come for deer's meat; we will leave some hanging on trees around our camping places."

The first day they killed a deer they hung the meat on trees and left the bones on the ground.

In one day old Wûlkûtska ate all that had been left in the house; then he made Tskel sleep and started to track his sons. He found the bones and he pounded and ate them. That night, when the brothers were making a camp in the bushes, they came upon a cave. In the morning they told Pitoíois to stay in the cave while they were hunting, and not to go out; that there were snakes around, and she mustn't go to sleep, for if she did they would bite her.

When Tskel woke up and found that the old man was not in the house, he was frightened, and he ran out to find him. He followed his tracks till he came to where he was pounding and eating bones.

"Why did you come here?" asked Tskel. "Didn't your sons tell you to stay at home?"

The old man didn't listen to Tskel's words; he kept on pounding. Tskel hurried along to overtake the brothers. When he came to their camp, he asked: "Where do you leave your wife while you are hunting?"

"We hide her."

"You must be careful. Your father is tracking you; he means to kill her. I left him eating bones, but he will be here soon."

Just then Tskel screamed out: "I see him now! There he is, peeping over that mountain."

Old Wûlkûtska was on the farther side of the mountain, looking over. He threw his mortar at Pitoíois, but she saw it coming and dodged. That minute the old man was there at the camp.

"I am sweating. It's awful hot!" said he.

" You have been eating bones," said his sons, and they began to scold him.

Pitoíois gave him meat and bones, then said to the brothers: " Let us leave him and go over two mountains." At the foot of the second mountain there was a large river.

" Are there any fish in this river? " asked Pitoíois.

" A great many," said the eldest brother. When she took off two of her dresses to go into the water, the youngest brother said: " Put on your dresses; they will get stiff and hard."

" I can fix them," said Pitoíois, and she began to catch fish with her basket. Soon she saw her father-in-law watching her. Just his forehead and eyes were above the top of the mountain.

He thought: " I will have her now; she hasn't seen me yet." That time the old man talked to his mortar, said: " Hit her if you can, but if you can't, fall on the ground. Don't fall in the water." He threw the mortar, but Pitoíois saw it coming and dodged. The mortar fell on the ground with a terrible noise. The brothers were roasting meat; they heard the noise and ran toward the river. Pitoíois dropped her basket and fish, and ran toward the camp, crying.

" What noise was that? " asked the brothers.

" It was your father's mortar. It struck near me. He is trying to kill me."

" It is your fault," said the brothers. " When he was dead, you brought him to life."

" I don't hate him, I want him to live," said Pitoíois.

That minute Wûlkûtska came puffing along. " I am sweating. It's awful hot! " said he.

All night the brothers watched the old man for fear he would kill Pitoíois.

" You needn't bother," said Pitoíois. " I am willing to die, but I want to see my brothers again."

" We will go home," said the eldest brother.

" It makes me feel lonesome to go home. It was you who wanted to come," said the youngest brother.

The second brother was mad; he snatched his father's mortar and threw it into the river. The old man chased him and threw the pounder at him; it just missed him. The young man picked it up and threw it back. It hit the old man and killed him, for his mortar was in the water and he was getting weak. The brothers were glad that he was dead.

"I can't do without the old man," said little Tskel, and he began to cry.

Pitoíois was sorry for Tskel. When the youngest brother saw how sorry Pitoíois and Tskel were, he asked Pitoíois if she could do anything to bring the old man to life.

She said: "I can bring him to life and give him a better mind. If I bring him to life now, he won't use his mortar again, and hereafter everyone will be as he will be,—when they grow old they will be like children."

She got the mortar, then she made a plate out of braided grass and sprinkled it with water. She spread the plate on the old man and stepped over him five times. He grew warm, but didn't come to life. Then she said to Tskel: "Strike him with your medicine stick." Tskel struck him twice on the head. "Strike him twice across the breast," said Pitoíois. At the second blow the old man got up; he was well again, and his mind was good.

The next morning Pitoíois had a little boy. Old Wûlkûtska called it grandson and was glad. The youngest brother and Pitoíois went to live with her brothers and the old man went with them. The four other Wûlkûtska brothers started off to hunt for a wife, and little Tskel went with them.

Pitoíois' brothers asked her: "Have you seen any young women where you have been?"

"There are not many women in the world," said Pitoíois.

"We will go and get the woman Kāhkaas told us about."

"Can you live with her?" asked Pitoíois. "Her home is under the water. You want a wife who can live on dry land. Don't go for her; she is not a good wife for you."

They asked their brother-in-law to go with them. Pitoíois didn't want him to go, but they started and he went with them. They traveled toward the southwest. When the brothers got tired and wanted water to drink, the brother-in-law dug a well for them with his hands, and said: "This well will always be here. The people to come will call it Wûlkûtska Ámpo after me."

On the south side of Klamath Lake they saw old man Kûlta.

"Why do you come here?" asked he.

"We have come for your daughter."

"My children are on that island over there. I have a place ready for each one of them; I make deep holes under the water, where they can watch the fish. My daughter wouldn't like you. She travels on trails under the water. You are land people; you mustn't go to my island, for my children would kill you."

The brothers climbed a high mountain. Near the top of it they found a lake. In the water at the edge of the lake was another old man like the first one. They saw him come out of the water with his mouth full of fish; they had never seen any one fish in that way before. When he saw them coming, he was frightened, and jumped into the water. They called to him and he turned around; then he knew they were Pitoíois' brothers. He called them "cousins" and asked: "Where are you going?"

"We are looking for a woman. Do you know where we can find one?"

"I don't know, for I live in the water. If I travel on land I get dry; I should die if I went far from water. Maybe if you go toward the west you will find people."

"We must go home," said the brothers; "our sister will be lonesome."

They found Pitoíois crying; she said: "It's useless for you to travel around; there are no women, except far away in the north."

The elder brother went to the top of a mountain and cried all day. His sister was sorry for him; she said: "There are people in the north. Maybe you will find a wife there."

"I will go north," said he, "and my brother will go with me." His medicine was the feather of a white eagle. He put a feather on the top of his little nephew's head, twisted his hair around it, and said: "If this feather comes off while we are gone, you will know that we shall never come back."

"You must watch for Wus," said the brother-in-law. "He is mad at us and will kill you if he can."

Before they got to the first mountain, the feather fell out of the baby's hair and flew away on the wind.

Pitoíois screamed and said to her husband: "Hurry and overtake our brothers and tell them that as soon as they were out of sight their medicine feather fell out of the baby's hair."

He went very fast, but the brothers were over five mountains. He couldn't overtake them, so he turned back.

The brothers came to a brook running through a wide meadow; there were trees on each side of the brook. They sat down under a tree and began to cry. The younger brother said: "I feel lonesome, as though I were going to die."

"I feel so, too," said the elder brother. "Let us travel fast; maybe we can get there to-day."

They started, but hadn't gone far when they saw Wus coming toward them. The younger brother screamed, and said: "I think this is the person you have been hunting for."

When Wus met them, he asked: "Where are you going?"

"We are just traveling around."

"You are like me; I have no home, I travel all the time. Who are you?"

"We can't tell you who we are, but we are people."

"Whose brothers are you?"

"We are brothers to nobody."

"I know whose brothers you are," said Wus. "Pitoíois is your sister; she hates me as if I had no life in me, and I hate her. I know your brother-in-law, the great arrow man."

"Where are there people?" asked the elder brother.

"Near here. Will your brother-in-law come behind you?"

"We don't know," said the younger brother.

Wus was mad. "You will no longer be living people," said he. "You will be birds and wander around nights."

Wus made night come quickly. The brothers got separated and lost in the darkness. They called to each other, but they couldn't get together, and to this day they wander around alone.

ILYÚYU AND KULTA'S SISTERS

CHARACTERS

Kûlta . . . . Otter
Ilyúyu . . . .

KÛLTA'S wife had one grown-up brother, and a number of little brothers and sisters. Her grown-up brother had a pet wolf, — same as people have pet dogs now. — Its name was Ilyúyu Watcagû, and the young man was called by the same name.

When Kûlta's wife went to visit her father and mother, and carry them the nice things Kûlta had paid for her, her brother wanted to go home with her. She said: " My brother, it is a bad place there. They eat snake heads and frog heads. If you don't eat with them, maybe they will kill you. There are bad women there, too; they will make fun of you and tease you." But the young man kept asking her to let him go, and at last she said: " Get some tula straws and roll them up in little balls. When the women give you snake heads to eat, put a ball on the dish; then they can't hurt you."

When they got to the house, one of Kûlta's sisters brought a dish of snake heads and gave it to Ilyúyu. Some of the heads were dry, others were fresh and alive. His sister said: " Put a ball on the plate." But Ilyúyu was so frightened that he couldn't move.

The women made fun of him, and said: " He doesn't call our brother 'brother-in-law.' We are as good as he is, but he won't eat with us." They took the plate away and said to him: " You came here to peek around and see how we lived; you will be sorry for it. Your head may get home, but your body will be destroyed."

Kûlta had two sisters. Ilyúyu gave each one of them a nice bone scratcher; then he said: " You needn't think you won't be sorry, too. Those bones will scratch all the flesh off your body."

Kûlta's wife was crying; she gathered up a sackful of nice beads and gave them to her brother; then she gave him a bow and arrow, and he started for home. As he went, he called: "Come, Ilyúyu! Come, Ilyúyu!" and the little wolf followed him. He talked to Ilyúyu, said: "We went to take our sister back to her husband, but now what trouble we are in." And he began to sing to himself in a crying voice: "We met trouble from going home with our sister, we met trouble from going home with our sister." After he had gone a little way, he said: "I wonder what is so heavy." He stopped, took the sack off his back, untied it, and threw away some of the nice beads his sister had given him. Then he called: "Come on, Ilyúyu!"

Ilyúyu cried; he was sorry to have his master lose such beautiful beads.

The young man said: "Come on, Ilyúyu. Don't cry for the beads. I have plenty of beads at home." When he had gone a little farther, his pack grew heavy again. He took it off and threw away more of the beads. Ilyúyu picked them up and carried them in his mouth. "Come on, Ilyúyu!" called his master. "Don't mind those beads; I have plenty of beads at home."

Soon the young man said: "I wonder what is so heavy." He threw away his bow and arrows. Ilyúyu cried. He picked up the bow and carried it in his mouth. "Come on, Ilyúyu," said his master. "Don't cry, I have another bow at home." Soon he said: "I wonder what is so heavy." And he threw away his quiver.

Kûlta's wife knew what the women were doing to her brother. She took a basket and followed him. When he threw away his quiver, she was there behind him; she picked up the quiver and put it in her basket. She felt badly. She cried hard and thought: "Poor brother, they will kill you."

The young man said: "There are too many beads on my moccasins; they are so heavy I can hardly step." He threw away one of the moccasins, and called: "Come on, Ilyúyu!"

(He didn't see his sister, and Ilyúyu didn't see her.) Soon he pulled off the other moccasin and threw it away. He threw away his belt. Ilyúyu picked it up and tried to carry it in his mouth. He dragged it a while, then dropped it. After a time the young man said: "What have I got on that is so heavy?" He took off his beaded shirt and threw it away. When Ilyúyu cried, his master called: "Come on, Ilyúyu, I have another shirt at home." He threw away his beaded leggings; then he was naked. Ilyúyu was crying. "Come on, Ilyúyu," said his master. Soon he pulled off one arm and threw it away. Ilyúyu tried to drag the arm along with his teeth, but his master called: "Come on, Ilyúyu, come on!" and he left it. His sister put it in her basket. Soon he said: "I wonder what is so heavy." And he threw away the second arm. He pulled off his legs; then he was only a body and head. He went on a little way, then said: "I wonder what is so heavy." His body fell off, and he was only a head. He became Núsdilausniyas (Rolling Head) and could travel fast. He crossed a mountain at a bound, then rolled along in the air. He had big eyes and long hair that waved behind him.

When he got to the river near his home, he struck the ground, and said: "Dum! dum!" Then he called in a loud voice: "Mother, come and take me across!" "Where are you?" asked his mother; she couldn't see him.

"I am here waiting. Come and get me!" When she didn't come, he got mad, flew across the river and came down in the house: "Dum! dum!" Then he flew at the people, hit them, and killed them.

Ilyúyu was crying; the river was swift and he couldn't cross. Soon the sister came. She found a canoe, crossed the river, and went to the house. She looked in through the smoke hole and saw the Head eating the body of her mother. She was terribly scared. She ran to the village to tell the people; she knew that after the Head had eaten her father and mother, it would fly to the village and kill everybody there.

The Head felt dust scatter in at the smoke hole, and knew that somebody was on the top of the house. It went out, saw tracks, and followed the woman. When Ilyúyu saw his master, just a great bloody Head, he felt so badly and was so afraid that he ran off to the mountains and wandered around, crying all the time.

When the sister told the people that her brother had turned to a man-eater, the two oldest women in the village said to them: " You must paint your faces with the pitch out of cedar trees, and be strong; maybe we can save you."

The two made a basket as tight and firm as they could. They waxed their hands so they could hold the Head. Then they rowed to the other side of the river and waited; soon they heard the Head coming, with a terrible whizzing and noise. It struck the bank: " Dum! dum! " and called out: " Come and take me over! " When it saw the two old women, it asked: " Why didn't young people come for me? "

" They are afraid of you," said one of the old women.

" They must come. I won't cross with you; you will throw me into the river."

" No, we won't. We want to put you in our basket and take you over in the right way, so people in later times won't make fun of you."

" How can I look out and see what you are doing? "

" You can look through the cracks in the basket."

" Will you carry me into your house when you get over? "

" Yes, we will take good care of you."

At last the Head said: " I'll go. Take me up carefully." When they got the Head into the basket, it screamed and tried to get out, said: " I can't see. Let me out! "

" We are almost over," said the women. " Keep still; you are all right. Now we are going to get out of the canoe. We are across the river."

They were only in the middle of the river. They took up the basket and dropped it into the water. It went up and down many times, for the Head was trying hard to get out. When the basket got near the bank, people pushed it away with long poles. After a while it got so heavy with water that it sank.

Then the old women said: " This world wasn't made for such things as you are. Hereafter you will only show yourself to scare doctors; you will be their medicine, and tell them what to do."

When the Head was drowned, the sister went back to Kûlta's house. Kûlta was off on the mountains, roaming around; when he saw his wife coming he was glad, and went to meet her. He said: "My sisters were proud of their scratching sticks. They scratched their arms, scratched till all the skin and flesh was off, then they scratched their legs and bodies, scratched till only bones were left, then they died. I was scared, and ran away."

Kûlta built a big fire and burned up his sister's bones, and the sacks of dried snake heads and frog heads. When the snakes came to life and tried to get out of the fire Kûlta and his wife pushed them in, but they couldn't watch all of them; some got away and ran off among the rocks, and that is why there are so many snakes in the world now.

When the fire had burned down, and only ashes were left, Kûlta said: "I can't stay here where my sisters died. I will make a house south of here, by the river."

While the woman was poking in the ashes, a big rattlesnake sprang at her. Kûlta heard the snake rattle. He struck it with a long pole, and it ran away. Then the woman began to vomit up all kinds of terrible stuff, pieces of snake skin and fish skin, and pieces of snake heads. Kûlta said: "This is always the way when women eat snake heads, and such things, but with men it is different."

When the woman was through vomiting, she found the snake and killed it. She said: "Hereafter, you will have no power. You will want to bite people, but you will tell them where you are; you can't help it. They will kill you with stones but will never eat your head; they will say you are dirty."

Every day the woman heard little Ilyúyu crying on the mountain. She felt so sorry that Kûlta said: "I will find him and bring him home." When he got near the place where his brother-in-law's sack grew heavy and he put it down to throw away some of the beads, he saw Ilyúyu sitting by the trail, but when the little fellow saw Kûlta he ran off, crying like a person. Kûlta saw him at the place where his brother-in-law had thrown away his quiver. He called: " Come here, Ilyúyu! Don't be afraid! Come and go home with me." But Ilyúyu ran away. Kûlta followed him all day but couldn't catch him. When he went home, he said to his wife: " To-morrow you must go for Ilyúyu. Maybe he will come when you call him."

The next morning Kûlta heated stones and his wife sweated. Then she listened. She heard Ilyúyu's cry and followed the sound, calling all the time: " Ilyúyu, Ilyúyu! " He would stop and wait for her to come up near him, but when she put out her hands to catch him he ran away. She followed him a good many days. When she camped he would come and lie down near her, but when she moved he would go away. She followed him till she was only skin and bones, then she said to him: " I am going home now. If you want to be wild you can. You will kill deer, and people will say, ' Ilyúyu, Kûlta's brother-in-law, did that.' "

Ilyúyu ran off to the mountains and Kûlta's wife never heard his cry again.

NANIHLAS[1]

CHARACTERS

Blaiwas	Eagle	Maûk	Fly
Kaiutois	Wolf	Múkus	Owl
Näníhläs	Bat		

Two Näníhläs brothers and their sister lived together. The brothers were small men. They had no way of killing deer, so they tried to trap them. They dug a hole so deep that if a deer fell into it, it couldn't get out.

One morning when the brothers went to their trap, they found a deer in it. "We don't want to shoot this deer," said the elder brother.

"Why not?" asked the younger.

"Because we want the skin for a dress for our sister. If we make a hole in it, her body will show through. We must catch the deer by the throat and choke him to death."

"I don't think we can kill him in that way," said the elder brother, "but we can try."

They caught hold of the deer's throat. The deer ran around in the pit and tried to get out.

"Hold on tight," said the younger brother. "He will soon die."

After a while the deer got out of the pit and ran off, but the brothers held on. The deer ran to a mountain where there were trees and tall brush; the blankets and caps of the Näníhläs brothers were torn off and their bodies were scratched, but the younger brother kept calling: "Hold on tight; we will kill him."

At last the elder brother let go of the deer and dropped to the ground. He went back and picked up his cap and the

[1] When Indians tell this story, they talk down in their throats, to imitate the Näníhläs people.

pieces of his blanket. He pinned the pieces together with sticks and mended his moccasins with sticks.

The younger brother clung on for a good while, then he hit against a tree, and got such a blow that he fell off and lay on the ground for a long time. At last he got up, and started for home; as he went along, he picked up the pieces of his blanket and fastened them together with sticks. He was mad at his brother for letting go so soon. When they met, they quarreled a while, then made up and went on. Soon they saw a number of women coming toward them; each woman was carrying a basketful of roots. The brothers sat down and waited.

When the women came, they put their baskets on the ground, put some roots in a small basket, and gave the basket to the elder brother. He called to his brother: " Come and eat some of these roots." The brother didn't go; he made believe that he was mad; he didn't say a word. The elder brother called him a second time; the third time he called, the younger brother said: " I won't eat those roots. The women gave them to you; they didn't give me any."

The women were afraid; they knew that those brothers were cross and powerful. One of the women asked: " What is the matter? Why are you mad? What are you quarreling about? "

The two began to fight. Each brother had a piece of burnt fungus; they chewed the fungus and rubbed it on their faces and heads to frighten the women. The women were so scared that they left their baskets and ran off.

Then the brothers stopped fighting and laughed. They took the roots and went home. They had a sister married to a man on the other side of Klamath Lake. They started off to visit her. The elder brother asked: " What will you do when we get there? "

The younger said: " I don't know; what will you do? "

" I will make the young men fight; the chief's son will get shot in the eye. Everybody will run off to see him, and while they are gone, we will steal all they have in their houses."

When they got to their sister's house she cried because she

had nothing to give them to eat. She began to pound fish bones for them. The younger brother asked: "Why do you cry? I will make those bones good." He made the fish bones into nice sweet seeds just by thinking hard. After a while, the young men of the village began to quarrel and then to fight, and right away the chief's son was shot in the eye. Everybody ran to see what had happened. The two brothers stole all there was in the village, — blankets, beads, everything, — made packs of them; made the packs small and put them under their finger nails; then they started off in their canoe, taking their sister with them.

When the people went back to their houses and found their things gone, they knew that the brothers had stolen them. They followed them in their canoes, and were catching up when the elder brother asked: "What shall we do now?"

"I will make ice," said the younger brother. Right away there was thick ice.

"What will you do with our canoe?"

"I will put it under one of my finger nails." He did that.

The men, finding their canoes fast in the ice, got out and ran after the brothers.

The elder brother asked: "What shall we do now?" "I will break up the ice and those men will drown." Right away the ice melted. All the men were drowned, but the brothers and their sister got home safe.

Blaiwas and Kaiutois and a good many hunters lived near the Näníhläs brothers. One day the younger brother said: "I am going to drive all the deer in the world into a great pit and keep them for ourselves." He had only to think hard and the pit was there and the deer were in it; not one deer was left outside. That was the kind of man he was.

The hunters wondered where the deer had gone. They couldn't find one, and soon they were starving. Maûk lived with the hunters; he scented the deer to the house of the Näníhläs brothers and found where they had them shut up. Then the hunters sent Múkus to watch the brothers. He went to their house, sat down by the fire, and pretended to fall asleep. The younger brother looked at Múkus' eyes, ran a stick into his nose, and put a coal of fire on the top of his head. Múkus didn't move or wink. They thought he was sound asleep. They wanted to kill a deer.

When they opened the pit, the deer were scared and made a great noise. The brothers caught one of them, brought it out of the pit, and fastened up the place. They killed the deer and skinned it, hid some of the meat, and roasted the rest.

Mûkus saw everything. The brothers thought: "He sees nothing; he is asleep."

Múkus went home and told the hunters that five great rocks fastened up the pit where the deer were. That the rocks were so big that it would take a great many people to move them, but the brothers rolled them over the hole by thinking. The hunters found Tcúititi and hired him to break the rocks. He broke them by flying up to the sky and falling down against them. He did that five times, and the five rocks fell to pieces. The deer came out and scattered over the whole world. The hunters were watching, and as the deer passed them, they chose the biggest bucks and killed them. The brothers didn't try again to hide the deer.

THE BRINGING TO LIFE OF THE WUS BROTHERS

CHARACTERS

Kaiutois	Gray Wolf
Wus	Black Fox

TEN Wus brothers and ten Kaiutois brothers lived together; they were kin. Each man had five daughters, except the youngest Wus brother; he wasn't married. The Wus brothers had a sister; she was nice-looking, but she had such a long neck that she couldn't eat meat; she ate the neck bones of deer; ate five at a time. Everybody in the world knew about her.

One day, when the eldest Wus brother was hunting, he took his drill out of his quiver to start a fire. He put the drill on the ground and the next minute it was gone; he couldn't find it anywhere. That night he said to his brothers: "I was alone all day, but when I put down my fire drill it went away. I hunted everywhere, but I couldn't find it. That means trouble is coming to us; I don't think we will live long."

The next morning when some of the brothers wanted to track deer, the eldest Wus brother said: "We must stay at home to-day. I feel scared about my drill; something bad is going to happen."

Old woman Kaiutois was sick in a little straw house near the big house where her sons lived. She called to them, and said: "I hear people around in the mountains; I think that they are coming to kill us. They are people from the north. I don't know what they say, but they are coming nearer and nearer all the time."

Just then a crowd of men with bows and arrows came down from the mountain. They came to fight the Wus brothers.

There were so many that they filled the house, and the brothers couldn't do anything; they were all killed except the youngest Wus brother. He got on the top of the house, made a long leap, then ran as fast as he could.

The strangers killed old woman Kaiutois, but they left Wus' mother alive. They said: "She is old, she won't have any more children; let her stay here."

They cut each man open and took out his heart. They put the hearts on the end of a long pole, burned the house, and started off, taking all the women with them except Wus' mother. When they were out of sight, Wus came home. He found his mother, and asked: "Did they leave the bodies?"

"Yes, but they cut them open and carried the hearts away."

"Don't feel lonesome," said Wus. "I have two minds; I can do anything. I will pay those people for killing my brothers."

The old woman had covered her head with pitch and ashes. Wus told her to go to the river and wash it off. While she was gone, he thought hard and right away there was a new house where the old one had been. It was large and nice, and was full of baskets and mats. He told his mother to make him ten pairs of moccasins.

"Why do you want moccasins?" asked the old woman. "I don't know where to get skin to make them with." She had a rabbit-skin dress on and he told her to cut ten pieces out of it. Right away the ten pieces were ten pairs of beautiful, beaded moccasins.

The old woman said: "You must be careful. Those men are strong. Maybe they will kill you."

"I am not afraid," said Wus. "I have more power than they have. I am going to find my sister. Maybe I will be gone a long time. Every day you must put down new mats and throw away the old ones." Then he said to the mats: "There must be new mats here each day."

Wus started. He traveled fast. Each pair of new moccasins lasted ten days. When there was a hole in the heel of one moccasin, he threw the pair away. He wore out five pairs; then he was near the house where the strangers lived. He climbed a high mountain and stayed there all day, watching the people in the valley. He saw his sister; she was almost dead. Men were throwing captives back and forth across a fire; their bodies were burned and black with smoke. At dark the men began to whoop and scream, and to dance around the fire.

Wus thought hard, and made something long and bright. When he raised it up, it blazed like fire. He called it golóbis. When he held it and looked far off, he could see everything. He saw the people throwing his sister back and forth like a ball, across the fire. The pole his brothers' hearts were on was stuck in the ground near the fire. He cried when he looked at his sister and his kin. He said: " I want to have long hair, and I want it covered with nice beads and bones, and I want a blanket, and leggings covered with porcupine quills." Right away his hair touched the ground, and he had a blanket and leggings covered with beautiful quills. At midnight he went where the people were and stood looking at the fire.

" Who is that? " asked one of the men.

" Maybe that is Wus," said another.

Wus took his bow and arrow and began to whip the bow string with the arrow. It made nice music. Right away the long-necked girl knew that the man was her brother. When he went nearer to the fire, people called out: " Wus! Wus! That man is Wus! " and they were frightened.

" Why do you call me Wus? " asked he.

" I feel as if Wus were looking at me," said the chief's son. " Where did you come from? We have never seen a man dressed as you are. Who are you? "

" You mustn't ask such questions," said Wus. " Everybody has heard of me. I live near you. My house is among the rocks. I have come to visit you. Where did you get those hearts and those young women? "

" Off in the south, where there are two lakes together. They are the hearts of the chiefs of that place. We killed nine of the Wus brothers, and all of the Kaiutois brothers, and took their wives and sisters."

" I am glad those men are dead," said Wus. " They made

me an orphan, and they almost killed my old grandmother, who lives north of here." Wus began to cry.

The people didn't quite believe him; they said: "You are Wus."

"Why do you say that?" asked Wus. "You make me feel badly."

"We missed the youngest Wus brother; maybe you are he."

"I will tell you about that young man," said Wus. "He can do anything he wants to. He can change into different things. He can turn people into rocks, or old stumps, or ashes. He wouldn't come here and talk to you; he would turn you into birds, or trees, or anything else he wanted to. He doesn't talk to people. I wish I could kill him, but I haven't power enough. I am afraid to go near him. I am glad you have killed his brothers."

People said: "Don't listen to that man; he is Wus."

Wus said: "Wait and see what will become of you when Wus comes. He will be here soon. He will come to kill you and take his sister home. Didn't you take all the nice clothes those brothers had? When their youngest brother ran away, was he dressed as I am? Can't I stay and play with those hearts and with the daughters of the men who killed my father and mother? I will dance five nights over those hearts; I am glad to see them hanging up there."

Some of the people said: "Let him stay. We will watch him. He can stay one day, then if he doesn't do any harm, we will let him stay longer. He isn't Wus."

Wus knew their thoughts. He began to dance and to throw the women across the fire. He meant to make them stronger. As he threw them, he talked to them in his heart, and they answered him in their hearts. He said aloud: "I am glad to throw you over the fire. Your kin killed my father and mother! I want the fire to burn you."

He danced all night and threw the women faster than any other man; but each time he threw them they were stronger.

In the morning he said: "You must let me sleep till the sun goes down; then I will show you how glad I am that those brothers are dead. My grandmother thinks that I am off hunting for deer. You must give me one of those hearts to carry home to her; then she will be glad, too."

After Wus had slept a while, one of the men woke him up and said: "You are hungry; here are seeds to eat." To one another they said: "If he is Wus, he won't eat our water seeds." He knew what they said. He ate the seeds and went to sleep again; slept till it was almost dark. Then he helped the men build a big fire. He loosened his hair and it floated around him, it was so long and thick. He had a woman braid it and tie it up with strings of beads. Then he called out: "I want everybody to come and see me dance!" The men sat around and looked at him. He danced well and he sang his own songs. He danced for three nights; by the middle of the third night everybody was tired. Wus said: "You should sleep so you will be strong enough to dance to-morrow." He was taking their minds away from them; they thought of nothing; they liked Wus and did as he told them.

The fourth night everybody was sleepy. Wus said: "Why don't you sleep now and dance in the daytime? People used to dance when the sun was bright so everybody could see what they were doing."

The next morning they danced till midday, then rested. Wus said: "This is the last night I'll dance. I am going home."

They began early. Wus pounded the hearts on the poles. He pulled the women around, rubbed them against the hearts, and said: "Those are the hearts of your fathers and of your kin." He whooped and screamed and danced till midnight. Then all the men were falling asleep, they were so tired.

"What makes you so sleepy?" asked Wus. "When Wus comes, you'll not do as you are doing now. Wus has power; when he comes, he won't leave one of you alive." He kicked the men to make them get up and dance; then he said: "You didn't let me know you were going off to kill those men; now you must give me this long-necked woman. Those men didn't do you any harm, but they killed all my people." He began to sing, and as he sang, every man fell sound asleep.

Wus said to the women: "When I hold up my golóbis,

you must start and run toward the east. Run as fast as you can." He took the string of hearts and wound it around his waist. Then he held the golóbis — a great red ball — in his hand and went around among the sleeping men. The ball killed them all, burned their lives up; when he turned the ball over, it went out. The men lay there dead; Wus cut them open and took out their hearts.

When Wus caught up with the women, he gave each woman one moccasin. Right away each moccasin became a pair. As he traveled, he picked up the old moccasins he had thrown away when coming. There were no holes in them now. They were beautiful and new.

When Wus and the women were half-way home, they came to a place where their brothers and kin used to hunt deer. The women felt lonesome and began to cry. Wus said: "You needn't feel lonesome; I am going to bring all of our people to life."

Now old woman Wus dreamed that she saw a whole string of hearts come in at the top of the house, like snakes. When she woke up, she felt scared; she rubbed herself in ashes and thought: "As I have dreamed, it will be. Nobody can change a dream."

When near home, the long-necked girl began to sing; her song was like the song of a fly. The old woman heard it and was glad; she knew that her daughter was coming, for nobody that lived in the world could sing her song

When they got to the house, the women hurried to get wood and build a fire, so that their grandmother could boil the hearts Wus had brought. When everything was ready, the old woman said: "You must all stay outside while I do my work."

Wus said: "Why do you have them stay outside? The spirits of the men will be out there talking. If the women answer, your work will be spoiled, and my brothers will never come to life."

The old woman put the hearts in a basket of water and put hot stones around the basket. Then she tied blankets around the women and made them lie down in one corner of the house. She said: "When your brothers begin to come back, they will talk to you; they will ask: 'Are you glad to see us?' 'Have we been gone long?' 'What are you lying there for?' 'Get up and give us something to eat; we are hungry;' but don't answer, don't say a word. If you do, there won't be anything but hearts in the basket."

When the water began to boil, the spirits of the men whose hearts were in the basket began to talk in the brush outside the house; then they went into the house and talked to the women. When the women didn't answer, they pushed them and scolded. But the women didn't look up, didn't speak. After a while, there was a great noise, laughing and talking, then each man took his place by the fire.

The old woman said to them: "You should keep still; you have made me feel lonesome. You have been dead; I put ashes on my head and mourned for you."

The eldest Wus said: "Why did you feel lonesome? You knew our brother had power, that nobody could kill him and that he could save us."

They were glad when they saw their sister. She said: "Those men treated me badly; they wouldn't give me anything to eat, and they threw me back and forth across the fire."

"I am glad they didn't make you eat our hearts," said the eldest brother. "Those people sometimes make their captives eat the hearts of their own brothers and kin."

LOK AND KÉKINA

CHARACTERS

Lok	Bear
Kékina	Lizard
Wus	Fox

FIVE Lok brothers and their sister lived in a house on a mountain near Klamath Lake; not far away lived old woman Wus with her two nephews, the Kékina brothers. They were orphans; the Lok brothers had killed their father and their mother. In summer Wus had had the children gather roots and store them in a tree for winter. When winter came the younger boy went three times each day to the top of the tree to eat a few of the roots. As he went, he called out: " Spring is coming! Spring is coming! "

Lok's sister had a big pile of roots hidden under the ground. She never gave any to Wus; she was always watching around to see what Wus taught the boys. Wus didn't teach them anything. She didn't dare to; but the elder boy knew how to make poison arrows.

One morning when little Kékina ran out to the tree, he cried: " Spring is coming! Spring is coming! " and brought down a few roots for his brother.

The Lok woman heard him, and asked: " Why do you tell such a lie? Spring isn't coming. It is winter. When you see smoke on the mountains, then spring will come." To the elder brother Lok said: " You are good for nothing; you sit all day making arrows, but you can't kill anything."

Old woman Wus cried, but the boy told her and his little brother not to answer Lok; if they did, Lok would tell her brothers, and they might come and kill them.

Once when the little boy was outside, Lok said to him:

"Little boy, I feel mean toward you; you tell lies about spring coming." That evening Lok watched him and was mad when he called out: "Spring is coming! Spring is coming!" for every time he called, it hurried spring along, and she liked winter. She went to the tree where the roots were hidden, spat on her hands, took hold of the top of the tree, pulled it down, rolled the roots in a ball, and swallowed them.

The next morning, when little Kékina called: "Spring is coming! Spring is coming!" and ran to the tree, he found that all his roots were gone. He saw Lok's tracks and knew that she had stolen them. He rolled around on the ground and cried, he felt so badly. Then he went in and lay down by his brother, who was making poison arrows. The brother said: "Keep still, I am going to talk to my arrows and tell them what to do." He held the arrows over the fire, and said: "Arrows, you must go right through the bodies of the big-handed people; the people that never get enough to eat."

Old woman Lok was listening around; she said: "You are talking about the people who killed your father and mother, and will kill you."

When her brothers came home, she said: "I hate to hear that Kékina boy talk about killing you."

The eldest brother said: "Somebody makes him mad; maybe you have been boasting that we killed his father and mother." He scolded the woman till she said: "I am going off; I sha'n't come back till night."

While she was gone, old woman Wus stole half of her roots, dug a hole and hid them, and then made mole tracks around, little hills of dirt.

In Lok's house the chief slept in the middle, near the fire; two brothers slept on one side of him and two on the other; the sister slept by the ladder. That night, when the brothers were asleep, little Kékina crept into their house. He passed his hands over them and they all slept soundly, they couldn't wake up. He cut off the chief's foot, put the end of his leg on the log in the fire, and said to it: "Don't you waken the chief till you are half burned up." He took the foot home. Wus roasted it, and she and her nephews ate it. Then she put out the fire, rubbed ashes on her mouth to hide the grease, and began to cry as if she were hungry.

When the leg was half consumed, the chief woke up and screamed: " My leg is burning! My leg is burning! " His sister said: " This is Kékina's work," but the chief said: " No, I went to sleep with my feet on the log." He died the next day.

When his brothers were going to burn the body, old woman Wus said: " People will make fun of you if you burn your brother. You must put him in the ground with his burnt leg sticking out. If you feel badly, you can go away. I will watch, I won't let anything come to eat him."

When the Lok brothers had put the chief in the ground and gone off, Wus dug up the body and cooked it for her nephews to eat; then she stuck a chunk of burnt wood where the leg had been.

The next day old woman Lok said: " I am afraid Wus and those boys will dig up our brother's body and eat it." And she went to see. She didn't go far, for she saw the chunk sticking up out of the ground and thought it was the leg.

The elder Kékina brother said to Wus: " You must go and find out what the Loks are doing. You can tell them that I have driven you away."

When Wus got where the Loks were camped, she began to cry.

They asked: " What are you crying for? "

" My nephews have driven me out," said Wus; " they won't let me stay with them."

The Loks believed her and let her stay around. When they asked: " Where are you going to live? " she said: " I have other kin, I am going to them. Their house is straight east."

That night Lok had a dream. The dream said: " Your brother's body has been stolen." In the morning she started off to find out if it had. When she got back, she said: " Just as my dream told me, somebody has carried off our brother."

Wus said: " I know nothing about it."

Lok said: " Yes, you do; those boys did it."

Wus said: " No, they moved away when you did. You can go and kill them if you want to. I am going east."

She started, but when she was a little way off, she turned and went west. When she got home, she said to her nephews: " The Loks are coming to fight you."

" I'm not afraid of the Loks," said the elder brother. " You must go off to the mountain. I will put my brother in a crack of the house, then I will fight the Loks with knives." He had five knives under one arm; his bow and arrows were hanging up.

When the four Lok brothers and their sister came, one of the brothers caught Kékina in his mouth and swallowed him. Kékina stuck a knife in Lok's heart, killed him, and came out. The second brother swallowed him; he killed him and came out; the third swallowed him and was killed. The fourth brother bit Kékina, then swallowed him. Kékina was hurt; he stayed in Lok's body a good while before he could get strength enough to stick his knife in Lok's heart and run out. He didn't cut Lok's heart open, and Lok jumped up and swallowed him again. That time Lok choked, and Kékina nearly smothered; but he made himself small and rolled out of Lok's throat.

Old woman Lok said: " I told you those boys would kill you. Now all our brothers are dead." Just then Lok saw Kékina. He caught him and swallowed him again. That time Kékina cut Lok's heart open and he died.

Old woman Lok jumped at Kékina to bite him, but he ran down her throat before she could bite; he ran out, and she caught him; again she was going to bite him, but he ran down her throat and came out. The next time he slipped down quickly; he cut her heart open, and she died.

Wus came home; they had lots of meat now, and she was glad. When spring came, little Kékina wanted to dig roots. Wus said: " Don't go far. The Lok brothers had a great many kin. You must keep away from them."

Kékina said: " When I find sweet roots, I want to lie down by them, and eat them; sometimes I feel like staying all night."

"You must be careful," said Wus. "The Loks like the same things that you do. One might come along and eat the roots and you with them, without knowing that you were there."

One night little Kékina didn't come home. The next morning his brother began to hunt for him. Off on a flat he saw men digging roots; they were Loks. He went up to one of them, and asked: "Have you seen my brother?"

"No," said Lok, "he hasn't been here."

He asked ever so many men, and each one said: "He hasn't been here." One man said: "We could eat him and not know it; for sometimes we dig up great roots with our hands, and he might be with them. There is a Lok over there; he came ahead of us. Maybe he saw your brother."

When Kékina asked him, he said: "What makes you ask questions? I don't want to talk," and he started off.

Kékina followed him, and said: "Open your mouth."

"Why should I open my mouth? I am sick. Let me alone."

Kékina kept following him. At last Lok opened one side of his mouth; then Kékina made him open the other side. In Lok's teeth he had found one of little Kékina's hairs; he got it out and wound it around the head of his arrow. Then he began to fight with the Loks. One after another they swallowed him; he cut each one's heart open and killed him. He left only one Lok alive, — the poorest and oldest. He said to that one: "I will not kill you, but you will no longer be a person; you will be a common bear and scare people."

Kékina took the hair home. Wus told him to sprinkle her medicine basket and put it over the hair, then step over the basket five times. He did, and his brother came to life. Then the two brothers and Wus lived together as before.

GRASSHOPPER IN LOVE WITH DEER

CHARACTERS

Djáhdjai	Grasshopper
Djihens	Ant
Wiĕs	Deer

A MAN had two wives, Djáhdjai and Djihens. When it came root-digging time, the two women went out every morning to dig roots, but they went in different directions; they didn't dig on the same flat.

At midday Djihens always went home with a basketful of nice, white roots. Djáhdjai never went home till it was getting dark, and then she had only a few roots in the bottom of her basket. Each night she took Djihens' basket and picked out all the longest and best roots, and when her husband came from hunting deer, she said: " I dug these! "

The man loved Djáhdjai better than he did Djihens, but Djáhdjai didn't love him; she loved Wiĕs.

Each morning, as soon as she got to the flat, she began to dance and to chirp her love song. Her song said: " Come this way, Big Head! Come this way; I want to see you! "

Wiĕs listened, and as soon as he heard the song, he came up on the rocks and looked down on the flat. He looked all around, as if counting the trees and bushes to see that everything was right, that there was nobody around, then he went to Djáhdjai.

Each evening the husband asked his wives if their moccasins were worn out. Djihens always answered: " No, I don't kick the ground all the time and wear my moccasins out."

Djáhdjai always had holes in her moccasins.

Her husband scolded, and asked: " How do you wear out your moccasins so? I haven't made moccasins for Djihens since we came here."

"I can't stand still when I dig; I have to jump around and stand hard on the ground. I dig roots among the rocks, where they are long and sweet. Djihens digs on the flat, and her roots are not as long as mine, or as nice."

"Well," said the man, "I don't know how you can wear out a pair of moccasins every day. Your feet eat up moccasins as stones do."

One morning, when Djáhdjai started off with her basket and digging stick, Djihens thought she would watch and see where she went. So she followed her. Every little while Djáhdjai turned around to find out if anybody was looking at her. Djihens was hiding in the grass; she couldn't see her. When Djáhdjai got near the mountain, she stopped and began to sing her love song. The song drew Wiĕs to the rocks. Djihens hid under the grass, so he couldn't see her. He looked all around, then he started toward Djáhdjai.

The Wiĕs people had two trails up the mountain, one for men, the other for women. Djáhdjai always waited for him at the end of the men's trail.

Djihens thought: "Now I know why she comes home with an empty basket. She comes here to see Wiĕs; she draws him to her with her love song. How nice it sounds!"

After a while Djihens crept away, went off to the flat to dig roots. The next morning she followed Djáhdjai again. She listened to her love song and saw Wiĕs come to meet her. That night she said to her husband: "Don't make new moccasins for Djáhdjai; she doesn't care for you." The man didn't believe her; he thought she was jealous of Djáhdjai.

Djihens always knew what he thought. She said, "If you don't believe me, go and listen to her love song." Then she told him how Djáhdjai stole her roots and said she had dug them herself.

The next day, after Djihens had carried her roots home, she went to watch Djáhdjai. The woman spent the whole day with Wiĕs, then she dug a few roots and went home.

The man had been a good hunter, but after Djáhdjai fell in love with Wiĕs, he couldn't find a deer, couldn't find even a fresh track. One day he went home early and asked Djihens:

"Where does Wičs come from when he comes to meet Djáhdjai?"

"I don't know," said Djihens. "I see him first on the rocks. He looks around, then he comes straight down the mountain."

When Djáhdjai came home and found her husband there, she said to Djihens: "Why did you leave me and come to the house? I hunted a long time for you."

The man said nothing. He made believe he loved Djáhdjai more than ever. But he said to Djihens: "To-morrow I will watch her myself."

The next morning Djáhdjai said: "I am going to dig roots to-morrow; to-day I will stay at home and rest." When she didn't see her husband, she asked where he had gone.

Djihens said: "He can't find any deer on this side of the mountain. He is going to the other side. That is why he started so early."

Djáhdjai said she was going to stay at home, but as soon as Djihens was gone, she started off toward the mountain.

The man hid by the side of the trail Wičs came on. He hunted for his most poisonous arrow and was going to shoot him. Then he thought: "No, I will just watch them to-day." Soon he heard Djáhdjai singing. When he saw a big man stand on the rocks and look down at her, he was so jealous that he cried. After a while he went home.

That day Djáhdjai said to Wičs: "My husband hunts all the time. I am afraid he will see you."

The next morning the man got up early and went to the mountain. As he went, he talked to the mountain and to the earth; said: "Draw him toward me. You, Earth, see everything; you know everything; you know what Wičs has done. I want to punish him. Draw him to me."

That day Djáhdjai wanted to stay at home. She didn't know why her husband went off so early mornings, but Djihens said: "I am sick. One of us must dig roots; you had better go."

The man tracked Wičs, then sat down to watch him and see where his life was. As Wičs went toward the top of the mountain, the man saw that he kept his life in his neck. He shot at him. Wiěs ran off northeast and fell among the trees. The man found him, cut up his body, and carried home some of the flesh.

Djáhdjai looked up at the mountain and sang her love song; she sang a long time, but Wiěs didn't come. When she got home, she said to her husband: " You have killed a deer. Why don't you cook some meat for me? "

He gave her a plateful. She ate it all; she liked it. Then he said: " That was Wiěs' flesh. Did you like it? " The woman was scared. When she tried to run away, the man shot her through the body. The arrow went in under one arm, and came out under the other. It left a hole in each side.

Then he said: " Hereafter you will be nothing but a grasshopper, but your name will be what it is now, Djáhdjai. I hope that in later times a man will never have such a wife as you were."

To this day grasshoppers have a hole in each side.

KAI AND HIS FATHER-IN-LAW, NATANATAS

CHARACTERS

Kai	Rabbit (Jack)
Góshgoise	Rabbit (Small)
Natanatas	

KAI and his little brother, Góshgoise, went to Natanatas' house. Kai wanted to marry Natanatas' daughter. He left Góshgoise outside. Old woman Natanatas gave Góshgoise seeds and roots, but he wouldn't eat them.

" What does Góshgoise eat? " she asked.

" He likes the tips of grass and of weeds," said Kai. She gathered some and gave them to him; then he ate.

Old man Natanatas thought: " My sons want something to eat. I don't like this man Kai; I will kill him, and they can eat him." He knew that Kai didn't eat fish and never went to catch them; but he said: " Sometimes I get so many fish that I can't make the canoe go; the net is too heavy. I want you to come and help me."

Kai went with his father-in-law; he didn't like to refuse.

When they got to the lake, Natanatas said: " Get into the canoe; I fish out in the lake."

When they were in the middle of the lake, the old man said: " I feel tired. We will sleep a little while; then we will feel better and can work."

Natanatas lay down in one end of the canoe and Kai in the other. Kai slept a long time; when he woke up, he shook the old man, and said: " Here, old man, wake up; the wind blows. We are going to get tipped over and drowned."

Natanatas pretended to be asleep, but he was making the wind blow; he wanted to tip the canoe over and drown Kai.

Kai screamed: " Wake up! The canoe is full of water."

Natanatas didn't move. Kai pulled him around, shook

him and pounded him. The wind blew harder and harder. Kai was scared; he was wet and freezing, but no matter what he did, he couldn't waken the old man. Just then a white eagle feather that was flying along the bank called to Kai: "Why do you stay out there? Old Natanatas is trying to kill you. Pull five strands of seaweed from the bottom of the the canoe, tie them together, twist them, and throw them into the water; then jump on to them and come ashore."

Kai did that, and got to land. He dried himself and went back to old Natanatas' house.

Some of Natanatas' sons lived under the water; when their father drowned a man, they caught and ate him.

Natanatas didn't know which way Kai went. He said to himself: "Maybe he fell into the lake, and my sons have eaten him." He was glad. He made the wind stop blowing. Then he rowed to the bank, pulled his canoe out of the water, and went home. When he went into the house, he asked: "Has Kai come?" Just then he saw him lying by the fire, asleep.

When Kai woke up, the old man said: "I didn't know where to hunt for you. The wind blew so hard I thought you were drowned. I felt badly. I went all around the lake looking for you. I thought you were dead and I cried."

The next morning Natanatas went for rocks; he wanted to heat them and sweat. When he came home, he said to Kai: "I saw a big deer right here near the house; you could track it, but you haven't anything to kill it with."

Kai's wife cried; she said: "Father is trying to kill you. He kills every man who comes here. He doesn't want a son-in-law."

Soon the old man said to Kai: "You must go to the lake and get some reeds. I will make you arrows to shoot deer and ducks with; I am tired of eating fish."

Kai went to the lake, but he couldn't see any reeds. He looked all around; then he saw some growing on an island out in the middle of the lake. He sat down and thought of what he was to do, thought for a long time. Then white eagle feathers called out to him: "Why do you sit there so long?

You should think of us, then you would get the reeds." When he thought of the feathers, he rose up in the air and went to the island. He got the reeds and went home.

When Kai gave the reeds to Natanatas, the old man made believe he was glad. He said: "You thought it was far; you didn't want to go, but you found it was easy. Now you must bring me two round stones to straighten the arrows. There is only one place to get them; that is down by the river."

Kai went to the river. It was deep and ran very fast. Under the water he saw the stones his father-in-law wanted. He didn't know how to get them. He looked for others, but couldn't find them; then he sat down and thought about what he was to do. He felt lonesome; he knew Natanatas was trying to kill him.

Then white eagle feathers called out: "Why do you sit there so long? The old man is waiting. Why don't you think of us?"

He thought of white feathers. Right away the river dried up. Kai took the stones and went home.

Old Natanatas made believe he was glad; he said: "Those are like the stones I used when I was a young man. Now I must have feathers to put on the arrows. In a tree near here there is an eagle's nest; I saw eggs in the nest. Maybe the little eagles are big enough to have long feathers. You must go and see."

When Kai got to the tree, he looked up and saw an eagle in the nest. He took off his clothes and began to climb. As he climbed, the tree grew. Kai didn't look back; he didn't know that the tree was getting taller and taller. He climbed for a long time. At last he got to the nest. When he looked down and saw how high up he was, he was scared and began to cry.

Soon somebody said right there near him: "Why do you sit here crying? Pull feathers out of the young eagles; then think of us and you will go down the way we do."

Kai pulled the feathers, then he floated down as feathers do. When he got home, the old man said he was glad, said:

"There is where I used to get my feathers; those eagles always have a nest in that tree."

Natanatas had the bow and arrows ready. He gave them to Kai, and said: "Now you must kill a deer, and we shall have sinew to tie the feathers on with. I will show you a place where deer always come." He went with Kai, showed him deer tracks, and said: "Sit down here. I will go farther and scare deer so they will run this way."

Old Natanatas had a son under the ground, and he went to get him to help kill Kai. When Kai was alone, he got up and went off; he didn't stay where the old man told him to.

The old man told his son to take the form of a deer and run at Kai and kill him. "Put your heart in your foot," said he. "Kai can't shoot at your foot." Then he called out: "A deer is coming! A deer is coming!"

Góshgoise's heart was with his brother and it kept calling to him: "Pets, pets, pets! Pets, pets, pets!" (Foot, foot, foot!) It did that to help Kai and tell him that he must shoot the deer in the foot, for its life was there.

When the deer got near, Kai thought: "Maybe my brother is telling me to shoot the deer in the foot." He shot; the arrow went through the deer's foot and killed him.

When the old man came, he asked: "Where is the deer?"

"I fell asleep," said Kai; "the deer passed me."

"I told you to sit still, and watch for it."

"I shot at it once," said Kai. "Maybe I hit it."

"Where is it?"

Kai told him and he went to hunt for the deer. When he found it, he felt badly. He tried to look glad, but he didn't say much. He only said: "We won't cut up this deer till we kill another one. There are five paths here where deer run. I will show you a good place. This time you must sit still; you mustn't lie down and go to sleep." When they got to the place, Natanatas said: "Sit here and watch; I will go and scare the deer."

When a deer ran toward Kai, he hid. The deer looked for

him, and the old man called: "Deer is coming! Deer is coming!" Again little Góshgoise said, "Pets, pets, pets!"

The deer couldn't see Kai. Kai shot it in the foot and killed it.

When Natanatas came, Kai said: "A deer ran by. I shot once; maybe I killed it. We will go and see."

When the old man saw the dead deer, he said: "It's almost dark; we will leave the deer here till morning."

When they got home, Kai's wife scolded her father; she said: "You will kill all my brothers trying to kill Kai, but you won't kill him. He has more power than you have."

The next morning Natanatas said: "My son-in-law, you are afraid of a deer. He has horns and you think he will hit you. He won't hurt you. Sit right still and shoot when you see him coming."

Kai thought: "This time I will sit where he puts me."

The deer saw Kai, but Kai shot it in the foot and killed it. When the old man asked: "Where is the deer?" Kai said: "It saw me and ran off. I shot once, but maybe I missed him."

Natanatas thought: "I have only two sons left, but I will try once more." Tears were running down his face. He said to Kai: "I have been running; I am sweating."

Kai killed two more of the old man's sons. Natanatas wouldn't let Kai touch the deer. He said: "We will come to-morrow and cut them up." (He was going to bring them to life.)

Little Góshgoise was getting lonesome; he thought: "If my brother is going to stay around here, I will go home. He is away every day, and I am alone all the time."

The next morning old Natanatas said: "There are big fish in the lake; we will go and spear one." (He had turned his sons to fish, and they were in the lake.)

This time Kai took Góshgoise with him. He knew that his brother was lonesome.

The old man said to his sons: "As soon as you see Kai's spear, catch hold of it and pull him into the water. Then eat him."

When Kai got to the lake, he was frightened, and thought: " I won't spear fish." Then he thought: " I must do everything the old man tells me to do."

Soon he saw a big fish coming. It threw up water in great waves. It caught Kai's spear and pulled, pulled hard, but Góshgoise took hold of the spear and helped Kai. They pulled the fish out on to the sand, and Kai sent his brother to tell the old man to come and see it. When Natanatas saw the fish, he said: " You have done enough for to-day; we will go home and play games."

The old man said to one of his sons: " I am going to run a race with Kai. When we run along the bank of the river, you must make a river on the other side of us, and as we go between the rivers, you must push Kai into the water. Your brothers will catch him and eat him."

When Kai and old Natanatas were between the rivers where the trail was narrow, Natanatas' son sprang out of the water, ran up behind Kai, and gave him a push. Kai was falling into the water when white eagle feathers saw his trouble, and called out: " Think of us! "

Kai did, and right away he floated off in the air. Then Kai called to his father-in-law: " You can't beat me! "

The next time they ran the old man said: " You must run on the left side of the trail."

" No, I will go on the right side," said Kai. He went on the right side, and when they came to a deep place and his brother-in-law ran up behind him, he turned and pushed him into the river. The brothers, who were waiting to eat Kai, ate their brother.

The old man said to Kai: " I will run with you again, but you must run on the left side."

Kai ran on the left side; his father-in-law pushed him off many times, but he didn't strike the water. He floated away, a feather, and when the old man looked back, there was Kai. At last he pushed Natanatas into the water.

Natanatas called out: " Don't eat me! Don't eat me! " His sons thought he was Kai and they ate him, but his spirit escaped and he was alive again. He scolded his sons, said:

" Why don't you kill this man? You must run with him and kill him. We have more power than he has."

Kai ran another race, pushed his brother-in-law into the water, and his brothers ate him up.

Then the old man said: " We won't run again. My sons feel badly, their brother is dead."

Kai's wife scolded her father, told him he had killed his sons, that she didn't like him any longer, and wouldn't stay where he stayed. Then she and Kai and Góshgoise crossed a high mountain, and came down to a meadow. They built a house and lived there always.

THE SPIRIT OF THE TULA GRASS

CHARACTERS

Blaiwas	Eagle
Ndukis	Hawk
Tusasás	Joker (Skunk)

NOT far from Knekuks lived a woman and her little grandson, the last one left of her kin. The boy often wanted to go to the village, but his grandmother said: "You are too small; you might get lost, or those people might kill you. They killed your father and mother."

One day the boy started off without saying anything to his grandmother. When she found that he had gone, she cried and felt badly. Tusasás lived in the village; he saw the boy and said: "I will take that little fellow for a servant; he can bring water for me."

"Keep still," said Blaiwas; "you talk too much."

The man who killed the boy's father was there; he said: "That boy has come to see me. Maybe he wants to kill me." He was making fun of him.

The boy went into each house to find out what people would say to him. Some were sorry for him; others drove him away. When he went home, his grandmother said: "Those people are waiting for you to grow up a little; then they will kill you."

After the first time, he went away every evening. One evening he saw, on the trail, an old dry spear of tula grass. He stepped on it and broke it; the spear screamed out, just as a person does when hurt. The boy stepped off from it quickly, and said: "Well, well, I never heard anything of this kind scream before." He picked up the pieces of grass. That minute he fell down. The grass made him fall; it was the spirit of a skoks.

The boy lost his mind and was almost dead. He thought the spirit said: " You have broken my back; now I want you to fix me and use me for a cane. If you meet enemies, use me against them."

When the boy got back his mind, his mouth was bloody. It is always that way when a child is going to be a doctor. (Medicines sometimes travel evenings to meet young boys.) He got up and went home.

When his grandmother saw him, she was scared; she said: " I don't like to see you this way. Doctors are killed as well as men who fight; you won't live long if you are this kind."

That night the boy dreamed that the tula cane told him how to make a regular medicine cane. He made the cane, and the next time he went to the village he took it with him. It was stronger than the tula grass cane.

Tusasás said: " Little boy, I am glad you brought me a cane; I will sing for it."

Blaiwas said: " You shouldn't make fun of that boy; let him alone."

" If we let him alone, he will kill us all," said Tusasás.

The man who killed the boy's father tied feathers in the boy's hair to make fun of him, and said: " I want to eat you, but if I don't eat you, you will have to carry water for me."

Tusasás said: " He is mine; I will make him work when he is a little larger."

Everywhere the boy went they made fun of him because he was so small. One night he said: " Grandmother, I want you to fix my head." She shaved off all of his hair but one tuft on the top of his head; that she braided, and it stuck up straight. She painted his head and his face red.

" Haven't I any name? " asked the boy.

" No," said his grandmother. " You have never given yourself a name."

" Call me Sápkokis " (the name of the twist of hair on top of his head). " And call me by my name every time I come in or go out; it will make me stronger each time I hear it."

The next night he stuck his medicine cane over the place where he slept, took down his tula cane, and said to his grandmother: " I am going to the place where they make fun of me. If my medicine cane falls, it will be a sign that I am in trouble."

When he got to the place, the man who killed his father asked: " Why do you come so often? I wish you would keep away from me. I don't like you; you look just like your father. Give me your cane! "

Sápkokis wouldn't give up his cane. He ran off to old woman Ndukis' house. She said: " Why do you come to this village so often? That man over there will kill you." When he didn't start for home, she screamed to him to hurry, that the man was following him. She tore a hole in her house and told the boy to crawl out and run home as quickly as he could.

Sápkokis crawled out, but he went around on one side and struck the man with his tula cane. The man fell in two pieces.

The people said to the dead man: " That comes of your talking so big! " They shot at Sápkokis, but couldn't hit him; he darted around and hit men with his tula cane. Each man he hit died right away. One man said: " I never killed any of your people; I have always been kind to you." He let that man live.

Sápkokis went home whooping and singing; he was glad. The women of the village told all the people living what the boy had done.

Sápkokis said to his grandmother: " I am going to a place where there is high grass; I am not going to stay here and fight people."

He went to the mountain and stood in the high grass on one side of the trail. A great many men started out to kill Sápkokis. When he saw them coming, he met them, and asked: " Where are you going? " No one answered. He said: " Here is the best place to fight." They tried to kill him, but his cane never failed; it killed every man.

In the evening Sápkokis went home whooping and singing. When his grandmother saw him coming, she said: " He has killed everybody; that is why he whoops and runs so fast. It was bad enough to make him an orphan, not to make him think of his people. That is the way: if they know, they can never forget. Those people should have let him alone."

Sápkokis traveled around and everybody knew that he was a great fighter. One day he told his grandmother he was going to see Kûlta. She said: " If you go, don't harm him; he is your kin."

Kûlta said: " My grandson, I am glad to see you. I hear women mourning. You must be on the watch; somebody may come here and kill you. You must cover your father and mother and relatives enough so you won't think any more about them." (He meant that he must kill all of his enemies.)

Sápkokis asked: " Do you feel lonesome for people? "

" No," said Kûlta, " my sons never did any harm, but men killed them. I am glad to have you kill those men."

When Sápkokis went home, Kûlta carried the old grandmother fish. He was glad that his grandson was such a strong man.

Sápkokis said: " You mustn't make any tracks around here. If you do people will think that you taught me all these things."

After this, Sápkokis and his grandmother lived in peace. There were only women and children left around their place.

A MEDICINE STORY. NUMBER I

CHARACTERS

Blaiwas . . . . Eagle		Skoksun Kalo . The Land of Spirits
Ktilisúnak . . . Ktilis' Son		
Skoks . . . . . Spirit		

KTILISÚNAK (Ktilis' son) was so young that he couldn't talk plainly. He lived with his grandmother. His sister was married and lived on a broad flat near the mountains. The grandmother was tired of taking care of the boy, and one evening she threw the little fellow out; then she threw him his bow and arrows, and said:

"Go off now! Maybe you will be a big chief and have many wives!"

The boy was naked and cold, but he got up and started off to see if he could find his sister's house. He cried all the way. When he got to the flat, he saw a woman coming with a great pack of old ragged mats on her back. The boy was scared; he trembled all over. He could see the woman's head and pack, but he couldn't see below her waist. He thought: "That isn't a living person," and he grew as cold as ice.

When he thought: "That isn't a living person," the woman screamed out, and right away the boy changed. He could see the woman, and he said: "I am not afraid of you now. My grandmother has thrown me out; I will give myself to anybody I meet."

The woman was a Skoks, and she came in a whirlwind. As the boy looked, she grew taller and taller. At last her head reached the sky. She screamed a second time. The boy's eyes were big from looking at her. The third time she screamed, she was there by him. She tried to pass him on the right side, but he pushed hard to the other side. As she passed him, he fell on his back; blood came out of his mouth and he lost his mind. Skoks had pulled his heart out and carried it off. (If she had passed on the left side she would have taken his spirit and carried it to Skoksun Kalo.)

Skoks went off in the air till she came to where the sun goes down; she stopped there just above the earth. Her hand was shut tight, and she held the boy's heart in it; she talked to the heart, and laughed.

She said: "Heart, I am trying you to see if you will be like me," and she laughed again.

The boy lay on the ground as if dead, but his spirit heard the Skoks talk to his heart, as she sat on the air and held the heart in her hand. After a while she opened her hand and let go of the heart. Then the little boy thought he saw a bird coming from the west. It came to him and lighted on his breast. That moment he jumped up and went toward his sister's house. He had changed; he wasn't a little boy; he was a young man.

His sister didn't know him. When he called her "sister," she asked: "What has changed you so?" She was scared. He didn't answer; he only laughed.

"Why don't you speak?" she asked.

Then he said: "Out on the flat I saw a tall woman with a big pack of old ragged mats on her back."

Right away the sister knew that he had seen a Skoks; she said: "My brother, why did you come so far alone?"

"My grandmother threw me out," said the boy. "I thought I was going to die."

The sister cried; she felt sorry for her brother.

He began to be sleepy. Skoks made him feel that way; she was coming to him again. She was going to be his medicine and make him a great doctor. He rubbed ashes on the right side of his face; on the left side he made stripes with a black coal, then he asked his sister to sing for him. She didn't want to sing, for the first person who sings for a doctor must go with him always, and sing for him. When he asked the second time, she sang. They didn't see the Skoks, but Ktilisúnak knew she was there.

Every evening the young man called out as Skoks called, when he met her on the flat; then he fell to the ground and was senseless till Skoks got through talking to him. Each time his sister asked: " What does your medicine want? "

" I see a crowd of medicines around me," said he. " They want somebody to sing and talk for them. You must go and ask old men to come and talk five days for them."

The sister went to Blaiwas' village, where there were many old men. They came and sang and told the medicine spirits what they must do. They said: "If you want this young man to work for you, you must be good to him; you mustn't make him crazy." Then they asked each medicine what it wanted. Skoks wanted a cap made of tula grass, and two grass plates. Eagle medicine wanted eagle feathers, and fish-hawk medicine wanted fish-hawk feathers. Each bird medicine wanted its own kind of feathers.

The old men got all of those feathers, and tied them on a long pole. There is a dream medicine, and the man who has it can cure himself, but he can't cure others. That medicine came to Ktilisúnak.

When the old men finished singing and talking, they said to the sister: " You mustn't cook or sweep or have any dust around when your brother is in the house. In the evening don't stir the ashes or let them fly up when you put wood on the fire; if you do, he will die; he is afraid of his medicines. Don't tease him to eat; let him eat when he wants to. If his medicines trouble him, we will come and talk to them."

The young man lay in the house day after day. — Doctors don't go out often; they go only when sick people send for them.

Near the sister's house there was a sick man who was only skin and bones. He sent for Ktilisúnak. The young man told his sister to sing for Skoks. Skoks came, but nobody could see her. When the three got to the house, the man was dying. Ktilisúnak put a hand each side of him, front and back, and caught his life, didn't let it get out of his body. In half a day the man was well.

When the sister got home, the medicines heard her say:

" Oh, I am tired! " In the night they said to the young man: " We didn't think she would get tired of us so soon."

The next morning Ktilisúnak asked his sister if she was tired of his medicines. She said: " I am tired of singing so much."

" I am tired, too," said the young man, " but I wouldn't live long if I didn't work for my medicines."

The next night Ktilisúnak sang for himself. Skoks was angry because the brother and sister were tired. The other medicines said to him: " We didn't know you felt so. We thought you would be glad to have us for servants. Hereafter you will be a common man; you will have no power to cure people."

The medicines left him. As soon as they were gone, he began to feel sick; he cried and sang for his medicines, but they didn't hear him, they had gone far away. The old men came, and sang and called to them, but they didn't come. When Ktilisúnak told the old men how he and his sister had got tired of singing, they said: " We will try once more."

" It's no use," said Ktilisúnak. " Skoks has got my life." He grew thin and died. People brought nice beads and mats and burned them with his body.

Blaiwas said to the sister: " It is as if you had killed your own brother. Haven't old people told you that medicines listen to what we say and that they can hear, even when they are a long way off? "

The sister felt badly. She burned up her house and went to another place. As soon as Ktilisúnak died, his old grandmother knew it. She was sorry that she had thrown him out, and three times each night she walked around the sister's house crying. Her voice sounded like the voice of a spirit. The sister wrapped herself up tight when she heard her grandmother around. Once, when she saw her, there were red tears on one side of the old woman's face and black tears on the other. At last she called out: " My granddaughter, I am going to the mountains. I don't want to be a person any longer, and hereafter you will not be a person; you will be a bird, and appear to doctors." They both became birds.

A MEDICINE STORY. NUMBER II

A MAN and his wife went off hunting and left their little boy at home. The mother said: "Stay here and watch things; don't go away anywhere."

The boy was afraid; he didn't want to stay alone. The father and mother had not been gone long when the boy heard a noise like a whirlwind in tall grass. A Skoks had come for him, but he didn't know that. He looked out, looked over his left shoulder, and saw a kind of grayish white fog. In that fog was a woman; one side of her face was painted in black streaks, the other side was the color of ashes. She called out to the boy: "Come here, little fellow!" The child didn't go; he screamed and fell dead.

The mother heard him scream and she ran home. When she found the boy dead and cold as ice, she cried, and called for somebody to come.

Old Koé heard her and came; she took off the child's clothes and rubbed his body with ashes, then she put black coal on one side of his face and white ashes on the other, and called for her Skoks. (Skoks was old Koé's medicine.)

Koé said to the mother: "A Skoks came for your child, but the little fellow turned his left shoulder. If he had turned his right shoulder, the Skoks would have taken his spirit away; but she didn't get hold of it; she called and it followed her. My Skoks will go for it."

The boy's spirit hadn't gone far. Koé's Skoks went right in front of it and brought it back, and the child came to life. When the mother asked how the Skoks looked, the boy said: "She had finger-nails longer than her hand. I couldn't see her plainly, but I heard her call me."

The mother wanted to give Koé nice things, beads and porcupine quills, but Koé said: "I don't want any of those things; I only want to bring back as many spirits as I can."

The little boy grew fast; he was a great kiúks. When men asked how his Skoks looked when she awakened him out of dreams, he said: " She has red eyes, like fire in the night, and her nails are longer than her fingers. She has hot ashes for her paint. One side of her face is white; on that side are black tears, on the other side are red tears, like blood."

A SKOKS STORY

On the shore of Tula Lake many chiefs were living,—the first people. (They are now turned to fowls and animals.) With them lived an old woman and her grandson. The boy was called "Big Belly;" Tusasás rubbed dirt on him and laughed at him because he was small and fat.

A Skoks traveled every evening along the eastern side of the lake. The Skoks wore a straw blanket, and made a great noise, crying as he went along. The minute anybody saw him, he vanished. If he passed a man whose right shoulder was toward him, that man died at once, for the spirit stole his life, but if the spirit passed on the other side, the person was senseless a while and then came to life.

One evening people heard the Skoks coming. It made such a noise that they heard it when it was a long way off. They were scared; they crowded together and each person wanted to be inside. Tusasás wanted to be under all the rest; they pulled him up and threw him out, but he crawled under again. The people shivered; it was so cold they were nearly frozen. It was always cold when that Skoks screamed; he made it so. Fires went out and grass wouldn't burn.

The old woman took the hull of seeds and made a fire for the little boy. She cried while she was making it, and said: "My grandson, all the people here are going to die." The little boy didn't seem to know what she meant; he got up and stood by the fire. She said: "Sit down, my grandson, you mustn't stand up or go out; if you meet this Skoks, you are sure to die." The old woman threw ashes toward the voice of the Skoks.

The little boy told his grandmother to tie a skin around him and roll him up so he could go and meet the Skoks.

"My grandson," said the old woman, "what can you do? You have no power." But she got a duckskin blanket, tied it around him, and said: " Don't let the Skoks pass on the right side; be sure that your left shoulder is toward him. He will try to make you go on the other side, but don't you go."

Every time the Skoks shouted, it was like throwing ice into the house, and Tusasás cried out: " Oh, let me go under; I am cold."

When the boy started, his grandmother said: " You must take some ordure in your hand, and if the Skoks tries to make you go on the wrong side, throw it at him."

Soon the boy saw the Skoks. His head reached the sky and he looked as if he were carrying a load of clouds. One side was painted white, the other black. He came very fast. The boy had hard work to get by. When he pushed into Skoks, Skoks darted forward. At last both fell, and their bodies turned to rock, but their spirits came out of the rocks. The boy was holding up the ordure, and that turned to rock, too.

When the sun rose the next morning, the boy's spirit went home. He was a young man now and wore a panther-skin blanket that came to his feet. (After a person meets a Skoks, he looks strange; he loses his old body.) As soon as the young man got home, it was warm; fires burned, and right away it was summer. The people made him chief and he had control of the place.

After that two men went north to visit their kin; one of the men was killed. When the people heard about it, they asked the chief if they should demand pay for the man's life. He said: " Yes, and if they don't pay, I will punish them." The men refused to pay, and messengers were sent to the chief.

He took a long obsidian knife and started. When nearly there, he said to his men: " Don't be frightened; the Skoks is getting mad and ready to move." (The Skoks was the chief's medicine.)

When the chief came to the enemy, they said: " We are men, not women; we are not afraid of you. We won't pay for the man we killed."

Both sides were ready to fight. The chief said to his men: " When I shout, fall on the ground and don't move." He shouted like Skoks and all of his people fell. His enemies were terribly frightened. Right away they were freezing. — The chief could see the Skoks, but nobody else could see him. — The chief killed a great many men; they were so cold they couldn't run away; he cut them to pieces with his obsidian knife.

After that, there was no trouble with the northern people; they had found that there was a powerful chief in the south, a man who could kill them easily.

A DOCTOR STORY

CHARACTER

Kiúks . . . . Doctor

A KIÚKS and his old mother were living at Dokwa, near Klamath Lake. The kiúks had a tall pole standing outside the house and on the top of the pole was a dead eagle. Inside of the house he had a dead fish-hawk and all kinds of dead birds.

The kiúks shouted and sang. The minute he stopped singing, the dead eagle came to life and screamed; when the eagle stopped screaming, the fish-hawk and all the dead birds inside the house came to life and screamed together. As soon as they were through screaming, the kiúks fed them. After they were fed, they died and remained dead till he called them to life again.

This man was a terrible kiúks; he could kill anybody. Nobody ever went to his house; everyone was afraid of him. When he called, and the eagle and all the birds answered, the earth began to tremble, and it trembled as long as the birds screamed. Everywhere people felt the earth shake, and it scared them. At such times they said: " The kiúks is singing, and the birds are screaming."

Men began to talk and to try to think of some way to kill the kiúks. One morning he hung up a wooden comb, and said to his mother: " I am going to Gombät; if this comb falls, you may know that somebody has killed me." He had a ska (a sharp stone about three feet long); he gave it to her and said: " As soon as the comb falls, take this ska and strike the ground near the fire five times, and strike the fire five times."

People had been wishing that this kiúks would go somewhere,

but he had always stayed at home. There were men watching, and when he came out of his house, they followed him. Before he got to Gombät, they killed him, shot arrows into his body, and cut him to pieces with flint knives.

When the comb fell, the mother knew that her son was dead. She took the ska and struck the ground five times, and the fire five times, as he had told her to do. That minute the men who had killed him fell dead, and the eagle and all the birds inside the house came to life and screamed.

The old woman went to Gombät; she found the pieces of her son, carried them home, and burned them; then his spirit went into her. She became just such a kiúks as he had been. She had been only a common old woman; now she used the eagle, fish-hawk, and birds just as her son had used them. People were scared, but they said to her: "You mustn't do as your son did, you mustn't kill people; if you do, we shall kill you as we killed him."

Her son gained strength when the birds screamed and the earth trembled, but the people frightened the old woman so she was afraid to sing for the birds; she grew weak and died. As soon as she was dead, the birds came to life and flew off to the woods.

The people left her body in the house and burned the house and body together.

THE END.

NOTES

LÁTKAKÁWAS

LÁTKAKÁWAS is evidently a sun myth. The young man who wooed Látkakáwas could run in the air and under the ground (Indians thought that the sun traveled from west to east underground). He was beautiful and bright, brighter than anything else in the world. He was immortal while he had the disk. When Kumush stole the disk Látkakáwas' husband died. The disk became a part of Kumush and he was immortal. His body was reduced to ashes, but he rose up anew, for the disk remained.

There is a condition, however, incident to the resurrection of the sun; he must be called. Some one must rouse him. The morning star has that duty, and will never be freed from it. While the sun exists, the morning star must call him. At the summons of the star the disk springs from the pile of ashes; the sun (represented as Kumush) is renewed completely and goes forth to run his course till consumed again.

Kumush is killed and his body is eaten by crows; only the disk remains. The morning star sees the disk, and calls out: "What are you doing, old man? Get up!" Kumush springs up, through virtue of the immortal disk and the compelling word of the star.

Many Indian tribes have myths in which the morning star figures as the Light-bearer.

The morning star of the Modocs is the same character as the Lucifer of the Latins.

THE FIVE BROTHERS OF LÁTKAKÁWAS

The five brothers marry and nothing more is known about them. Gáukos, the orphan boy, becomes the principal character.

At sunset Gáukos — the moon — is thrown out of his sister's house. He is a little boy, but as soon as he is outside he increases in size. He enters a ravine, and when he comes out at the opposite end he is a full-grown man. Later every one sees him; his body is bright and beautiful. When pursued by his sister, he crosses a valley at a step, springs from one mountain to another, and early in the morning reaches the first house, the home of two women, who have the power of making themselves young.

The Modocs have lost the name of Gáukos' elder sister, and they do not know the meaning of the name of the younger sister, Lĭsgaga. The elder sister is, probably, Daylight; she travels as Gáukos does, a valley at a step. In a Wintu creation myth, Sanihas (Daylight) is one of the principal characters.

In a Gaelic myth, the son of the King of Light is Day or Daylight, the Lady of Green Insh is Night, and her yellow-haired son is Dawn.

In this Modoc myth the power of the word was with Gäk. He said to Lóluk: " Hereafter, you will be kin to no man, you will burn all alike," and as he spoke Lóluk became common fire.

ISIS AND YAULILIK'S DAUGHTERS

Isis, the son of Látkakáwas, is the son of Kumush because Kumush has the disk, and the disk is Isis' father. The Indians do not know the meaning of the word Isis — or Áisis, as pronounced by some of the Modocs — or of Látkakáwas. — These names occur only in the myths connected with the disk. — Isis is the greatest hunter and the greatest runner in the world. He has long, bright red hair. When he builds a fire the smoke from it goes straight up; it does not scatter, or waver. Isis has some of the attributes of his father, the sun.

Kumush personates Isis and deceives Yaulilik's elder daughter. In mythology one character frequently personates another. — There is an example of this in Wintu: Klakherrit (Lightning) personates Pitis (Quail), deceives Pitis' family, and kills every member of it.

In Indian myths, whenever two sisters are sent to some place and warned by father or mother against a deceiver, who is likely to meet them on the way, the elder sister is generally ready to become a victim, the younger is the wise one.

Cogátkis is an interesting character; like Samson, his strength was in his hair. Through the power of his hair, he could see at a great distance, and he could talk to his mother though she was far away.

I have never found a myth in which the method of taking life is similar to that described in this myth. Isis had two children; the elder died; he took the younger in his arms, put the top of its head to his mouth and drew a long breath, drew the child's breath, its life, into himself. He said to his wives, " The children are half mine, and half yours. I have taken their breath into myself; you may have their bodies."

In an Algonkin myth a character similar to Látkakáwas is the " Earth maiden." The Sun looks at her and she brings forth a daughter, who becomes the mother of a great hero.

KUMUSH AND HIS DAUGHTER

Many of the Modocs firmly believe that their tribe originated as described in this myth. They call Kumush father, and live by the rules he laid down for them. They believe that he gave the race all gifts that support existence, that it is through him that the Indians live and prosper. He has many of the attributes of Zeus.

This myth and many of the myths in this volume are as sacred for Indians as Bible stories are for Christians. When old men are asked what their ideas are regarding life hereafter they tell of Kumush's visit to the great house in the underground world; of what he saw there, and of the terrible effort he made to bring spirits to the upper world, and create Indians.

The underground house of the Modoc dead is in the West.

When Kumush had done all that he could for mankind he went to the place where the sun rises. He traveled on Sun's road till he came to the middle of the sky, and there he built his house.

STEALING FIRE

This tale belongs to the first cycle of Indian myth-tales, tales which relate the adventures of living creatures, plants, elements, objects and phenomena in this world before they became what they are as we see them. Among living creatures man is not reckoned, for man does not appear in any of these myths.

In most cases the tales are simple and transparent; it is easy to recognize the heroes either by their names or their actions or both. The value of Indian myths lies in the fact that they represent the mental labor of men who lived ages before those who recorded their thoughts on papyrus, baked brick or burnt cylinders.

Sickness was a person and owned fire. Sun, whose home was in the West, also owned fire. A council was called and the first people sent Wus to secure fire for " the people who are to come." The first people knew that another race was coming and that they themselves were to be changed.

Many mythologies give an account of the stealing of fire. — In Nosa, Au Mujaupa, the master of fire, lived in the South. Ahalamila went there and stole a few coals. The struggle to escape with the coals was as strenuous as that described in the Modoc tale, but the Nosas do not know who Au Mujaupa was.

HOW SICKNESS CAME INTO THE WORLD

This version of how sickness scattered over the world is noteworthy. It is not known who the Glatcówas brothers were. When asked, the Modocs said: " Glatcówas is just a name." The little men possessed great power; they could turn into any conceivable thing. Keis got angry and made poisonous diseases. Wéwenkee reproached him, told him that sickness belonged to Nébăks, that it was only loaned to him, that he had no right to let it out. Kéis did not listen, and, as a result of his rage, sickness spread over the world.

HOW OLD AGE CAME INTO THE WORLD

It would be interesting to know who the five brothers were, but the knowledge is lost. Their first notable encounter was with Storm, a person who could kill any one whom he could catch and draw under water.

The brothers traveled till they came to a country where they found only one man and one woman. The man said: " You cannot destroy us. We shall live always." When the brothers tried to kill him, and could not, they were frightened and ran away. Komúchass followed them to their own country, and killed them. The Indian woman who related this myth believed that if the brothers had let Komúchass alone, there would have been no such thing as old age.

LEMÉIS AND NUL-WE

In this myth Leméis is described as a man-eater. In Indian myths lightning, thunder, earthquake, and cyclone are man-eaters. Every effort was made to find out who Nul-we and his grandmother were. Old Ko-a-lák-ak-a, who told the story, said that when she was young she knew, but she had forgotten. In a Nosa myth, somewhat similar in construction, but where Lightning is the chief personage, the old grandmother is Pom, the earth.

WIND AND THUNDER

For ages the reverence and enthusiasm of primitive men have been given to elemental heroes, and they are given them yet by every tribe which preserves its ancient beliefs and ideas.

Fortunately we know all of the characters in this story of the elements.

Tcûskai, who represents spring, thought that he could cut off North Wind's head. When Wind put his head out Tcûskai died.

Tskel killed South Wind, made a cap of his skin, put it on and went to North Wind's house and killed him.

Since the death of North Wind and South Wind the wind that comes from the south is South Wind's spirit, and the wind that comes from the north is North Wind's spirit.

The Warm Spring Indians of Oregon have a beautiful myth about the Southwest Wind brothers and the Northeast Wind brothers and their sister, Tekstye. When Southwest Wind had killed Tekstye's brothers she ran away. Southwest Wind overtook her just as she reached a river; he struck her and she fell into the water. Then he said: "You'll no longer be a person and freeze people. You can blow once in a while, then I will come and overpower you. Rain will be your enemy, too. You will blow and freeze up everything, then he and I will come, we will thaw out the ground, warm it up, and make it green and beautiful.

GÁUKOS AND KÛLTA

Gáukos, the moon, is afraid of the big-mouthed people, the grizzly bears (clouds). He takes Weketas to protect him. He says: "If only a bit of me is left in Lok's mouth Weketas can bring me to life." In the old time nearly every tribe of Indians on the western continent believed that an eclipse was caused by an animal's attempt to swallow the sun, or the moon. Some tribes believe it yet and think that the animal is a grizzly bear. In Guatamala, when there is an eclipse, the Indians assemble in their villages, beat on drums, scream and make as much noise as possible, "to scare the bear away."

In "Tulchuherris," a Wintu myth, Olelbis, the creator, warns Sas, the Sun, against the grizzlies; he says: "While coming from the east you will see thick brush along the road. In that brush are grizzly bears. Be on your guard against them; they will kill you if they can."

DJÁKALIPS — RED CLOUDS

In this myth it is not told who the two sisters are, but in most myths that describe rope-makers it is stated that when the great change came they turned to spiders. The Kaltsik (spider) people play a prominent part in "The Star Brothers." In a Wintu Myth Norwanchakus hires the spider people to go to Sun's house and ask where Keriha is. In Látkakáwas they made a basket and would have fastened it to the sky, but misfortune came from looking back.

MOASÄM BEPS, THE DAUGHTER OF SOUTH WIND

Moasäm Beps is a myth in which Winter and Spring are the characters. The fate of Tsákiak is pathetic, but we may be sure that if we knew what he represented, and had all the details of the myth, we should find it consistent, and true to nature.

WEST WIND'S WIVES

Is a beautiful myth. The mind that conceived it was full of poetic thought.

THE STAR BROTHERS

Ko-a-lák-ak-a, the woman who told this myth-tale, thought that Tekewas was a cloud — the red cloud that in morning heralds a storm, for she was often seen, a red cloud, lying on the top of a mountain watching the valley below. Her family were afraid of her. Even the sun feared her.

There are valuable elements in the myth: hastening the course of the sun; the destruction caused by looking back; two newly born children pressed into one (we do not know what phenomena or force the children represent); the one, by the blow of an arrow, made two.

The heroes had many adventures. The elder wrestled with Yahyáhaäs, killed him, and condemned his spirit to wander forever on mountains, and along rivers and brooks. The moment the victor pronounced the curse the conquered said: "You will no longer be a person. You and your brother will be stars." Thereupon they became what their opponent had made them. When the word had been uttered nothing in the universe could turn it aside or resist it.

Ko-a-lák-ak-a thought that Yahyáhaäs personified fog. Captain John said that Yahyáhaäs was lightning, and the people who wrestled with him were clouds.

Yahyáhaäs appears in a number of myths. He always has the same characteristics and the same power. His only way of killing an enemy is by wrestling with him. His spirit goes to the sky and becomes Leméis, thunder.

THE RAINMAKER

The people who lived in the world before this had all the weaknesses of the people of the twentieth century; they were jealous, unfaithful, and revengeful. But not in the beginning. For untold ages those " first people " lived in peace and harmony. " No man knows, no man can tell, how long they lived in that way." Then, by degrees, a change came.

Gáhga, old, and blind, and jealous, " could have destroyed " (drowned) " all the people in the world had he so willed." He was Rain. A similar character in Gaelic mythology is called " Wet Mantle." His power was in his mantle, which was rain itself.

WUS KUMUSH AND TSMUK

Tsmuk is darkness, and his daughter, whose name is given in another version of the story, is Iúnika, Twilight.

In this myth there is a fine description of Wus. He could make people old; he could change them to animals or to anything he chose. He was the greatest trickster in the world; he delighted in deceiving people. He made Tsmuk look toward the east; immediately Tsmuk's body became a black cloud. A west wind came and carried the cloud away; it was daylight. Wus said to Tsmuk, "You'll no longer be a person. You'll be darkness, and people will sleep when you are here. But I shall not sleep. I will sleep in the daytime and travel at night." The last part of Wus' declaration must be an interpolation, for Wus is connected with light. In the mythology of one of the Pacific coast tribes a personage with many of the characteristics of Wus is known to be that warm light which in fine weather we see waving and dancing above the earth. He leads persons astray, and is full of mischief and deceit.

FROST AND THUNDER (YAHYÁHAÄS).

This is the only myth in the collection in which Frost is a known character. Wus steals Gowwá's wife, Gowwá gets her back, then the Lok people (clouds) steal her, Gowwá kills the Loks and rescues his wife only to have her stolen by Yahyáhaäs, who carries her to his home under the rocks. All the strong people in the world assemble to aid Gowwá, but they cannot break the rocks. Then Tckumhûs, or Tsasgips, as he is familiarly called, — a little man who looks puny and powerless, — says that he can break the rocks. He blows on them and they fall apart.

YAHYÁHAÄS

Yahyáhaäs makes the sun hasten its course. In this myth the misfortune which results from looking back is clearly stated: " If you look back you will die." — Usually the person who looks back is turned to stone, as in the Bible Lot's wife was turned into a pillar of salt.

YAHYÁHAÄS AND THE KÚJA SISTERS

As usual in Indian myth-tales, the younger sister has the most power.

Yahyáhaäs boasted that he could conquer the Kúja sisters. The eldest, to show her power, stuck a woodpecker's feather in the ground and it came up a streak of fire in Yahyáhaäs' cane.

Kûlta had been dead a long time. Kúja washed his body and stretched it, then, by stepping over it, brought it to life.

Bringing to life is one of the most familiar performances in American and in Oriental mythology. The Mongolian hero sprinkles a pile of bones with the Water of Life taken from a spring near a silver-leafed aspen tree. Immediately the bones resume their old connections and take on flesh; the man rises and proceeds on his journey as though nothing had happened.

It should be remembered that, whatever be the names of the myth-tale heroes at present, the original heroes were not human; they perform deeds which no man could perform, which only one of the forces of nature could perform, if it had the volition and desires of a person. In a beautiful myth of the Warm Spring Indians of California, Summer, a long time dead, is brought to life by the South Wind.

TSMUK AND GÓSHGOISE

When asked who the Yaukûl people were the story-teller said: " They were stone people." The Modoc word for stone is bondak, that for rock is gowan. In a fragment of a variant of this myth Frost is one of the characters. The Modocs had a name for the different manifestations of frost; it is possible that Yaukûl is one of those names.

Góshgoise personifies spring. His grandmother made him a bright blue quiver out of her own hair. Then she made a spear that would last always and never get old, — lightning. He killed the Yaukûl people, then battled with the Kaudokis and the Juljulcus. He gave his spear, long lightning, to Juljulcus, and took Juljulcus' spear, heat lightning, " that lightning which flashes around the sky in warm weather." He went to Tsmuk's house, and Iúnika (Twilight), Tsmuk's daughter, who owned the moon, became his wife.

In this myth the idea that " bad thoughts " bring misfortune is brought out very strongly. A bad thought causes much trouble.

WAR BETWEEN BEASTS AND BIRDS

This myth recalls the fables of the great Russian writer, Kriloff. Whoever determines to be always, right or wrong, with the winning side, is likely to be left alone, as was Bat, who has no friend either among those that fly or those that walk.

LOK SNEWÉDJAS

Lok Snewédjas was a cloud, a snow storm and a whirlwind. The mountain was her father and the earth was her mother. In Wintu Wimaloimis, the grizzly-bear cloud woman, was not as good a mother as Lok Snewédjas, for she tried to eat her sons, Thunder and Lightning. Lok Snewédjas, when her child was in danger, rushed down the mountain in a whirlwind that tore big rocks from under the ground and threw them around as though they were tiny stones.

Lok Snewédjas owned all the yĕlalwek there was in the world. " No one had ever eaten any seed like it, or will ever eat any like it again." No matter how much was eaten the same amount remained. From a handful all the people in a village were fed and the handful remained.

This myth shows what power the Indians thought their " medicine men " possessed: if they called to the spirit of a dead man before the spirit reached the place where the sun goes down, it would came back to the body.

HOW KALASLÁKKAS WON HIS WIFE

In this myth-tale Tusasás, who, wherever he appears, is always the same worthless, shiftless mischief-maker and boaster, is well described. The importance of dreams is also well brought out.

THE BAD BROTHER

The hero is Rain. He drowns his mother, then sends his sister to Kówe, who in other myths is described as having control of all the springs in the world: " She lives under the water, she is in every spring. She is our grandmother. If she gets mad she can dry up the deepest water." The sister marries Djáudjau. Djáudjau visits his brother-in-law, and on leaving he gets green twigs, rubs himself with them, then rubs the twigs on the ground, and says: " I have brought away some of my brother-in-law's bad thoughts; now, Earth, take them all." He talks to the mountains and forgets his brother-in-law. A description of a similar act appears in several Modoc myths.

MINK AND WEASEL

Tskel and Tcûskai are great characters. In every myth in which they appear they are brothers and Skóûks is Tskel's wife; Tcûskai is always small, mischievous and inquisitive. Tskel, to punish Tcûskai for giving his blanket to Gopher (Pshageknik), who is North Wind, hid water. Tcûskai found it and was drinking it up when Tskel came. Had he drunk it all there would be no water in the world. Tskel made a cap of the skin of Gopher's head, and putting it on, went to Thunder's house and killed the five brothers.

Tcûskai, though he was so small that he could camp in a woodpecker's hole, pursued Wŏn, a creature that had to bend down to bite off the tops of trees. He wrestled with Sukas, a man-eater, who drew people in with his breath and swallowed them. — A wave.

PITOÍOIS

Pitoíois is now a bird (English name unknown). The old father-in-law is lightning. His life is in the stone mortar which he throws at persons whom he wishes to kill. If the mortar is broken he presses the pieces to his breast and it is whole again, but if it is buried in the ground under water he dies.

ILYÚYU

Ilyúyu became a head. The head crossed a mountain at a bound and rolled along in the air; it flew at men and killed them. — Among the Iroquois a cyclone is represented as a great head, the name of which, in Seneca, is Dagua Noenyent.

LOK AND KÉKINA

Is an attractive myth. Kékina is early Spring. Every time the little fellow calls: " Spring is coming. Spring is coming! " he hurries Spring along. The Loks are clouds; they prefer winter.

GRASSHOPPER IN LOVE WITH DEER

Is an illustration of unfaithfulness and deceit.

KAI AND HIS FATHER-IN-LAW

Old Ko-a-lák-ak-a, who told this myth, did not know who Natanatas was, but she thought that he represented Wind. He could cause a storm, and when a storm was raging, by wishing hard he could quell it. Natanatas gave his son-in-law what he thought to be impossible tasks. — The giving of tasks to a new son-in-law is a feature in many Indian myths, and also in Aryan myths.